Lecture Notes in Computer Science   12310

Formal Methods

Subline of Lectures Notes in Computer Science

More information about this series at http://www.springer.com/series/7407

Frank de Boer · Antonio Cerone (Eds.)

Software Engineering and Formal Methods

18th International Conference, SEFM 2020
Amsterdam, The Netherlands, September 14–18, 2020
Proceedings

 Springer

Editors
Frank de Boer
Informatica
Centrum voor Wiskunde
en Informatica (CWI)
Amsterdam, The Netherlands

Antonio Cerone 🆔
Department of Computer Science
Nazarbayev University
Astana, Kazakhstan

ISSN 0302-9743   ISSN 1611-3349 (electronic)
Lecture Notes in Computer Science
ISBN 978-3-030-58767-3   ISBN 978-3-030-58768-0 (eBook)
https://doi.org/10.1007/978-3-030-58768-0

LNCS Sublibrary: SL1 – Theoretical Computer Science and General Issues

This Springer imprint is published by the registered company Springer Nature Switzerland AG
The registered company address is: Gewerbestrasse 11, 6330 Cham, Switzerland

Preface

This volume contains the proceedings of the 18th International Conference on Software Engineering and Formal Methods (SEFM 2020), which was originally planned to take place during September 14–18, 2020, in Amsterdam, The Netherlands (hosted by the Centrum Wiskunde & Informatica – CWI). Because of the COVID-19 pandemic, SEFM 2020 could not take place physically but had to be replaced by a virtual event (still held during September 14–18, 2020).

The general aim of the conference is to bring together leading researchers and practitioners from academia, industry, and government to advance the state of the art in formal methods, to facilitate their uptake in the software industry, and to encourage their integration within practical software engineering methods and tools.

There were 58 full paper submissions, which were reviewed for quality, correctness, originality, and relevance. Each submission was reviewed by four Program Committee Members and an online post-reviewing discussion, open to the entire Program Committee, was held to make the final decisions. The committee decided to accept 16 papers (27.6% acceptance rate). This volume contains the revised versions of those 16 papers, which cover a wide variety of topics, including testing, formal verification, program analysis, runtime verification, meta-programming, and software development and evolution. The papers address a wide range of systems, such as IoT systems, human-robot interaction in healthcare scenarios, navigation of maritime autonomous systems, and operating systems.

The conference program also featured three keynote talks by Paola Inverardi (University of L'Aquila, Italy), Roberto Di Cosmo (Paris Diderot University, France), and Eelco Visser (Delft University of Technology, The Netherlands). This volume includes an extended abstract of Paola Inverardi's talk titled "A Software Exoskeleton to Protect Ethics and Privacy of Users in the Digital World" and a full paper of Eelco Visser's talk titled "Multi-Purpose Syntax Definition with SDF3" – co-authored by Luís Eduardo de Souza Amorim.

We would like to thank Paola Inverardi, Roberto Di Cosmo, and Eelco Visser for accepting our invitations to give keynote talks, and the authors who submitted their work to SEFM 2020. We are grateful to the members of the Program Committee and the external reviewers for providing timely and insightful reviews, as well as for their involvement in the post-reviewing discussions. We would also like to thank the SEFM Steering Committee for their advices and support, the workshop co-chairs Loek Cleophas (TU/e, The Netherlands) and Mieke Massink (ISTI, Italy), Jacopo Mauro (SDU, Denmark) for taking care of the publicity, and Hans-Dieter Hiep and Benjamin Lion (CWI, The Netherlands) for setting up and maintaining the conference web pages. We would like to thank all people involved in SEFM 2020 for their contributions in these exceptional circumstances of the COVID-19 pandemic.

We greatly appreciated the convenience of the EasyChair system for handling the submission and review processes, and for preparing these proceedings. Finally, we gratefully acknowledge the technical support from CWI.

July 2020

Frank de Boer
Antonio Cerone

Organization

Program Co-chairs

Frank de Boer   CWI, The Netherlands
Antonio Cerone   Nazarbayev University, Kazakhstan

Steering Committee

Frank de Boer   CWI, The Netherlands
Radu Calinescu   University of York, UK
Antonio Cerone (Chair)   Nazarbayev University, Kazakhstan
Rocco De Nicola   IMT Lucca, Italy
Peter Ölveczky   University of Oslo, Norway
Gwen Salaün   University of Grenoble Alpes, France
Marjan Sirjani   Malardalen University, Sweden

Program Committee

Erika Abraham   RWTH Aachen University, Germany
Wolfgang Ahrendt   Chalmers University of Technology, Sweden
Alessandro Aldini   University of Urbino, Italy
Luís Soares Barbosa   University of Minho, Portugal
Maurice H. ter Beek   ISTI-CNR, Italy
Dirk Beyer   LMU Munich, Germany
Frank de Boer   CWI, The Netherlands
Ana Cavalcanti   University of York, UK
Antonio Cerone   Nazarbayev University, Kazakhstan
Alessandro Cimatti   Fondazione Bruno Kessler, Italy
Marieke Huisman   University of Twente, The Netherlands
Alexander Knapp   Universität Augsburg, Germany
Tiziana Margaria   Lero, Ireland
Paolo Masci   National Institute of Aerospace (NIA), USA
Jacopo Mauro   University of Oslo, Norway
Peter Müller   ETH Zurich, Switzerland
Hans de Nivelle   Nazarbayev University, Kazakhstan
Catuscia Palamidessi   Inria, France
Anna Philippou   University of Cyprus, Cyprus
Ka I. Pun   Western Norway University of Applied Sciences, Norway
Grigore Rosu   University of Illinois at Urbana-Champaign, USA
Gwen Salaün   University of Grenoble Alpes, France
Augusto Sampaio   Federal University of Pernambuco, Brazil

Ina Schaefer	Technische Universität Braunschweig, Germany
Gerardo Schneider	Chalmers—University of Gothenburg, Sweden
Roberto Segala	University of Verona, Italy
Marjan Sirjani	Malardalen University, Sweden
Martin Steffen	University of Oslo, Norway
Meng Sun	Peking University, China
Silvia Lizeth Tapia Tarifa	University of Oslo, Norway
Simone Tini	University of Insubria, Italy
Elena Troubitsyna	KTH Royal Institute of Technology, Sweden
M. Birna van Riemsdijk	University of Twente, The Netherlands
Heike Wehrheim	University of Paderborn, Germany
Gianluigi Zavattaro	University of Bologna, Italy
Peter Ölveczky	University of Oslo, Norway

Additional Reviewers

Abbaspour Asadollah, Sara
Amadini, Roberto
Antonino, Pedro
Attala, Ziggy
Bagheri, Maryam
Basile, Davide
Baxter, James
Bordis, Tabea
Broccia, Giovanna
Bugariu, Alexandra
Castiglioni, Valentina
Chimento, Jesus Mauricio
Cledou, Guillermina
Clochard, Martin
Din, Crystal Chang
Eilers, Marco
Enoiu, Eduard Paul
Filipovikj, Predrag
Fontaine, Pascal
Friedberger, Karlheinz
Giallorenzo, Saverio
Haltermann, Jan
Hnetynka, Petr
Holzner, Stephan
Iyoda, Juliano
Khamespanah, Ehsan
Knüppel, Alexander
Kouzapas, Dimitrios
Krishna, Ajay

Kristensen, Lars
König, Jürgen
Lanotte, Ruggero
Lathouwers, Sophie
Lee, Nian-Ze
Lemberger, Thomas
Lu, Yuteng
Madeira, Alexandre
Mallozzi, Piergiuseppe
Matheja, Christoph
Mazzanti, Franco
Miranda, Breno
Monti, Raúl E.
Mota, Alexandre
Neves, Renato
Nieke, Michael
Oortwijn, Wytse
Park, Daejun
Pauck, Felix
Paulson, Lawrence
Rasouli, Peyman
Richter, Cedric
Runge, Tobias
Safari, Mohsen
Sankaranarayanan, Sriram
Schlatte, Rudolf
Sedaghatbaf, Ali
Serwe, Wendelin
Sewell, Thomas

Sharma, Arnab
Spiessl, Martin
Steffen, Bernhard
Steffen, Martin
Steinhöfel, Dominic
Stolz, Volker
Sun, Weidi
Syeda, Hira
Tschaikowski, Max

Turin, Gianluca
Tveito, Lars
Valencia, Frank
van den Bos, Petra
Vandin, Andrea
Wendler, Philipp
Windsor, Matt
Zhang, Xiyue
Zhang, Yi

A Software Exoskeleton to Protect Ethics and Privacy of Users in the Digital World (Abstract of a Keynote Talk)

Paola Inverardi

Università dell'Aquila, L'Aquila, Italy

Abstract. In recent years there has been an increasingly amount of interest on the impact that the digital society can have on the fundamental rights of individual, citizens and societies. Starting from the raising of the economy of data to the appearance of the present and future AI fueled autonomous systems the level of attention has lifted from privacy concerns to more general ethical ones [6, 7]. Although there is a general consensus on the vulnerability of users and societies this perspective has been only followed by the regulatory approach that by putting at work new regulations, notably GDPR has effectively enhanced the protection of users. Differently, in research the approach is mainly focusing on AI and concerns the systems/software developers and companies by proposing code of ethics and guidelines for the development of trustworthy systems in order to achieve transparency, accountability and explainability of decisions [1, 5].

Therefore, despite the claim for a human centric AI and the recommendation to empower the user, the user is left unpaired in her interactions with digital systems beyond the basic choice of accepting or not accepting the interaction with a system with all the consequences this might imply. From the case of privacy preferences in the app domain [12] to the more complex case of autonomous driving cars [4] the average user is unprotected and inadeguate in her interaction with the digital world. In the talk I will present the approach and preliminary results undertaken in the project EXOSOUL [2, 8–11] that stands on the side of users. EXOSOUL aims at equipping humans with an automatically generated exoskeleton, a software shield that protects and empowers them and their personal data in all interactions with the digital world by mediating or discarding those ones that would result in unacceptable or morally wrong behaviors according to the user's ethical and privacy preferences [3].

Keywords: Ethics · Privacy · Software exoskeleton

Supported by organization Università dell'Aquila.

References

1. European commission: White paper on artificial intelligence. https://ec.europa.eu/info/sites/info/files/commission-white-paper-artificial-intelligence-feb2020-en.pdf
2. Autili, M., DiRuscio, D., Inverardi, P., Pelliccione, P., Tivoli, M.: A software exoskeleton to protect and support citizen's ethics and privacy in the digital world. IEEE Access **7**, 62011–62021 (2019). https://doi.org/10.1109/access.2019.2916203
3. Autili, M., Inverardi, P., Spalazzese, R., Tivoli, M., Mignosi, F.: Automated synthesis of application-layer connectors from automata-based specifications. J. Comput. Syst. Sci. **104**, 17–40 (2019). https://doi.org/10.1016/j.jcss.2019.03.001
4. Awad, E., et al.: The moral machine experiment. Nature **563**, 59–64 (2018). https://doi.org/10.1038/s41586-018-0637-6
5. Commission, E.: High-level expert group on artificial intelligence: Ethics guidelines for trustworthy ai (2019)
6. Floridi, L.: Soft ethics and the governance of the digital. Philos. Technol. **31**(1), 1–8 (2018). https://doi.org/10.1007/s13347-018-0303-9
7. Inverardi, P.: The european perspective on responsible computing. Commun. ACM **62**(4), 64–64 (2019). http://doi.acm.org/10.1145/3311783
8. Migliarini, P., Scoccia, G.L., Autili, M., Inverardi, P.: On the elicitation of privacy and ethics preferences of mobile users. In: 7th IEEE/ACM International Conference on Mobile Software Engineering and Systems (MOBILESoft 2020), Vision Track (2020)
9. Scoccia, G.L., Autili, M., Inverardi, P.: A self-configuring and adaptive privacy-aware permission system for android apps. In: 1st IEEE International Conference on Autonomic Computing and Self-Organizing Systems (ACSOS 2020) (2020)
10. Scoccia, G.L., Fiore, M.M., Pelliccione, P., Autili, M., Inverardi, P., Russo, A.: Hey, my data are mine! active data to e mpower the user. In: IEEE/ACM 39th International Conference on Software Engineering (ICSE 2017) (ICSE2020-NIER) (2020)
11. Scoccia, G.L., Malavolta, I., Autili, M., DiSalle, A., Inverardi, P.: Enhancing trustability of android applications via user-centric flexible permissions. IEEE Trans. Softw. Eng. (2019). https://doi.org/10.1109/tse.2019.2941936
12. Scoccia, G.L., Ruberto, S., Malavolta, I., Autili, M., Inverardi, P.: An investigation into android run-time permissions from the end users' perspective. In: 5th IEEE/ACM International Conference on Mobile Software Engineering and Systems (MOBILESoft 2018) (2018)

Contents

Multi-purpose Syntax Definition
with SDF3

Luís Eduardo de Souza Amorim[1] and Eelco Visser[2(✉)]

[1] Australian National University, Canberra, Australia
[2] Delft University of Technology, Delft, The Netherlands
`e.visser@tudelft.nl`

Abstract. SDF3 is a syntax definition formalism that extends plain context-free grammars with features such as constructor declarations, declarative disambiguation rules, character-level grammars, permissive syntax, layout constraints, formatting templates, placeholder syntax, and modular composition. These features support the multi-purpose interpretation of syntax definitions, including derivation of type schemas for abstract syntax tree representations, scannerless generalized parsing of the full class of context-free grammars, error recovery, layout-sensitive parsing, parenthesization and formatting, and syntactic completion. This paper gives a high level overview of SDF3 by means of examples and provides a guide to the literature for further details.

Keywords: Syntax definition · Programming language · Parsing

1 Introduction

A syntax definition formalism is a formal language to describe the syntax of formal languages. At the core of a syntax definition formalism is a *grammar formalism* in the tradition of Chomsky's context-free grammars [14] and the Backus-Naur Form [4]. But syntax definition is concerned with more than just phrase structure, and encompasses all aspects of the syntax of languages.

In this paper, we give an overview of the syntax definition formalism SDF3 and its tool ecosystem that supports the multi-purpose interpretation of syntax definitions. The paper does not present any new technical contributions, but it is the first paper to give a (high-level) overview of all aspects of SDF3 and serves as a guide to the literature. SDF3 is the third generation in the SDF family of syntax definition formalisms, which were developed in the context of the ASF+SDF [5], Stratego/XT [10], and Spoofax [38] language workbenches.

The first SDF [23] supported modular composition of syntax definition, a direct correspondence between concrete and abstract syntax, and parsing with the full class of context-free grammars enabled by the Generalized-LR (GLR) parsing algorithm [44,56]. Its programming environment, as part of the ASF+SDF MetaEnvironment [40], focused on live development of syntax definitions through incremental and modular scanner and parser generation [24–26] in order to provide fast turnaround times during language development.

© The Author(s) 2020
F. de Boer and A. Cerone (Eds.): SEFM 2020, LNCS 12310, pp. 1–23, 2020.
https://doi.org/10.1007/978-3-030-58768-0_1

The second generation, SDF2 encompassed a redesign of the internals of SDF without changing the surface syntax. The front-end of the implementation consisted of a transformation pipeline from the rich surface syntax to a minimal core (kernel) language [58] that served as input for parser generation. The key change of SDF2 was its integration of lexical and context-free syntax, supported by Scannerless GLR (SGLR) parsing [60,61], enabling composition of languages with different lexical syntax [12].

SDF3 is the latest member of the family and inherits many features of its predecessors. The most recognizable change is to the syntax of productions that should make it more familiar to users of other grammar formalisms. Further, it introduces new features in order to support multi-purpose interpretations of syntax definitions. The *goals of the design of SDF3* are (1) to support the definition of the concrete and abstract syntax of formal languages (with an emphasis on programming languages), (2) to support *declarative* syntax definition so that there is no need to understand parsing algorithms in order to understand definitions [39], (3) to make syntax definitions *readable and understandable* so that they can be used as reference documentation, and (4) to support *execution* of syntax definitions as parsers, but also for other syntactic operations, i.e to support *multi-purpose* interpretation based on a single source. The focus on multi-purpose interpretation is driven by the role of SDF3 in the Spoofax language workbench [38].

In this paper, we give a high-level overview of the features of SDF3 and how they support multi-purpose syntax definition. We give explanations by means of examples, assuming some familiarity of the reader with grammars. We refer to the literature for formal definitions of the concepts that we introduce. Figure 1 presents the complete syntax definition of a tiny functional language (inspired by OCaml [42]), which we will use as running example without (necessarily) referring to it explicitly.

2   Phrase Structure

A programming language is more than a set of flat sentences. It is the structure of those sentences that matters. Users understand programs in terms of structural elements such as expressions, functions, patterns, and modules. Language designers, and the tools they build to implement a language, operate on programs through their underlying (tree) structure. The productions in a context-free grammar create the connection between the tokens that form the textual representation of programs and their phrase structure [14]. Such productions can be interpreted as parsing rules to convert a text into a tree. But SDF3 emphasizes the interpretation of productions as definitions of structure [39].

A sort (also known as non-terminal) represents a syntactic category such as expression (Exp), pattern match case (Case), or pattern (Pat). A production defines the structure of a language construct. For example, the production

```
Exp.Add = Exp "+" Exp
```

```
module fun                          module lex
imports lex
context-free start-symbols Exp      lexical sorts ID
sorts Exp Case Bnd Pat              lexical syntax
context-free syntax                   ID = [a-zA-Z] [a-zA-Z0-9]*
  Exp     = <(<Exp>)> {bracket}     lexical restrictions
  Exp.Int = INT                       ID -/- [a-zA-Z0-9]
  Exp.Var = ID
  Exp.Min = [-[Exp]]                lexical sorts INT
  Exp.Sub = <<Exp> - <Exp>> {left}  lexical syntax
  Exp.Add = <<Exp> + <Exp>> {left}    INT = [\-]? [0-9]+
  Exp.Eq  = <<Exp> == <Exp>> {left} lexical restrictions
  Exp.Fun = [fun [ID*] -> [Exp]]      INT -/- [0-9]
  Exp.App = <<Exp> <Exp>> {left}    context-free restrictions
  Exp.Let = <                         "-" -/- [0-9]
    let <{Bnd "\n\n"}*>
      in <Exp>                      lexical sorts AST EOF
  >                                 lexical syntax
  Exp.IfE = <                         LAYOUT = [\ \t\n\r]
    if <Exp> then
      <Exp>                           LAYOUT = Com
    else                              Com    = "/*"
      <Exp>                                    (~[\*] | Ast | Com)*
  >                                            "*/"
  Exp.IfT = <                         Ast    = [\*]
    if <Exp> then
      <Exp>                           LAYOUT = "//" ~[\n\r]*
  >                                              ([\n\r] | EOF)
  Exp.Match = <                       EOF    =
    match <Exp>                     lexical restrictions
      with <{Case "\n"}+>             AST -/- [\/]
  > {longest-match}                   EOF -/- ~[]
  Bnd.Bnd   = <<ID> = <Exp>>
  Case.Case = [| [Pat] -> [Exp]]    context-free restrictions
  Pat.PVar  = ID                      LAYOUT? -/- [\ \t\n\r]
  Pat.PApp  = <<Pat> <Pat>> {left}    LAYOUT? -/- [\/].[\/]
  Pat       = <(<Pat>)> {bracket}     LAYOUT? -/- [\/].[\*]
context-free priorities
  Exp.Min > Exp.App               ────────────────────────────
  > {left: Exp.Sub Exp.Add}        let // length of a list
  > Exp.Eq > Exp.IfE > Exp.IfT       len = fun xs ->
  > Exp.Match > Exp.Fun > Exp.Let,     match xs
  Exp.App <1> .> Exp.Min                 with | nil -> 0
template options                            | cons x xs -> 1 + len xs
  ID = keyword {reject}            in len (cons 1 (cons 2 nil))
  keyword -/- [a-zA-Z0-9]
```

Fig. 1. Syntax of a small functional language in SDF3 and an example program.

defines that an addition expression is one alternative for the Exp sort and that
it is the composition of two expressions. A production makes the connection
with sentences by means of literals in productions. In the production above, the
two expressions making an addition are separated by a + operator. Finally, a
production defines a constructor name for the abstract syntax tree structure of
a program (Add in the production above). The pairs consisting of sort and constructor names should be unique within a grammar and can be used to identify
productions. (Such explicit constructor names are new in SDF3 compared to
SDF2.) A set of such productions is a grammar.

The productions of a grammar generate a set of well-formed syntax trees.
For example, Fig. 2 shows a well-formed tree over the example grammar. The
language defined by a grammar are the sentences obtained by taking the yields
of those trees, where the yield of a syntax tree is the concatenation of its leaves.
Thus, the sentence corresponding to the tree in Fig. 2 is (fun x -> x + 3) y.

The grammars of programming languages frequently feature lists, including
lists of statements in a block, lists of field declarations in a class, and lists of
parameters of a function. SDF3 supports direct expression of such list sorts by
means of Kleene star and plus operators on sorts. In Fig. 1 the formal parameters
of a Fun is defined as ID*, a list of zero or more identifiers. Other kinds of list
include A+ (one or more As), {A sep}* (zero or more As separated by seps),
and {A sep}+ (one or more As separated by seps). Lists with separators are
convenient to model, for example, the arguments of a function as {Exp ","}*,
i.e. a list of zero or more expressions separated by commas.

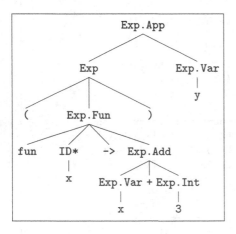

Fig. 2. Concrete syntax tree

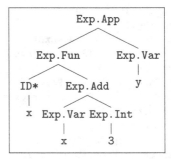

Fig. 3. Abstract syntax tree

Abstract Syntax. Concrete syntax trees contain irrelevant details such as keywords, operator symbols, and parentheses (as identified by the bracket attribute
on productions). These details are irrelevant since the constructor of a production of a node uniquely identifies the language construct concerned. Thus, from

a concrete syntax tree we obtain an *abstract syntax tree* by omitting such irrelevant details. Figure 3 shows the abstract syntax tree obtained from the concrete syntax tree in Fig. 2. Abstract syntax trees can be represented by means of first-order terms in which a constructor is applied to a (possibly empty) sequence of sub-terms. For example, the abstract syntax tree of Fig. 3 is represented by the term.

```
App(Fun(["x"], Add(Var("x"), Int("3"))), Var("y"))
```

Note that lists are represented by sequences of terms between square brackets.

Signatures. A grammar is a schema for describing well-formed concrete and abstract syntax trees. That is, we can check that a tree is well-formed by checking that the subtrees of a constructor node have the right sort according to the corresponding production, and a parser based on a grammar is guaranteed to produce such well-formed trees. To further process trees after parsing, we can work on a generic tree representation such as XML or ATerms [6], or we can work with a typed representation. The schemas for such typed representations can be derived automatically from a grammar. For example, the Statix language for static semantics specification [3] uses algebraic signatures to describe well-formed terms. The following signature in Statix defines the algebraic signature of a selection of the constructors of the example language:

```
signature
sorts Exp
constructors
Fun : list(ID) * Exp -> Exp
Add : Exp * Exp -> Exp
App : Exp * Exp -> Exp
Var : ID -> Exp
Int : INT -> Exp
```

The SDF3 compiler automatically generates signatures for Statix [3], Stratego [10], and DynSem [57].

3 Declarative Disambiguation

Multiple trees over a grammar can have the same yield. Or, vice versa, a sentence in the language of a grammar can have multiple trees. If this is the case, the sentence, and hence the grammar is *ambiguous*.

One strategy to disambiguate a grammar is to transform it to an unambiguous grammar that describes the same language, but has exactly one tree per sentence in the language. However, this may not be easy to do, may distort the structure of the trees associated with the grammar, and changes the typing scheme associated with the grammar. SDF3 supports the disambiguation of an ambiguous grammar by means of declarative disambiguation rules. In this section we describe disambiguation by means of associativity and priority rules. In the next section we describe lexical disambiguation rules.

Disambiguation by Associativity and Priority Rules. Many language reference manuals define the disambiguation of expression grammars by means of priority and associativity tables. SDF3 formalizes such tables as explicit associativity and priority rules over the productions of an ambiguous context-free grammar. While grammar formalisms such as YACC also define associativity and priority rules, these are defined in terms of low-level implementation details (e.g. choosing sides in a shift/reduce conflict.) The semantics of SDF3 associativity and priority rules has a direct formal semantics that is defined independently of a particular implementation [53]. The semantics is defined by means of *subtree exclusion*, that is, disambiguation rules are interpreted by *rejecting* trees that match one of the subtree exclusion patterns generated by a set of disambiguation rules. If a set of rules is sound and complete (there is a rule for each pair of productions), then disambiguation is sound and complete, i.e. assigns a single tree to a sentence. (Read the fine print in [53].)

A priority rule `A.C1 > A.C2` defines that (the production identified by the constructor) `A.C1` has higher priority than (the production identified by the constructor) `A.C2`. This means that (a tree with root constructor) `A.C2` cannot occur as a left, respectively right recursive child of (a tree node with constructor) `A.C1` if `A.C2` is right, respectively left recursive. A left associativity rule `A.C1 left A.C2` defines that `A.C1` and `A.C2` are mutually left associative. This means that `A.C2` cannot occur as a right recursive child of `A.C1`. (Right associativity is defined symmetrically.)

Figure 1 defines the disambiguation rules for the example language. According to these rules the expression `a - b + c == d` should be parsed as `((a - b) + c) == d` (since `Sub` and `Add` are left associative and have higher priority than `Eq`) and the expression `match a with | b -> c + d` should be parsed as `match a with | b -> (c + d)` (since `Add` has higher priority than `Match`).

The semantics of priority shown above is particularly relevant for prefix and postfix operators. A prefix operator (such as `Match`) may occur as right child of an infix operator (such as `Sub`), even if it has lower priority, since such a combination of productions is not ambiguous. For example, the expression `a - match b with | c -> d` has only one abstract syntax tree.

This semantics is safe, i.e. it does not reject any sentences that are in the language of the underlying context-free grammar. However, with the rules defined so far the semantics is not complete. As an example consider two of the trees for the sentence `a - match b with | c -> d + e` in Fig. 4. Both these trees are conflict free according to the rules above; a `Match` may occur as right hand child of a `Sub` and `Sub` and `Add` are left associative. The problem is that the conflict between `Match` as a left child of `Add` is hidden by the `Sub` tree. To capture such *deep conflicts*, the priority rule involving `Add`, `Sub` and `Match` is amended to require that a right-most occurrence of a production `A.C2` in the left recursive argument of a production `A.C1` is rejected if `A.C1 > A.C2`. (And symmetrically for left-most occurrences in right recursive arguments.) Thus, the priority rules of Fig. 1 select the left tree of Fig. 4.

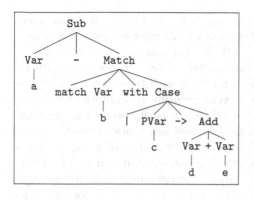 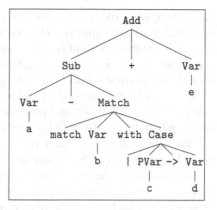

Fig. 4. Concrete syntax trees for the expression a - match b with | c -> d + e.

The longest-match attribute of the Match production is a short hand for deep priority conflicts for lists. The Match construct gives rise to nested pattern match clauses such as the following

```
match a with | d -> match e with | f -> g + h | i -> j + k
```

The longest match attributes disambiguates such nested lists by associating trailing cases with the nearest match statement.

Afroozeh et al. [1] showed that semantics of disambiguation in SDF2 [7,61] was not safe. They define a safe interpretation of disambiguation rules by means of a grammar transformation. Amorim and Visser [53] define a direct semantics of associativity and priority rules by means of subtree exclusion including prefix and postfix operators, mixfix productions, and indirect recursion. They show that the semantics is safe and complete for safe and complete sets of disambiguation rules for expression grammars without overlap. They also discuss the influence of overlap on disambiguation of expression grammars. For example, in Fig. 1, the productions Min, Sub, and App have overlap. The expression x - y can be parsed as App(Var("x"), Min(Var("y"))) or as Sub(Var("x"), Var("y")). This is not an ambiguity that can be solved by means of safe associativity and priority rules. The *indexed* priority rule Exp.App <1> .> Exp.Min solves this ambiguity by forbidding the occurrence of Min as second argument of App. (The index is 0 based.)

Amorim et al. show that deep conflicts are not only an artifact of grammars, but do actually occur in the wild, i.e. that they do occur in real programs [52]. One possible implementation of disambiguation with deep conflicts is by means of data dependent parsers. Amorim et al. show that such parsers can have near zero overhead when compared to disambiguation by grammar rewriting [55].

Parenthesization. In the previous section we saw that parentheses, i.e. productions annotated with the bracket attribute, are omitted when transforming a concrete syntax tree to an abstract syntax tree (Fig. 3). Furthermore, by using declarative disambiguation, the typing scheme for abstract syntax trees allows arbitrary combinations of constructors in well-formed abstract syntax trees. This is convenient, since it allows transformations on trees to create new trees without regard for disambiguation rules. Before formatting such trees (Sect. 5), parentheses need to be inserted in order to prevent creating a sentence that has a different (abstract) syntax tree when parsed. That is, we want the equation parse(format(t)) = t to hold for any well-formed abstract syntax tree.

The advantage of declarative disambiguation rules is that they can be interpreted not only to define disambiguation during parsing, but can also be interpreted to detect trees that need disambiguation. For example, without parenthesization the tree `Add(Eq(Var("a"), Var("b")), Var("c"))` would be formatted as `a == b + c`, which would be parsed as `Add(Var("a"), Eq(Var("b"), Var("c")))`. Parenthesization recognizes that the first tree has a priority conflict between `Add` and `Eq` and inserts parentheses around the equality expression, such that the tree is formatted as `(a == b) + c`, which has the original tree as its abstract syntax tree. The implementation of SDF3 in Spoofax supports parenthesization following the disambiguation semantics of Amorim and Visser [53].

4   Lexical Syntax

The lexical syntax of a language concerns the lexemes, words, or tokens of the language and typically includes identifiers, numbers, strings, keywords, operators, and delimiters. In traditional parsers and parser generators, parsing is divided into a lexical analysis (or scanning) phase in which the characters of a program are merged into tokens, and a context-free analysis phase in which a stream of tokens is parsed into phrase structure. Inspired by Salomon and Cormack [45], SDF2 adopted *character-level grammars* using the single formalism of context-free productions to define lexical and context-free syntax, supported by scannerless parsing [60]. SDF3 has inherited this feature.

Character-Level Grammars. In character-level grammars, the terminals of the grammar are individual characters. In SDF3, characters are indicated by means of character classes. For example, the definition of identifiers uses the character class `[a-zA-Z0-9]` comprising of lower and upper case letters and digits. Tokens are defined using the same productions that we use for context-free phrase structure, except that it is not required to associate a constructor with a lexical production. For example, the syntax of identifiers is defined using the production `ID = [a-zA-Z] [a-zA-Z0-9]*`, i.e. an identifier starts with a letter, which is followed by zero or more letters or digits. In a production such as `Exp.Let = "let" Bind* "in" Exp` it appears that `"let"` and `"in"` are terminals. However, SDF3 defines such literals by means of a lexical production in which the literal acts as a sort, which is defined in terms of character classes. Thus, the use of the literal `"let"` implies a production `"let" = [l] [e] [t]`. SDF3 also supports case-insensitive literals; in this case, the literal `'let'` implies a production `'let' = [lL] [eE] [tT]`.

Lexical Disambiguation. Just as phrase structure, lexical syntax may be ambiguous, requiring lexical disambiguation. The root cause of lexical ambiguity is overlap between lexical categories. For example, an identifier ab overlaps with the prefix of a longer identifier abc and let may be an identifier or a keyword. The two common lexical disambiguation policies are (1) prefer longest match, and (2) prefer one category over another. In scanner specification languages such as LEX [43] these policies are realized by (1) preferring the longest match and by (2) ordering the definitions of lexical rules and selecting the first rule that applies. This works well when recognizing tokens independent of the context in which they appear.

In a character-level grammar that approach does not work, since tokenization may depend on the phrase structure context (see also the discussion on language composition below), and due to modularity of a syntax definition, there is no canonical order of lexical rules. Thus, lexical disambiguation is defined analogously to subtree exclusion for phrase structure in the previous section, by defining what is not allowed using *follow restrictions* and *reject productions*. We discuss an example of each. The expression ab can be a single identifier or the application of a to b, i.e. App(Var("a"),Var("b")). This ambiguity is solved by means of the follow restriction ID -/- [a-zA-Z0-9] which states that an identifier cannot be followed directly by a letter or digit. The expression if x then y can be an if-then expression, i.e., IfT(Var("x"), Var("y")), or it can be the application of the variable if to some other variables, i.e.,

```
App(App(App(Var("if"), Var("x")), Var("then")), Var("y"))
```

This ambiguity is solved by means of reject productions ID = "if" {reject} and ID = "else" {reject} to forbid the use of the keywords if and else as identifiers.

Layout. Another aspect of lexical syntax is the whitespace characters and comments that can appear between tokens, which are known as 'layout' in SDF. The definition of layout is a matter of lexical definition as that of any other lexical category. Module lex in Fig. 1 defines layout as whitespace, multi-line comments (delimited by /* and */), and single-line comments (starting with //). The multi-line comments can be nested to enable commenting out code with comments. This is not supported by scanner generators based on regular expressions. Note the use of follow restrictions to ensure that an asterisk within a multi-line comment is not followed by a slash (which should be parsed as the end of the comment), and to characterize end-of-file as the empty string that is not followed by any character (which is in turn defined as the complement of the empty character class).

What is special about layout is that it can appear between any two ordinary tokens. In a scanner-based approach layout tokens are just skipped by the scanner, leaving only tokens that matter for the parser. A character-level grammar needs to be explicit about where layout can appear. This would result in boiler-plate code as illustrated by the following explicit version of the Exp production

```
syntax
  Exp-CF.Var = ID-CF
  Exp-CF.Add = Exp-CF LAYOUT?-CF "+" LAYOUT?-CF Exp-CF {left}
  ID-CF      = ID-LEX
  ID-LEX     = [\65-\90\97-\122] [\48-\57\65-\90\97-\122]*-LEX
  "+"        = [\43]
  LAYOUT?-CF =
  LAYOUT?-CF = LAYOUT-CF
  LAYOUT-CF  = LAYOUT-CF LAYOUT-CF {left}
  LAYOUT-CF  = LAYOUT-LEX
  LAYOUT-LEX = [\9-\10\13\32]
restrictions
  LAYOUT?-CF -/- [\9-\10\13\32]
  ID-LEX     -/- [\48-\57\65-\90\97-\122]
```

Fig. 5. Normalized syntax and restrictions for a selection of productions from Fig. 1.

```
  Exp.Fun = "fun" LAYOUT? ID* LAYOUT? "->" LAYOUT? Exp
```

To avoid such boilerplate, the SDF3 compiler applies a transformation to productions in context-free syntax sections in order to inject optional layout [61]. Figure 5 shows the result of that normalization to a small selection of productions from Fig. 1. Note that in lexical productions (such as for ID-LEX) no layout is injected, since the characters of tokens should not be separated by layout. Note the use of -LEX and -CF suffixes on sorts to distinguish lexical sorts from context-free sorts (This transformation is currently applied to the entire grammar, which may hinder grammar composition between modules specifying different layout.)

Layout Sensitive Syntax. In Sect. 3 we showed how associativity and priority rules can be used to disambiguate an ambiguous grammar. For example, we saw how longest match for Match ensures that a match case is always associated with the nearest match. Similarly, Fig. 1 disambiguates the dangling-else ambiguity between IfT and IfE such that an else branch is always associated with the closest if.

An alternative approach to disambiguation is to take into account the layout of a program. For that purpose, SDF3 supports the use of *layout constraints*, which pose requirements on the two dimensional shape of programs [17,54]. We illustrate layout constraints with layout-sensitive disambiguations of the Match and IfE productions in Figs. 6 and 7.

The layout constraints in Fig. 6 require that the if and else keywords of the IfE production are aligned. The examples in the figure show how the else branch can be associated with either if by choosing the layout. In addition, the indent constraints require that the conditions and branches of the IfT and IfE constructs appear to the right of the if and else keywords. Figure 7 disambiguates the association of the match cases with a match by requiring that the

```
Exp.IfE = "if" exp1:Exp "then" exp2:Exp "else" exp3:Exp {
  layout(align "if" "else" && indent "if" "then"
         && indent "if" exp1 && indent "if" exp2 && indent "else" exp3)
}
Exp.IfT = "if" exp1:Exp "then" exp2:Exp {
  layout(indent "if" "then" && indent "if" exp1 && indent "if" exp2)
}
```

`if a then`
`  if b then`
`    c`
`  else`
`    d`
	`IfT(`
	`    Var("a")`
	`, IfE(Var("b"), Var("c"), Var("d"))`
	`)`

`if a then`
`  if b then`
`    c`
`else`
`  d`
	`IfE(`
	`    Var("a")`
	`, IfT(Var("b"), Var("c"))`
	`, Var("d")`
	`)`

Fig. 6. Layout-sensitive disambiguation of dangling-else.

```
Exp.Match = "match" Exp "with" cases:Case+ {
  layout(indent "match" "with" && indent "match" exp
         && align-list cases)
}
```

`match a` ` with	d -> match e` ` with	f -> g` `	i -> j`	`match a` ` with	d -> match e` ` with	f -> g` `	i -> j`

`Match(`
`  Var("a")`
`, [ Case(`
`    PVar("d")`
`  , Match(`
`      Var("e")`
`    , [ Case(PVar("f"),Var("g"))`
`    , Case(PVar("i"),Var("j"))`
`    ]`
`    )`
`  )`
`  ]`
`)`
	`Match(`
	`  Var("a")`
	`, [ Case(`
	`    PVar("d")`
	`  , Match(`
	`      Var("e")`
	`    , [Case(PVar("f"),Var("g"))]`
	`    )`
	`  )`
	`  , Case(PVar("i"),Var("j"))`
	`  ]`
	`)`

Fig. 7. Layout-sensitive disambiguation of longest match for nested match cases.

```
1 let length = fun xs → match xs
2                        with nil → 0
3                          | cons x xs → 1 + length xs
4      name = first + last
5      from = select address from Person where ~name == name
6 in length (cons $Exp from)
7                    ⊹ Var                        if $Exp then
                     ⊹ IfE                           $Exp
                     ⊹ Eq                         else
                     ⊹ A...                          $Exp
                     ⊹ Int
```

Fig. 8. Syntax-aware editor for the **fun-query** language with syntax highlighting, parse error recovery, error highlighting, and syntactic completion.

cases are aligned. Thus, one can obtain the non-longest match (second example) without using parentheses.

Syntax Highlighting. The Spoofax language workbench [38,64] generates a syntax-aware editor from a syntax definition. Based on the lexical syntax, it derives syntax highlighting for programs by assigning colors to the tokens in the syntax tree as illustrated in Fig. 8. The default coloring scheme assigns colors to lexical categories such as keywords, identifiers, numbers, and strings. The coloring scheme can be adjusted in a configuration file by associating colors with sorts and constructors.

Language Composition. SDF3 supports a simple module mechanism, allowing large syntax definitions to be divided into a collection of smaller modules, and allowing to define a library with reusable definitions. For example, the **lex** module provides a collection of common lexical syntax definitions. A module may extend the definition of syntactic categories of another module. This can be used, for example, to organize the syntax definition for a language as a collection of components (such as variables, functions, booleans, numbers) that each introduce constructs for a common set of syntactic categories (such as types and expressions).

Another application of the module mechanism is to compose the syntax definitions of different languages into a composite language. For example, Fig. 9 defines a tiny query language in module **query** and its composition with the **fun** language of Fig. 1. The composition introduces the use of a query as an expression, and a quoted expression as a query identifier. The languages have a different lexical syntax, i.e. the keywords of the **fun** language are not reserved in the **query** language, and vice versa. Thus, **from** can be used as a variable in a **fun** expression, while it is a keyword in a query (see Fig. 8). Language composition with SDF2/3 has been used for the embedding of domain-specific languages [12], for the embedding of query and scripting languages [9], and for the organization of composite languages such as AspectJ [11] and WebDSL [27,62].

A consequence of merging of productions for sorts with the same name and injecting layout between symbols of a production, is that the layout of com-

```
module query                              module fun-query
sorts Query lexical sorts QID             imports fun query
lexical syntax                            context-free syntax
  QID = [a-zA-Z0-9]+                        Exp.Query = Query
lexical restrictions                       QID.Exp = [~[Exp]]
  QID -/- [a-zA-Z0-9]                       ID = [select] {reject}
context-free syntax
  Query.Select = <
    select <QID*> from <QID*> where <Cond>
  >
  Cond.Eq = <<QID> == <QID>>
template options
  QID = keyword {reject}
  keyword -/- [a-zA-Z0-9]
```

Fig. 9. Composition of languages with different lexical syntax.

posed languages is unified. It is future work to preserve the layout of composed languages.

5 Formatting

Formatting is the process of mapping abstract syntax trees to text. This can be used to improve the layout of a manually written program, or it can be used to turn a generated or transformed abstract syntax tree into a program text. Formatting is preceded by parenthesization to correctly insert parentheses such that parsing the formatted text preserves the tree structure (see Sect. 3).

Template Productions. Formatting comes in two levels. The basic level of formatting, also known as ugly-printing, is concerned with inserting the 'irrelevant' notational details that were removed in the translation to abstract syntax. After ugly-printing, parsing the generated text should produce the original abstract syntax tree. This translation can be obtained from a grammar mechanically. For example, the Stratego/XT transformation tool suite featured a 'pretty-print' table generator [35] that formalized for each constructor a mapping to these notational details.

The second level of formatting, also known as pretty-printing, is concerned with producing white space to make the generated program text readable. The Box language [8,34] provides abstractions for horizontal and vertical composition and horizontal (e.g. indentation) and vertical (line breaks) spacing. This is a useful intermediate representation for formatting, which allows the pretty-printer writer to abstract from an actual pretty-print algorithm. (Libraries for pretty-printing are built on the same principle [29].) Still, a mapping from abstract syntax trees to Box expressions requires human judgement and cannot be derived mechanically from a grammar. The pretty-print table generator mentioned above featured heuristics for associating Box expressions with language constructs. However, in many cases, it was necessary to edit the table to produce useful results, creating a bidirectional update problem to reflect changes to the grammar. SDF3 solves this problem by means of *template productions*, originally motivated to support syntactic completion (see below) [63]. (Template productions are a signature feature of SDF3, as they changed the syntax of productions from defined non-terminal on the right in SDF and SDF2, to defined non-terminal on the left, and the template quotes have a distinct influence on the typography of syntax definitions.)

A regular context-free grammar production (Sect. 2) such as

```
Exp.IfE = "if" Exp "then" Exp "else" Exp
```

combines sorts and literals. Sorts are identifiers referring to other productions and become the sub-terms of an abstract syntax tree node. Literals are quoted strings and are removed in the mapping to abstract syntax, needing to be restored during pretty-printing. Sorts and literals are implicitly separated by layout as discussed in Sect. 4.

In a template production the usual quotation is inverted. Consider the template version of the `IfE` production in Fig. 10. The outer quotes (`<if ...>`), quote a literal piece of text. The inner quotes (`<Exp>`) are escapes to sorts. A template not only captures literals and sorts, but also captures a two dimensional shape. For the purposes of parsing this shape is ignored. That is, whitespace between symbols is turned into optional layout analogous to the transformation discussed in Sect. 4. (For the purpose of

```
Exp.IfE = <
  if <Exp> then
    <Exp>
  else
    <Exp>
>
```

Fig. 10. Template production

layout-sensitive parsing it would be interesting to interpret the layout in a template as layout constraints, but it is not easy to distinguish which layout should be enforced, and which layout is incidental.)

For the purpose of pretty-printing, the two dimensional shape is interpreted as horizontal and vertical composition and spacing. That is, newlines are interpreted as vertical space and spaces are interpreted as indentation (with respect to the first non-whitespace character of the template). The template in Fig. 11 shows how the spacing of list elements can be configured with whitespace in the separator.

```
Exp.Let = <
  let <{Bnd "\n\n"}*>
  in <Exp>
>
```

Fig. 11. Separator layout

Templates are translated to a transformation from abstract syntax terms to Box expressions. Thus, after every change to the grammar, the pretty-printer is automatically regenerated and up-to-date, without requiring a bidirectional update process. Plain productions with quoted literals can also be obtained automatically from template productions.

The formatters derived from SDF3 templates have some limitations, which are partly due to (the interpretation of) the Box intermediate representation.

First, formatting is fairly rigid. It does not take into account the composition and size of expressions, but formats a language construct always in the same manner. Furthermore, it is not customizable with user preferences, as is customary in integrated development environments such as Eclipse. When formatting manually written programs to improve their layout, or when formatting a program after applying some transformation (e.g. a refactoring), it can be important to preserve the layout (comments and/or whitespace) of the original program. De Jonge and Visser [32] developed a layout preserving formatting algorithm with heuristics for moving comment blocks. This algorithm is currently not integrated in the SDF3 tool suite.

Completion. Formatting is also an issue when proposing and inserting syntactic completions in an editor. The first version of Spoofax [38] featured syntactic completion templates instructing the editor what to do on particular triggers, which redundantly specified syntactic patterns. Vollebregt et al. [63] introduced template productions with the goal to automatically generate completion templates and support a program completion workflow in the style of structured editors. Amorim et al. [51] generate explicit placeholder syntax for all syntactic sorts in order to explicitly represent incomplete programs. Syntactic completion becomes a matter of generating completion proposals for placeholders based on the productions of the grammar. The resulting editor behaves like a combination of text editor and structure editor as illustrated in Fig. 8.

6   Parsing

Finally, we discuss the parsing strategy of SDF3. Character-level grammars do not fit in restricted grammar classes such as LL or LR grammars; deciding which alternative to take may require an unbounded number of characters of lookahead [61]. Furthermore, only the full class of context-free grammars is closed under composition [28], i.e. the composition of two LL or LR grammars is not necessarily an LL or LR grammar. Thus, SDF3 uses a generalized parsing algorithm that can deal with the full class of context-free grammars.

Lazy Parse Table Generation. The SDF3 compiler first transforms a modular syntax definition to a monolithic and normalized syntax definition, which makes layout and deep priority conflicts explicit in the grammar [53,61]. A static analysis checks whether all used sorts are defined and warns for missing associativity and priority rules. A parser generation algorithm is used to generate a shift/reduce parse table from the normalized grammar. The algorithm is based on SLR parse table generation [28] adapted to deal with shallow priority conflicts [59]. Follow restrictions are implemented by restricting the follow set of non-terminals in the parse table. Follow restrictions that are longer than one character are added as dynamic checks. The resulting table may contain shift/reduce conflicts.

```
a + b == c + d
```
```
amb([
  Add(Var("a"), amb([ Add(Eq(Var("b"), Var("c")), Var("d"))
                    , Eq(Var("b"), Add(Var("c"), Var("d")))]))
  , Add(amb([ Eq(Add(Var("a"), Var("b")), Var("c"))
            , Add(Var("a"), Eq(Var("b"), Var("c")))]), Var("d"))
  , Eq(Add(Var("a"), Var("b")), Add(Var("c"), Var("d")))
])
```

Fig. 12. Sentence and abstract syntax tree with (shared) ambiguities.

LR parse table generation is a non-local operation, requiring the entire grammar, implying that separate compilation is not possible. If one module of the syntax definition is changed, it needs to be recompiled entirely. This is a disadvantage for scenarios that depend on language extension [12,16]. Bravenboer and Visser developed a representation and algorithm for parse table composition that realized a form of separate compilation for syntax definitions [13]. However, the algorithm did not support cross-module priority declarations and was not adopted in practice. As a more pragmatic approach, Amorim et al. [52] adopted lazy parse table generation [26], which starts with an empty parse table, and only generates those states that are needed at parse time. This ensures fast turnaround times during development of syntax definitions.

Scannerless Generalized LR Parsing with Error Recovery. The shift/reduce parse tables generated from SDF3 definitions are not deterministic, i.e. may have shift/reduce conflicts due to proper ambiguities or unbounded lookahead. To handle both these cases, SDF3 uses a Scannerless Generalized-LR (SGLR) parsing algorithm [60].

The GLR algorithm handles conflicts in the parse table by forking off separate parsers for each alternative of a conflict [44]. If the parser has encountered a genuine ambiguity, the parallel parsers will eventually end up in the same parse state, and the branches give rise to alternative parse trees. The result of parsing is a *parse forest*, a compact representation of all possible parse trees. A language engineer using SDF3 can inspect the ambiguities of a grammar by inspecting the (abstract) syntax trees with ambiguities, instead of inspecting shift/reduce conflicts. Figure 12 shows an abstract syntax tree with ambiguities for an expression in the example language using a syntax definition without disambiguation rules.

Another reason for shift/reduce conflicts is the limited lookahead of the parser generator. For example, consider parsing the expression a == b /* a comment */ + c. After reading the identifier b, the parser can reduce to create Eq(Var("a"),Var("b")) or it can shift, expecting to eventually parse some subexpression of Eq, i.e. resulting in a term of the form Eq(Var("a"),?(Var("b"), ...)). This decision can only be made when parsing the + operator. But before the parser sees that operator, it first needs to process the comment. Forking

```
module matching
language mpsd-sdf3
start symbol Exp
test match longest match [[
  match a with | b -> match c with | e -> f | g -> h
]] parse to [[
  match a with | b -> (match c with | e -> f | g -> h)
]]
```

Fig. 13. Testing longest match disambiguation of the match-with expression.

the parser allows delaying the decision. Eventually only one of the parsers will survive and produce a tree without ambiguities.

A GLR parser becomes a scannerless parser by reading characters as tokens and handling lexical disambiguation such that invalid forks are prevented or killed as early as possible [60]. Follow restrictions are handled by means of a dynamic lookahead check on reductions. Reject productions are implemented by rejecting states that are reached with a reject production. That requires postponing the reduction from *rejectable* states until it is certain no reject productions will appear.

The SGLR algorithm is extended to support parse error recovery and produce a parse tree even if a program text contains syntactic errors [30,33,36]. This is important in interactive settings such as editors in an integrated development environment in order to enable editor services such as syntax highlighting and type analysis for programs with errors, as arise during program development. Error recovery is realized by an extension of SDF3 with recovery productions, which are only used in case normal parsing fails. There are two main categories of recovery rules. Inspired by island grammars [31], so called *water productions* turn normal tokens into layout, which allows skipping some tokens when they cannot be parsed otherwise. Productions such as ")" = {recover} allow the insertion of missing literals (or complete sorts). The SDF3 normalizer automatically generates a permissive grammar with recovery rules, but such rules can also be added manually. Error recovery is the basis for reporting syntax errors. Improving the localization and explanation of error messages is a topic for future work.

An extension of SGLR to support incremental parsing based on the work of Wagner et al. [65] is under development [49].

Testing. Testing SDF3 syntax definitions is supported by the Spoofax Testing (SPT) language, a domain-specific language for testing various aspects of language definitions, including parsing [37]. An SPT test quotes a language fragment and specifies a test expectation. For testing syntax, the expectations are parse succeeds, parse fails, and parse to a specific term structure. Figure 13 illustrates the testing of disambiguation in SPT by specifying the disambiguated expression as parse result.

7   Related Work

We have referred to previous and related work throughout this paper. The papers that we cited about particular aspects of SDF3 provide extensive discussions of related technical work, which is beyond the scope of this paper. Here we provide a couple of high-level pointers to related efforts.

The design and implementation of SDF3 is motivated by its use in the Spoofax language workbench [38,64]. Erdweg et al. [18,19] give an overview of general concerns of the design and implementation of language workbenches.

SDF3 is bootstrapped, i.e. the syntax of SDF3 has been defined in SDF3. Other significant applications of SDF3 are the NaBL2 [2] and Statix [3] languages for type system specification, the IceDust language for data modeling [20–22], and the FlowSpec language for data-flow analysis specification [50]. Many languages originally developed with SDF2 are being ported to SDF3, including the Stratego transformation language [10].

Several syntax definition languages share aims with SDF3, in particular regarding the support for language composition. The syntax definition sublanguage of the RASCAL meta-programming language [41] has a common root in SDF2. RASCAL has adopted generalized GLL parsing [48] instead of GLR parsing. The syntax definition language of the Silver [66] attribute grammar system takes a different approach to language composition. Instead of relying on scannerless generalized parsing, it relies on context-aware scanners and restrictions on grammars in order to guarantee absence of ambiguities in composed grammars [46]. Based on these restrictions it can support parse table composition for language composition [47]. The Eco editor [15] supports language composition using language boxes, where the editor keeps track of transitions between languages, avoiding the composition of grammars.

8   Conclusion

In this paper we have presented SDF3, a mature language for the definition of syntax. The design and implementation of SDF3 are based on many years of research and engineering, fed by the experience of numerous researchers, developers, and students. The multi-purpose interpretation of SDF3 specifications allows quick prototopying of language designs and enables testing these designs in a full-fledged environment with a syntax aware editor.

Acknowledgment. We would like to thank our numerous co-authors (see the References section) for their contributions to the SDF family of languages. We would like to thank Peter Mosses for comments on this paper.

References

1. Afroozeh, A., van den Brand, M., Johnstone, A., Scott, E., Vinju, J.: Safe specification of operator precedence rules. In: Erwig, M., Paige, R.F., Van Wyk, E. (eds.) SLE 2013. LNCS, vol. 8225, pp. 137–156. Springer, Cham (2013). https://doi.org/10.1007/978-3-319-02654-1_8

2. van Antwerpen, H., Néron, P., Tolmach, A.P., Visser, E., Wachsmuth, G.: A constraint language for static semantic analysis based on scope graphs. In: Erwig, M., Rompf, T. (eds.) Proceedings of the 2016 ACM SIGPLAN Workshop on Partial Evaluation and Program Manipulation, PEPM 2016, St. Petersburg, FL, USA, January 20–22, 2016, pp. 49–60. ACM (2016). https://doi.org/10.1145/2847538.2847543

3. van Antwerpen, H., Poulsen, C.B., Rouvoet, A., Visser, E.: Scopes as types. Proc. ACM Program. Lang. 2(OOPSLA), 1–30 (2018). https://doi.org/10.1145/3276484

4. Backus, J.W.: The syntax and semantics of the proposed international algebraic language of the Zurich ACM-GAMM conference. In: IFIP Congress. pp. 125–131 (1959)

5. van den Brand, M.G.J., et al.: The ASF+SDF meta-environment: a component-based language development environment. In: Wilhelm, R. (ed.) Compiler Construction, 10th International Conference, CC 2001 Held as Part of the Joint European Conferences on Theory and Practice of Software, ETAPS 2001 Genova, Italy, April 2–6, 2001, Proceedings. Lecture Notes in Computer Science, vol. 2027, pp. 365–370. Springer (2001). https://doi.org/10.1016/S1571-0661(04)80917-4

6. van den Brand, M.G.J., de Jong, H.A., Klint, P., Olivier, P.A.: Efficient annotated terms. Softw.: Pract. Exp. 30(3), 259–291 (2000)

7. van den Brand, M.G.J., Scheerder, J., Vinju, J.J., Visser, E.: Disambiguation filters for scannerless generalized LR parsers. In: Horspool, R.N. (ed.) CC 2002. LNCS, vol. 2304, pp. 143–158. Springer, Heidelberg (2002). https://doi.org/10.1007/3-540-45937-5_12

8. van den Brand, M.G.J., Visser, E.: Generation of formatters for context-free languages. ACM Trans. Softw. Eng. Methodol. 5(1), 1–41 (1996). https://doi.org/10.1145/226155.226156

9. Bravenboer, M., Dolstra, E., Visser, E.: Preventing injection attacks with syntax embeddings. Sci. Comput. Program. 75(7), 473–495 (2010). https://doi.org/10.1016/j.scico.2009.05.004

10. Bravenboer, M., Kalleberg, K.T., Vermaas, R., Visser, E.: Stratego/XT 0.17. A language and toolset for program transformation. Sci. Comput. Program. 72(12), 52–70 (2008). https://doi.org/10.1016/j.scico.2007.11.003

11. Bravenboer, M., Tanter, É., Visser, E.: Declarative, formal, and extensible syntax definition for AspectJ. In: Tarr, P.L., Cook, W.R. (eds.) Proceedings of the 21th Annual ACM SIGPLAN Conference on Object-Oriented Programming, Systems, Languages, and Applications, OOPSLA 2006, pp. 209–228. ACM (2006). https://doi.org/10.1145/1167473.1167491

12. Bravenboer, M., Visser, E.: Concrete syntax for objects: domain-specific language embedding and assimilation without restrictions. In: Vlissides, J.M., Schmidt, D.C. (eds.) Proceedings of the 19th Annual ACM SIGPLAN Conference on Object-Oriented Programming, Systems, Languages, and Applications, OOPSLA 2004, pp. 365–383. ACM, Vancouver (2004). https://doi.org/10.1145/1028976.1029007

13. Bravenboer, M., Visser, E.: Parse table composition. In: Gašević, D., Lämmel, R., Van Wyk, E. (eds.) SLE 2008. LNCS, vol. 5452, pp. 74–94. Springer, Heidelberg (2009). https://doi.org/10.1007/978-3-642-00434-6_6

14. Chomsky, N.: Three models for the description of language. IRE Trans. Inf. Theory 2(3), 113–124 (1956). https://doi.org/10.1109/TIT.1956.1056813

15. Diekmann, L., Tratt, L.: Eco: a language composition editor. In: Combemale, B., Pearce, D.J., Barais, O., Vinju, J.J. (eds.) SLE 2014. LNCS, vol. 8706, pp. 82–101. Springer, Cham (2014). https://doi.org/10.1007/978-3-319-11245-9_5

16. Erdweg, S., Rendel, T., Kästner, C., Ostermann, K.: Sugarj: library-based syntactic language extensibility. In: Lopes, C.V., Fisher, K. (eds.) Proceedings of the 26th Annual ACM SIGPLAN Conference on Object-Oriented Programming, Systems, Languages, and Applications, OOPSLA 2011, part of SPLASH 2011, Portland, OR, USA, October 22–27, 2011, pp. 391–406. ACM (2011). https://doi.org/10.1145/2048066.2048099

17. Erdweg, S., Rendel, T., Kästner, C., Ostermann, K.: Layout-sensitive generalized parsing. In: Czarnecki, K., Hedin, G. (eds.) SLE 2012. LNCS, vol. 7745, pp. 244–263. Springer, Heidelberg (2013). https://doi.org/10.1007/978-3-642-36089-3_14

18. Erdweg, S., et al.: The state of the art in language workbenches. In: Erwig, M., Paige, R.F., Van Wyk, E. (eds.) SLE 2013. LNCS, vol. 8225, pp. 197–217. Springer, Cham (2013). https://doi.org/10.1007/978-3-319-02654-1_11

19. Erdweg, S., et al.: Evaluating and comparing language workbenches: existing results and benchmarks for the future. Comput. Lang. Syst. Struct. **44**, 24–47 (2015). https://doi.org/10.1016/j.cl.2015.08.007

20. Harkes, D., Groenewegen, D.M., Visser, E.: IceDust: incremental and eventual computation of derived values in persistent object graphs. In: Krishnamurthi, S., Lerner, B.S. (eds.) 30th European Conference on Object-Oriented Programming, ECOOP 2016, July 18–22, 2016, Rome, Italy. LIPIcs, vol. 56. Schloss Dagstuhl - Leibniz-Zentrum fuer Informatik (2016). https://doi.org/10.4230/LIPIcs.ECOOP.2016.11

21. Harkes, D., Visser, E.: Unifying and generalizing relations in role-based data modeling and navigation. In: Combemale, B., Pearce, D.J., Barais, O., Vinju, J.J. (eds.) SLE 2014. LNCS, vol. 8706, pp. 241–260. Springer, Cham (2014). https://doi.org/10.1007/978-3-319-11245-9_14

22. Harkes, D., Visser, E.: IceDust 2: derived bidirectional relations and calculation strategy composition. In: Müller, P. (ed.) 31st European Conference on Object-Oriented Programming, ECOOP 2017, June 19–23, 2017, Barcelona, Spain. LIPIcs, vol. 74. Schloss Dagstuhl - Leibniz-Zentrum fuer Informatik (2017). https://doi.org/10.4230/LIPIcs.ECOOP.2017.14

23. Heering, J., Hendriks, P.R.H., Klint, P., Rekers, J.: The syntax definition formalism SDF - reference manual. SIGPLAN Not. **24**(11), 43–75 (1989). https://doi.org/10.1145/71605.71607

24. Heering, J., Klint, P., Rekers, J.: Incremental generation of parsers. IEEE Trans. Softw. Eng. **16**(12), 1344–1351 (1990)

25. Heering, J., Klint, P., Rekers, J.: Incremental generation of lexical scanners. ACM Trans. Program. Lang. Syst. **14**(4), 490–520 (1992). https://doi.org/10.1145/133233.133240

26. Heering, J., Klint, P., Rekers, J.: Lazy and incremental program generation. ACM Trans. Program. Lang. Syst. **16**(3), 1010–1023 (1994). https://doi.org/10.1145/177492.177750

27. Hemel, Z., Groenewegen, D.M., Kats, L.C.L., Visser, E.: Static consistency checking of web applications with WebDSL. J. Symb. Comput. **46**(2), 150–182 (2011). https://doi.org/10.1016/j.jsc.2010.08.006

28. Hopcroft, J.E., Motwani, R., Ullman, J.D.: Introduction to Automata Theory, Languages, and Computation, 3rd edn. Addison-Wesley, Boston (2006)

29. Hughes, J.: The design of a pretty-printing library. In: Jeuring, J., Meijer, E. (eds.) AFP 1995. LNCS, vol. 925, pp. 53–96. Springer, Heidelberg (1995). https://doi.org/10.1007/3-540-59451-5_3

30. de Jonge, M., Kats, L.C.L., Visser, E., Söderberg, E.: Natural and flexible error recovery for generated modular language environments. ACM Trans. Program. Lang. Syst. **34**(4), 15 (2012). https://doi.org/10.1145/2400676.2400678
31. de Jonge, M., Nilsson-Nyman, E., Kats, L.C.L., Visser, E.: Natural and flexible error recovery for generated parsers. In: van den Brand, M., Gašević, D., Gray, J. (eds.) SLE 2009. LNCS, vol. 5969, pp. 204–223. Springer, Heidelberg (2010). https://doi.org/10.1007/978-3-642-12107-4_16
32. de Jonge, M., Visser, E.: An algorithm for layout preservation in refactoring transformations. In: Sloane, A., Aßmann, U. (eds.) SLE 2011. LNCS, vol. 6940, pp. 40–59. Springer, Heidelberg (2012). https://doi.org/10.1007/978-3-642-28830-2_3
33. de Jonge, M., Visser, E.: Automated evaluation of syntax error recovery. In: Goedicke, M., Menzies, T., Saeki, M. (eds.) IEEE/ACM International Conference on Automated Software Engineering, ASE 2012, Essen, Germany, September 3–7, 2012, pp. 322–325. ACM (2012). https://doi.org/10.1145/2351676.2351736
34. de Jonge, M.: A pretty-printer for every occasion. In: The International Symposium on Constructing Software Engineering Tools (CoSET2000). University of Wollongong, Australia (2000)
35. de Jonge, M.: Pretty-printing for software reengineering. In: 18th International Conference on Software Maintenance (ICSM 2002), Maintaining Distributed Heterogeneous Systems, 3–6 October, 2002, Montreal, Quebec, Canada, pp. 550–559. IEEE Computer Society (2002)
36. Kats, L.C.L., de Jonge, M., Nilsson-Nyman, E., Visser, E.: Providing rapid feedback in generated modular language environments: adding error recovery to scannerless generalized-LR parsing. In: Arora, S., Leavens, G.T. (eds.) Proceedings of the 24th Annual ACM SIGPLAN Conference on Object-Oriented Programming, Systems, Languages, and Applications, OOPSLA 2009, pp. 445–464. ACM (2009). https://doi.org/10.1145/1640089.1640122
37. Kats, L.C.L., Vermaas, R., Visser, E.: Integrated language definition testing: enabling test-driven language development. In: Lopes, C.V., Fisher, K. (eds.) Proceedings of the 26th Annual ACM SIGPLAN Conference on Object-Oriented Programming, Systems, Languages, and Applications, OOPSLA 2011, Part of SPLASH 2011, Portland, OR, USA, October 22–27, 2011, pp. 139–154. ACM (2011). https://doi.org/10.1145/2048066.2048080
38. Kats, L.C.L., Visser, E.: The Spoofax language workbench: rules for declarative specification of languages and IDEs. In: Cook, W.R., Clarke, S., Rinard, M.C. (eds.) Proceedings of the 25th Annual ACM SIGPLAN Conference on Object-Oriented Programming, Systems, Languages, and Applications, OOPSLA 2010, pp. 444–463. ACM, Reno/Tahoe (2010). https://doi.org/10.1145/1869459.1869497
39. Kats, L.C.L., Visser, E., Wachsmuth, G.: Pure and declarative syntax definition: paradise lost and regained. In: Cook, W.R., Clarke, S., Rinard, M.C. (eds.) Proceedings of the 25th Annual ACM SIGPLAN Conference on Object-Oriented Programming, Systems, Languages, and Applications, OOPSLA 2010, pp. 918–932. ACM, Reno/Tahoe (2010). https://doi.org/10.1145/1869459.1869535
40. Klint, P.: A meta-environment for generating programming environments. ACM Trans. Softw. Eng. Methodol. **2**(2), 176–201 (1993). https://doi.org/10.1145/151257.151260
41. Klint, P., van der Storm, T., Vinju, J.J.: RASCAL: a domain specific language for source code analysis and manipulation. In: Ninth IEEE International Working Conference on Source Code Analysis and Manipulation, SCAM 2009, Edmonton, Alberta, Canada, September 20–21, 2009, pp. 168–177. IEEE Computer Society (2009). https://doi.org/10.1109/SCAM.2009.28

42. Leroy, X., Doligez, D., Frisch, A., Garrigue, J., Rémy, D., Vouillon, J.: The OCaml system release 4.10 (2020)
43. Lesk, M.E.: Lex–a lexical analyzer generator. Tech. rep. CS-39. AT&T Bell Laboratories, Murray Hill, N.J. (1975)
44. Rekers, J.: Parser generation for interactive environments. Ph.D. thesis, University of Amsterdam, Amsterdam, The Netherlands (January 1992)
45. Salomon, D.J., Cormack, G.V.: Scannerless NSLR(1) parsing of programming languages. In: PLDI, pp. 170–178 (1989)
46. Schwerdfeger, A., Wyk, E.V.: Verifiable composition of deterministic grammars. In: Hind, M., Diwan, A. (eds.) Proceedings of the 2009 ACM SIGPLAN Conference on Programming Language Design and Implementation, PLDI 2009, Dublin, Ireland, June 15–21, 2009, pp. 199–210. ACM (2009). https://doi.org/10.1145/1542476.1542499
47. Schwerdfeger, A., Van Wyk, E.: Verifiable parse table composition for deterministic parsing. In: van den Brand, M., Gašević, D., Gray, J. (eds.) SLE 2009. LNCS, vol. 5969, pp. 184–203. Springer, Heidelberg (2010). https://doi.org/10.1007/978-3-642-12107-4_15
48. Scott, E., Johnstone, A.: GLL parsing. Electron. Notes Theor. Comput. Sci. **253**(7), 177–189 (2010). https://doi.org/10.1016/j.entcs.2010.08.041
49. Sijm, M.P.: Incremental scannerless generalized LR parsing. In: Smaragdakis, Y. (ed.) Proceedings Companion of the 2019 ACM SIGPLAN International Conference on Systems, Programming, Languages, and Applications: Software for Humanity, SPLASH 2019, Athens, Greece, October 20–25, 2019, pp. 54–56. ACM (2019). https://doi.org/10.1145/3359061.3361085
50. Smits, J., Visser, E.: FlowSpec: declarative dataflow analysis specification. In: Combemale, B., Mernik, M., Rumpe, B. (eds.) Proceedings of the 10th ACM SIGPLAN International Conference on Software Language Engineering, SLE 2017, Vancouver, BC, Canada, October 23–24, 2017, pp. 221–231. ACM (2017). https://doi.org/10.1145/3136014.3136029
51. de Souza Amorim, L.E., Erdweg, S., Wachsmuth, G., Visser, E.: Principled syntactic code completion using placeholders. In: van der Storm, T., Balland, E., Varró, D. (eds.) Proceedings of the 2016 ACM SIGPLAN International Conference on Software Language Engineering, Amsterdam, The Netherlands, October 31–November 1, 2016, pp. 163–175. ACM (2016). https://doi.org/10.1145/2997364.2997374
52. de Souza Amorim, L.E., Steindorfer, M.J., Visser, E.: Deep priority conflicts in the wild: a pilot study. In: Combemale, B., Mernik, M., Rumpe, B. (eds.) Proceedings of the 10th ACM SIGPLAN International Conference on Software Language Engineering, SLE 2017, Vancouver, BC, Canada, October 23–24, 2017, pp. 55–66. ACM (2017). https://doi.org/10.1145/3136014.3136020
53. de Souza Amorim, L.E., Visser, E.: A direct semantics of declarative disambiguation rules. In: ACM TOPLAS (2020). under revision
54. de Souza Amorim, L.E., Steindorfer, M.J., Erdweg, S., Visser, E.: Declarative specification of indentation rules: a tooling perspective on parsing and pretty-printing layout-sensitive languages. In: 0005, D.P., Mayerhofer, T., Steimann, F. (eds.) Proceedings of the 11th ACM SIGPLAN International Conference on Software Language Engineering, SLE 2018, Boston, MA, USA, November 05–06, 2018, pp. 3–15. ACM (2018). https://doi.org/10.1145/3276604.3276607
55. de Souza Amorim, L.E., Steindorfer, M.J., Visser, E.: Towards zero-overhead disambiguation of deep priority conflicts. Programming Journal **2**(3), 13 (2018). https://doi.org/10.22152/programming-journal.org/2018/2/13

56. Tomita, M.: An efficient context-free parsing algorithm for natural languages. In: IJCAI, pp. 756–764 (1985)
57. Vergu, V.A., Néron, P., Visser, E.: DynSem: a DSL for dynamic semantics specification. In: Fernández, M. (ed.) 26th International Conference on Rewriting Techniques and Applications, RTA 2015, June 29 to July 1, 2015, Warsaw, Poland. LIPIcs, vol. 36, pp. 365–378. Schloss Dagstuhl - Leibniz-Zentrum fuer Informatik (2015). https://doi.org/10.4230/LIPIcs.RTA.2015.365
58. Visser, E.: A family of syntax definition formalisms. In: van den Brand, M.G.J., Estrela, V.V. (eds.) ASF+SDF 1995. A Workshop on Generating Tools from Algebraic Specifications. Technical report P9504, Programming Research Group, University of Amsterdam (May 1995)
59. Visser, E.: A case study in optimizing parsing schemata by disambiguation filters. In: International Workshop on Parsing Technology (IWPT 1997), pp. 210–224. Massachusetts Institute of Technology, Boston (September 1997)
60. Visser, E.: Scannerless generalized-LR parsing. Tech. rep. P9707, Programming Research Group, University of Amsterdam (July 1997)
61. Visser, E.: Syntax definition for language prototyping. Ph.D. thesis, University of Amsterdam (September 1997)
62. Visser, E.: WebDSL: a case study in domain-specific language engineering. In: Lämmel, R., Visser, J., Saraiva, J. (eds.) GTTSE 2007. LNCS, vol. 5235, pp. 291–373. Springer, Heidelberg (2008). https://doi.org/10.1007/978-3-540-88643-3_7
63. Vollebregt, T., Kats, L.C.L., Visser, E.: Declarative specification of template-based textual editors. In: Sloane, A., Andova, S. (eds.) International Workshop on Language Descriptions, Tools, and Applications, LDTA 2012, Tallinn, Estonia, March 31–April 1, 2012, pp. 1–7. ACM (2012). https://doi.org/10.1145/2427048.2427056
64. Wachsmuth, G., Konat, G., Visser, E.: Language design with the Spoofax language workbench. IEEE Softw. **31**(5), 35–43 (2014). https://doi.org/10.1109/MS.2014.100
65. Wagner, T.A., Graham, S.L.: Efficient and flexible incremental parsing. ACM Trans. Program. Lang. Syst. **20**(5), 980–1013 (1998). https://doi.org/10.1145/293677.293678
66. Wyk, E.V., Bodin, D., Gao, J., Krishnan, L.: Silver: an extensible attribute grammar system. Sci. Comput. Program. **75**(1–2), 39–54 (2010). https://doi.org/10.1016/j.scico.2009.07.004

Finding and Fixing a Mismatch Between
the Go Memory Model
and Data-Race Detector
A Story on Applied Formal Methods

Daniel Schnetzer Fava[⊠]

Department of Informatics, University of Oslo, Oslo, Norway
danielsf@ifi.uio.no

Abstract. Go is an open-source programming language developed at
Google. In previous works, we presented formalizations for a weak memory model and a data-race detector inspired by the Go specification. In
this paper, we describe how our theoretical research guided us in the process of finding and fixing a concrete bug in the language. Specifically, we
discovered and fixed a discrepancy between the Go memory model and
the Go data-race detector implementation—the discrepancy led to the
under-reporting of data races in Go programs. Here, we share our experience applying formal methods on software that powers infrastructure
used by millions of people.

1 Introduction

Go is an open-source programming language designed for concurrency. Developed at Google, the language has gained traction in the areas of cloud computing [6], where it is used to implement various client-server applications and
container management systems, such as Docker [12] and Kubernetes [2].

One of the language's main features are light-weight threads, called *goroutines*, which are spawned during function invocation. Any function can be made
to execute asynchronously by simply prepending the keyword go to the function's
name during invocation. Go's approach to synchronization also stands out. *Do
not communicate by sharing memory; instead, share memory by communicating* [8]—is a catchphrase among Go programmers. The language's feature-mix
encourages a style of programming where (1) variables are implicitly owned
by goroutines, and (2) variables are shared when this ownership is transferred
through direct communication. So, in contrast to locks, which favor synchronization via mutual exclusion, Go has channels, which typically enforce a happens-
before relation [10] between a message sender and its receiver.

The discipline prescribed by Go's *share by communicating* slogan is not,
however, enforced at compile time.[1] It is, therefore, possible for programs to

---

[1] There are good reasons why a type checker cannot enforce such a discipline without
seriously restricting the language.

© Springer Nature Switzerland AG 2020
F. de Boer and A. Cerone (Eds.): SEFM 2020, LNCS 12310, pp. 24–40, 2020.
https://doi.org/10.1007/978-3-030-58768-0_2

harbor data races. Since data races often lead to counter intuitive behavior, the Go programming language comes with a data-race detector built into its toolchain.

The Go memory model is relaxed and its specification describes the behavior of well-synchronized programs. In [4], we gave a small-step operational semantics of a memory model inspired by Go's. There, we proved the DRF-SC guarantee, which states that data-race free (DRF) program executions behave sequentially consistently (SC) under the proposed model. Given the importance of flagging data races, in [5] we explore the use of our semantics for the sake of data-race detection. Armed with these formalisms, we turned our attention to Go's implementation. With that, we discovered that the Go data-race detector was not strictly abiding by the rules of the Go memory model specification. This oversight lead to the under-reporting of data races in Go programs. We then proposed and implemented a fix in conjunction with the Go community. Here, we discuss how the theoretical modeling of the language helped us find and address this issue.

In Sects. 2 and 3, we will visit the Go memory model and explore examples of synchronization via channel communication. Having covered this background, we discuss how the Go data-race detector is built into the language (Sect. 4). In Sect. 4.1, we show that the detector's implementation inadvertently mismatched rules governing channel communication. We address the issue in Sect. 5 and share lessons we learned in Sect. 6.

2 Synchronization via Channel Communication

Two concurrent memory accesses constitute a data race if they reference the same memory location and at least one of the accesses is a *write*. Data races can be eliminated through synchronization, that is, the enforcement of an order between conflicting memory accesses. In Go, synchronization is performed via channel communication. Go channels assure FIFO communication from a sender to a receiver sharing the channel's reference. Channels can be dynamically created and closed—their type and finite capacity are fixed upon creation.

When attempting to receive from an empty channel, a thread blocks until, if ever, a value is made available by a sender. A thread also blocks when attempting to send on a channel that is full. According to the Go memory model specification [7], the following two main rules govern synchronization. Given a channel c with capacity C:

I. A send on c happens-before the corresponding receive from c completes.
II. The kth receive from c happens-before the $(k + C)^{th}$ send on c completes.

The first rule establishes a causal relationship between a sender and its communicating partner. In contrast, the second rule establishes a relationship between a sender and some past receiver, without there being any message transmission between the two goroutines. Note also that the second rule accounts for channel capacity: a current sender is able to place a new message because some past receiver, by taking an older message out, has made space in the channel's buffer.

Figure 1a is an example of synchronization via rule (I), and Fig. 1b is an example via rule (II). Throughout the paper, we will follow the syntax in [4], which closely matches Go's. The term $c \leftarrow v$, with the arrow pointing into c, stand for the sending of value v over channel c. Let $\leftarrow c$, with the arrow pointing away from c, stand for the reception of a value from the channel. Assuming a channel of capacity one, Fig. 1a is the classic message passing example, while Fig. 1b enforces mutual exclusion.

$T0$	$T1$		$T0$	$T1$
$z := 42$	$\leftarrow c$		$c \leftarrow 0$	$c \leftarrow 0$
$c \leftarrow 0$	load z		$z := 42$	$z := 43$
			$\leftarrow c$	$\leftarrow c$

(a) Message passing example.   (b) Mutual exclusion example.

Fig. 1. Synchronization via channel communication (channels of capacity one).

In the message passing example, the goroutine $T0$ writes to a shared variable z and, by sending a message over a channel, the routine transfers its implicit ownership of z. Goroutine $T1$ blocks until a message is ready to be received. Once a message has been received, $T1$ proceeds to load from z. This program is properly synchronized, which means $T1$ necessarily loads the value of 42 as opposed to potentially observing an uninitialized variable value. Using the happens-before (HB) rules of the Go memory-model specification, we can show that the memory accesses are properly synchronized as follows:

$$z := 42 \quad \sqsubset_{hb} \quad c \leftarrow 0 \qquad \qquad \text{via program order} \quad (1)$$
$$c \leftarrow 0 \quad \sqsubset_{hb} \quad \leftarrow c \qquad \qquad \text{via channel rule (I)} \quad (2)$$
$$\leftarrow c \quad \sqsubset_{hb} \quad \text{load } z \qquad \qquad \text{via program order} \quad (3)$$
$$z := 42 \quad \sqsubset_{hb} \quad \text{load } z \qquad \text{via (1), (2), (3) and transitivity of HB.}$$

While Fig. 1a and rule (I) account for direct communication, Fig. 1b relies on rule (II) and the use of channels as locks. The example in Fig. 1b involves two threads attempting to write to the same shared variable. Before writing, a thread sends a message onto a channel. Because the channel has capacity one, all subsequent attempts to send again will block until the prior message is received. Therefore, it is not possible for $T0$ and $T1$ to execute their critical sections at the same time. The send is thus analogous to acquiring a lock, and the receive to releasing the lock. Again, we can use the Go memory model to reason about this example. Without loss of generality, assume $T0$ sends its message first, then

$$z := 42 \quad \sqsubset_{hb} \quad \leftarrow c \text{ by } T0 \qquad\qquad \text{via program order} \qquad (4)$$
$$\leftarrow c \text{ by } T0 \quad \sqsubset_{hb} \quad c \leftarrow 0 \text{ by } T1 \qquad\qquad \text{via channel rule (II)} \qquad (5)$$
$$c \leftarrow 0 \text{ by } T1 \quad \sqsubset_{hb} \quad z := 43 \qquad\qquad \text{via program order} \qquad (6)$$
$$z := 42 \quad \sqsubset_{hb} \quad z := 43 \qquad \text{via (4), (5), (6) and transitivity.}$$

While mutual exclusion is ensured, we cannot ascertain the final value of z. If $T0$ sends a message before $T1$, then z equals 43; otherwise, $z = 42$. Note also that, in this example, rule (I) is obviated by the *program order;* therefore, the rule has no synchronization effect here.[2]

The Go memory model is described plain and succinctly in English [7]. The word "completes," present in both rules (I) and (II), can easily be overlooked. By overlooking the distinction between an operation and its completion, the Go data-race detector over-synchronizes and, therefore, fails to report certain races. The bug, which we describe in detail in the next section, is related to the following question: Is it possible for the detector to account for the mutex paradigm (Fig. 1b) and, at the same time, observe the distinction between a channel operation and its completion?

3   The Go Memory Model: Every Word Counts

The completion of a channel operation, in addition to the operation itself, is an important part of the Go memory model. In rule (I), it is not the case that a send happens-before the corresponding receive. Instead, the send happens-before the *completion* of the corresponding receive. Similar for rule (II), involving a past receive and the *completion* of a current send. To illustrate, consider Fig. 2, where each vertical arrow represents the execution of a thread (flowing from top to bottom). Both the top and the bottom diagrams depicts consecutive send sd and receive rv operations on a channel of capacity one—the operations are indexed as to show their order of execution.

According to the Go memory model, channel operations are related as shown in Fig. 2a. The operations are broken into two halves of a circle: the top is the operation and the bottom its completion. The arrows in the diagram represent the happens-before relation—arrows are labeled with the memory-model rule that justify their existence. According to rule (I), the 0th send happens-before the completion of the 0th receive—this relation is captured by the arrow starting at the top half-circle on the far left (sd^0) and ending at the bottom half-circle to the right (completion of rv^0). The next arrow establishes the happens-before relation

---

[2] The relation below can be derived by both program-order as well as by rule (I). Similar for the send and receive operations performed by $T1$.

$$c \leftarrow 0 \text{ by } T0 \quad \sqsubset_{hb} \quad \leftarrow c \text{ by } T0$$

between receive rv^0 and send sd^1 according to rule (II), and so forth. Note from Fig. 2a that an operation is related to its immediate predecessor. There is no chain of happens-before starting from the "distant" past. For example, although sd^0 is related to the completion of rv^0, and rv^0 is related to the completion of sd^1, it is not the case that sd^0 and sd^1 are related to each other.

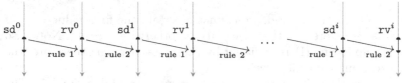

(a) Depiction of rules (I) and (II) on a channel of capacity one.

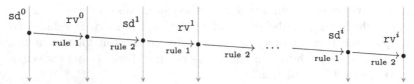

(b) Alternate formulation of rules (I) and (II) with no distinction between an operation and its completion.

Fig. 2. The Go memory model specification, *every word counts*.

Figure 2b captures an alternative formulation of the happens-before rules (I) and (II) where the word "completes" is left out. Sends and receives are not split into the operation and the operation's completion. Instead, sends and receives happen-before each other. This formulation leads to a chain starting at the very first send, and connecting every send and receive operation ever performed onto the channel. From an application programmer's perspective, this chain leads to an accumulation of happens-before information: after interacting with a channel, a goroutine's behavior is now dependent, not only on its communicating partner but, on every thread that has previously interacted with the channel. From the point of view of data races, this alternate formulation leads to over-synchronization.

The Go data-race detector's implementation matches the behavior of Fig. 2b and, therefore, deviates from the Go memory model specification. Note that the over-synchronization on the part of the detector is not the result of careful deliberation, for example when false-negatives are accepted in exchange for lower runtime overheads. Rather, the implementation springs from an interpretation of synchronization from the perspective of locks rather than of channels. As will be discussed in Sect. 5, addressing this issue not only eliminates false-negatives but also yields lower runtime overhead.

4   The Go Data-Race Detector

By adding -race to the command line, a Go program can be compiled and run with data-race detection enabled. The Go data-race detector is based on TSan, the Thread Sanitizer library [9]. The library is part of the LLVM infrastructure [11] and was originally designed to find races in C/C++11 applications.

When data-race detection is enabled, each thread becomes associated with an additional data structure. This data structure keeps track of the operations that are in happens-before from a thread's point of view. In most data-race detectors, including TSan, this data structure is a *vector clock* (VC) [10]. Vector-clocks offer a compact representation of the relative order of execution between threads. With this bookkeeping, data-race detectors are able to find synchronization issues in programs—where synchronization means the transfer of happens-before information between threads.

In the setting of locks, a thread performs an *acquire* operation in order to "learn" the happens-before information stored in a lock. By performing a *release* operation, a thread deposits its happens-before information onto a lock. In the setting of channels, we can think of happens-before as being transferred via sends and receives.

Listing 1.1: Send.		Listing 1.2: Receive.	

```
1   func chansend(c *hchan,            func chanrecv(c *hchan,                 1
2            ep unsafe.Pointer,                 ep unsafe.Pointer,            2
3            block bool,                        block bool)                   3
4            callerpc uintptr)                  (selected,                    4
5            bool {                             received bool) {              5
6     ...                                 ...                                 6
7     lock(&c.lock)                       lock(&c.lock)                       7
8     ...                                 ...                                 8
9     if c.qcount < c.dataqsiz {          if c.qcount > 0 {                   9
10      qp := chanbuf(c, c.sendx)           qp := chanbuf(c, c.recvx)         10
11      if raceenabled {                    if raceenabled {                  11
12        raceacquire(qp)                     raceacquire(qp)                 12
13        racerelease(qp)                     racerelease(qp)                 13
14      }                                   }                                 14
15                                          if ep != nil {                    15
16      typedmemmove(c.elemtype, qp, ep)      typedmemmove(c.elemtype, ep, qp) 16
17                                          }                                 17
18                                          typedmemclr(c.elemtype, qp)       18
19      c.sendx++                           c.recvx++                         19
20      if c.sendx == c.dataqsiz {          if c.recvx == c.dataqsiz {        20
21        c.sendx = 0                         c.recvx = 0                     21
22      }                                   }                                 22
23      c.qcount++                          c.qcount--                        23
24      unlock(&c.lock)                     unlock(&c.lock)                   24
25      return true                         return true, true                 25
26    }                                   }                                   26
27    ...                                 ...                                 27
28  }                                   }                                   28
```

Fig. 3. Snippets of Go's send and receive operations from runtime/chan.go.

Figure 3 contains snippets from Go's implementation of the send and receive operations. Unsurprisingly, Go implements a channel of capacity C as an array of length C. This array is contained in a struct called hchan. Struct member sendx is the index where a new message is to be deposited, while recvx is the index of the next message to be retrieved. Function chanbuf takes a channel struct and an index—the function returns a pointer to the channel's array at the given index. Note from lines 19 to 22 that a channel array is treated as a circular buffer.

When data-race detection is enabled, each channel array entry becomes associated with a vector-clock. Also, when detection is enabled, a send operation (Listing 1.1) generates calls to acquire and release—lines 11 to 14. The acquire causes the sender to "learn" the happens-before (HB) information associated with the channel entry at c.sendx. The release causes the thread's HB information to be stored back into that entry.[3] The receive operation is similarly implemented and shown in Listing 1.2.

In light of the implementation described above, we now revisit the message passing and mutual exclusion examples of Sect. 2. In the case of message passing, a thread sends a message onto a channel of capacity one, then another thread receives this message before accessing a shared resource—see Fig. 1a. According to the data-race detector's implementation, the channel array entry at index 0 observes an *acquire* followed by *release* on behalf of the sender. Then, again, a sequence of *acquire* followed by *release* on behalf of the receiver. In effect, the happens-before information of the sender is transferred to the receiver: specifically, the *release* by $T0$ followed by the *acquire* by $T1$ places $T0$'s write operation in happens-before relation with respect to $T1$'s read operation. The message passing example of Fig. 1 is thus deemed properly synchronized by the Go data-race detector.

We can reason about the mutual exclusion example of Fig. 1b in similar terms. A thread sends onto a channel, accesses a shared resource, and then receives from the channel. With the receive operation, this thread deposits its happens-before information onto the channel—line 13 of Listing 1.2. The second thread then acquires this happens-before information when it sends onto the channel—line 12 of Listing 1.1. Again, the Go data-race detector's implementation correctly deems the example as properly synchronized.

4.1 The Bug

Although the Go data-race detector behaves correctly on the message-passing and mutual-exclusion examples, the detector's implementation does not reflect the Go memory model specification. The acquire/release sequence performed on behalf of send and receive operations follows the typical lock usage. Channel

---

[3] In the implementation of the send operation, a message is moved from the sender's buffer to a receiver's buffer ep on line 16. The index c.sendx is incremented in line 19 and the increment wraps around based on the length of the array—lines 20 to 22. The number of elements in the array is incremented, the lock protecting the channel is unlocked and the function returns—lines 23 to 25.

programming is, however, different from lock programming. The current implementation of the detector leads to an accumulation of happens-before information associated with channel entries. This monotonic growth of happens-before information, however, is not prescribed by the Go memory model.

In the example that follows, we illustrate the mismatch between (1) the implementation of the data-race detector and (2) the memory model specification. We show how this mismatch leads to over-synchronization and the under reporting of data races.

$$
\begin{array}{ccc}
T0 & T1 & T2 \\
c \leftarrow 0 & c \leftarrow 0 & \leftarrow c \\
z := 42 & & \text{load } z \\
\leftarrow c & &
\end{array}
$$

Fig. 4. Example that highlights a mismatch between the Go memory model and the Go data-race detector implementation. (Capacity of channel c equals one).

Let c in Fig. 4 be a channel of capacity one. The example is then a mix of mutual exclusion and message passing: $T0$ is using the channel as a lock in an attempt to protect its access to a shared variable,[4] and we can interpret $T1$ as using the same channel to communicate with $T2$.[5] Now, consider the interleaving in which $T0$ runs to completion, followed by $T1$, then $T2$—shown in Trace 7. Is the write to z by $T0$ in a race with the read of z by $T2$?

$$
(c \leftarrow 0)_{T0} \quad (z := 42)_{T0} \quad (\leftarrow c)_{T0} \quad (c \leftarrow 0)_{T1} \quad (\leftarrow c)_{T2} \quad (\text{load } z)_{T2} \quad (7)
$$

The original Go data-race detector does not flag these accesses as racy:[6] $T0$ releases its happens-before (HB) by sending on the channel. This HB is stored in the vector-clock associated with c's 0th array entry. The send by $T1$ performs an acquire followed by a release, at which point the VC associated with the entry contains the union of $T0$'s and $T1$'s happens-before. Finally, the receive by $T2$ performs an acquire and a release, causing $T2$ to learn the happens-before of $T0$ and $T1$. Formally, the data-race detector derives a happens-before relation between the write and the read as follows:

$$
\begin{array}{lll}
z := 42 & \sqsubseteq_{hb} \ \leftarrow c \text{ by } T0 & \text{via program order} \\
\leftarrow c \text{ by } T0 & \sqsubseteq_{hb} \ c \leftarrow 0 \text{ by } T1 & \text{release by } T0, \text{ acquire by } T1 \\
c \leftarrow 0 \text{ by } T1 & \sqsubseteq_{hb} \ \leftarrow c \text{ by } T2 & \text{release by } T1, \text{ acquire by } T0 \\
\leftarrow c \text{ by } T2 & \sqsubseteq_{hb} \ \text{load } z & \text{via program order} \\
z := 42 & \sqsubseteq_{hb} \ \text{load } z & \text{via transitivity of HB}
\end{array}
$$

---

[4] The send operation by $T0$ is analogous to acquire and the receive to release.
[5] Recall that the mutual exclusion and message passing patterns were introduced in Fig. 1 and discussed in Sect. 2.
[6] GitHub issue https://github.com/golang/go/issues/37355.

According to the Go memory model specification, however, the receive from c in $T0$ is not in happens-before relation to the send in $T1$. Instead, the receive is in happens-before relation to the *completion* of the send! Information about the write to z by thread $T0$ is transmitted to $T1$, but this information is only incorporated into $T1$ *after* the thread has transmitted its message to $T2$. Therefore, $T2$ does not receive $T0$'s happens-before information. In other words, according to the Go memory model, there is no chain of happens-before connecting $T0$ to $T2$. The trace captured by Eq. (7) is thus racy, with the race depicted in Fig. 5. Specifically, the race is captured by the absence of a path between the write to z in $T0$ and the load of z in $T2$.

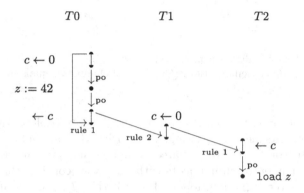

Fig. 5. Partial order on events according to the Go memory model. The HB relation is represented by arrows labeled with the Go memory model rule justifying the arrow's existence. The top part of the half-circle corresponds to a channel operation and the bottom to its completion.

The Go memory model calls for a mix between channel communication as described by Lamport [10] and lock programming. Lamport [10] was studying distributed systems in the absence of shared memory: the shared resources were the channels themselves, and the absence of races (of channel races) was related to determinism. In contrast, Go employs channels as a primitive for synchronizing *memory accesses*. In Go, some happens-before relations are forged solely between communicating partners—these relations are derived from rule (I), which is also present in [10]. Similar to lock programming, some happens-before relations are the result of an accumulation of effects from past interactions on a channel. This accumulation occurs when we incorporate rule (II), which is not present in [10]. So, while the language favors a discipline where an implicit notion of variable ownership is transferred via direct communication, as prescribed by rule (I), by incorporating rule (II), Go also supports the use of channels as locks.

5   The Fix: Capturing the Semantics of Channels

The repair to the Go data-race detector's deviation from the memory model specification comes from acknowledging that a primitive, different from acquire and release, can better fit the semantics of synchronization via channel communication. We propose the primitive depicted in Fig. 6, which we call *release-acquire-exchange* or `rea`. Let $\mathbb{T}_t$ be the happens-before information of thread t, m be the channel entry where a message will be deposited or retrieved, and $\mathbb{C}_m$ be the happens-before information associated with m. The primitive is implemented with a thread releasing onto a place-holder and then acquiring from $\mathbb{C}_m$. The happens-before in $\mathbb{C}_m$ is then overwritten with the HB information from the place-holder.[7] We added this new synchronization primitive into TSan, the data-race detection library that powers the Go data-race detector. With the new primitive in place, changes to the Go sources became trivial:[8] it involved changing sequences of acquire/release calls with a call to *release-acquire-exchange*.

$$\frac{\mathbb{C}'_t := \mathbb{C}_t \sqcup \mathbb{L}_m \qquad \mathbb{L}'_m := \mathbb{C}_t}{(\mathbb{C}_t, \mathbb{L}_m) \Rightarrow^{\text{rea}(t,m)} (\mathbb{C}'_t, \mathbb{L}'_m)}$$

Fig. 6. Semantics of "release-acquire-exchange," a new primitive added to TSan.

Given the addition of `rea` into TSan, let us revisit trace (7). While the original implementation of the Go data-race detector did not flag this trace as racy, the updated version does. Given the detector's updated implementation, we can reason about the race as follows. Let $\mathbb{T}_{T0}$, $\mathbb{T}_{T1}$, and $\mathbb{T}_{T2}$ be data-structures storing happens-before information of threads $T0$, $T1$, and $T2$. Let $\mathbb{C}_{c[0]}$ be the happens-before associated with the 0th array entry of channel c. We denote the write event to z as $!z$ and, for simplicity, we represent happens-before information as a set of memory events. The race-detector state is then the tuple $[\mathbb{T}_{T0}, \mathbb{T}_{T1}, \mathbb{T}_{T2}, \mathbb{C}_{c[0]}]$, with initial state $[\{\}, \{\}, \{\}, \{\}]$. The data-race detector performs the following transitions as the program executes:

---

[7] The place-holder is a variable local to a function in TSan, as opposed to an extra memory region allocated in Go.

[8] Changes in Go https://golang.org/cl/220419 and TSan https://reviews.llvm.org/D76300.

$$\begin{array}{cccc}
\mathbb{C}_{T0} & \mathbb{C}_{T1} & \mathbb{C}_{T2} & \mathbb{L}_{c[0]}
\end{array}$$

$$[\ \{\}, \quad \{\}, \quad \{\}, \quad \{\}\ ] \Rightarrow^{(c \leftarrow 0)_{T0}}$$
$$[\ \{\}, \quad \{\}, \quad \{\}, \quad \{\}\ ] \Rightarrow^{(z:=42)_{T0}} \tag{8}$$
$$[\{!z\}, \quad \{\}, \quad \{\}, \quad \{\}\ ] \Rightarrow^{(\leftarrow c)_{T0}} \tag{9}$$
$$[\{!z\}, \quad \{\}, \quad \{\}, \quad \{!z\}] \Rightarrow^{(c \leftarrow 0)_{T1}} \tag{10}$$
$$[\{!z\}, \quad \{!z\}, \quad \{\}, \quad \{\}\ ] \Rightarrow^{(\leftarrow c)_{T2}} \tag{11}$$
$$[\{!z\}, \quad \{!z\}, \quad \{\}, \quad \{\}\ ] \Rightarrow^{(\mathtt{load}z)_{T2}} \tag{12}$$

The write to z by $T0$ places $!z$ into $\mathbb{T}_{T0}$—transition from Eq. (8) to (9). Sends and receives are interpreted according to their formal semantics in Fig. 6. The receive by $T0$ places the write event into the channel-entry's happens-before—Eqs. (9) and (10). The send by $T1$ places the write event into the thread's happens-before and overwrites the channel-entry's happens-before with the empty set—Eqs. (10) and (11). The receive by $T2$ retrieves the empty happens-before information— Eqs. (11) and (12). Therefore, at the time $T2$ loads from the shared variable, the write to z by $T0$ is not in happens-before with respect to $T2$. In conclusion, the execution is racy.

Note that the fix to the Go data-race detector does not invalidate the use of channels as locks. Without loss of generality, let the trace below be an execution of the mutual exclusion example of Fig. 1b.

$$(c \leftarrow 0)_{T0} \quad (z := 42)_{T0} \quad (\leftarrow c)_{T0} \quad (c \leftarrow 0)_{T1} \quad (z := 43)_{T1} \quad (\leftarrow c)_{T1} \tag{13}$$

The detector's execution, from initial state $[\mathbb{T}_{T0}, \mathbb{T}_{T1}, \mathbb{C}_{c[0]}] = [\{\}, \{\}, \{\}]$, is

$$\begin{array}{ccc}
\mathbb{T}_{T0} & \mathbb{T}_{T1} & \mathbb{C}_{c[0]}
\end{array}$$

$$[\ \{\}, \quad \{\}, \quad \{\}\ ] \Rightarrow^{(c \leftarrow 0)_{T0}}$$
$$[\ \{\}, \quad \{\}, \quad \{\}\ ] \Rightarrow^{(z:=42)_{T0}}$$
$$[\{!z\}, \quad \{\}, \quad \{\}\ ] \Rightarrow^{(\leftarrow c)_{T0}}$$
$$[\{!z\}, \quad \{\}, \quad \{!z\}] \Rightarrow^{(c \leftarrow 0)_{T1}}$$
$$[\{!z\}, \quad \{!z\}, \quad \{\}\ ]$$

Note that the event $!z$ capturing the write by $T0$ is contained in $\mathbb{T}_{T1}$ before $T1$ attempts to write to z. In other words, the writes are ordered by happens-before and the execution is properly synchronized. Thus, the answer to the question raised at the end of Sect. 2, *"is it possible to support the use of channels as locks (as in the mutex example) and still avoid over-synchronization?"* is yes.

We implement the new synchronization primitive **rea** in TSan with one pass, as opposed to two passes, over the data-structure storing happens-before information. Therefore, the updated data-race detector implementation provides better performance than the original sequence of *acquire* followed by *release*. Another consequence of our fix is a potential reduction in the memory footprint associated with data-race detection. This savings comes from the fact that vector clocks associated with channel entries no longer observe as large of an accumulation of happens-before information—this point was previously touched upon in Sect. 3, Fig. 2. We include a short experimental evaluation in Appendix A.

5.1 From Small-Step Operational Semantics to rea

The *release-acquire-exchange* primitive comes from our previous formalizations of Go channels. It is conceptually useful to distinguish between happens-before information transmitted on behalf of rule (I) versus (II). In our earlier formalization of a memory model inspired by the Go specification [4], a channel c is split into two: a forward and a backward one. The forward channel c_f holds messages and thread-local information to be transmitted, as prescribed by rule (I), from a sender to its corresponding receiver. The backward channel c_b, which flows from a prior receiver to a current sender, captures rule (II) of the memory model.[9]

In [4], threads or goroutines $p\langle\sigma, t\rangle$ have a unique identifier p, contain thread-local information σ, and a term t corresponding to the program under execution. When it comes to data-race detection, thread-local information σ is composed of *happens-before* data. This data could be stored in a vector-clock or, more simply, it could be a set of read- and write-events that are in happens-before with respect to the thread. Synchronization, therefore, entails the exchange of thread-local information σ via channel communication.

$$\frac{\neg closed(c_f[q_2]) \qquad \sigma' = \sigma + \sigma''}{c_b[q_1 :: \sigma''] \parallel p\langle\sigma, c \leftarrow v; t\rangle \parallel c_f[q_2] \quad \rightarrow \quad c_b[q_1] \parallel p\langle\sigma', t\rangle \parallel c_f[(v, \sigma) :: q_2]} \text{ R-Send}$$

$$\frac{v \neq \bot \qquad \sigma' = \sigma + \sigma''}{c_b[q_1] \parallel p\langle\sigma, \texttt{let } r = \leftarrow c \texttt{ in } t\rangle \parallel c_f[q_2 :: (v, \sigma'')] \quad \rightarrow} \text{ R-Rec}$$
$$c_b[\sigma :: q_1] \parallel p\langle\sigma', \texttt{let } r = v \texttt{ in } t\rangle \parallel c_f[q_2]$$

Fig. 7. Send and receive reduction rules in the calculus of [4].

Configurations consist of the parallel composition of goroutines, memory events, and channels. The semantics of [4] is operational. We give the reduction rules for sends and receives in Fig. 7—other rules are omitted and can be found in the original paper. The let-construct in R-Rec is a binder for the local variable r in a term t. In the case of R-Rec, the let-construct allows t to refer to the value obtained when receiving from a channel.

---

[9] As noted in [5], "the interplay between forward and backward channels can also be understood as a form of flow control. Entries in the backward channel's queue are not values deposited by threads. Instead, [these entries] can be seen as tickets that grant senders a free slot in the communication channel.".

According to reduction rule R-SEND, when a thread sends a value v, the thread's local state σ is placed on the forward channel alongside v. The rule captures captures the placement of the message (v, σ) onto the forward channel as follows: if q_2 is the content of the forward channel before transmission, $(v, \sigma) ::$ q_2 are the contents after. The transmission of σ models rule (I) of the Go memory model: a receiver who receives (v, σ) will learn about the sender's actions up to the given send operation.

Besides transmitting, a sender also learns HB information in accordance to rule (II). Precisely, the $(k + C)^{th}$ sender obtains, from the backward channel, thread-local state from the kth receiver. This is captured by the update $\sigma' = \sigma + \sigma''$ with the state σ'' coming from the backward channel. Thus, if the contents of the backward channel were $q_1 :: \sigma''$ before the send, the channel is left with q_1 after the send. Note that the update to the sender state occurs *on completion* of the send operation: the update "occurs after" the sender has deposited its message onto the forward channel—concretely, the send transmits the thread state σ as opposed to the updated thread state σ'.

When receiving, a goroutine obtains a value v as well as a state σ'' from a sender. As dictated by rule (I), the receiver updates its state given the corresponding sender state: $\sigma' = \sigma + \sigma''$. The sender also deposits its state onto the backward channel. Similar to R-SEND, the original thread state σ is deposited as opposed to the updated thread state σ'.

For both reduction rules R-SEND and R-REC, local thread state σ is deposited onto a channel as opposed to the update thread state σ'. This discipline creates a distinction between an operation and its completion. In effect, the reduction rules do not cause the over-synchronization observed by the Go data-race detector.

5.2 Why Not *acquire* and *release*?

The formalization in [4] speaks of synchronization in terms of channel communication. Since TSan operates at the level of locks, we might be tempted to implement the reduction rules with acquire and release operations. The reduction rule R-SEND could be implemented with a thread releasing its happens-before information into the forward queue, and *then* acquiring happens-before information from the backward queue. Similarly, R-REC can be implemented with a release to the backward queue, followed by an acquire from the forward queue.

One invariant of the semantics in [4] is that the number of elements in the forward and backward queues equals the capacity of the channel. Since a thread must first release its HB into the channel before acquiring from the channel, there would be more than C entries in the queues while a send or receive is in-flight. In fact, when using acquire and release operations as primitives, the Go data-race detector would need to allocate an array of length $C + 2$ for a channel of capacity C. Given such an array, sends and receives can be implemented with acquire/release operations as shown on Listings 1.3 and 1.4. Recall that `c.sendx` and `c.recvx` are the indices into the array where the next message is to be deposited and retrieved respectively. Recall also that `chanbuf` returns a pointer to a channel's array at a given index.

Listing 1.3. Implementation of send.

```
1   idx := c.sendx+1
2   if idx == C+2
3       idx = 0
4   qf := chanbuf(c, c.sendx)
5   qb := chanbuf(c, idx)
6   racerelease(qf)
7   raceacquire(qb)
```

Listing 1.4. Implementation of receive.

```
idx := c.recvx−1                    1
if c.recvx == 0                     2
    idx = C+1                       3
qf := chanbuf(c, c.recvx)           4
qb := chanbuf(c, idx)               5
racerelease(qb)                     6
raceacquire(qf)                     7
```

Although correct, there are major downsides to the solution of Listings 1.3 and 1.4. First, it requires additional memory allocation. Second, because the Go runtime expects a channel of capacity C to be implemented with an array of length C, the solution would require intrusive changes. Third, from a timing perspective, in order to implement a single channel operation, the solution performs two passes over the data-structure storing happens-before information—we want a solution that performs less passes.

Compared to *acquire* and *release*, the *release-acquire-exchange* primitive requires no additional allocation in Go, involves minimal changes to the Go runtime, and has lower overhead.

6 Lessons Learned

When we started looking at TSan's source code, our goal was to improve Go's data-race detector by expressing synchronization in terms of channels as opposed to locks [5]. We began reading the source code of Go and TSan in November 2019. In January 2020, we started experimenting by compiling the projects from source and making modifications in order to gain experience and intuition. This tinkering lead us to find, in early and mid February, a small Go compiler bug[10] and a small performance bug in TSan.[11] Shortly after, around late February, we found the bug described in this paper.

Given our experience formalizing the calculus in [4], we could see similarities between our reduction rules and the Go implementation.[12] The implementations of send and receive, however, stood out. The bug was thus found by inspection. We created a test (Fig. 4) to showcase what we believed was discrepancy between the detector and the memory model. From there, we filed an issue on GitHub and started interacting with the Go community. With this interaction, which

---

[10] https://github.com/golang/go/issues/37012.

[11] https://reviews.llvm.org/D74831.

[12] For example, the closing of channels in both [4] and in Go cause happens-before information to be deposited onto the channel, regardless of whether the channel is full.

went until May, an initial patch was iteratively improved until being accepted for future release.

In this section, we collect insights drawn from our experience in both (1) formalizing aspects of the Go programming language and (2) interacting with the TSan and Go communities.

Models Do Not Have to Be Right, They Have to Be Useful. In [4], we developed a memory model based on the Go specification. Before embarking on studying the Go source code, we found ourselves at cross-roads. Since our model is not as relaxed as Go's, more theoretical research remained to be done. We pondered whether to continue working on formalizations or whether to investigate how the current model fits the "real world." Both avenues are interesting to us. By taking, for now, the second avenue, we learned that *models do not have to be right, they have to be useful.* Our memory model formalization in [4] *is not* the memory model of Go, but it is close enough to allow us to reason about Go and its implementation.

Mind the Gap. In one hand, we have the concept of a data-race according to the synchronization rules of the Go memory model specification. The specification is expressed in English. On the other hand, we have the Go data-race detector implementation, with thousands of lines of code spawning different projects and repositories and involving at least three languages (Go, C/C++, and assembly). These are two ends of a spectrum. Our model was useful, in part, because of where it sits in this spectrum. When developing the model in [4], we followed the English text of the Go memory model specification very closely. Our model, however, is expressed in structural operational semantics—its rules form an executable implementation. Our calculus, therefore, forms a bridge between source code and the specification expressed in natural language.[13]

Bad News Is Good News. The effort in formalizing and proving a nontrivial property of a software system is often high. Before finding the issue described in this paper, we had been working on formalisms related to Go for over two years. This high barrier of entrance is both good and bad. It is good, less obviously so, because it opens opportunities for collaboration between industry and academia. While industry excels at delivering software, academia can provide artifacts, such as formalisms and proofs, which are still not as commonly produced in industry.[14]

---

[13] Our observation about the representational different between specification and implementation is not new. The idea of bridging specification and implementation has been tackled by many fronts, for example [1].

[14] Because of stigma, the "formal" qualifier has been de-emphasized when disseminating formal methods in industry [13]. This stance has shifted dramatically [3].

7   Conclusion

The bug described in this paper evaded skilled developers for about six years, nearly since the data-race detector was bolted onto the Go runtime. In this paper, we share how formal methods played an integral role in bringing the issue to light, and giving it closure.

Acknowledgments. I would like to thank Martin Steffen for his feedback on this manuscript, Dmitry Vyukov for his feedback and guidance on incorporating the proposed changes into Go and TSan, Keith Randall for rebuilding the TSan library files that ship with Go, and everyone who gave constructive feedback during the code review process. I would also like to thank the reviewers for their comments on this manuscript, and reviewer 2 in particular.

A   Memory Footprint

Here we illustrate how our fix to the Go data-race detector leads to a smaller memory foot-print. Consider an in-place parallel sorting algorithm where an array is recursively split, up to some depth, in approximately half. Each region of the array is assigned to a thread for sorting. When a thread completes sorting, it signals its parent. The parent merges, in-place, the consecutive array regions previously assigned to its children.

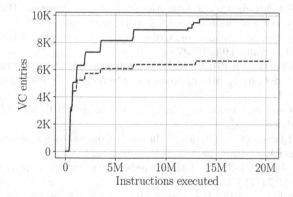

Fig. 8. Number of VC entries associated with channels during the execution of an in-place parallel sorting algorithm: before (solid line) and after (dashed line) the introduction of release-acquire-exchange.

We tracked the number of entries in the vector-clocks associated with channel array entries. Measurements of the number of VC entries were taken multiple times during the program's execution. For ease of collecting and plotting the data, we modified TSan to call out to a reference data-race detector implemented

in Python.[15],[16] Figure 8 shows the number of VC entries before and after the
fix to the data-race detector—meaning, with a race detector that performed an
acquire followed by *release* versus a race detector that implements the *release-
acquire-exchange* primitive. The x-axis is the number of instructions executed,
the y-axis is the number of vector-clock entries consumed so far in the execution.
As the program makes progress, more entries accumulate in the vector-clocks
associated with channel entries. This accumulation is much more accentuated
before the fix to the data-race detector. In fact, for this workload, the fix lead to
larger than 30% reduction in the number of VC entries after 12.5M instructions
were executed.

References

1. Back, R., von Wright, J.: Refinement Calculus - A Systematic Introduction. Graduate Texts in Computer Science. Springer, Heidelberg (1998). https://doi.org/10.
   1007/978-1-4612-1674-2
2. Brewer, E.A.: Kubernetes and the path to cloud native. In: Ghandeharizadeh, S.,
   Barahmand, S., Balazinska, M., Freedman, M.J. (eds.) Proceedings of the Sixth
   ACM Symposium on Cloud Computing, SoCC 2015, Kohala Coast, Hawaii, USA,
   August 27–29, 2015, p. 167. ACM (2015)
3. Cook, B.: Formal reasoning about the security of amazon web services. In: Chockler, H., Weissenbacher, G. (eds.) CAV 2018. LNCS, vol. 10981, pp. 38–47. Springer,
   Cham (2018). https://doi.org/10.1007/978-3-319-96145-3_3
4. Fava, D., Steffen, M., Stolz, V.: Operational semantics of a weak memory model
   with channel synchronization. J. Log. Algebr. Methods Program. **103**, 1–30 (2019).
   An extended version of the FM 18 publication with the same title
5. Fava, D.S., Steffen, M.: Ready, set, Go! data-race detection and the Go language.
   Sci. Comput. Program. **195**, 102473 (2020)
6. Go Developer Survey (2019). https://blog.golang.org/survey2019-results
7. Go Memory Model (2014). https://golang.org/ref/mem. Accessed May 31. covering
   Go version 1.9.1
8. Go Share Memory by Communicating. The Go blog (2010). https://blog.go-lang.
   org/codelab-share
9. Google.thread.sanitizer   (2015).   https://github.com/google/sanitizers/wiki/
   ThreadSanitizerAlgorithm
10. Lamport, L.: Time, clocks, and the ordering of events in a distributed system.
    Commun. ACM **21**(7), 558–565 (1978)
11. Lattner, C., Adve, V.: LLVM: a compilation framework for lifelong program anal-
    ysis & transformation. In International Symposium on Code Generation and Opti-
    mization, 2004, CGO 2004, pp. 75–86. IEEE (2004)
12. Merkel, D.: Docker: lightweight Linux containers for consistent development and
    deployment. Linux J. **2014**(239), 2 (2014)
13. Newcombe, C., Rath, T., Zhang, F., Munteanu, B., Brooker, M., Deardeuff, M.:
    How Amazon web services uses formal methods. Commun. ACM **58**(4), 66–73
    (2015)

---

[15] https://github.com/dfava/paper.go.mm.drd.
[16] Because of differences in how vector clocks are allocated and managed, the memory
gains reported by the reference data-race detector may be different from TSan's.

Formal Verification of COLREG-Based Navigation of Maritime Autonomous Systems

Fatima Shokri-Manninen[1]([⊠]), Jüri Vain[2], and Marina Waldén[1]

[1] Åbo Akademi University, Turku, Finland
{fatemeh.shokri,marina.walden}@abo.fi
[2] Tallinn University of Technology, Tallinn, Estonia
juri.vain@taltech.ee

Abstract. Along with the very actively progressing field of autonomous ground and aerial vehicles, the advent of autonomous vessels has brought up new research and technological problems originating from the specifics of marine navigation. Autonomous ships are expected to navigate safely and avoid collisions following COLREG navigation rules. Trustworthy navigation of autonomous ships presumes applying provably correct navigation algorithms and control strategies. We introduce the notion of maritime game as a special case of Stochastic Priced Timed Game and model the autonomous navigation using UPPAAL STRATEGO. Furthermore, we use the refinement technique to develop a game model in a correct-by-construction manner. The navigation strategy is verified and optimized to achieve the goal to safely reach the manoeuvre target points at a minimum cost. The approach is illustrated with a case study inspired by COLREG Rule 15.

Keywords: Verification · Refinement · Maritime autonomous systems · COLREG rules · Collisions avoidance · Navigation · Safety · Optimization · Game theory · UPPAAL STRATEGO

1 Introduction

The demand for unmanned ships has risen aiming at reducing operation costs due to minimal crew on board and safety at sea but also promoting remote work. Autonomous ships are expected to make more and more decisions based on their current situation at sea without direct human supervision. This means that an autonomous ship should be able to detect other vessels and make appropriate adjustments to avoid collision by maintaining maritime traffic rules. However, the existence of a 'virtual captain' from the shore control centre (SCC) is still a must to perform critical or difficult operations [2] and there is a need for reconfirmation when inconsistent or corrupted commands are detected by the onboard system.

© Springer Nature Switzerland AG 2020
F. de Boer and A. Cerone (Eds.): SEFM 2020, LNCS 12310, pp. 41–59, 2020.
https://doi.org/10.1007/978-3-030-58768-0_3

The connectivity between ships and SCC has to guarantee sufficient communication for sensor monitoring and remote control [10] when SCC intervention is needed. This connectivity also plays an important role for the safety of operations concerning collision avoidance in the remote-controlled scenarios for transforming the data and receiving information regarding the decision from SCC. Sub-second reaction time is, however, not critical regarding safe navigation in the maritime sector as it takes up to minutes for the ship to change its course in case of detection of another ship or an obstacle. In this paper the goal is to model maritime autonomous systems so that the unmanned ships learn a safe and optimal strategy for navigation pursuing collisions avoidance.

One of the most critical safety issues in the development of autonomous vehicles and self-driving cars is their poor performance under adverse weather conditions, such as rain and fog due to sensor failure [15]. However, when modelling maritime specification, we do not take into account sensor inaccuracies and possible transmission errors, since there are standard sensor redundancy design and error correction measures applied on modern vessels to ensure that ships notice each other in a timely manner. For safety assurance, a ship is able to communicate with another ship or shore via VHF radio, satellite services, etc.

For unambiguous navigation protocol, the International Maritime Organization (IMO) [11] published navigation rules to be followed by ships and other vessels at sea which are called Convention On the International Regulations (COLREG).

When developing the autonomous ship navigation system, quality assurance via tool supported model-based control synthesis and verification is of utmost importance. UPPAAL STRATEGO [9] is a branch of the UPPAAL [6] synthesis and verification tool family. It uses machine learning and model checking techniques to synthesize optimal control strategies. Hence, it is a good candidate for control synthesis tool which satisfies above mentioned needs.

In our research, we aim at adapting formal modelling with UPPAAL STRATEGO for verifying and synthesizing safe navigation of autonomous ships. As an additional contribution, we improve the autonomous ships navigation performance regarding its safety and security at the same time planning for optimal route and scheduling maneuvers according to COLREG rules.

2   Related Work

There has been a variety of studies on autonomous ship navigation obeying COLREG rules. Among these fuzzy logic [17], interval programming [7], and 2D grid map [22] could be mentioned. However, the previous approaches do not deal with verification for safe navigation. Moreover, (potentially) nondeterministic behaviour of autonomous ships, communication delays, sensor failure and weather conditions are not considered in their models.

Recently, in MAXCMAS project [23], COLREG rules have been implemented in collision avoidance module (CAM) software where collision avoidance decision is generated and action taken as soon as collision risk is detected. In spite of their various simulation tools, verification methods are discussed only implicitly. Furthermore, to the best of our knowledge, our work is the first one that synthesizes a safe and optimal navigation strategy that also takes into account some of the weather conditions.

There is a fair number of publications on autonomous navigation control synthesis methods and tools that rely on various sets of assumptions - for example continuous, discrete and hybrid dynamics, as well as piece-wise linear and non-linear processes [12,16,18]. The main issue of the controller synthesis is the scalability of synthesis methods in case of complex control objects. Hierarchical control architectures, e.g. in SCADA are addressing this issue. While low-level control typically should tackle with continuous (often nonlinear) processes the upper control layers deal with the abstract representation which typically describes hybrid or discrete dynamics. In this work, we model the vessels dynamics on a high level of abstraction using discrete state space and continuous time.

Among the tools that are oriented to timed discrete-state models and timed game based control synthesis, UPPAAL STRATEGO has proven its relevance in several case studies, where optimal strategies have been generated using Statistical Model Checking (SMC) and machine learning. Examples include, for instance, adaptive cruise control [16], railway systems [13] and autonomous driving systems [4,5].

In [16] the authors synthesize a safe control strategy with the goal of maintaining a safe distance between vehicles where one of them is considered to be uncontrollable by the given controller. Railway control systems, are modelled as a Stochastic Priced Timed Game in [13] by using game theory, where a set of trains considered as an environment and lights, points and sections in the railway, are assumed to be controllable. In [5] the authors also model a railway signalling system with autonomously moving blocks as a Stochastic Priced Timed Game, but in addition they consider stochastic delays in the communication. A safe and optimal driving strategy for the model is synthesised in UPPAAL STRATEGO. In [4], on the other hand, SMC has been used for formal modelling uncertainty in autonomous positioning systems. The safety of the position of a tram is proved with the levels of uncertainty and possible hazards induced by onboard satellite positioning equipment.

In our work, we introduce the notion of a maritime game for control synthesis that is based on navigation specification of the ship where weather conditions are integrated. We model the navigation problem as a special case of Stochastic Priced Timed Game with a goal of collisions avoidance between two ships. Furthermore, we use the refinement technique [3] for a stepwise development of the model for avoiding complexity and ambiguity in the modelling.

3   Case Study and Navigation Specification

3.1   Overview of the Case Study

When modelling navigation manoeuvres of autonomous ships, we focus on standard situations, addressed in COLREG. As an example, let us consider a scenario where two ships have intersecting courses as depicted in Fig. 1.

In this example, in spite of the existence of remote monitoring from the SCC, we assume also that ships have autonomous navigation capability. According to Rule 15 of COLREG [19]; when two power driven vessels have intersecting courses with the risk of collision, the vessel which has the other on her own starboard (right) side shall keep out of the way and avoid crossing ahead of the other vessel. In this case the vessel giving way should adjust its speed and/or course to pass behind the approaching vessel. The adjustment will therefore be made to the starboard side. In the case depicted in Fig. 1, shipB should give way while shipA maintains its direction and speed.

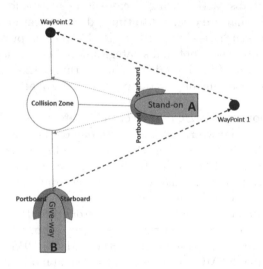

Fig. 1. Autonomous navigation of ships

The navigation control of shipB has a choice to slow down instead of altering its path to pass shipA. By doing this, the expected arrival time might not be as late as when following a redirected route. However, if for some reason shipA is slowing down, then the controller should navigate shipB safely to another route through a sequence of waypoints [1] (see Fig. 1).

3.2   Ship Waypoints (WP) and Path Plan

For safe navigation of vessels, we consider a set of waypoints along the route which define the routing subgoals and that the ship has to traverse during the maneuver. When a vessel plans the voyage from the current position to its next waypoint position, a course change may occur. In case of rerouting to a waypoint, a new heading should be calculated. Figure 2 shows the heading relationship between the ship and waypoint.

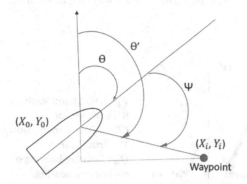

Fig. 2. Heading relation between ship and waypoint

Assume that (X_0, Y_0) is the initial position of the ship and (X_i, Y_i) are the coordinates of the targeted waypoint, the bearing angle ψ of the waypoint from the ship is calculated as follows [1]:

$$\theta' = a \tan 2 \frac{(Y_i - Y_0)}{(X_i - X_0)} \tag{1}$$

$$\psi = \theta' - \theta \tag{2}$$

where θ is the heading of the ship, θ' is the encountering angle of the waypoint from the vertical axis. Here, if the value of ψ becomes negative, then 2π (360) is added to make it positive.

To calculate the position of the ship after altering the course based on the new heading of the ship (ψ), the following calculations should be performed:

$$X = X_0 + V \cos(\psi) \quad Y = Y_0 + V \sin(\psi) \tag{3}$$

where (X_0, Y_0) is the initial position of the ship, (X, Y) are the coordinates of the next position of the ship and V is the speed of the ship.

In our scenario with two ships assuming that (X_A, Y_A) are the coordinates of shipA and (X_B, Y_B) are the coordinates of shipB, the distance between the two ships is calculated as Euclidean distance. This could require an update of the position of either one or both ships following Eqs. 1, 2 and 3. After the update, the distance between the ships should be re-calculated to evaluate whether the risk of collision still remains.

3.3   Influence of Wind on the Ship Navigation

When the ship moves in the presence of wind in addition to navigating along the true course (heading), it will also drift as a consequence of wind which is called leeway [24]. Thus, leeway (α) is the angle between the heading (TC) and the drift track (CG). Figure 3 shows the leeway angle with the presence of wind.

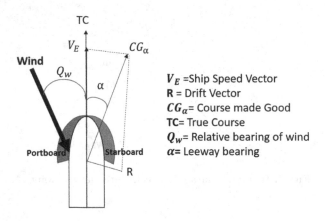

Fig. 3. Leeway angle (α)

If the wind pressure comes from portboard, it deviates the angle of the ship heading to the right then α is positive '+'. In case of the pressure from starboard the α is negative '-'. The leeway is calculated as follows [24].

$$\alpha = K(\frac{V_W}{V_E})^2 \sin Q_w \qquad (4)$$

where, V_W is the speed of the wind and V_E is the speed of the ship. In this formula Q_w is the relative bearing of the wind whereas K is the leeway coefficient. After calculating the drift angle based on the wind conditions, the heading of the ship should be corrected periodically.

4   Reinforcement Learning and Game Theory

To analyze the navigation options of autonomous ships, and more importantly, to verify the navigation decisions, especially in combination with the other ships we use game theory as a base formalism for modelling and for optimizing the games.

Reinforcement learning (RL) is commonly used for solving Markov-decision processes, where an agent interacts with the world and collects rewards [21]. RL is a powerful method for learning an optimal strategy for the agent from trial and error. UPPAAL STRATEGO [9] uses RL and model checking by combining the

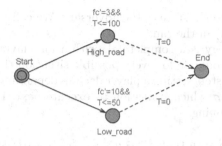

Fig. 4. An example of a timed game automaton in the UPPAAL STRATEGO

techniques to synthesize optimal control strategies. Any of the moves (modeled
as transitions) which the agent chooses in its current state, incurs a cost, e.g.
fuel consumption (fc). In Fig. 1, the first time derivative of fc is denoted fc'. In
this setting, the priced timed game [8] defines an infinite-state Markov (reward)
decision process with the goal of finding a strategy that will minimize the cost
to reach the goal state.

Reinforcement learning can be considered in the context of a game, often for
one player (agent) or as a two-player game in which the other player is typically
the environment. The agent playing against the environment tries to learn a
policy that maximizes the agent's reward in the environment.

Our ship navigation control model is based on a game G = (S, E), consisting
of a set S of states and a set E of directed edges between those states, the state
transitions. Since there are two players in the considered game, where the agent
(player) plays against the environment (Agent vs. Env), we also have two types
of transitions, controllable and uncontrollable. As can be seen from the example
in Fig. 4, the driver as the playing agent can choose one of the two alternative
roads which are represented as controllable transitions (indicated by the solid
line). However, the actual travel-time depends on the intensity of traffic (environment) on a particular day, which is reflected as the upper time-bounds in the
invariants of locations *High_road* and *Low_road*. Since the outgoing edges from
these locations are uncontrollable (indicated by the dashed line), leaving these
locations may occur latest at these time-bounds. Such a two-player (possibly
antagonistic) game is represented by a tuple G= (S, →, --→, s_0, *Bad*, *Goal*)
where [13],

- →⊆ $S \times S$: set of controllable transitions (Player).
- --→⊆ $S \times S$: set of uncontrollable transitions (Environment).
- $s_0 \in S$: initial state.
- *Bad* ⊆ S: set of states where player loses the game.
- *Goal* ⊆ S: set of states where player wins the game.
  We assume that sets *Bad* and *Goal* do not intersect.

In game theory, a run is a finite or infinite sequence of states $r =$
$(s_0, s_1, s_2, \dots)$. In case of a finite sequence of states, the player reaches its terminal state that can be a goal state that is a winning state, or a bad state that

corresponds to the winning state of the adversary. We call a run safe, if there is no bad state ($s \in Bad$) in the run.

The player's strategy is a complete algorithm for playing the game, telling what move a player should do for every possible situation throughout the game. In a state transition system setting a player decides depending on its current state ($s \in S$) and strategy σ which transition to execute next. Formally, a strategy for the player is a mapping,

$$\sigma : S \to S \text{ such that } \forall r \in \rho, r.s \in S : (r.s, \sigma(r.s)) \in E,$$

where ρ is a set of runs, such that from any state s of a run r in ρ, strategy σ chooses the next state reachable by an outgoing edge of s.

A strategy is called safe if in the run, any of the outgoing transitions in the state ($s \in S$) does not lead to bad states:

$$\sigma_{safe} = \{(s_i, s_j) \,|\, s_i, s_j \in S \wedge (s_i, s_j) \in E \wedge s_j \notin Bad\}.$$

A strategy is feasible if it is a safe strategy and reaches the goal state ($s \in Goal$) in the run:

$$\sigma_{feasible} = \{(s_i, s_j) \,|\, (s_i, s_j) \in \sigma_{safe} \wedge (\exists s : s \in S \wedge s = s_j \wedge s \in Goal)\}.$$

Similarly we define a feasible run. A run r is feasible if it is finite of length $|r|$, safe and reaches a goal state ($s \in Goal$):

$$r_{feasible} = \{r | (\forall s_i : s_i \in r, i \in [1, |r| - 1] : s_i \notin Bad) \wedge$$
$$(\exists s_j : s_j \in r \wedge j = |r| \wedge s_j \in Goal)\}.$$

A run is called optimal, if it is feasible and reaches the goal state ($s \in Goal$) in the run with a minimum cost:

$$r_{optimal} = \{r | r \in r_{feasible} \wedge cost(r) \le min(ran(cost))\}.$$

where cost function $cost : \rho \to \mathbb{R}$ assigns a real-valued number to each run.

A winning strategy is optimal, if it is a safe and feasible strategy and there is a run ending up in goal state ($Goal$) with a minimum cost:

$$\sigma_{optimal} = \{(s_i, s_j) \,|\, (s_i, s_j) \in \sigma_{feasible} \wedge (\exists r : r \in r_{optimal} \wedge s_i \in r \wedge s_j \in r)\}.$$

5 Maritime Game

To formally model the navigation problem, we formalise it in the game tuple $G_M = (S, \to, \dashrightarrow, s_0, Bad, Goal)$ where,

- S: is a set of states of the ships. To grant the decidability of G_M, we consider S as a finite set.
  In principle, S consists of as many partitions as there are ships involved in the game. For the two ships in the paper we consider $S = S_A \times S_B$, where

S_A denotes the state component of shipA and S_B of shipB. Both S_A and S_B are composed of the same set of variables and the state vector of a ship has the following structure:

$$<P, WP, H, HS, Vel, WW, WS>$$

where the state variables and their domains are defined as follows:

- $P \in \{(x,y)|x \in X \wedge y \in Y\}$: Position of the ship in the 2D coordinate system. The position will be updated periodically based on the heading and speed of the ship.
- $WP \in \{(x_{wp0}, y_{wp0}), (x_{wp1}, y_{wp1}), \ldots, (x_{wpn}, y_{wpn})\}$: Ordered set of way-points of the ship in the coordinate system. The next waypoint for a ship may change in case the ship changes course.
- $H \in [0, 360]$: Heading of the ship in the degree interval. Heading of the vessel will be updated in case of rerouting.
- $HS \in \{initial, deviated\}$: Heading Status of the ship. Before changing course, the value of the heading status is $initial$. As soon as the heading becomes updated due to navigation to the waypoint, it will be assigned to $deviated$. If the heading of the ship is $deviated$, the ship needs to do a rerouting to go back to the initial path and original heading.
- $Vel \in [0, 10]$: Velocity of the vessel in the normalized integer interval. During navigation at sea, vessels can accelerate, decelerate or continue its voyage with the same speed. The discrete interval $[0, 10]$ is a reasonable approximation for the speed, since we mainly consider big cargo ships with a cruising speed of about 12 knots. Moreover, the approximated speed has always been rounded up to the worst case.

In addition to the above state variables, we introduce new variables used in the model refinement.

- o (Refinement) $WW \in BOOL$: Windy Weather condition in boolean expressions. If Windy Weather has the value true, it means that weather is windy. It is introduced in the refinement step, we introduce environmental condition which affects the vessel course. We consider that the heading of the ship is drifted due to the wind pressure.
- o (Refinement) $WS \in V_W \times Q_w$: Wind Specification of vessels. For calculation of drift angle by Eq. 4 when the wind pressure is present, we need to know the wind speed (V_W) and angle of the wind (Q_w) that comes to the vessel.

Thus, at each time instant the state variables of the ships' state vectors acquire one value from their domain as determined by the transition relations, either $\rightarrow$ or $--\rightarrow$. We use the same navigation specifications for both ships in the game, with the difference that shipA does not contain the controllable navigation variables WP and HS that shipB has or weather features WW and WS that affect the vessel. This is because we are interested in capturing the behaviour of shipB as an agent under different circumstances.

- $\rightarrow$, $--\rightarrow$: The transition relations are defined as $\rightarrow \subseteq S \times G(V) \times Act \times S$ and $--\rightarrow \subseteq (S \times G(V) \times Pr \times Act \times S)$ where,

- $G(V)$: is the set of constraints in guards and V denotes the set of integer and boolean variables.
- Act: is a sequence of assignment actions with integer and boolean expressions. According to player preference, one of the enabled transitions will be chosen in the current state. We define four functions that define the effect of player actions. The functions for player transitions are as follows:
  - $Update\_Heading$: $(P, WP) \rightarrow H$ is a function that calculates a angle for the ship's heading angle H from the ship's current position P and its next waypoint WP.
  - $Update\_Speed$: $(Vel, [-2, 2]) \rightarrow Vel$ is a function that assigns a new velocity to the vessel based on the current velocity Vel and a value in the interval $[-2, 2]$. This interval indicates the acceleration/deceleration of 0-2 speed units.
  - $Update\_Position$: $(H, Vel, P) \rightarrow P$ is a function that gives a new position for the ship given its previous position P, heading H and velocity Vel.
  - (Refinement) $Leeway\_angle$: $(WS, Vel) \rightarrow H$ is a function that assigns a calculated drift angle for the ships's heading H, depending on the wind specification WS and velocity Vel.
- Pr: denotes the set of integer-valued probabilities.

In this two-player game, we model shipB with its controller as a player. As a consequence, all transition for this player are considered to be controllable. However, we assume shipA as an Environment for shipB with the same functionality except that shipA has some stochastic transitions with probability (Pr) in addition to normal transitions.

- $s_0 \in s_{B0} \times s_{A0}$: is initialized with random speed, initial position and heading of ships. For analyzing concrete incidents these initial values could be based on values from existing datasets.
- Bad: is the state where two ships get to collision zone (see Fig. 1).
- $Goal$: is the state that is reached when two ships have passed each other within a safe distance.

6   Model Development in UPPAAL STRATEGO

We model the navigation problem[1] as a Stochastic Priced Timed Game using the tool UPPAAL STRATEGO where the controller of shipB should dynamically plan its maneuver, while the opponent (shipA) moving according to its preset trajectory forces shipB to change its route. In this game, we define the fuel consumption (fc) as a the price to be minimized under the safe strategy. The change in velocity of the ship is directly related to fc, so that the consumption of fuel increases if the ship slows down and speeds up again rather than changes the route, causing the price to increase.

The goal is that the ships move to their target positions in a safe way (without the risk of a collision) while at the same time optimizing the fuel consumption.

---

[1] The game model is found in: https://github.com/fshokri/Game-model.

To avoid ambiguity, we use refinement [3], which enables the system to be created in a stepwise manner gradually adding details into the model and proving that each refinement step preserves the correctness of the previous steps. Models can be refined either via *superposition refinement* [14,20], where new features are added to the automaton, or by *data refinement*, where abstract features are replaced by more concrete ones.

The current refinement process of the model consists of one abstract model with one refinement step using both superposition and data refinement. The abstract model presents the general view of safe navigation with given waypoints. In the refinement step, we introduce weather conditions windy or clear for the ship navigation. We assume that strong wind from shipB starboard increases fuel consumption when turning right. The two step timed automata model introduced here should be seen as a modeling step towards an implementation.

6.1   An Abstract Model of Autonomous Ships

For synchronizing the state transitions of the two ships, shipB and shipA the scheduler template is created with two channels for each ship; *ShipBgo!*, *ShipAgo!* as well as *Update_B!* and *Update_A!* (see Fig. 5). The first channel enables each ship to move while the second one updates their positions after moving action. We define two functions in this automaton namely *initialize()* and *UpdateDistance()*. The former initializes two ships with initial headings and positions in the coordinate system. The latter calculates the distance between two ships after movement. If the distance becomes smaller than the defined safe distance, it means that the ship collides with another ship and the game is over. For restarting the game, we add one transition from state *End* to *Init*. In this template, we also add exponential rates where the process may be delayed an arbitrary long time in the worst case. The user-supplied rate (here 5) has been chosen as an expert estimate for unbounded delays but it can be tuned according to a particular situation.

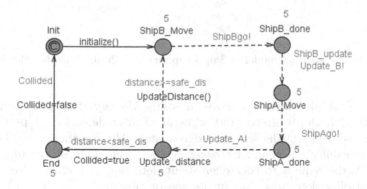

Fig. 5. The scheduler in UPPAAL STRATEGO

In the abstract model the behaviour of shipB is depicted in Fig. 6 where the model is divided into ship (upper) and controller (lower) automata templates. In the shipB template, we model the different states of a ship that are reachable from the initial state (*Moving*), while in the controller we only consider events for giving permissions to take actions. Since shipB is the player in this game, all transitions for shipB and its controller are considered to be controllable.

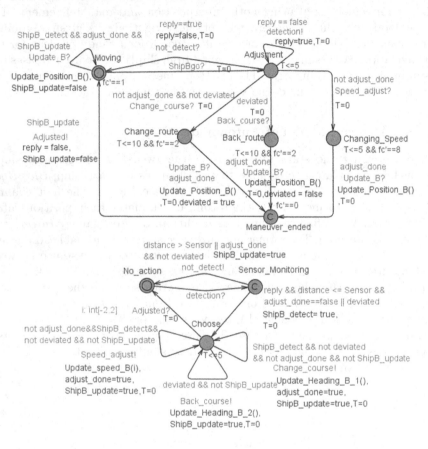

Fig. 6. The abstract model of ShipB (upper) and ShipB controller (lower)

In Fig. 6, shipB starts its move in state *Moving* if it gets permission via *ShipBgo*? If shipB already did adjustment after detection, it periodically updates its position via the self-loop edge of state *Moving* that is synchronized with the scheduler via channel *Update_B*? (see Fig. 5). In state *Adjustment* shipB sends the request to controller about detection (*detection*!) (see Fig. 6). If the controller detects a ship by its sensor (*distance* <= *sensor*) then it will non-deterministically change speed or change course. In case of rerouting, the new heading will be calculated by functions *Update_Heading_B()_1* and $Update\_Heading\_B()\_2$ in the controller, and the new position of the ship will be updated in shipB by $Update\_Position\_B()$. Note that the implementation of the two functions is the same, the only difference is that the function $Update\_Heading\_B()\_1$ uses $waypoint1$ for calculating the new heading, while $waypoint2$ is used for the function $Update\_Heading\_B()\_2$. Since the UPPAAL tool has limited support for simulation of double values, we convert the integer values to ones of double type by multiplying them by 1.0 (see Fig. 7) in the arc tangent formula in the function $Update\_Heading\_B()\_1$.

When shipB moves to the maneuver waypoint, it deviates from its original path and the heading status becomes $deviated$. If the heading of the ship is $deviated$, the ship needs to go back to its original path ($waypoint2$) by moving to state $Back\_route$ after the collision risk has been removed.

As can be seen from Fig. 6, we add the continuous variable (fc') as a hybrid clock in the invariant of the states having non zero duration, i.e. states $Change\_route$, $Back\_route$ and $Changing\_Speed$, to show how much fuel the ship consumes for adjustment. As the value for the states $Change\_route$ and $Back\_route$ are smaller than state $Changing\_Speed$, they will consume less fuel. Function $Update\_Heading\_B$ uses Eq. 1 and 2 to calculate the new heading whereas we use Eq. 3 in function $Update\_Position\_B()$. Figure 7 shows the implementation of function $Update\_Heading\_B_1$ according to the Eq. 1 and 2. While Fig. 8 shows the updating of the position of the ship according to Eq. 3 (left) and calculating the Euclidean distance between two ships (right).

```
// Changing route needs to update the heading
void Update_Heading_B()_1{
    double degree
    int deg, newHeading;
    degree= atan2(Wpy*1.0-Pos_y_B*1.0, Wpx*1.0-Pos_x_B*1.0);
    deg = fint(degree);
    newHeading= deg-headingB;
    if (newHeading >= 0)
       headingB = newHeading;
    else
       headingB = newHeading + 360;}
```

Fig. 7. C function for updating the heading of the ship

We model shipA as an environment for shipB. For this reason, all transitions in shipA automaton are uncontrollable. We follow the same structure as above for the shipA template (see Fig. 9), except that in shipA both the ship template and its controller template are integrated to one. Moreover, we consider a stochastic behaviour for shipA. According to COLREG, shipA should maintain its direction and speed. For this reason, shipA keeps moving straight on with the probability $weight = 8$ to indicate that this should happen with a high probability. The parameters for these probability distributions are defined from common practice.

void Update_Position_B(){
int x, y;
x=fint(round(cos(headingB)));
y=fint(round(sin(headingB)));
Pos_x_B= x* SpeedB +Pos_x_B;
Pos_y_B= y * SpeedB +Pos_y_B;}
	// calculating distance between two ships
	void UpdateDistance{
	double diffx, diffy;
	diffx = pow(Pos_x_A - Pos_x_B, 2);
	diffy = pow(Pos_y_A -Pos_y_B, 2);
	distance = fint(sqrt(diffx + diffy}

Fig. 8. C function for updating the position (left) and the distance (right) of the ship

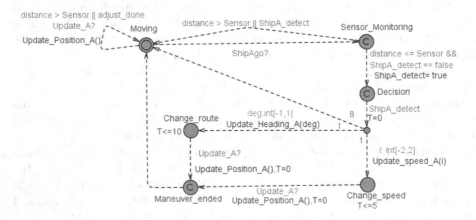

Fig. 9. The abstract model of ShipA in UPPAAL STRATEGO

6.2   Introducing Weather Conditions

In the refinement step, we consider the impact of weather conditions on shipB navigation using the boolean variable *windy* which is non-deterministically assigned a value true or false in the scheduler template. For shipB, we add two new states *Change_route_drift* and *Back_route_drift* where the rerouting includes the drifting due to windy weather (see Fig. 10). We assume that the fuel consumption for these states ($fc' == 5$) is greater than in clear weather ($fc' == 2$) as strong wind from shipB starboard increases fuel consumption when turning right. Changing course even in the windy weather is a better choice than changing speed due to less fuel consumption. State *Changing_Speed* remains unchanged in windy weather, since wind cannot considerably change the speed of the ship [24].

The correction of the ship heading under windy circumstances is performed by functions *Update_HeadB_wind*1() and *Update_HeadB_wind*2() in the controller by updating the heading of the ship from the new calculated drift angle by function *leeway_angle*() (Eq. 4). The difference between updating heading functions in windy weather (*Update_HeadB_wind*1(), *Update_HeadB_wind*2()) and without wind (*Update_Heading_B*()_1, *Update_Heading_B*()_2) (see Fig. 7) is only that leeway angle is added to the new heading of ship.

$$newHeading = deg - headingB + leeway;$$

For the controller template, we add two new transitions in the *Choose* state regarding windy weather where drift angle will be considered in case of changing course.

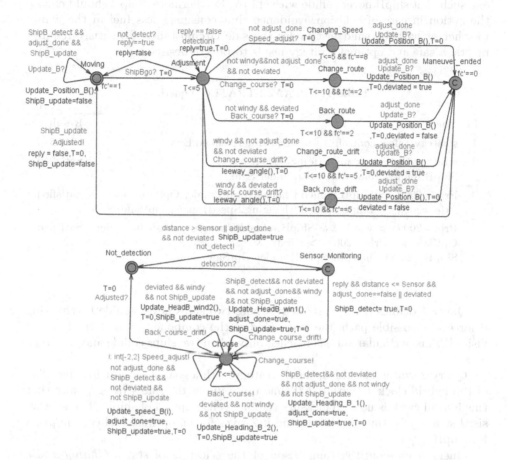

Fig. 10. The refined model of ShipB and controller in UPPAAL STRATEGO

The weather conditions are superimposed as a new feature to the abstract model by strengthening the guards in the model and adding assignments to the variables of the new feature. The variables of the heading are data refined to take the leeway into account but otherwise, the behaviour of the model remains the same.

6.3 Verification and Validation

UPPAAL STRATEGO provides an extended query language, where strategies can be verified and optimized (by reinforcement learning) for stochastic priced timed games. The constructed strategies can be used as constraints in performing

SMC of a game (like Query 3 and 4 in Table 1). Table 1 presents verified Queries 1 to 4.

The main objective of the maritime game model is to synthesise a safe strategy such that shipB never collide with shipA. Furthermore, ShipB should choose the action in case of collision avoidance that consumes less fuel in the windy weather or without wind just under the safe circumstance. To satisfy requirements, a safe and optimal strategy needs to be synthesised.

Table 1. UPPAAL STRATEGO queries

Id	Query	Result
1	strategy Safe= control: A[] not Scheduler_refined.End	Satisfied
2	strategy OptSafe = minE(fc)[<=200]: <> ShipB_refined.Maneuver_ended under Safe	Satisfied
3	Pr[<=200](<> ShipB_refined.Change_route) under OptSafe >= Pr[<=200](<> ShipB_refined.Changing_Speed) under OptSafe	Satisfied
4	Pr[<=200](<> windy && ShipB_refined.Change_route_drift) under OptSafe >= Pr[<=200](<> windy && ShipB_refined.Changing_Speed) under OptSafe	Satisfied

Query 1 defines the Safe strategy where two ships never collide by checking if for every possible path, the state *End* of the component *Scheduler* is never visited. This particular state is reached only when two ships collide and the game is over.

Query 2 synthesizes the optimal strategy with a goal of minimizing the value of the hybrid clock fc within 200 time units under the safe strategy. Note that this hybrid clock is used to measure the fuel consumption of shipB. The synthesised strategy is, thus, both safe and it strives for an optimal fuel consumption for shipB.

Query 3 presents the comparison of the selection of states *Change_route* and *Changing_Speed* by shipB in case of adjustment after detecting the other ship within 200 time units under the previously computed Opt (near-optimal) strategy. The probability of state *Change_route* to get selected are greater than *Changing_Speed*. This is because *Change_route* has a lower fc' rate compared to other locations. UPPAAL STRATEGO executes this query for 62 runs and estimates the probability to be true (value=1) with confidence 0.95.

Query 4 presents the same comparison as Query 3 with the difference that weather conditions are taken into account. It states that the likelihood for shipB to opt for action *Change_route_drift* in windy weather within 200 time units under the safe and optimal strategy is higher than selection of *Changing_Speed*. UPPAAL STRATEGO executes this query for 582 runs and estimates the probability for it to be true with confidence 0.95.

Note that Queries 1 to 3 are proved both in the abstract and the refined models. Query 4 is provable only in the refinement model, because of the new variable *windy* and the new state $Change\_route\_drift$ introduced in the refinement.

7 Conclusions and Future Work

The novelty of this paper is introducing the notion of maritime game as a special case of Stochastic Priced Timed Game and constructing the respective model of the autonomous navigation using UPPAAL STRATEGO. The practical usability of our approach (maritime game) is to develop the theory of autonomous ships safe navigation and for that purpose to analyze the navigation problem in a rigorous state-based model setting. We use the refinement technique to develop a game model in a correct-by-construction manner. The stepwise refinement approach helps to avoid ambiguity in the modelling to verify the satisfiability of the safety requirements of the model.

In this paper, the approach for the strategy synthesis of safe navigation has been presented as a stochastic two players priced game with the goal of collision avoidance. Taking into account several practically important side constraints such as wind, currents, navigation mistakes by the vessel of the adversary, and involvement of other obstacles (nautical signs, small boats) complicates the synthesis task and presumes the validation of the approach under extra constraints not studied in standard game-theoretic setting yet. Though limited with two ships navigating in offshore scenarios, our work is the first attempt to synthesize a safe and optimal navigation strategy that also takes into account weather conditions. The navigation problem is exemplified based on navigation specification and COLREG Rule 15. Further developing the Maritime theory to capture multi-vessel navigation situations in traffic-intensive harbour zones and integration of winter navigation remain as future work.

Acknowledgments. This study has been partly supported by the project ESC funded by the Academy of Finland (grant No.308980) and the Estonian Ministry of Education and Research institutional research grant no. IUT33-13. We would like to thank Marius Mikučionis for his assistance with UPPAAL STRATEGO. We also thank the anonymous reviewers for their inputs and suggestions.

References

1. Ahmed, Y.A., Hasegawa, K.: Fuzzy reasoned waypoint controller for automatic ship guidance. IFAC-PapersOnLine **49**(23), 604–609 (2016)
2. Ahvenjärvi, S.: The human element and autonomous ships. TransNav Int. J. Mar. Navig. Saf. Sea Transp. **10** (2016)
3. Back, R.-J., von Wright, J.: Refinement Calculus: A Systematic Introduction. Graduate Texts in Computer Science. Springer, Heidelberg (1998). https://doi.org/10.1007/978-1-4612-1674-2

4. Basile, D., Fantechi, A., Rucher, L., Mandò, G.: Statistical model checking of hazards in an autonomous tramway positioning system. In: Collart-Dutilleul, S., Lecomte, T., Romanovsky, A. (eds.) RSSRail 2019. LNCS, vol. 11495, pp. 41–58. Springer, Cham (2019). https://doi.org/10.1007/978-3-030-18744-6_3

5. Basile, D., ter Beek, M.H., Legay, A.: Strategy synthesis for autonomous driving in a moving block railway system with UPPAAL STRATEGO. In: Gotsman, A., Sokolova, A. (eds.) FORTE 2020. LNCS, vol. 12136, pp. 3–21. Springer, Cham (2020). https://doi.org/10.1007/978-3-030-50086-3_1

6. Behrmann, G., David, A., Larsen, K.G.: A tutorial on UPPAAL. In: Bernardo, M., Corradini, F. (eds.) SFM-RT 2004. LNCS, vol. 3185, pp. 200–236. Springer, Heidelberg (2004). https://doi.org/10.1007/978-3-540-30080-9_7

7. Benjamin, M.R., Curcio, J.A., Leonard, J.J., Newman, P.M.: Navigation of unmanned marine vehicles in accordance with the rules of the road. In: Proceedings 2006 IEEE International Conference on Robotics and Automation, ICRA 2006, pp. 3581–3587. IEEE (2006)

8. David, A., Jensen, P.G., Larsen, K.G., Legay, A., Lime, D., Sørensen, M.G., Taankvist, J.H.: On time with minimal expected cost!. In: Cassez, F., Raskin, J.-F. (eds.) ATVA 2014. LNCS, vol. 8837, pp. 129–145. Springer, Cham (2014). https://doi.org/10.1007/978-3-319-11936-6_10

9. David, A., Jensen, P.G., Larsen, K.G., Mikučionis, M., Taankvist, J.H.: UPPAAL STRATEGO. In: Baier, C., Tinelli, C. (eds.) TACAS 2015. LNCS, vol. 9035, pp. 206–211. Springer, Heidelberg (2015). https://doi.org/10.1007/978-3-662-46681-0_16

10. Höyhtyä, M., Huusko, J., Kiviranta, M., Solberg, K., Rokka, J.: Connectivity for autonomous ships: architecture, use cases, and research challenges. In: 2017 International Conference on Information and Communication Technology Convergence (ICTC), pp. 345–350. IEEE (2017)

11. IMO: Convention on the international regulations for preventing collisions at sea (COLREGs) (1972)

12. Jenie, Y.I., van Kampen, E.-J., Remes, B.: Cooperative autonomous collision avoidance system for unmanned aerial vehicle. In: Chu, Q., Mulder, B., Choukroun, D., van Kampen, E.J., de Visser, C., Looye, G. (eds.) Advances in Aerospace Guidance. Navigation and Control, pp. 387–405. Springer, Heidelberg (2013). https://doi.org/10.1007/978-3-642-38253-6_24

13. Karra, S.L., Larsen, K.G., Lorber, F., Srba, J.: Safe and time-optimal control for railway games. In: Collart-Dutilleul, S., Lecomte, T., Romanovsky, A. (eds.) RSSRail 2019. LNCS, vol. 11495, pp. 106–122. Springer, Cham (2019). https://doi.org/10.1007/978-3-030-18744-6_7

14. Katz, S.: A superimposition control construct for distributed systems. ACM Trans. Program. Lang. Syst. (TOPLAS) 15(2), 337–356 (1993)

15. Kutila, M., Pyykönen, P., Holzhüter, H., Colomb, M., Duthon, P.: Automotive LIDAR performance verification in fog and rain. In: 2018 21st International Conference on Intelligent Transportation Systems (ITSC), pp. 1695–1701. IEEE (2018)

16. Larsen, K.G., Mikučionis, M., Taankvist, J.H.: Safe and optimal adaptive cruise control. In: Meyer, R., Platzer, A., Wehrheim, H. (eds.) Correct System Design. LNCS, vol. 9360, pp. 260–277. Springer, Cham (2015). https://doi.org/10.1007/978-3-319-23506-6_17

17. Lee, S.-M., Kwon, K.-Y., Joh, J.: A fuzzy logic for autonomous navigation of marine vehicles satisfying COLREG guidelines. Int. J. Control Autom. Syst. 2(2), 171–181 (2004)

18. Mühlegg, M., Dauer, J.C., Dittrich, J., Holzapfel, F.: Adaptive trajectory controller for generic fixed-wing unmanned aircraft. In: Chu, Q., Mulder, B., Choukroun, D., van Kampen, E.J., de Visser, C., Looye, G. (eds.) Advances in Aerospace Guidance, Navigation and Control, pp. 443–461. Springer, Heidelberg (2013). https://doi.org/10.1007/978-3-642-38253-6_27
19. Perera, L.P., Carvalho, J.P., Soares, C.G.: Autonomous guidance and navigation based on the COLREGs rules and regulations of collision avoidance. In: Proceedings of the International Workshop Advanced Ship Design for Pollution Prevention, pp. 205–216 (2009)
20. Snook, C., Waldén, M.: Refinement of statemachines using Event B semantics. In: Julliand, J., Kouchnarenko, O. (eds.) B 2007. LNCS, vol. 4355, pp. 171–185. Springer, Heidelberg (2006). https://doi.org/10.1007/11955757_15
21. Sutton, R.S., Barto, A.G.: Reinforcement Learning: An Introduction. MIT Press, Cambridge (2011)
22. Teo, K., Ong, K.W., Lai, H.C.: Obstacle detection, avoidance and anti collision for MEREDITH AUV. In: OCEANS 2009, pp. 1–10. IEEE (2009)
23. Varas, J.M., et al.: MAXCMAS project: autonomous COLREGs compliant ship navigation. In: Proceedings of the 16th Conference on Computer Applications and Information Technology in the Maritime Industries (COMPIT), pp. 454–464 (2017)
24. Wuchen, S., Renxiang, B., Yong, L., Xinyu, L., Liangqi, L., Pengfei, F.: Prediction of leeway and drift angle based on empirical formula. In: Proceedings of the Asia-Pacific Conference on Intelligent Medical 2018 & International Conference on Transportation and Traffic Engineering 2018, pp. 196–199 (2018)

End-to-End Verification of Initial
and Transition Properties of GR(1)
Designs in SPARK

Laura R. Humphrey[1]([⊠]), James Hamil[2], and Joffrey Huguet[3]

[1] Air Force Research Laboratory, Wright-Patterson Air Force Base, OH 45433, USA
laura.humphrey@us.af.mil
[2] LinQuest Corp., Beavercreek, OH 45431, USA
james.hamil.ctr@us.af.mil
[3] AdaCore, 75009 Paris, France
huguet@adacore.com

Abstract. Manually designing control logic for reactive systems is time-consuming and error-prone. An alternative is to automatically generate controllers using "correct-by-construction" synthesis approaches. Recently, there has been interest in synthesis from Generalized Reactivity(1) or GR(1) specifications, since the required computational complexity is relatively low, and several tools exist for synthesis from GR(1) specifications. However, while these tools implement synthesis approaches that are theoretically "correct-by-construction," errors in tool implementation can still lead to errors in synthesized controllers. We are therefore interested in "end-to-end" verification of synthesized controllers with respect to their original GR(1) specifications. Toward this end, we have modified Salty – a tool that produces executable software implementations of controllers from GR(1) specifications in a variety of programming languages – to produce implementations in SPARK. SPARK is both a programming language and associated set of verification tools, so it has the potential to enable the "end-to-end" verification we desire. In this paper, we discuss our experience to date using SPARK to implement controllers and verify them against a subset of properties comprising GR(1) specifications, namely system initial and system transition properties. We also discuss lessons learned about how to best encode controllers synthesized from GR(1) specifications in SPARK for verification, examples in which verification found unexpected controller behaviors, and caveats related to the interpretation of GR(1) specifications.

Keywords: Reactive synthesis · End-to-end verification · Functional verification

---

Supported by AFRL contract FA8650-16-C-2642 and AFOSR grant RQCOR20–35. Distribution Statement A. Approved for public release: distribution unlimited. Case #88ABW-2020-0649.

F. de Boer and A. Cerone (Eds.): SEFM 2020, LNCS 12310, pp. 60–76, 2020.
https://doi.org/10.1007/978-3-030-58768-0_4

1 Introduction

Reactive systems must be capable of correctly responding to various inputs, e.g. originating from human users or events in the system's operational environment. The process of manually designing the control logic for such systems is both time-consuming and error prone. An alternative is to use "correct-by-construction" synthesis approaches to automatically generate a system's control logic directly from specifications, which can reduce both the amount of time needed for design and the likelihood of errors [1,8,10,14]. In general, *synthesis* is the process of automatically generating a design from a specification. More specifically, *reactive synthesis* approaches generate designs in the context of an uncontrolled environment, assumptions about which are encoded in the specification. Reactive synthesis approaches tend to have high computational complexity, so there is particular interest in synthesis from Generalized Reactivity(1) or GR(1) specifications, the complexity of which is only polynomial in the size of the game graph encoded by the specification [3]. Synthesis from GR(1) specifications has been used to generate digital circuits [5] and controllers for teams of unmanned vehicles [2], ground robots [13], software-defined networks [16], and aircraft power distribution systems [18], to name a few.

GR(1) is a fragment of linear temporal logic. A GR(1) specification φ takes the form $\varphi = \varphi^e \rightarrow \varphi^s$, where φ^e encodes assumptions about the *environment* in which a system is to operate, and φ^s encodes guarantees the *system* should make under those assumptions [6]. More specifically, φ takes the form $\varphi = (\varphi_i^e \wedge \varphi_t^e \wedge \varphi_l^e) \rightarrow (\varphi_i^s \wedge \varphi_t^s \wedge \varphi_l^s)$, where φ_i^e and φ_i^s are *initial* properties, φ_t^e and φ_t^s are *transition* or safety properties, and φ_l^e and φ_l^s are *liveness* properties. For inputs in the set $\mathcal{I}$ controlled by the environment and outputs in the set $\mathcal{O}$ produced by the system, terms are defined as:

φ_i^e, φ_i^s - Boolean formulas over $\mathcal{I}$ and $\mathcal{O}$, respectively, that characterize the initial state of the environment and system.

φ_t^e, φ_t^s - Formulas of the form $\bigwedge_{j \in J} \Box B_j$, where each B_j is a Boolean combination of variables from $\mathcal{I} \cup \mathcal{O}$ and expressions of the form $\bigcirc v$, where $v \in \mathcal{I}$ for φ_t^e and $v \in \mathcal{I} \cup \mathcal{O}$ for φ_t^s. These encode properties that should always hold as well as rules for how inputs and outputs are allowed to change based on most recent input and output values.

φ_l^e, φ_l^s - Formulas of the form $\bigwedge_{j \in J} \Box \Diamond B_j$, where each B_j is a Boolean formula over $\mathcal{I} \cup \mathcal{O}$. These encode properties that should hold infinitely often.

In this context, the temporal operators $\Box$ "always," $\Diamond$ "eventually," and $\bigcirc$ "next" have the following meanings. A formula of the form $\Box b$ holds if b is true at every time step, $\Diamond b$ holds if b is eventually true at some future time step, $\Box \Diamond b$ holds if b is true infinitely often in the future, and $\bigcirc b$ holds if b is true at the next time step. It is assumed that at each time step, the environment chooses an input from $\mathcal{I}$, then the system chooses an output from $\mathcal{O}$ in response. Synthesis from GR(1) specifications can therefore be viewed as a two-player game between the system and the environment, where the goal is for the system to satisfy φ^s as long as the environment satisfies φ^e. If this goal is achievable, then we say the specification is realizable, and the result is a *control protocol* or *strategy* for the system that can be expressed as a Moore machine.

Several tools for synthesis from GR(1) specifications are available. For example, RATSY [4] has a focus on circuit design and synthesizes designs encoded in BLIF, Verilog, and HIF. Similarly, Anzu [12] produces circuit designs in Verilog. LTLMoP [9] is focused on control of robots modeled as hybrid systems, and it synthesizes designs as hybrid controllers with handler modules to help connect controllers to simulated or real-world systems. TuLiP [17] has a similar focus and can synthesize controller implementations in Python. Slugs [6] is architected to allow users to tailor synthesis algorithms, e.g. to optimize criteria such as quick response, cost-optimality, and error-resilience, and it produces mathematical representations of controller designs. Salty [7] provides a front-end to Slugs that makes specifications easier to write and debug and a back-end that turns controller designs into executable software implementations in a variety of programming languages, including Python, C++, Java, and now SPARK. Though all of these tools implement synthesis algorithms that are theoretically "correct-by-construction," tool implementation errors could still result in errors in synthesized controllers. We are therefore interested in "end-to-end" verification of such controllers. Toward this end, we have extended Salty to produce software implementations of synthesized controller designs in SPARK.

SPARK, which is based on the Ada programming language, is both a programming language with a specification language and an associated verification toolset [11]. Though SPARK aims to perform fully automated verification, manual adaptation of the source code is in general necessary. For example, if one were to translate source code originally written in Ada to SPARK, one would have to remove unsupported features such as functions with side-effects, aliased variable names, exception handlers, etc. Formal verification of user-specified properties also requires manually writing specifications at the level of the source code in the form of contracts, e.g. preconditions and postconditions that summarize the assumptions and guarantees provided by individual subprograms.

There are different levels to which one can use SPARK to verify a program [15]. Generally, the level of verification performed during development is incremental, going from lowest to highest. Verification at the lowest level, colloquially referred to as *stone level*, is achieved when code is accepted by SPARK, since SPARK has stricter legality rules than Ada. Verification at the *bronze level* is achieved when flow analysis returns with no error; flow analysis checks for errors such as reads of uninitialized data or violations of user-specified data flow contracts. Verification at the *silver level* ensures that there will be no runtime errors when executing the program, e.g. division by zero or numeric overflow/underflow. Verification at the *gold level* consists of verifying key user specifications, such as type invariants and subprogram preconditions and postconditions; however, at this level, the specifications only partially specify the desired behavior of the code. Verification at the *platinum level* consists of verifying a complete set of specifications. At the moment, the SPARK code generated by Salty proves at gold level. In particular, SPARK is able to prove the system initial and system transition portions of the original GR(1) specification, where proof of system transition properties requires also proving a type invariant on the underlying Moore machine representation of the controller; this type invariant encodes that each state is reached by a specific set of input values and produces a specific set of output values. Platinum level would be reached if the liveness properties were expressed and proved, which we leave for future work.

In what follows, in Sect. 2 we describe the structure of synthesized controller implementations in SPARK by walking through a simple example involving a traffic light. To evaluate whether verification of synthesized SPARK controllers is feasible and has utility, we collected a corpus of examples from various sources. In Sect. 3, we take a detailed look at one of these examples, a controller that coordinates the actions of a team of unmanned air vehicles performing an escort mission, and we describe how SPARK revealed an error in the controller's specification. In Sect. 4, we give an overview of results for the rest of the examples, with a focus on scalability. In Sect. 5, we discuss lessons learned, including how to best structure synthesized controllers for proof. We end with concluding remarks in Sect. 6, including a discussion of future work.

2   Implementation and Verification of Synthesized Controllers in SPARK

We have extended the open source tool Salty[1] to produce software implementations of controllers synthesized from GR(1) specifications in SPARK. Given a GR(1) specification in Salty format, Salty does some preprocessing to sanity check, optimize, and translate the specification to Slugs format. Salty then calls Slugs to synthesize a controller design. Slugs provides the option of returning the controller design as a Moore machine expressed in text format, which is what Salty uses to create an executable software implementation of the controller. This Moore machine encodes all the states of the controller. It also encodes the transition relation between states, i.e. the controller's next state given the current state and the next set of input values. Every state then encodes a set of output values to be produced each time the controller transitions to that state. As in all Moore machines, each state produces exactly one set of output values. Controllers synthesized from GR(1) specifications have the additional property that for each state, there is a unique set of input values that brings the controller into that state, regardless of what the previous state was.

If SPARK is chosen as the target programming language, Salty translates this textual Moore machine representation of the controller to an implementation in SPARK. To give a brief overview, the Moore machine representing the controller is encoded as a record (analogous to a struct in C) that stores the controller's current state and a copy of the current input and output values, i.e. the values associated with the most recent transition. There is then a "move" procedure that implements the transition relation. This procedure changes the

---

[1] https://github.com/GaloisInc/salty/.

controller's state based on the next set of input values, produces the next set of output values, and updates its internal copy of current input and output values based on these most recent input and output values. Salty also synthesizes all of the annotations necessary to encode the specifications of interest and verify that the controller satisfies those specifications. In terms of specifications, we seek to prove that the controller satisfies the system initial properties φ_i^s and system transition properties φ_t^s. Recall that GR(1) specifications take the form $(\varphi_i^e \wedge \varphi_t^e \wedge \varphi_l^e) \rightarrow (\varphi_i^s \wedge \varphi_t^s \wedge \varphi_l^s)$. Note however that for controllers synthesized from GR(1) specifications, system initial and transition properties should hold regardless of whether environment liveness properties hold. We are therefore interested in showing that $(\varphi_i^e \wedge \varphi_t^e) \rightarrow (\varphi_i^s \wedge \varphi_t^s)$. For the SPARK implementation, Salty therefore generates functions corresponding to φ_i^e and φ_t^e, which are used in the precondition for the move procedure. It also generates functions corresponding to φ_i^s and φ_t^s, which are used in the postcondition for the move procedure. If SPARK can verify that the move procedure satisfies the postcondition given the precondition, this verifies $(\varphi_i^e \wedge \varphi_t^e) \rightarrow (\varphi_i^s \wedge \varphi_t^s)$. In terms of additional annotations needed to prove this property, Salty generates "state to input mapping" and "state to output mapping" functions that encode which input and output values are associated with each state; these are used to define a type invariant on the controller. This is essentially all that is required to prove system initial and system transition properties of synthesized controllers in SPARK.

To understand synthesized SPARK controllers and annotations in more detail, consider a simple example involving a traffic light controller. Let the controller's single input be *tick*. Color changes occur in every state in which *tick* is true. The traffic light's color cycles infinitely over the sequence red → green → yellow → red → .... Let the output variables then be *red*, *yellow*, and *green*. The environment specifications are $\varphi_i^e = \top$, $\varphi_t^e = \top$, $\varphi_l^e = \Box\Diamond tick$, i.e. *tick* can be true or false in the initial state and has no constraints on how it transitions from state to state, but it must be true infinitely often. The system initial and liveness specifications are $\varphi_i^s = red \wedge \neg yellow \wedge \neg green$ and $\varphi_l^s = \Box\Diamond green$, i.e. the light starts as red but should infinitely often be green. The system transition specification is

$$\Box(\bigcirc((red \wedge \neg yellow \wedge \neg green) \vee (\neg red \wedge yellow \wedge \neg green) \vee (\neg red \wedge \neg yellow \wedge green)) \wedge \quad (1)$$

$$(red \wedge \bigcirc tick \rightarrow \bigcirc green) \wedge (green \wedge \bigcirc tick \rightarrow \bigcirc yellow) \wedge (yellow \wedge \bigcirc tick \rightarrow \bigcirc red) \wedge \quad (2)$$

$$(red \wedge \bigcirc \neg tick \rightarrow red) \wedge (green \wedge \bigcirc \neg tick \rightarrow green) \wedge (yellow \wedge \bigcirc \neg tick \rightarrow yellow)) \quad (3)$$

That is, the light should only be one color at a time (1); the color should change from red → green → yellow → red → ... whenever *tick* is true (2); and the color should remain the same whenever *tick* is false (3).

In SPARK, subunits consist of a specification and a body. The package specification for this traffic light example is shown in Fig. 1. Type `Controller` encodes a Moore machine representing the synthesized controller. In the public part of the specification, `Controller` (line 2) is declared as a private type so that the user

```
 1   package TrafficLight with SPARK_Mode is
 2      type Controller is private;
 3
 4      type System is record
 5         red: Boolean; yellow: Boolean; green: Boolean;
 6      end record;
 7
 8      function Is_Init(C: Controller) return Boolean;
 9      function Env_Init(tick: Boolean) return Boolean is (True);
10      function Sys_Init(S: System) return Boolean is
11         (S.red and not S.yellow and not S.green) with Ghost;
12
13      function Env_Trans(C: Controller; tick: Boolean) return Boolean
14         with Pre => (not Is_Init(C));
15      function Sys_Trans(C: Controller; tick: Boolean; S: System)
16         return Boolean with Pre => (not Is_Init(C)), Ghost;
17
18      procedure Move(C: in out Controller; tick: in Boolean; S: out System)
19      with
20         Pre => (if Is_Init(C) then Env_Init(tick) else Env_Trans(C, tick)),
21         Contract_Cases =>
22            (Is_Init(C) => Sys_Init(S) and (not Is_Init(C)),
23             others     => Sys_Trans(C'Old, tick, S) and (not Is_Init(C)));
24
25   private
26      function State_To_Input_Mapping(C: Controller) return Boolean
27         with Ghost;
28      function State_To_Output_Mapping(C: Controller) return Boolean
29         with Ghost;
30
31      subtype State_Num is Integer range 1 .. 7;
32
33      type Controller is record
34         State: State_Num := State_Num'Last; tick: Boolean; S: System;
35      end record
36         with Type_Invariant => (State_To_Input_Mapping(Controller) and
37                                 State_To_Output_Mapping(Controller));
38
39   end TrafficLight;
```

Fig. 1. SPARK specification for a traffic light controller.

cannot arbitrarily manipulate its state. In the private part of the specification,
Controller (lines 33–37) is a record that stores the controller's internal state
number, current input value(s), and current output value(s). The internal state
number is always initialized to the last possible state number, i.e. the largest
value for State_Num; this "controller initialization" state encodes the status of
the controller before any inputs are received, and the only transition(s) out of
this state are those allowed by φ_i^e. In this example, each input and output is of
type Boolean. (Salty also allows for enumerations and integers, to be discussed
later.) When there are multiple inputs or outputs, they are wrapped in a record
of type Environment (not used here) or System (lines 4–6), respectively. There
is only one input in this example, so it is not wrapped in a record, which is
why there is no Environment record in Fig. 1. Since Controller is a Moore
machine, for each internal state, there is exactly one set of output values produced in that state. Furthermore, recall that controllers synthesized from GR(1)
specifications have the additional property that there is exactly one set of input
values that brings the controller into each state. Controller therefore includes
a type invariant (lines 36 37) that captures this property, where functions

`State_To_Input_Mapping` and `State_To_Output_Mapping` evaluate whether the controller's state corresponds to the expected input and output value(s), respectively. Both of these functions are declared (lines 26–29) with aspect `Ghost`, indicating that they are intended mainly for proof purposes, i.e. they will create verification conditions related to type `Controller` but will not be executed in the actual program, unless it is specified during compilation that they should be. Executing ghost code is often used for debugging, e.g. to check an unproved property through testing. In this case, removing the ghost code can save significant memory, since `State_To_Input_Mapping` and `State_To_Output_Mapping` internally encode large lookup tables that have to store information on every state of the controller, which is often thousands of states or even millions of states for the largest example in our database. The logic for these functions is given in the body (not shown), but for instance when `C.State = 1`, `State_To_Input_Mapping(C)` returns `True` if and only if `C.tick = False`, since *tick* being false brings the system into state 1; and `State_To_Output_Mapping(C)` returns `True` if and only if `C.S = System'(red => True, yellow => False, green => False)`, since *red* is true and *yellow* and *green* are false in state 1.

The public function `Is_Init` (line 8) checks whether the controller is in its initialization state, i.e. no inputs have yet been received. The public function `Env_Init` (line 9) checks whether input(s) satisfy φ_e^i. It is implemented as an expression function, i.e. the implementation is given directly in the specification, because all terms needed to define it are visible in the public part of the specification. In this example, since $\varphi_e^i = \top$ in the Salty specification, this automatically generated function always simply returns `True`. The public function `Sys_Init` (lines 10–11) checks whether outputs(s) satisfy φ_s^i. It is implemented as an expression function for the same reason. From the Salty specification, $\varphi_i^s = red \wedge \neg yellow \wedge \neg green$, so this function returns the value of the expression `S.red and not S.yellow and not S.green`. But unlike `Is_Init` and `Env_Init`, it is marked with aspect `Ghost` because it is mainly used for proof and does not need to be executed. `Is_Init` and `Env_Init` are used for proof but are also callable in functional code. We chose to make these functions non-ghost functions for reasons related to the meaning of GR(1) specifications. Recall that GR(1) specifications have the form $\varphi_e \rightarrow \varphi_s$. If φ_e ever becomes false, i.e. if the environment produces input value(s) that violate φ_e, then the specification as a whole is satisfied regardless of whether the system produces output value(s) that satisfy φ_s. In theory, the system could then produce arbitrary outputs and still satisfy the overall specification. In practice, we believe a user would generally want to know that the environment violated its specification, so that the user could either choose the system output value(s) explicitly or fall back to some other routine. Therefore, a user needs to be able to check inputs with `Env_Init` if `Is_Init` returns true, which is why both are callable. At the moment, they are not used in the code of the `Move` procedure. Public functions `Env_Trans` and `Sys_Trans` (lines 13–16) check whether the next set of input value(s) and output value(s) satisfy φ_e^t and φ_s^t, respectively. For the same reasons as above, `Sys_Trans` is a ghost function but `Env_Trans` is not. Note that `Env_Trans` has a precondition that the controller must not be in its initialization state, since φ_e^t can depend on both the current and next set of input value(s). This precondition is similarly necessary for `Sys_Trans`, since it can depend on both current and next input and output value(s). As with `Env_Init` and `Sys_Init`, the logic for these functions is synthesized from the Salty specification and implemented in the body (not shown), since they make use of input and output values stored in the `Controller`, whose fields are private.

The public procedure `Move` (lines 18–23) transitions the `Controller` based on its current internally stored values (i.e. state number and most recent input and output values) and next set of input value(s), and it produces the next set of output value(s). It has a precondition that if `Controller` is in its initialization state (i.e. it has not yet received any inputs), inputs must satisfy φ_e^i; otherwise they must satisfy φ_e^t. The aspect `Contract_Cases` specifies additional sets of preconditions paired with postconditions, where the set of all preconditions must be mutually exclusive and exhaustively cover the entire input space. The `others` keyword can be used to cover the set of all input conditions not covered in any explicit cases of the contract. Note that for the left-hand side of each case (i.e. left of `=>`), variable names refer to values before evaluation of the subprogram; for the right-hand side, they refer to values after evaluation. Therefore, the aspect `Old` can be used on the right to reference the value of a variable before evaluation of the subprogram. Combined with the previous precondition, `Contract_Cases` asserts that if the controller is in its initialization state, then after execution of `Move`, the first set of output value(s) produced should satisfy φ_s^i and the controller should no longer be in its initialization state. If the controller is not in its initialization state, then the output value(s) produced should satisfy φ_s^t, which is evaluated based on the most recent input and output values stored in `C'Old`, the next input value(s) just provided (in this case stored in `tick`), and the next output values just generated (in this case stored in the record `System`). This set of contract cases embodies our main proof goal, i.e. verification of system initial and transition properties from the original GR(1) specification.

A fragment of the body of `Move` is shown in Fig. 2. Note that there are cases that can lead to `Program_Error`. This is because case statements require all possible cases to be covered, so we programmatically use `others` to cover all possible input combinations that would not be allowed due to φ_e^i or φ_e^t. In the traffic light example, these are unnecessary because all possible combinations of input values are allowed out of each state. In any case, SPARK will prove that such cases are not reachable if the preconditions of `Move` are met, i.e. if the environment satisfies its specification.

We briefly note that Salty includes language features that can result in different constructs being used to represent inputs and outputs in synthesized controllers, including enumerations and integers. For instance, enumerations encode that an enumerated input or output can have exactly one of a set of values at a time, as in the traffic light being exactly one color as expressed in φ_s^i and part (1) of φ_s^t. In such cases, enumerations or integers can make both specifications and code more compact and easier to read and understand. As a technical aside,

```
procedure Move(C: in out Controller; tick: in Boolean; S: out System) is
begin
  case C.State is
    when 1 =>
      case tick is
        when False =>
          C.State := 1;
          C.S.red := True; C.S.yellow := False; C.S.green := False;
        when True =>
          C.State := 3;
          C.S.red := False; C.S.yellow := False; C.S.green := True;
        when others =>
          raise Program_Error;
      end case;
      ...
    when 7 =>
      case tick is
        when False =>
          C.State := 1;
          C.S.red := True; C.S.yellow := False; C.S.green := False;
        when True =>
          C.State := 2;
          C.S.red := True; C.S.yellow := False; C.S.green := False;
        when others =>
          raise Program_Error;
      end case;
  end case;
  C.tick := tick; S := C.S;
end Move;
```

Fig. 2. The body of the Move procedure.

during synthesis, enumerations and integers are translated to a bit vector representation along with additional initial and transition specifications that encode properties inherent to these types, such as values being mutually exclusive and rules for addition and subtraction over integers. Once synthesis is complete, values are translated back to their original enumeration or integer representation.

3   Example Controller for a Team of UAVs

In order to evaluate the feasibility and utility of our approach, we collected GR(1) specifications from a variety of sources. This includes the Salty repository, which contains examples of GR(1) specifications for control of teams of unmanned air vehicles (UAVs) performing different missions. One of these encodes the rules for a "VIP Escort" mission, in which one UAV is designated as a "very important person" (VIP) that must always be "escorted" by a friendly surveillance UAV when it moves, and it must also be protected from an "enemy" UAV. The VIP and surveillance UAVs are controlled by the system, while the enemy UAV is controlled by the environment. The mission map contains regions that the UAVs can move between. "Escorting" consists of ensuring that 1) the VIP only enters regions previously visited by a surveillance UAV and 2) whenever the VIP changes regions, a surveillance UAV "tracks" it, i.e. moves with it between regions. "Protection" consists of ensuring that the VIP is never in the same region as the enemy UAV. Additional rules include constraints and liveness requirements on how the UAVs can move between regions and which regions they start in.

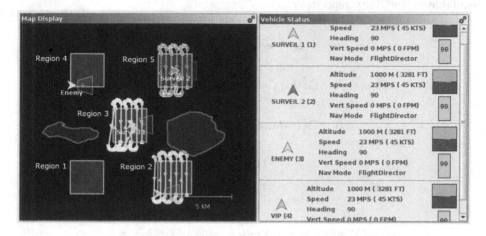

Fig. 3. A VIP escort multi-UAV mission as simulated in OpenAMASE using a Salty-synthesized controller that issues commands to the UAVs through OpenUxAS.

A particular instantiation of this mission is shown in Fig. 3, as depicted in the open source Aerospace Multi-Agent Simulation Environment (OpenA-MASE)[2]. It includes the VIP, two surveillance UAVs numbered 1 and 2, one enemy UAV, and five regions numbered 1 to 5. Environment inputs include integer variable $loc_e \in \{1\ldots5\}$, which encodes the current region of the enemy UAV, and Boolean variables sr_i for $i = \{1\ldots5\}$, where sr_i is true if and only if region i has been visited at some point by a surveillance UAV. System outputs include integer variables $loc_v, loc_{s1}, loc_{s2} \in \{1\ldots5\}$, which indicate the current region of the VIP and surveillance UAVs 1 and 2, and Boolean variables $vTrack_1$ and $vTrack_2$, which indicate whether surveillance UAVs 1 and 2 are executing a behavior to follow the VIP. Note that low-level control, e.g. waypoint planning and sensor steering, is implemented by the open source Unmanned Systems Autonomy Services (OpenUxAS)[3]. The controller synthesized by Salty implements high-level decision logic, and OpenUxAS monitors the state of the controller and translates its current output values to a set of UAV commands that are simulated in OpenAMASE. For example, when loc_v changes value to 2, OpenUxAS commands the VIP to follow a path from its current region to region 2, or when $vTrack_1$ changes from false to true, OpenUxAS commands surveillance UAV 1 to fly next to the VIP. The high-level controller synthesized

---

[2] https://github.com/afrl-rq/OpenAMASE.
[3] https://github.com/afrl-rq/OpenUxAS.

by Salty makes some assumptions about the low-level behaviors implemented by OpenUxAS, in this case, mainly that all UAVs move at the same speed and transition to new regions at the same time. A workflow for connecting Salty-implemented controllers with OpenUxAS and OpenAmase is described in [7], and all of the scripts, configuration files, etc. needed to run this example are available on the Salty repository.

For this mission, the GR(1) specifications for the environment are:

$$\varphi_e^i = \quad (loc_e = 4) \wedge \neg sr_1 \wedge \neg sr_2 \wedge sr_3 \wedge \neg sr_4 \wedge sr_5 \tag{4}$$

$$\varphi_e^t = \bigwedge_{i=\{1...5\}} \Box\Big((loc_{s1} = i) \vee (loc_{s2} = i) \rightarrow \bigcirc sr_i\Big) \wedge \tag{5}$$

$$\bigwedge_{i=\{1...5\}} \Box\Big((\neg(loc_{s1} = i) \wedge \neg(loc_{s2} = i) \wedge \neg sr_i \rightarrow \bigcirc \neg sr_i) \wedge \tag{6}$$

$$\Big(sr_i \rightarrow \bigcirc sr_i\Big)\Big) \wedge \tag{7}$$

$$\Box\neg(loc_e = 1) \wedge \Box\neg(loc_e = 2) \tag{8}$$

$$\varphi_e^l = \Box\Diamond\neg(loc_e = 3) \wedge \Box\Diamond\neg(loc_e = 4) \wedge \Box\Diamond\neg(loc_e = 5). \tag{9}$$

These express that (4) the enemy UAV starts in region 4, and regions 3 and 5 start as surveilled; (5) a region is considered to be surveilled after either one of the surveillance UAVs is in it; (6) a previously unsurveilled region remains unsurveilled if neither surveillance UAV is in it; (7) once a region is surveilled, it remains surveilled; (8) the enemy UAV cannot go to regions 1 or 2; and (9) the enemy UAV must infinitely often not be in each region 3, 4, and 5.

GR(1) specifications for the system are:

$$\varphi_s^i = \quad (loc_v = 2) \wedge (loc_{s1} = 3) \wedge (loc_{s2} = 5) \wedge \neg vTrack_1 \wedge \neg vTrack_2 \tag{10}$$

$$\varphi_s^t = \Box\Big(\neg(loc_v = \bigcirc loc_v) \rightarrow (\bigcirc vTrack_1 \vee \bigcirc vTrack_2)\Big) \wedge \tag{11}$$

$$\bigwedge_{i=\{1...2\}} \Box\Big(vTrack_i \rightarrow (sloc_i = loc_v)\Big) \wedge \tag{12}$$

$$\bigwedge_{i=\{1...5\}} \Box\Big((loc_v = i) \rightarrow \neg(loc_e = i)\Big) \wedge \tag{13}$$

$$\bigwedge_{i=\{v,s1,s2\}} \Box\Big((\bigcirc(loc_i = 1) \rightarrow (loc_i = 1) \vee (loc_i = 2) \vee (loc_i = 3)) \wedge \tag{14}$$

$$(\bigcirc(loc_i = 2) \rightarrow (loc_i = 1) \vee (loc_i = 2) \vee (loc_i = 3)) \wedge \tag{15}$$

$$(\bigcirc(loc_i = 3) \rightarrow \bigvee_{j=\{1...5\}} (loc_i = j)) \wedge \tag{16}$$

$$(\bigcirc (loc_i = 4) \rightarrow (loc_i = 3) \vee (loc_i = 4) \vee (loc_i = 5)) \wedge \qquad (17)$$

$$(\bigcirc (loc_i = 5) \rightarrow (loc_i = 3) \vee (loc_i = 4) \vee (loc_i = 5))) \qquad (18)$$

$$\varphi_s^l = \ \Box\Diamond(loc_v = 1) \wedge \Box\Diamond(loc_v = 5). \qquad (19)$$

These express that (10) the VIP starts in region 2, surveillance UAV 1 in region 3, and surveillance UAV 2 in region 5, with neither surveillance UAV tracking the VIP; (11) the VIP does not change regions unless a surveillance UAV is tracking it; (12) a surveillance UAV can only track the VIP if they are in the same region at the same time; (13) the VIP cannot be in the same region as the enemy UAV at the same time; (14) and (15) the VIP and surveillance UAVs can move from regions 1 or 2 to regions 1, 2, or 3; (16) the VIP and surveillance UAVs can move from region 3 to any other region; (17) and (18) the VIP and surveillance UAVs can move from regions 4 or 5 to regions 3, 4, or 5; and (19) the VIP must go to regions 1 and 5 infinitely often.

We have chosen to describe this particular example in detail because during the process of extending Salty to produce SPARK implementations, we discovered a previously undetected problem with this example's specification. As written, the specification is realizable and produces what appears at a glance to be a reasonable controller with 97 states. In fact, we had previously run this example with OpenAMASE, OpenUxAS, and a Python controller synthesized by Salty. However, we did not originally notice in the Python implementation that 34 of the controller's 97 states do not have successors. Since no special logic was added to Salty to handle this situation, the generated SPARK code included empty case statement alternatives in the Move procedure. For example, in state 2 the case statement alternative is simply when 2 =>, with no statements in the body. This code failed to compile, since SPARK does not allow for fall-through behavior in case statements (nor does Ada); explicit statements are expected for each case statement alternative. In Python, this error went undetected; the transition relation for the controller is encoded as a map, and entries corresponding to states without successors simply had an empty list of "next state" values. We briefly note that if we had encoded the controller using a map in SPARK, the error would still have been detected through SPARK analysis rather than a syntactic check of the code; the case statement encoding was chosen for efficiency reasons to be discussed in Sect. 5.

This error is the result of a subtlety of the semantics of GR(1) specifications. Recall that GR(1) specifications take the form $\varphi_e \rightarrow \varphi_s$. Obviously a specification of this form is satisfied if φ_e and φ_s are both true, but it is also satisfied if φ_e is false. Also recall from the introduction that GR(1) specifications are interpreted in the context of a two-player game in which the environment takes its turn first and the system takes its turn second. The issue here is that the environment is able to take transitions that will necessarily cause it to violate φ_e^t in the next time step. Note that φ_e^t contains terms of the form $\Box \ \psi$, specifically

$\Box\neg(loc_e = i)$ for $i = \{1, 2\}$ (8). Note that a term of the form $\Box\neg p$ is not the same as a term of the form $\Box \bigcirc \neg p$. The distinction is important. If the environment chooses p for the "next" time step, this does not violate $\Box\neg p$ in the "current" time step. However, once the next state is reached, p becomes the new "current" value, and $\Box\neg p$ will now be violated no matter what the environment chooses. Generally, specifications should follow the latter form $\Box \bigcirc \neg p$, which prohibits the environment from choosing p in the "next" time step. This was indeed an error in these specifications, so we changed $\Box\neg(loc_e = 1) \wedge \Box\neg(loc_e = 2)$ to $\Box \bigcirc \neg(loc_e = 1) \wedge \Box \bigcirc \neg(loc_e = 2)$ in (8). However, we also modified Salty to **raise Program_Error** in cases with no successors and checked that we were still able to prove $\varphi_e \to \varphi_s$ (since reaching these cases would require violating the precondition φ_e). Such cases amount to instances in which the precondition on **Move** would have to be violated, which is why we allow the user to execute **Env_Trans** as discussed in Sect. 2. We also plan to have Salty issue a warning when there are states with no successors, since such cases are likely unintended.

4   Results

To further evaluate the utility and feasibility of our approach, we pulled additional example GR(1) specifications from a variety of sources including Anzu, LTLMoP, TuLiP, Slugs, and Salty, all of which make their examples publicly available for download. GR(1) specifications in Salty format, synthesized SPARK packages, and SPARK analysis results for all of these examples are available on the Salty GitHub repository, including the traffic light example of the previous section. We note that while some examples are small and simple, e.g. demos along the lines of the traffic light example, there are many in our collection that are more realistic. For instance, Anzu has controller specifications for a generalized IBM buffer and an AMBA bus. LTLMoP and TuLiP have specifications for robot controllers that have been demonstrated on simulated and/or real robots. And Salty has specifications for controllers to coordinate the actions of teams of vehicles that have been demonstrated in simulation.

Figure 4 shows the amount of time needed to analyze examples as a function of total number of transitions in the Moore machine representing the controller, with examples that could not be analyzed due to memory errors set to 1. Results were generated on a Linux VM given 24 GB RAM and 4 processors on a MacBook Pro with a 2.9 GHz Intel Core i9 with 32 GB RAM. We ran 40 examples in total. Results for 33 examples are plotted. On most examples with less than 4000 transitions, SPARK was able to completely verify/prove the synthesized code complies with its specification. Examples that had more than 4000 transitions (the 7 unplotted examples) required too much memory to analyze, resulting in errors when attempting to verify them in SPARK.

Of examples with less than 4000 transitions, two resulted in errors. These two examples had abnormally large specifications consisting of approximately 1000 atomic propositions each, whereas most other examples with a similar number of transitions had 500 or less. Such cases occur, e.g. when systems include a

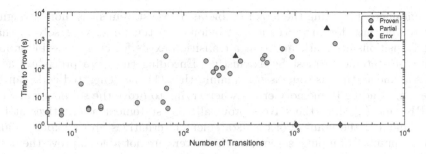

Fig. 4. Timing results for example SPARK controllers as a function of number of transitions in the controller. "Proven" examples were fully verified, "partial" examples were partially verified, and "error" examples were too big to analyze.

large number of inputs and/or outputs but have very tight specifications on how they can transition, leading to large specifications and therefore lengthy pre- and postconditions but relatively small controllers.

Two examples with less than 4000 transitions could only be partially proven. One was relatively large, with about 2000 transitions. The other had arithmetic terms in its specification (Salty and Slugs support integer inputs and outputs); we are investigating why this example does not fully prove, since we feel that SPARK should be capable of fully proving this example.

5 Lessons Learned

Throughout the process of synthesizing and attempting to verify controllers in SPARK, we learned several lessons, both about SPARK and about some of the finer points of GR(1) specifications.

In terms of encoding SPARK controllers for verification, we originally tried to mirror the approach taken in other Salty language targets by building a static lookup table for state transitions. To do this, we tried to create an array of `Formal_Hashed_Maps` indexed by `State_Num`, where keys were derived from environment input values and used to look up the next `State_Num` and corresponding system output values. Ghost functions consisting of nested quantified expressions were used to check that in each state, specification properties held using input and output values encoded by the current state and all states reachable as contained in the hashed maps. These functions comprised the postcondition of a function that initialized the controller's lookup table. The body of the `Move` procedure simply retrieved the outputs and next state from the lookup table using its stored `State_Num` and `Environment` input. The public portion of the SPARK specification was largely unchanged. This approach was only able to prove the smallest of examples in a reasonable amount of time.

While the use of formal containers was intuitive, they are more complex to reason about in terms of proof because they require reasoning about models of the containers. Encoding the lookup table as a case statement is more straight-forward, because for instance, it is "obvious" to the underlying solvers that state transitions are static and that a transition exists for every possible input, since case statements must be exhaustive. Encoding the `Move` procedure as a case statement still has some issues, mainly that (1) the generated code can be quite long, leading to memory errors when trying to prove the subprogram with SPARK, and (2) since the solvers prove all case statement alternatives at the same time and the number of case statement alternatives grows exponentially with the number of inputs, sometimes the solvers are not able to prove the post-condition. A solution to both problems could be to split the `Move` procedure into several smaller procedures. This would allow SPARK to apply modular analysis on several smaller procedures, thus enabling the proof on larger files. We are currently investigating ways to split up the procedure that does not accidentally create more difficulties for the underlying solvers.

The process of encoding and analyzing controllers in SPARK did reveal some unexpected behaviors. First, as discussed in Sect. 3, there were two example controllers[4] with specifications that resulted in states with no successors. As a result, these controllers contained empty case statements in the `Move` procedure. We had previously tested the Salty-synthesized controller in Python for the example in Sect. 3 and had not noticed the error, though it would have resulted in an unhandled runtime exception if one of the states without successors had been reached in the Python implementation. Second, a meta-analysis of SPARK timing results also revealed that other examples in our database did not have any inputs, i.e. they amounted to synthesizing a system independent of an environment. In those cases, we had specifications for a non-existent environment that were vacuous, and this caused SPARK to take an abnormally long amount of time to verify these controllers, given their relatively small size. These controllers did not have errors per se, but they were inefficiently encoded. We plan to modify Salty to handle such cases by removing the environment, functions over the environment, and all references to the environment in all pre- and postconditions. This greatly decreases verification time and also reduces the size and increases the efficiency of the code.

6   Conclusions

We were able to successfully use SPARK to verify safety and transition properties of moderately sized controllers synthesized by Salty from GR(1) specifications. Encoding the controllers and all of the annotations necessary for these controllers to prove automatically was relatively straighforward, and it was satisfying to be able to generate proofs using a single tool rather than having to use multiple tools to perform verification. Furthermore, the act of performing "end-to-end" verification with SPARK on such controllers was valuable because (1) it revealed a type of specification error in some examples that would result in runtime errors

---

[4] Salty's vip_orig.salt and Anzu's arbiter.salt.

in other Salty target languages, and (2) it revealed cases in which controllers were inefficiently encoded, i.e. when there is no environment.

In terms of future work, we can potentially improve the scalability of our approach by decomposing the Move procedure into several subprocedures, as discussed in the previous section. We are also interested in expressing and proving liveness properties. Liveness properties will be more challenging to verify because they necessarily require reasoning about future states beyond the "next" state. Verifying system liveness in SPARK will require something like encoding a lookahead buffer and showing that certain states will inevitably be reached when the environment satisfies its specification, which can itself also include liveness terms. This is likely to result in complex first-order formulas with alternating quantification over time, which are notoriously hard to handle in automated solvers, so discharging the resulting proof obligations may prove to be a challenge. To tackle this issue, collaboration with a model checker performing verification at the level of the input language might be more appropriate.

References

1. Alur, R., Moarref, S., Topcu, U.: Compositional synthesis of reactive controllers for multi-agent systems. In: Chaudhuri, S., Farzan, A. (eds.) CAV 2016. LNCS, vol. 9780, pp. 251–269. Springer, Cham (2016). https://doi.org/10.1007/978-3-319-41540-6_14
2. Apker, T.B., Johnson, B., Humphrey, L.R.: LTL templates for play-calling supervisory control. In: AIAA Infotech@Aerospace. AIAA (2016)
3. Bloem, R., Jobstmann, B., Piterman, N., Pnueli, A., Yaniv, S.: Synthesis of reactive(1) designs. J. Comput. Syst. Sci. **78**(3), 911–938 (2012)
4. Bloem, R., et al.: RATSY – a new requirements analysis tool with synthesis. In: Touili, T., Cook, B., Jackson, P. (eds.) CAV 2010. LNCS, vol. 6174, pp. 425–429. Springer, Heidelberg (2010). https://doi.org/10.1007/978-3-642-14295-6_37
5. Ehlers, R., Könighofer, R., Hofferek, G.: Symbolically synthesizing small circuits. In: IEEE Formal Methods in Computer-Aided Design (FMCAD), pp. 91–100. IEEE (2012)
6. Ehlers, R., Raman, V.: Slugs: extensible GR(1) synthesis. In: Chaudhuri, S., Farzan, A. (eds.) CAV 2016. LNCS, vol. 9780, pp. 333–339. Springer, Cham (2016). https://doi.org/10.1007/978-3-319-41540-6_18
7. Elliott, T., Alshiekh, M., Humphrey, L.R., Pike, L., Topcu, U.: Salty-a domain specific language for GR(1) specifications and designs. In: 2019 International Conference Robotics and Automation (ICRA), pp. 4545–4551. IEEE (2019)
8. Fainekos, G.E., Girard, A., Kress-Gazit, H., Pappas, G.J.: Temporal logic motion planning for dynamic robots. Automatica **45**(2), 343–352 (2009)
9. Finucane, C., Jing, G., Kress-Gazit, H.: LTLMoP: experimenting with language, temporal logic and robot control. In: IEEE/RSJ International Conference Intelligent Robots and Systems (IROS), pp. 1988–1993. IEEE (2010)
10. Guo, M., Tumova, J., Dimarogonas, D.V.: Cooperative decentralized multi-agent control under local LTL tasks and connectivity constraints. In: IEEE Conference Decision and Control (CDC), pp. 75–80. IEEE (2014)
11. Hoang, D., Moy, Y., Wallenburg, A., Chapman, R.: SPARK 2014 and GNATprove. Int. J. Softw. Tools Technol. Transfer **17**(6), 695–707 (2015)

12. Jobstmann, B., Galler, S., Weiglhofer, M., Bloem, R.: Anzu: a tool for property synthesis. In: Damm, W., Hermanns, H. (eds.) CAV 2007. LNCS, vol. 4590, pp. 258–262. Springer, Heidelberg (2007). https://doi.org/10.1007/978-3-540-73368-3_29
13. Kress-Gazit, H., Fainekos, G.E., Pappas, G.J.: Where's Waldo? sensor-based temporal logic motion planning. In: IEEE International Conference Robotics and Automation (ICRA), pp. 3116–3121. IEEE (2007)
14. Kupermann, O., Vardi, M.: Synthesizing distributed systems. In: IEEE Symposium Logic in Computer Science, pp. 389–398. IEEE (2001)
15. Moy, Y.: Climbing the software assurance ladder-practical formal verification for reliable software. Electron. Commun. EASST **76** (2019)
16. Wang, A., Moarref, S., Loo, B.T., Topcu, U., Scedrov, A.: Automated synthesis of reactive controllers for software-defined networks. In: IEEE Int. Conf. Network Protocols (ICNP). pp. 1–6. IEEE (2013)
17. Wongpiromsarn, T., Topcu, U., Ozay, N., Xu, H., Murray, R.M.: TuLiP: a software toolbox for receding horizon temporal logic planning. In: International Conference Hybrid Systems: Computation and Control, pp. 313–314. HSCC 2011, ACM (2011)
18. Xu, H., Topcu, U., Murray, R.M.: A case study on reactive protocols for aircraft electric power distribution. In: IEEE Conference Decision and Control (CDC), pp. 1124–1129. IEEE (2012)

Affine Systems of ODEs in Isabelle/HOL for Hybrid-Program Verification

Jonathan Julián Huerta y Munive[✉]

The University of Sheffield, Western Bank, Sheffield S10 2TN, UK
jjhuertaymunive1@sheffield.ac.uk

Abstract. We formalise mathematical components for solving affine and linear systems of ordinary differential equations in Isabelle/HOL. The formalisation integrates the theory stacks of linear algebra and analysis and substantially adds content to both of them. It also serves to improve extant verification components for hybrid systems by increasing proof automation, removing certification procedures, and decreasing the number of proof obligations. We showcase these advantages through examples.

Keywords: Hybrid systems · Formal verification · Proof assistants

1 Introduction

With the increased number of computers controlling physical mechanisms, also known as cyber-physical systems, proofs of their correctness become more relevant. An important approach is differential dynamic logic ($d\mathcal{L}$) [21]. It is an extension of dynamic logic with inference rules to reason about flows and invariants of ordinary differential equations (ODEs). Numerous case studies apply it and its domain-specific proof assistant, KeYmaera X [14,16]. Despite other approaches to verification [1,2], we focus on $d\mathcal{L}$-style deductive verification.

Our recent $d\mathcal{L}$-inspired components allow the verification of hybrid programs in the general purpose proof assistant Isabelle/HOL [7,17,19]. Using a shallow embedding and Kleene algebras instead of dynamic logics, the implementation of these components makes them modular and extensible. Their modularity has been explored before in various ways, however their extensibility for the benefit of proof performance has not yet been pursued. In particular, extensions of Isabelle's mathematical components for ordinary differential equations to specific classes promises significant benefits in this regard.

Linear and affine systems of ODEs, for example, those described by linear (resp. affine) transformations, are among the simplest and most studied variants. They enjoy desirable mathematical properties like existence and uniqueness of solutions to their associated initial value problems (IVPs), and come with various methods for solving them. In particular, there is an explicit way to compute the

This work was funded by CONACYT's scholarship no. 440404.

© Springer Nature Switzerland AG 2020
F. de Boer and A. Cerone (Eds.): SEFM 2020, LNCS 12310, pp. 77–92, 2020.
https://doi.org/10.1007/978-3-030-58768-0_5

general solution for their time-independent versions [10,22]. Although there is much work in extending both the ODE libraries [11–13] and the linear algebra libraries [6,23], there are no formalisations in Isabelle connecting both theory stacks and this reverberates in the verification process with our components. For instance, formalising existence and uniqueness results for affine and linear systems reduces the proofs that users have to supply. Also, where users have to find solutions to the time-independent versions, we can provide the general one.

Thus, inspired by the deductive approach to verification of hybrid systems, our main contribution is the first formalisation of linear and affine systems of ODEs in a proof assistant by combining the theory stacks of linear algebra and ODEs. We add to this integration by extending these libraries with properties about operator norms, diagonal matrices, and derivatives involving matrix-vector multiplication. In addition, we provide evidence that the study and analysis of these systems with a proof assistant is feasible.

Moreover, we extend the Kleene algebra verification components for hybrid systems by improving their tactics for checking if a function is a derivative of another one. We use these tactics to formalise the fact that all linear and affine systems of ODEs have unique solutions, and we certify the general solution for the time-independent case. In the cases where the linear transformation has a diagonalisable representation, we also prove lemmas that include a simpler representation of the general solution. Finally, we add proof automation for operations with the list-representation of $n \times n$ matrices.

The Isabelle formalisation itself forms a major contribution of this paper. It adds new mathematical components to an important field of analysis and improves our verification components for hybrid systems. The formalisations are available in the reviewed Archive of Formal Proofs [18].

2   Affine Systems of ODEs

We first review the mathematical definitions and results for differential equations needed for our formalisation.

Dynamical systems describe the time dependency of points in a state space S. Formally, they are monoid actions $\varphi : T \to S \to S$ that satisfy

$$\varphi\,(t_1 + t_2) = \varphi\,t_1 \circ \varphi\,t_2 \qquad \text{and} \qquad \varphi\,0 = id,$$

where the monoid $(T, +, 0)$ represents time. A dynamical system is a *flow* or *continuous* if $T = \mathbb{R}$ or $T = \mathbb{R}_+$, the non-negative real numbers. Flows emerge from solutions to systems of ordinary differential equations as explained below.

In a system of ODEs $X'\,t = f\,(t, X\,t)$, the function $f : T \times S \to \mathbb{R}^n$ is a *vector field*; it assigns a vector to each point in $T \times S$ with $T \subseteq \mathbb{R}$ and $S \subseteq \mathbb{R}^n$, it is continuous and it suffices to describe the system [10,22]. An *initial value problem* then consists of a vector field f and an initial condition $(t_0, s) \in T \times S$, where t_0 and s represent the initial time and state of the system. Therefore, a *solution* to this system is a continuously differentiable function $X : T \to S$ that satisfies $X'\,t = f\,(t, X\,t)$ for all $t \in T$. This function also solves the IVP if it satisfies $X\,t_0 = s$. Finally, if for each $s \in S$ there is a unique solution or *trajectory* $\varphi_s^f : T \to S$ to the IVP given by f and $(0, s)$, then the equation $\varphi\,t\,s = \varphi_s^f\,t$ defines the flow $\varphi : T \to S \to S$ of f. Geometrically, the trajectory φ_s^f is the only curve in S that passes through s and is always tangential to f.

Picard-Lindelöf's theorem guarantees local existence and uniqueness of solutions for some IVPs [10,22]. It requires the domain $T \times S$ of f to be open with $(t_0, s) \in T \times S$, and f to be locally Lipschitz continuous in S. That is, there must be $\varepsilon > 0$ and $\ell \geq 0$ such that for all $t \in \overline{B_\varepsilon(t_0)} \cap T$ and all $s_1, s_2 \in \overline{B_\varepsilon(s)} \cap S$,

$$\|f(t, s_1) - f(t, s_2)\| \leq \ell \|s_1 - s_2\|,$$

where $\|-\|$ denotes the euclidean norm in $\mathbb{R}^n$ and $\overline{B_\varepsilon(t)} = \{\tau \mid \|\tau - t\| \leq \varepsilon\}$. If these conditions are satisfied, then the theorem asserts the existence of an interval $T_s \subseteq T$ where a unique local solution $\varphi_s^f : T_s \to S$ for the IVP exists, that is $(\varphi_s^f)'\,t = f(t, \varphi_s^f\,t)$ and $\varphi_s^f\,t_0 = s$ for all $t \in T_s$. If $t_0 = 0$ and $T = \bigcup_{s \in S} T_s$, then the flow φ of f exists and is a monoid action [22].

An important class of vector fields with unique solutions are those representing *affine* systems of ODEs. They satisfy the equation

$$(\varphi_s^f)'\,t = A\,t \cdot \varphi_s^f\,t + B\,t,$$

for matrix-vector multiplication $\cdot$, $n \times n$ matrices $A\,t$ and vectors $B\,t$, where A and B are continuous functions on T. Equally important are the corresponding *linear* systems where $B\,t = 0$ for all $t \in T$.

Affine systems of ODEs are Lipschitz continuous with respect to the operator norm $\|M\|_{op} = Sup\,\{\|M \cdot s\| \mid \|s\| = 1\}$, where M is a matrix with real coefficients and Sup denotes the supremum of a set. Indeed, with Lipschitz constant $\ell = Sup\,\{\|A\,t\|_{op} \mid t \in \overline{B_\varepsilon(s)}\}$,

$$\|(A\,t) \cdot s_1 - (A\,t) \cdot s_2\| = \|(A\,t) \cdot (s_1 - s_2)\| \leq \|A\,t\|_{op} \|s_1 - s_2\| \leq \ell \|s_1 - s_2\|.$$

Constant ℓ exists by continuity of A and $\|-\|$, and compactness of $\overline{B_\varepsilon(s)}$. Picard-Lindelöf thus guarantees a unique local solution for the associated IVPs. In particular, in the time-independent or *autonomous* case where A and B are constant functions, their unique solutions are well-characterised and globally defined. That is, flows φ for autonomous affine systems exist and satisfy

$$\varphi\,t\,s = \exp(tA) \cdot s + \exp(tA) \cdot \int_0^t (\exp(-\tau A) \cdot B)\,d\tau,$$

where exp is the matrix exponential $\exp A = \sum_{i \in \mathbb{N}} \frac{1}{i!} A^i$.

Computing such exponentials may be computationally expensive due to the iteration of matrix multiplication. Exceptions are *diagonalisable matrices* A which are similar to a diagonal matrix D in the sense that there is an invertible P such that $A = P^{-1}DP$. For these matrices,

$$\exp A = \exp(P^{-1}DP) = P^{-1}(\exp D)P,$$

where exp D in the right hand side is diagonal and easy to characterise: its entries in the main diagonal are the exponential of those in D. Therefore, when working with solutions of autonomous affine (or linear) systems, it is preferable to work with those in diagonal form.

3   Isabelle Components for Affine Systems of ODEs

We describe our Isabelle formalisation of the mathematical concepts outlined in Sect. 2. More specifically, we explain our addendum of definitions and lemmas for an integration of the existing libraries for ODEs and linear algebra. We finish with an instance of Picard-Lindelöf's theorem for affine and linear systems.

As Isabelle only allows total functions, we formalise the type of vector fields as $real \Rightarrow 'a \Rightarrow ('a :: real\text{-}normed\text{-}vector)$, which by currying is isomorphic to $\mathbb{R} \times V \to V$, where V is a normed vector space over $\mathbb{R}$. We then restrict domains and codomains of solutions using our definition in [19].

definition $ivp\text{-}sols :: (real \Rightarrow 'a \Rightarrow ('a :: real\text{-}normed\text{-}vector)) \Rightarrow real\ set \Rightarrow 'a\ set \Rightarrow$
$real \Rightarrow 'a \Rightarrow (real \Rightarrow 'a)\ set\ (Sols)$
where $Sols\ f\ T\ S\ t_0\ s = \{X\ |X.\ (D\ X = (\lambda t.\ f\ t\ (X\ t))\ on\ T) \wedge X\ t_0 = s \wedge X \in T \to S\}$

The first conjunct $D\ X = (\lambda t.\ f\ t\ (X\ t))$ in the definiendum above translates to $X'\ t = f\ (t, X\ t)$, the second states that $X :: real \Rightarrow 'a$ is a solution to the associated IVP, and the third that X maps elements of T into S.

We use $\mathbb{R}^n$, with $n \geq 0$, as our default vector space. It is formalised using Isabelle's type $(real, 'n)\ vec$ (abbreviated as $real\hat{\ }'n$) of real valued vectors of dimension n. Isabelle's HOL-Library builds this type using a bijection to the type of functions $'n \Rightarrow real$ with finite $'n$. For $s :: real\hat{\ }'n$, the expression $s\$i$ denotes the ith coordinate of s. That is, $\$$ is the bijection from $real\hat{\ }'n$ to $'n \Rightarrow real$. Its inverse is written with a binder χ that replaces λ-abstraction. Thus, $\chi i.\ s\$i = s$ and $(\chi i.\ c)\$i = c$ for all $s :: real\hat{\ }'n$ and $c :: real$.

Matrices are then vectors of vectors—an $m \times n$ matrix A has type $real\hat{\ }'n\hat{\ }'m$. The product of matrix A with vector s is denoted $A *v s$; the scaling of vector s by real number c is written $c *_R s$. In Isabelle, a solution X to an affine system of ODEs with $A :: real \Rightarrow real\hat{\ }'n\hat{\ }'n$ and $B :: real \Rightarrow real\hat{\ }'n$ then satisfies the predicate $D\ X = (\lambda t.\ A\ t *v X\ t + B\ t)\ on\ T$.

We use a formalisation of Picard-Lindelöf's theorem from [19]. The locale *picard-lindeloef* groups its assumptions. If *picard-lindeloef* $f\ T\ S\ t_0$ holds, then T and S are open, $t_0 \in T$, $s \in S$, $\lambda t.\ f\ t\ s$ is continuous on T, and f is locally Lipschitz continuous. The context of the locale also contains the lemma *picard-lindeloef.unique-solution*, stating that any two functions solving an IVP

$$(D\ X = (\lambda t.\ f\ t\ (X\ t))\ on\ \{t_0\text{--}t\}) \qquad X\ t_0 = s \qquad X \in \{t_0\text{--}t\} \to S$$

are equal at $t \in T$. Here, $\{t_0\text{--}t\}$ is Isabelle notation for the set of all numbers between t and t_0 where t can be above or below t_0. Our following lemma then yields a generic instance of *picard-lindeloef.unique-solution* for affine systems.

lemma *picard-lindeloef-affine*:
  fixes $A :: real \Rightarrow real\char94'n\char94'n$
  assumes *Ahyp*: *matrix-continuous-on* T A
    and $\bigwedge \tau\ \varepsilon.\ \tau \in T \implies \varepsilon > 0 \implies$ *bdd-above* $\{\|A\ t\|_{op}\ |t.\ dist\ \tau\ t \leq \varepsilon\}$
    and *Bhyp*: *continuous-on* T B **and** *open* S
    and $t_0 \in T$ **and** *Thyp*: *open* T *is-interval* T
  shows *picard-lindeloef* $(\lambda\ t\ s.\ A\ t *v\ s + B\ t)\ T\ S\ t_0$
  $\langle proof \rangle$

Assumptions *Ahyp* and *Bhyp* state that functions A and B are continuous. The second one requires that the image of $\overline{B_\tau}(\varepsilon)$ for $\tau \in T$ under $\lambda t.\ \|A\ t\|_{op}$ is bounded above. The remaining ones are direct conditions of Picard-Lindelöf's theorem. Continuity in *Ahyp* is different from that in *Bhyp* because Isabelle's default norm for matrices $A :: real\char94'n\char94'm$ is the Euclidean norm, not the operator norm from Sect. 2. Thus, for the lemma above, we formalise the Lipschitz continuity argument at the end of Sect. 2 starting with the following definition.

abbreviation *op-norm* :: $('a::real\text{-}normed\text{-}algebra\text{-}1)\char94'n\char94'm \Rightarrow real\ (1\|\text{-}\|_{op})$
  where $\|A\|_{op} \equiv onorm\ (\lambda x.\ A *v\ x)$

Function *onorm* lives in Isabelle's HOL-Analysis library and it is an alternative definition of the operator norm $onorm\ f = Sup\ \{\|f\ x\| / \|x\| \mid x \in V\}$. However, for many proofs, the definition of $\|-\|_{op}$ in Sect. 2 is more convenient. Hence we formalise the equivalence as shown below.

lemma *op-norm-def*: $\|A\|_{op} = Sup\ \{\|A *v\ x\| \mid x.\ \|x\| = 1\}$
  $\langle proof \rangle$

We omit its proof because lack of automation for suprema in Isabelle/HOL makes it an 8-line script. We also show that $\|-\|_{op}$ satisfies the norm axioms.

lemma *op-norm-ge-0*: $0 \leq \|A\|_{op}$
  using *ex-norm-eq-1 norm-ge-zero norm-matrix-le-op-norm basic-trans-rules(23)* **by** *blast*

lemma *op-norm-zero-iff*: $(\|A\|_{op} = 0) = (A = 0)$
  unfolding *onorm-eq-0[OF blin-matrix-vector-mult]* **using** *matrix-axis-0[of 1 A]* **by** *fastforce*

lemma *op-norm-triangle*: $\|A + B\|_{op} \leq (\|A\|_{op}) + (\|B\|_{op})$
  using *onorm-triangle[OF blin-matrix-vector-mult[of A] blin-matrix-vector-mult[of B]]*
    matrix-vector-mult-add-rdistrib[symmetric, of A - B] **by** *simp*

lemma *op-norm-scaleR*: $\|c *_R A\|_{op} = |c| * (\|A\|_{op})$
  unfolding *onorm-scaleR[OF blin-matrix-vector-mult, symmetric] scaleR-vector-assoc* ..

With this norm, we can define continuity for time-dependent matrix functions and prove Lipschitz continuity.

definition *matrix-continuous-on* :: $real\ set \Rightarrow (real \Rightarrow ('a::real\text{-}normed\text{-}algebra\text{-}1)\char94'n\char94'm) \Rightarrow bool$
  where *matrix-continuous-on* T $A = \forall t{\in}T.\forall \varepsilon{>}0.\exists \delta{>}0.\forall \tau{\in}T.\ |\tau - t|{<}\delta \longrightarrow \|A\ \tau - A\ t\|_{op}{\leq}\varepsilon$

lemma *lipschitz-cond-affine*:
  fixes $A :: real \Rightarrow real\char94'n\char94'm$ **and** $T::real\ set$
  defines $L \equiv Sup\ \{\|A\ t\|_{op}\ |t.\ t \in T\}$
  assumes $t \in T$ **and** *bdd-above* $\{\|A\ t\|_{op}\ |t.\ t \in T\}$
  shows $\|A\ t *v\ x - A\ t *v\ y\| \leq L * (\|x - y\|)$
  $\langle proof \rangle$

Using the constant *UNIV*, the universal set for a given type, we prove the fact that solutions for the autonomous affine and linear case are globally defined. The proofs are just an instantiation of *picard-lindeloef-affine*.

lemma *picard-lindeloef* (λ *t s. A ∗v s + B*) *UNIV UNIV 0*
  using *picard-lindeloef-affine*[*of - λt. A λt. B*] **by** (*simp only: diff-self op-norm0, auto*)

lemma *picard-lindeloef* (λ *t.* (∗v) *A*) *UNIV UNIV 0*
  using *picard-lindeloef-affine-constant*[*of A 0*] **by** *force*

All the lemmas and abbreviations displayed above are part of a new addition to Isabelle's Archive of Formal Proofs [18]. Our work in this section covers over 10 pages of proofs and definitions about matrix limits, norms, and operations. This is equivalent to more than 600 lines of code. It also includes various tangential concepts to affine systems of ODEs like the maximum norm for matrices and its relation to the operator norm [22].

4   Flows for Affine Systems of ODEs in Isabelle

One part is still missing from our formalisation: the general solution for autonomous affine and linear systems of ODEs. This is the focus of this section. Moreover, we prove that these solutions are proper flows in the sense that they are defined over the entire monoid $\mathbb{R}$ and state space $\mathbb{R}^n$.

The general solution for autonomous affine systems was introduced in Sect. 2. Similarly, the general solution for the respective autonomous linear systems of ODEs is $X t = (\exp ((t - t_0) A)) \cdot s$ for $s \in \mathbb{R}^n$. The exponential operation $\exp x = \sum_{n \in \mathbb{N}} \frac{1}{n!} x^n$, however, is available in Isabelle only within the type-class *real-normed-algebra*-1 with an identity element 1 satisfying $\|1\| = 1$. As this is not true for *real*^'*n*^'*n*, because $\|(\chi\ i.\ 1)\| \neq 1$, we define a sub-type of square matrices and show that it is an instance of *real-normed-algebra*-1 and *banach*.

typedef '*m sq-mtx* = *UNIV*::(*real*^'*m*^'*m*) *set*
  morphisms *to-vec sq-mtx-chi* **by** *simp*

instance *sq-mtx* :: (*finite*) *real-normed-algebra-1*
  ⟨*proof*⟩

instance *sq-mtx* :: (*finite*) *banach*
  ⟨*proof*⟩

The command *morphisms* introduces the bijection *to-vec* and its inverse *to-mtx* between '*n sq-mtx* and *real*^'*n*^'*n*. Both instantiations require proving that matrices form normed vector spaces. Beyond that, the first instantiation requires showing that they also form a ring. The second instantiation formalises the fact that every Cauchy sequence of square matrices converges.

As many properties in previous sections apply to matrices as vectors of vectors, we lift various operations from this type to our new type of square matrices.

lift-definition *sq-mtx-ith* :: '*m sq-mtx* $\Rightarrow$ '*m* $\Rightarrow$ (*real*^'*m*) (**infixl** \$\$ *90*) **is** (\$).

lift-definition *sq-mtx-vec-mult* :: '*m sq-mtx* $\Rightarrow$ (*real*^'*m*) $\Rightarrow$ (*real*^'*m*) (**infixl** ∗v *90*) **is** (∗v).

lift-definition *sq-mtx-inv* :: ('*m*::*finite*) *sq-mtx* $\Rightarrow$ '*m sq-mtx* (-⁻¹ [*90*]) **is** *matrix-inv*.

This means that we can write $\$\$$ and $*_V$ instead of $\$$ and $*v$ respectively, and we can convert proofs between the new and the old type. We thus obtain the same results as before in the new type, including Picard-Lindelöf's theorem.

lemma *picard-lindeloef-sq-mtx-affine*:
  assumes *continuous-on T A* **and** *continuous-on T B*
    and $t_0 \in T$ *is-interval T open T* **and** *open S*
  shows *picard-lindeloef* $(\lambda t\ s.\ A\ t *_V s + B\ t)\ T\ S\ t_0$
  ⟨*proof*⟩

Next we extend the derivative tactics in [19] that determine whether one function is a derivative of another. We extend them by adding derivative rules for ($*_V$). This allows us to formalise the general solution for autonomous linear and affine systems of ODEs.

lemma *has-vderiv-on-sq-mtx-linear*:
  $D\ (\lambda t.\ exp\ ((t - t_0) *_R A) *_V s) = (\lambda t.\ A *_V (exp\ ((t - t_0) *_R A) *_V s))\ on\ \{t_0--t\}$
  by (*rule poly-derivatives*)+ (*auto simp: exp-times-scaleR-commute sq-mtx-times-vec-assoc*)

lemma *has-vderiv-on-sq-mtx-affine*:
  fixes t_0*::real* **and** A :: ($'a$*::finite*) *sq-mtx*
  defines *lSol c t* ≡ $exp\ ((c * (t - t_0)) *_R A)$
  shows $D\ (\lambda t.\ lSol\ 1\ t *_V s + lSol\ 1\ t *_V (\int_{t_0}^{t} (lSol\ (-1)\ \tau *_V B)\ \partial\tau))$
  $= (\lambda t.\ A *_V (lSol\ 1\ t *_V s + lSol\ 1\ t *_V (\int_{t_0}^{t} (lSol\ (-1)\ \tau *_V B)\ \partial\tau)) + B)\ on\ \{t_0--t\}$
  ⟨*proof*⟩

As no conditions on the parameter t are given, these general solutions are flows. We formalise these results with the locale *local-flow* of [19].

lemma *local-flow-sq-mtx-affine*: *local-flow* $(\lambda s.\ A *_V s + B)\ UNIV\ UNIV$
  $(\lambda t\ s.\ exp\ (t *_R A) *_V s + exp\ (t *_R A) *_V (\int_0^t (exp\ (-\tau *_R A) *_V B)\partial\tau))$
  ⟨*proof*⟩

lemma *local-flow-sq-mtx-linear*:
  local-flow (($*_V$) A) *UNIV UNIV* $(\lambda t\ s.\ exp\ (t *_R A) *_V s)$
  ⟨*proof*⟩

As reasoning with general solutions is easier for diagonalisable matrices, we formalise matrix invertibility, similarity and diagonal matrices from linear algebra. We also characterise the exponential of a matrix in terms of these concepts.

lemma *mtx-invertible-def*: *mtx-invertible A* ⟷ $(\exists A'.\ A' * A = 1 \wedge A * A' = 1)$
  ⟨*proof*⟩

definition *similar-sq-mtx* :: ($'n$*::finite*) *sq-mtx* ⇒ $'n$ *sq-mtx* ⇒ *bool* (**infixr** ∼ 25)
  where $(A \sim B)$ ⟷ $(\exists P.\ mtx\text{-}invertible\ P \wedge A = P^{-1} * B * P)$

definition *diag-mat f* = $(\chi\ i\ j.\ if\ i = j\ then\ f\ i\ else\ 0)$

lemma *exp-scaleR-diagonal1*:
  assumes *mtx-invertible P* **and** $A = P^{-1} * (diag\ i.\ f\ i) * P$
  shows $exp\ (t *_R A) = P^{-1} * (diag\ i.\ exp\ (t * f\ i)) * P$
  ⟨*proof*⟩

The first three concepts and related properties are available for matrices of type $real\char`^'n\char`^'n$ and $'n$ *sq-mtx*. The exponential is only available for the latter. For example, the notation (diag $i.\ f\ i$) is the $'n$ *sq-mtx* version of *diag-mat f*.

Our development of the type $'m$ $sq\text{-}mtx$ and the diagonalisation of square matrices is over 16 pages long. It spans over 900 lines of code or more than 200 lemmas whose proofs are long due to the various convergence arguments and instantiations. Yet, the substantial formalisation in this section is new and it allows Isabelle users to prove facts involving derivatives of matrix operations.

5 Working with Linear Systems in Isabelle

The mathematical development so far supports several ways of proving properties of affine systems of ODEs in Isabelle/HOL. In this section, we discuss various use cases of our components, including their limitations. Our classification depends on whether users know a solution to an affine system

$$X't = At \cdot Xt + Bt. \tag{1}$$

In the autonomous case $At = A$, it also depends on the diagonalisability of A.

Firstly, users may want to certify that a function $\varphi^f : T \to S$ solves system (1), with $T \subseteq \mathbb{R}$ and $S \subseteq \mathbb{R}^n$. If they formalise Eq. (1) in Isabelle by substituting φ^f for X, then they can use tactic $poly\text{-}derivatives$ to check that both sides of the equation reduce to the same expression as in lemma $has\text{-}vderiv\text{-}on\text{-}sq\text{-}mtx\text{-}linear$ of Sect. 4.

Alternatively, users might want to relate two different characterisations φ_1^f, φ_2^f of the solution to an IVP $X't = At \cdot Xt + Bt$ with $Xt_0 = s$. Using uniqueness, as provided by Picard-Lindelöf's theorem, they can convert easily between one characterisation to the other by firstly formalising that $\varphi_1^f t = \varphi_2^f t$ for all $t \in T \subseteq \mathbb{R}$. Our most general uniqueness lemma is $picard\text{-}lindeloef.unique\text{-}solution$ of Sect. 3, but we have derived specific instances for the autonomous affine case $X't = A \cdot Xt + B$, linear case $X't = A \cdot Xt$, and the case when $t_0 = 0$ and φ^f is the general solution in terms of the matrix exponential.

A particular case where our uniqueness lemmas are useful is in $d\mathcal{L}$-style verification of hybrid systems [21]. Its postconditions must hold for all the points in all solutions of an IVP or along all points of the flow [7,19,20]. Uniqueness therefore simplifies the verification procedure by restricting it to only one solution. We further explore this in Sects. 7 and 8.

So far we have covered cases where users have a solution to system (1). Otherwise, our formalisation provides the general solution for autonomous affine systems $X't = A \cdot Xt + B$ in terms of the matrix exponential with lemmas $has\text{-}vderiv\text{-}on\text{-}sq\text{-}mtx\text{-}affine$ and $has\text{-}vderiv\text{-}on\text{-}sq\text{-}mtx\text{-}linear$ for the type of matrices $'n$ $sq\text{-}mtx$ of Sect. 4.

A formalisation of the general solution for the non-autonomous case is harder and left for future work. The difficulty resides in that one usually needs a solution to the associated linear system $X't = At \cdot Xt$ [8] which can be difficult to find. With this solution, one can use the variation of parameters method to generate the corresponding solution to the affine system (1) [10]. An alternative approach consists in finding the solution to an equivalent linear system of ODEs in one more dimension. Indeed, the system

$$\begin{pmatrix} X't \\ 1' \end{pmatrix} = \begin{pmatrix} (At) & (Bt) \\ 0^\top & 0 \end{pmatrix} \cdot \begin{pmatrix} Xt \\ 1 \end{pmatrix} = \begin{pmatrix} At \cdot Xt + Bt \\ 0 \end{pmatrix}$$

subsumes system (1) in its first entry. Here, $0^\top$ is a transposed zero-vector with the same length as Bt and $0, 1 \in \mathbb{R}$. Thus, if the solution to any of those two linear systems is known, our components are the basis for solving the affine system of interest.

Yet, working with the general solution might require the simplifications at the end of Sect. 2 via the diagonalisation $A = P^{-1}DP$ provided that the associated diagonal D and change of basis P matrices are known. In Sect. 4, Lemma *exp-scaleR-diagonal1* includes the simplification based on this proviso.

If matrices are non-diagonalisable, the general solution is left for future work as we need Jordan Normal forms to formalise this result [22]. However, many non-diagonalisable matrices can still be tackled with our components. An example of this are nilpotent matrices that satisfy the condition $A^k = 0$ for some $k \geq 0$. If k is small, the exponential is still easy to characterise as $\exp A = \sum_{i=0}^{k} \frac{1}{i!} A^i$. We exemplify how to use our components in such cases in Sects. 6 and 8.

Finally, users may want to work with the flow $\varphi\,t\,s$ of the autonomous affine system of ODEs $X't = A \cdot (Xt) + B$ with initial condition $X\,0 = s$. For this, they must use the type $'n\ sq\text{-}mtx$ and the locale *local-flow* applied to the general solution. With this locale, users can change between characterisations of the flow via uniqueness theorems or use the lemma that formalises the monoid-action behaviour of the flow over $\mathbb{R}$.

6 Examples

In this section, we analyse two systems of ODEs and characterise their flows with our Isabelle formalisation. In the first example, we diagonalise the associated matrix and use this to describe the general solution more conveniently. For the second one, we construct the general solution by computing the associated matrix exponential directly.

Example 1 (Diagonalizable Matrix). An ubiquitous second order ODE in physics and engineering is

$$x''\,t = a(x\,t) + b(x'\,t).$$

Fixing $a = -\frac{k}{m}$ and $b = -\frac{d}{m}$ yields the damped harmonic oscillator equation of a mass m attached to a spring with constant k sliding along a horizontal track with damping factor d. Alternatively, with $a = \frac{1}{CL}$ and $b = \frac{R}{L}$, we obtain an ODE for modelling the current of a closed circuit where a resistor (R), inductor (L) and capacitor (C) are in series with a source of constant voltage [10].

Introducing variable y such that $x' \, t = y \, t$ yields the linear system

$$\begin{pmatrix} x' \, t \\ y' \, t \end{pmatrix} = \begin{pmatrix} 0 & 1 \\ a & b \end{pmatrix} \cdot \begin{pmatrix} x \, t \\ y \, t \end{pmatrix}.$$

In Isabelle, we use our function mtx that turns lists into the type $'n$ sq-mtx.

abbreviation mtx-$hOsc$ :: $real \Rightarrow real \Rightarrow 2$ sq-mtx (A)
   where $A \; a \; b \equiv mtx$
   $([0, \; 1] \; \#$
   $[a, \; b] \; \# \; [])$

We use WolframAlpha® to diagonalise it: generate its eigenvalues ι_1, ι_2 and its change of basis matrix P. Then we formalise these entities and certify the diagonalisation as follows.

abbreviation mtx-chB-$hOsc$ :: $real \Rightarrow real \Rightarrow 2$ sq-mtx (P)
   where $P \; a \; b \equiv mtx$
   $([a, \; b] \; \#$
   $[1, \; 1] \; \# \; [])$

lemma mtx-$hOsc$-$diagonalizable$:
   defines $\iota_1 \equiv (b - sqrt \; (b\hat{}2 + 4 * a))/2$ **and** $\iota_2 \equiv (b + sqrt \; (b\hat{}2 + 4 * a))/2$
   assumes $b^2 + a * 4 > 0$ **and** $a \neq 0$
   shows $A \; a \; b = P \; (-\iota_2/a) \; (-\iota_1/a) * (diag \; i. \; if \; i = 1 \; then \; \iota_1 \; else \; \iota_2) * (P \; (-\iota_2/a) \; (-\iota_1/a))^{-1}$
   $\langle proof \rangle$

Integrating a computer algebra system directly into Isabelle, so that inputs and certification are done automatically, is beyond our research goals in this article. Although we omit the proof, it is a simple 4-line script thanks to the addition of our lemmas about standard matrix operations to Isabelle's simplifier.

Finally, we use this diagonalisation to compute the general solution of the ODEs generated by $A \; a \; b$ and instantiate $local$-$flow$-sq-mtx-$linear$ to this result.

lemma mtx-$hOsc$-$solution$-eq:
   defines $\iota_1 \equiv (b - sqrt \; (b^2 + 4 * a))/2$ **and** $\iota_2 \equiv (b + sqrt \; (b^2 + 4 * a))/2$
   defines $\Phi \; t \equiv mtx \; ($
   $[\iota_2 * exp(t*\iota_1) - \iota_1 * exp(t*\iota_2), \quad exp(t*\iota_2) - exp(t*\iota_1)] \#$
   $[a * exp(t*\iota_2) - a * exp(t*\iota_1), \; \iota_2 * exp(t*\iota_2) - \iota_1 * exp(t*\iota_1)] \# [])$
   assumes $b^2 + a * 4 > 0$ **and** $a \neq 0$
   shows $P \; (-\iota_2/a) \; (-\iota_1/a) * (diag \; i. \; exp \; (t * (if \; i = 1 \; then \; \iota_1 \; else \; \iota_2))) * (P \; (-\iota_2/a) \; (-\iota_1/a))^{-1}$
   $= (1/sqrt \; (b^2 + a * 4)) *_R (\Phi \; t)$
   $\langle proof \rangle$

lemma $local$-$flow$-mtx-$hOsc$:
   defines $\iota_1 \equiv (b - sqrt \; (b\hat{}2 + 4 * a))/2$ **and** $\iota_2 \equiv (b + sqrt \; (b\hat{}2 + 4 * a))/2$
   defines $\Phi \; t \equiv mtx \; ($
   $[\iota_2 * exp(t*\iota_1) - \iota_1 * exp(t*\iota_2), \quad exp(t*\iota_2) - exp(t*\iota_1)] \#$
   $[a * exp(t*\iota_2) - a * exp(t*\iota_1), \; \iota_2 * exp(t*\iota_2) - \iota_1 * exp(t*\iota_1)] \# [])$
   assumes $b^2 + a * 4 > 0$ **and** $a \neq 0$
   shows $local$-$flow \; ((*_V) \; (A \; a \; b)) \; UNIV \; UNIV \; (\lambda t. \; (*_V) \; ((1/sqrt \; (b^2 + a * 4)) *_R \Phi \; t))$
   $\langle proof \rangle$

Our matrix operation lemmas make the proof of both results easy to tackle for the experimented Isabelle user. The last lemma yields an automated certification of the uniqueness and the monoid-action behavior of this flow. These results will be useful later in the verification of a simple hybrid program.

Example 2 (Non-diagonalizable Matrix). To derive the equations for constantly accelerated motion in one dimension, we start with the ODE $x''' \, t = 0$. This is equivalent to the linear system

$$\begin{pmatrix} x't \\ v't \\ a't \end{pmatrix} = \begin{pmatrix} 0 & 1 & 0 \\ 0 & 0 & 1 \\ 0 & 0 & 0 \end{pmatrix} \cdot \begin{pmatrix} xt \\ vt \\ at \end{pmatrix},$$

where x, v and a represent the position, velocity and acceleration of the motion. Although the matrix in this system is non-diagonalisable, it is nilpotent as formalised below.

abbreviation *mtx-cnst-acc* :: *3 sq-mtx* (*K*)
  where *K* ≡ *mtx* (
  [0,1,0] #
  [0,0,1] #
  [0,0,0] # [])

lemma *powN-scaleR-mtx-cnst-acc*: *n > 2* ⟹ *(t ∗ₙ K) ˆn = 0*
⟨*proof*⟩

We can use this fact to obtain the general solution and the kinematics equations for constantly accelerated motion with initial state $s = (s\$1, s\$2, s\$3)$.

lemma *exp-mtx-cnst-acc*: *exp (t ∗ₙ K) = ((t ∗ₙ K)²/ₙ 2) + (t ∗ₙ K) + 1*
  unfolding *exp-def* **apply**(*subst suminf-eq-sum[of 2]*)
  using *powN-scaleR-mtx-cnst-acc* **by** (*simp-all add: numeral-2-eq-2*)

lemma *exp-mtx-cnst-acc-vec-mult-eq*: *exp (t ∗ₙ K) ∗ᵥ s*
= *vector [s\$3 ∗ tˆ2/2 + s\$2 ∗ t + s\$1, s\$3 ∗ t + s\$2, s\$3]*
⟨*proof*⟩

Here, *vector* is a function that turns lists into vectors. From this, a simple instantiation shows that the kinematics equations describe the flow of the ODE.

lemma *local-flow-mtx-cnst-acc*:
  local-flow ((∗ᵥ) K) UNIV UNIV (λt s. ((t ∗ₙ K)²/ₙ 2 + (t ∗ₙ K) + 1) ∗ᵥ s)
  using *local-flow-sq-mtx-linear[of K]* **unfolding** *exp-mtx-cnst-acc*.

Throughout this section, formalisation and proofs are relatively simple. This is because our lemmas about matrix operations, if added to Isabelle's simplifier, improve proof automation.

7   Applications in Hybrid Program Verification

To illustrate an application of our formalisation, we use our Isabelle verification components for hybrid programs [17]. This approach starts with an algebra $(K, +, ; , 0, 1, ^*)$ for simple while-programs that also supports a boolean subalgebra $(B, +, ; , 0, 1, \neg)$ of tests such as a Kleene algebra with tests or a modal Kleene algebra [4,15]. With the interpretation of elements of K as programs, $+$ as nondeterministic choice, ; as sequential composition, * as finite iteration, and 0 and 1 as the aborting and ineffective programs respectively, the equations

$$\textbf{if } p \textbf{ then } \alpha \textbf{ else } \beta = p; \alpha + \neg p; \beta,$$
$$\textbf{while } p \textbf{ do } \alpha = (p; \alpha)^*; \neg p$$

model the behaviour of while-programs. These algebras allow us to write correctness specifications via Hoare-triples $\{-\} - \{-\}$ or weakest liberal preconditions wlp [3,9]. This means that we can derive the rules of Hoare-logic and/or those of the wlp-calculus. In Isabelle, this approach accelerates the verification process as our Kleene algebra components automatically generate domain-specific conditions by handling the program-structure without intervention from the user.

Moreover, these algebras have *state transformer* models where elements of the algebra are interpreted as functions of type $S \to \mathcal{P} S$ for a given set S. In this setting, Kleisli composition $(f \circ_K g) s = \bigcup \{g \, s' \mid s' \in f \, s\}$ interprets ;, + is pointwise union $\lambda s. \, f \, s \cup g \, s$, 0 is $\lambda s. \, \emptyset$, 1 is the Kleisli unit $\eta_S \, s = \{s\}$, and $*$ is $f^{*K} \, s = \bigcup \{f^n \, s \mid n \geq 0\}$, where $f^0 = \eta_S$ and $f^{n+1} = f^n \circ_K f$ [19].

Given a finite set of program variables V, the isomorphism between $\mathbb{R}^n$ and $\mathbb{R}^V$ allows us to work in the state transformer semantics of $S \subseteq \mathbb{R}^V$, effectively giving us hybrid stores. Defining $f[a \mapsto b] \, a = b$ and $f[a \mapsto b] \, t = f \, t$ if $t \neq a$, the function $\lambda s. \, \{s[x \mapsto e \, s]\}$ is a state transformer. It maps a store $s \in S$ to the singleton of that store with variable $x \in V$ updated to $e \, s$, for $e : S \to \mathbb{R}$. In particular, it models program assignments

$$(x := e) \, s = \{s[x \mapsto e \, s]\}.$$

Similarly, for an interval $U \subseteq T$ such that $0 \in U$, the *orbit* map $\gamma^\varphi : S \to \mathcal{P} S$ defined by $\gamma^\varphi \, s = \mathcal{P} \, \varphi_s^f \, U$ is a state transformer. It sends each $s \in S$ to the set of all the points in the trajectory φ_s^f for the IVP induced by f and $(0, s)$. However, for modelling boundary conditions, an alternative *G-guarded* version is better. For predicate $G : S \to \mathbb{B}$, we use the *evolution command* state transformer

$$(x' = f \, \& \, G) \, s = \{\varphi_s^f \, t \mid t \in U \land (\forall \tau \in \downarrow t. \, G \, (\varphi_s^f \, \tau))\},$$

where "$x' =$" is syntactic sugar to resemble ODEs, and $\downarrow t = \{\tau \in U \mid \tau \leq t\}$.

By adding assignments and evolution commands to the language of these algebras of programs, we get *hybrid programs*. In particular, we also have correctness specifications for these commands

$$\{\lambda s. \, Q \, (s[x \mapsto e \, s])\} \, x := e \, \{Q\},$$

$$\{\lambda s \in S. \, \forall t \in U. \, (\forall \tau \in \downarrow t. \, G \, (\varphi_s^f \, \tau)) \to Q \, (\varphi_s^f \, t)\} \, x' = f \, \& \, G \, \{Q\}.$$

The above definition of evolution commands requires uniqueness of the solution to the IVP $X' = f(t, X \, t)$ and $X \, 0 = s$. For a more general definition where this is not needed see [19]. Yet, affine and linear systems have unique solutions for specific IVPs. Thus, our formalisation of affine and linear systems is compositional with respect to the verification style described in [7,19].

8 Verification Examples

In this section, we verify two simple hybrid programs using the components of [19] and our formalisation of linear systems of ODEs. Both verifications follow directly from our results in Sect. 6.

Example 3 (Overdamped Door-Closing Mechanism). We use the system of ODEs

$$\begin{pmatrix} x' \, t \\ y' \, t \end{pmatrix} = \begin{pmatrix} 0 & 1 \\ a & b \end{pmatrix} \cdot \begin{pmatrix} x \, t \\ y \, t \end{pmatrix} = (A \, a \, b) \cdot \begin{pmatrix} x \, t \\ y \, t \end{pmatrix},$$

with $a = -\frac{k}{m}$ and $b = -\frac{d}{m}$ to model a damped harmonic oscillator as described in Example 1. The expression $b^2 + 4 \cdot a$ dictates the behaviour of the system. If $b^2 + 4 \cdot a < 0$, the damping factor is too big and there is no oscillation. Otherwise, the oscillation continues. Overdamping is a desired property of some oscillators inside door mechanisms where the engineer does not want the doors to slam or open on the opposite side.

We use Isabelle's $s\$1$ and $s\$2$ to formalise respectively the position (x) and velocity (y) of one of these door-oscillators. We represent a closed door with the equation $s\$1 = 0$. Hence, an open door immediately after being pushed by a person corresponds to the conjunction $s\$1 > 0 \land s\$2 = 0$. We can prove that once this happens, the door will never open on the opposite side, that is $s\$1 \geq 0$, if its oscillator is overdamped.

```
lemma overdamped-door:
  assumes b² + a * 4 > 0 and a < 0 and b ≤ 0 and 0 ≤ t
  shows PRE (λs. s$1 = 0)
  HP (LOOP
      (λs. {s. s$1 > 0 ∧ s$2 = 0});
      (x´=(*v) (A a b) & G on {0..t} UNIV @ 0)
      INV (λs. 0 ≤ s$1))
  POST (λs. 0 ≤ s $ 1)
  apply(rule fbox-loopI, simp-all add: le-fun-def)
  apply(subst local-flow.fbox-g-ode-ivl[OF local-flow-mtx-hOsc[OF assms(1)]])
  using assms apply(simp-all add: le-fun-def fbox-def)
  unfolding sq-mtx-scaleR-eq UNIV-2 sq-mtx-vec-mult-eq
  by (clarsimp simp: overdamped-door-arith)
```

Notation *PRE P HP X POST Q* is syntactic sugar for the Hoare triple $\{P\}X\{Q\}$, meaning that if the system starts satisfying precondition P, then after the execution of the hybrid program X, postcondition Q will hold. In the lemma above we assume $a < 0$ and $b \geq 0$ because $a = -\frac{k}{m}$, $b = -\frac{d}{m}$ and, in physics, the constants k, d and m are often positive. The condition $t \geq 0$ guarantees the verification for a positive lapse of time.

The hybrid program is the finite iteration of a discrete door-opening, modelled by the state transformer $\lambda s. \{s\$1 > 0 \land s\$2 = 0\}$, followed by the ODE $x' \, t = A \cdot (x \, t)$. The loop-invariant of this iteration is the same as the desired postcondition. As we do not deal with boundary conditions, we use variable G for the guard of the evolution command. The first two lines in the proof of this lemma apply the Hoare-rules for loops and evolution commands respectively. The remaining lines simplify the emerging proof obligations.

Example 4 (Automatic Docking). A space ship is aligned with its docking station d and approaching it with velocity $v_0 > 0$. The ship needs to stop exactly at d and its current position is x_0, where $d > x_0$. In order to do this, the ship calculates that it needs a constant deceleration of $a = -\frac{v_0^2}{2(d-x_0)}$. Its motion follows the system of Example 2,

$$\begin{pmatrix} x' \, t \\ v' \, t \\ a' \, t \end{pmatrix} = \begin{pmatrix} 0 \ 1 \ 0 \\ 0 \ 0 \ 1 \\ 0 \ 0 \ 0 \end{pmatrix} \cdot \begin{pmatrix} x \, t \\ v \, t \\ a \, t \end{pmatrix} = K \cdot \begin{pmatrix} x \, t \\ v \, t \\ a \, t \end{pmatrix}.$$

We formalise the position, velocity and acceleration of the ship with state $s = (s\$1, s\$2, s\$3)$ and its discrete behaviour with an assignment of $s\$3$ to the value of the safe acceleration. Under these assumptions, we need to guarantee that the ship will stop ($s\$2 = 0$) if and only if its position coincides with d ($s\$1 = d$). The formalisation is shown below.

lemma *docking-station-arith*:
  assumes $(d::real) > x$ **and** $v > 0$
  shows $(v = v^2 * t \ / \ (2 * d - 2 * x)) \longleftrightarrow (v * t - v^2 * t^2 \ / \ (4 * d - 4 * x) + x = d)$
  ⟨*proof*⟩

lemma *docking-station*:
  assumes $d > x_0$ **and** $v_0 > 0$
  shows $PRE \ (\lambda s. \ s\$1 = x_0 \land s\$2 = v_0)$
  $HP \ ((3 ::= (\lambda s. \ -(v_0 \hat{} 2/(2*(d-x_0))))); \ x\acute{} = (*_V) \ K \ \& \ G)$
  $POST \ (\lambda s. \ s\$2 = 0 \longleftrightarrow s\$1 = d)$
apply(*clarsimp simp: le-fun-def local-flow.fbox-g-ode[OF local-flow-sq-mtx-linear[of K]]*)
  unfolding *exp-mtx-cnst-acc-vec-mult-eq* **using** *assms* **by** (*simp add: docking-station-arith*)

In the proof of this hybrid program, as before, the first line applies the Hoare-rule for evolution commands. The second line simplifies the emerging proof obligation by calling the lemma *docking-station-arith* which we proved separately.

9   Conclusion

We have developed new mathematical components for affine and linear systems of ODEs that improve a modular semantic framework for verification of hybrid programs based on Kleene algebras [19] in Isabelle. These extend the tactics of the framework and simplify the verification procedure by eliminating uniqueness and existence requirements for solutions to these systems of ODEs.

As many systems in physics and engineering are linear, our work impacts a wide range of applications for our verification components. Furthermore, our extension showcases the advantages of using a general purpose proof assistant. It demonstrates that our components can handle exponentiation and other transcendental functions beyond first-order real arithmetic, to which traditional deductive verification of hybrid programs is confined [21].

Our work is also an extension to Isabelle's HOL-Analysis library as it adds lemmas from linear algebra and the theory of ODEs. Previous formalisations in Isabelle/HOL intersect with our components in both fields, but none of them combines them. For instance, there are two formalisations of Jordan Normal forms in Isabelle's archive of formal proofs (AFP) [6,23]. They have been combined and made executable in their exported versions to Standard ML or Haskell [5,6]. An integration of this work and our verification components to handle more than just diagonalisable matrices is a pursuable endeavour. On the other hand, there is much work in extending Isabelle's libraries for ODEs [11–13]. The AFP contains a definition for bounded linear operators and a proof that linear systems expressed with these have unique solutions [13]. However, the affine version of this result has not yet been formalised and it requires further work to make it compatible with the type of vectors $real\,\char`^\,'n$ and our components.

Yet, much work remains to make this approach widely-adoptable in current practice. The general solution for non-autonomous linear systems of ODEs using resolvent matrices remains to be formalised in a proof assistant. Also, our work can only certify diagonalisations and solutions, but the generation of these is left to the user. An alternative approach would automate our procedure in Example 1. That is, a computer algebra system (CAS) would obtain the solution (or diagonalisation) and another tool would generate the Isabelle theory with a certification of the solution provided. This is left for future work.

Acknowledgements. The author wishes to thank the reviewers for their insightful comments. He also thanks Georg Struth, Harsh Beohar, Rayna Dimitrova, Kirill Bogdanov and Michael Foster for discussions.

References

1. Althoff, M., et al.: ARCH-COMP19 category report: continuous and hybrid systems with linear continuous dynamics. In: ARCH19, pp. 14–40 (2019)
2. Alur, R.: Formal verification of hybrid systems. In: EMSOFT 2011, pp. 273–278. ACM (2011)
3. Armstrong, A., Gomes, V.B.F., Struth, G.: Building program construction and verification tools from algebraic principles. Form. Asp. Comput. **28**(2), 265–293 (2015). https://doi.org/10.1007/s00165-015-0343-1
4. Desharnais, J., Möller, B., Struth, G.: Algebraic notions of termination. Log. Meth. ods Comput. Sci. **7**(1) (2011)
5. Divasón, J., Aransay, J.: Gauss-Jordan algorithm and its applications. Archive of Formal Proofs (2014)
6. Divasón, J., Kunčar, O., Thiemann, R., Yamada, A.: Perron-Frobenius theorem for spectral radius analysis. Archive of Formal Proofs (2016)
7. Foster, S., Huerta y Munive, J.J., Struth, G.: Differential hoare logics and refinement calculi for hybrid systems with Isabelle/HOL. In: Fahrenberg, U., Jipsen, P., Winter, M. (eds.) RAMiCS 2020. LNCS, vol. 12062, pp. 169–186. Springer, Cham (2020). https://doi.org/10.1007/978-3-030-43520-2_11
8. Friedland, B., Director, S.W.: Control Systems Design: An Introduction to State-Space Methods. McGraw-Hill Higher Education, New York (1985)
9. Gomes, V.B.F., Struth, G.: Modal Kleene algebra applied to program correctness. In: Fitzgerald, J., Heitmeyer, C., Gnesi, S., Philippou, A. (eds.) FM 2016. LNCS, vol. 9995, pp. 310–325. Springer, Cham (2016). https://doi.org/10.1007/978-3-319-48989-6_19
10. Hirsch, M.W., Smale, S., Devaney, R.L.: Differential Equations, Dynamical Systems, and Linear Algebra. Academic Press, Cambridge (1974)

11. Immler, F.: Formally verified computation of enclosures of solutions of ordinary differential equations. In: Badger, J.M., Rozier, K.Y. (eds.) NFM 2014. LNCS, vol. 8430, pp. 113–127. Springer, Cham (2014). https://doi.org/10.1007/978-3-319-06200-6_9

12. Immler, F., Hölzl, J.: Numerical analysis of ordinary differential equations in Isabelle/HOL. In: Beringer, L., Felty, A. (eds.) ITP 2012. LNCS, vol. 7406, pp. 377–392. Springer, Heidelberg (2012). https://doi.org/10.1007/978-3-642-32347-8_26

13. Immler, F., Hölzl, J.: Ordinary differential equations. Archive of Formal Proofs (2012). https://www.isa-afp.org/entries/Ordinary_Differential_Equations.shtml

14. Jeannin, J., et al.: A formally verified hybrid system for safe advisories in the next-generation airborne collision avoidance system. STTT **19**(6), 717–741 (2017). https://doi.org/10.1007/s10009-016-0434-1

15. Kozen, D.: Kleene algebra with tests. ACM TOPLAS **19**(3), 427–443 (1997)

16. Loos, S.M., Platzer, A., Nistor, L.: Adaptive cruise control: hybrid, distributed, and now formally verified. In: Butler, M., Schulte, W. (eds.) FM 2011. LNCS, vol. 6664, pp. 42–56. Springer, Heidelberg (2011). https://doi.org/10.1007/978-3-642-21437-0_6

17. Huerta y Munive, J.J.: Verification components for hybrid systems. Archive of Formal Proofs (2019). https://www.isa-afp.org/entries/Hybrid_Systems_VCs.html

18. Huerta y Munive, J.J.: Matrices for odes. Archive of Formal Proofs (2020). https://www.isa-afp.org/entries/Matrices_for_ODEs.html

19. Huerta y Munive, J.J., Struth, G.: Predicate transformer semantics for hybrid systems: verification components for Isabelle/HOL (2019). arXiv:1909.05618

20. Huerta y Munive, J.J., Struth, G.: Verifying hybrid systems with modal Kleene algebra. In: Desharnais, J., Guttmann, W., Joosten, S. (eds.) RAMiCS 2018. LNCS, vol. 11194, pp. 225–243. Springer, Cham (2018). https://doi.org/10.1007/978-3-030-02149-8_14

21. Platzer, A.: Virtual Substitution & Real Arithmetic. Logical Foundations of Cyber-Physical Systems, pp. 607–628. Springer, Cham (2018). https://doi.org/10.1007/978-3-319-63588-0_21

22. Teschl, G.: Ordinary Differential Equations and Dynamical Systems. AMS, Premstätten (2012)

23. Thiemann, R., Yamada, A.: Matrices, Jordan normal forms, and spectral radius theory. Archive of Formal Proofs (2015)

Interoperability and Integration Testing Methods for IoT Systems: A Systematic Mapping Study

Miroslav Bures[1]([✉])[iD], Matej Klima[1][iD], Vaclav Rechtberger[1][iD],
Xavier Bellekens[2][iD], Christos Tachtatzis[2][iD], Robert Atkinson[2][iD],
and Bestoun S. Ahmed[1,3][iD]

[1] Department of Computer Science, FEE, Czech Technical University in Prague,
Karlovo namesti 13, Prague, Czech Republic
miroslav.bures@fel.cvut.cz
[2] Department of Electronic and Electrical Engineering, University of Strathclyde,
99 George Street, Glasgow, Scotland, UK
[3] Department of Mathematics and Computer Science, Karlstad University,
Universitetsgatan 2, 65188 Karlstad, Sweden
http://still.felk.cvut.cz

Abstract. The recent active development of Internet of Things (IoT) solutions in various domains has led to an increased demand for security, safety, and reliability of these systems. Security and data privacy are currently the most frequently discussed topics; however, other reliability aspects also need to be focused on to maintain smooth and safe operation of IoT systems. Until now, there has been no systematic mapping study dedicated to the topic of interoperability and integration testing of IoT systems specifically; therefore, we present such an overview in this study. We analyze 803 papers from four major primary databases and perform detailed assessment and quality check to find 115 relevant papers. In addition, recently published testing techniques and approaches are analyzed and classified; the challenges and limitations in the field are also identified and discussed. Research trends related to publication time, active researchers, and publication media are presented in this study. The results suggest that studies mainly focus only on general testing methods, which can be applied to integration and interoperability testing of IoT systems; thus, there are research opportunities to develop additional testing methods focused specifically on IoT systems, so that they are more effective in the IoT context.

Keywords: Internet of Things · Testing · Verification · Integration · Interoperability · Automated testing

1 Introduction

The Internet of Things (IoT) provides numerous advantages to its users in various application domains. However, extensive development of IoT systems in the

© Springer Nature Switzerland AG 2020
F. de Boer and A. Cerone (Eds.): SEFM 2020, LNCS 12310, pp. 93–112, 2020.
https://doi.org/10.1007/978-3-030-58768-0_6

last decade has led to a number of reliability and security challenges [12,31,33]. One of the challenges frequently reported by researchers as well as industry practitioners is the integration testing of IoT systems. In contemporary IoT projects, software developers work with network specialists and electronic experts for testing; however, these parties have different backgrounds and may be accustomed to using different methods of system testing (e.g., low-level testing vs. high-level functional testing). Moreover, different expectations may also play a role; for example, in a standard software system, lower layers (e.g., network or operating systems) are usually considered to be already tested and reliable; therefore, quality engineers focus on the application itself. In the case of an IoT system, the situation might differ and lower levels might also need to be tested properly. In addition, interoperability challenges are closely associated with integration testing; different devices using a variety of protocols need to cooperate in an appropriate manner, and this reliable cooperation has to be verified. Individual devices can have numerous versions and variants, which increases the difficulty of correct and seamless integration.

Integration testing and interoperability testing of IoT systems are considered to overlap for several cases even though semantic differences and different definitions can be pointed out. However, because these terms overlap in their common usage, we decided to cover both **interoperability** and **integration** testing in the scope of this study.

As mentioned earlier, there is an increased demand for more efficient interoperability and integration testing methods. Currently, the model-based testing (MBT) discipline naturally covers the area of integration testing through methods such as path-based testing [8,10,11], which is typical for E2E integration tests, or combinatorial [40] and constrained interaction testing [4], which is useful in unit integration testing and optimization of system configurations. Logically, in the recent period, researchers have attempted to tailor or apply formal verification and MBT techniques for IoT systems to increase system efficiency [3]. Interoperability and integration testing have significant importance in the IoT context and mapping current methods for IoT integration testing would provide valuable information to researchers for IoT and industrial quality assurance. Unfortunately, no systematic mapping study has been conducted yet in the field of integration testing for IoT systems. Hence, we attempt to bridge this gap through this study.

The contributions of this study are as follows:

1. It gives an overview of research and development activity in this field, identifying the active parties and individuals;
2. It also provides an overview of methods and approaches that are available for IoT integration testing;
3. It identifies research opportunities and discusses possible research directions.

This paper is organized as follows. Section 2 analyzes existing mapping studies and literature surveys in the fields of integration testing, IoT testing, quality assurance and IoT integration, which justifies the motivation of this study.

Section 3 explains the methodology used in this study, defines the research questions (RQs) to be answered, and the stages through which relevant studies are identified and analyzed. Section 4 presents the answers to individual RQs and related discussions. The last section presents the analysis of the possible threats to the validity of this study and concludes the paper.

2   Motivation and Related Work

The motivation of this study is twofold. The first is the importance of integration testing in the quality assurance process of IoT solutions [12,33] and the second is the fact that no previous systematic mapping study has addressed integration testing methods for IoT systems specifically.

In the field of general integration testing, there are several systematic literature surveys and mapping studies.

In 2007, Rehman et al. published a survey of issues and available techniques for general software integration testing [45]. Their study summarizes and classifies a variety of integration testing approaches, covering the fields of MBT, test automation frameworks, and methodological aspects; it also provides a good overview of available approaches and concepts that can be used in the definition of a test strategy. However, the study focuses on general software integration testing and is not IoT-specific. Moreover, the study was published more than a decade ago; new techniques and approaches might be available now. Moreover, modern integrated software applications may change as the systems are becoming more complex and demands for their real-time or almost real-time operation have increased. This will also be reflected in integration testing methods; therefore, a state-of-the-art survey is required.

A more recent study by Shashank et al. from 2010 also focuses on the field of integration testing of component-based software systems. However, the study, published as a conference paper, is limited in terms of its sample size; rather than an extensive classification, it provides an overview of available approaches and selected examples of approaches [49]. Despite the limited extent of the study, the brief classification of the state-of-the-art methods into established MBT and software verification categories provided in this study is valid.

Another recent survey and analysis on model-based integration testing was conducted by Haser et al. in 2014 [27]. Essentially, this study is not limited to software systems; the authors discuss integration testing methods that can be applied to a broader scope of cyber-physical systems, which also covers the IoT domain. In the study, an extensive sample of 718 papers is analyzed, and conclusions are obtained for the defined research questions on software paradigms, system assessment types, and usage of non-functional requirements. However, the study is limited to model-based integration testing with limited scope of defined research questions. For the field of IoT-specific integration testing methods, a broader study is required.

In the field of testing techniques that specifically focus on IoT systems and their specifics, a recent systematic mapping study by Ahmed et al. [3] focuses on general aspects of quality and quality assurance techniques designed for IoT systems. The scope of this study is broader than the field of integration testing and covers topics such as security, privacy, construction of testbeds, general MBT, and formal verification techniques. Integration testing is not discussed in depth in this study due to its general scope, and from this viewpoint, overlap with the scope of this study is minimal.

Another recent conference paper by Dias et al. briefly summarizes current testing tools for IoT systems; integration testing is included in the examined aspects of the problem [18]. However, the discussion is brief, and regarding the selected method in the study, all state-of-the-art methods in this field are not covered.

In 2019, Cortes et al. conducted a mapping study on software testing methods used for IoT systems [15]. The study categorizes and analyses publications discussing general testing approaches used in IoT systems. Unfortunately, the discussion of integration testing is very brief in this paper.

Another study by Garousi et al. focuses on the testing methods for embedded systems [23] (which may, to a certain extent, overlap with IoT systems discussed in this study). However, besides the fact that the field of embedded systems is not the same as the IoT field, the study focuses on general testing methods and approaches and does not concentrate on interoperability and integration testing specifically.

The most frequently addressed quality aspects of IoT systems in the last five years are security and privacy [3]. This is also clear from the availability of published literature surveys and systematic mapping studies. A meta-survey summarizing and analyzing 32 available surveys on security, privacy, and defensive mechanisms of cyber-physical systems (including IoT) was recently published by Giraldo et al. [24]. The study provides a good overview of previous works and motivates the reader to find relevant literature sources related to security and privacy problems.

Regarding the integration of IoT systems, a mapping study focusing on integration techniques and styles as well as related architectural aspects of integration was published by Cavalcante et al. [14]. However, this study does not discuss testing or quality assurance aspects of system integration.

To summarize, no current systematic mapping study is dedicated to integration testing techniques for IoT systems, discussing these techniques in the context of IoT domain and from the viewpoint of IoT quality challenges, which are frequent subjects of various reports [12,31,33]. This study aims to provide the missing information in this specific field.

3   Methodology

This systematic mapping study follows the methodology recommendations provided by Kitchenham and Charters [34]. The process of collection and analysis of relevant studies is divided into the following six stages:

1. Research scope determination and definition of RQs to be answered in the study.
2. Search for potentially relevant papers, which includes establishment of a search strategy and acquisition of the identified papers.
3. Identification of truly relevant papers from the initial selection based on the title, abstract, full-text, and quality assessments, which includes performing snowball sampling of other relevant studies.
4. Data extraction from the remaining papers to allow further detailed analyses.
5. Classification of papers and analyses of the extracted data to answer defined RQs.
6. Validity evaluation and discussion of the possible limitations of the study.

The main stages of the methodology are depicted in Fig. 1 and described in this section.

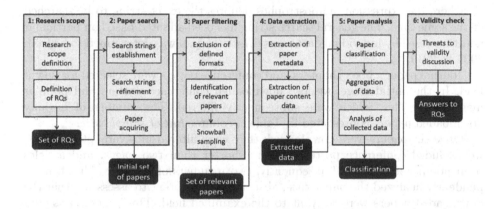

Fig. 1. Stages of the systematic mapping study methodology followed in this study

In this study, we define seven RQs for analyzing the field of integration testing methods for IoT systems from various viewpoints:

- **RQ 1:** What is the research trend in this field in terms of the number of studies published in recent years?
- **RQ 2:** Which researchers are currently conducting active research in this field?
- **RQ 3:** Which publication media (journals and conferences) publish papers in the field of integration testing for IoT systems?
- **RQ 4:** What are the topics and subproblems currently being dealt with in the field of IoT integration and interoperability testing?
- **RQ 5:** Which testing techniques and approaches are used in this field?
- **RQ 6:** What are the current challenges and limitations in the field of IoT integration testing?
- **RQ 7:** What are the possible future research directions in this field?

We do not limit the study to a particular class or type of subproblems, or testing techniques. Hence, *RQ 4* involves informal testing techniques as well as formal and MBT techniques.

To search for relevant papers in the field of integration testing for IoT systems, we decided to use the following four established publication databases: IEEE Xplore, ACM Digital Library, Springer Link, and Elsevier ScienceDirect.

To verify the completeness of the search strings, we randomly selected a set of 30 papers as control samples, which discussed interoperability and integration testing issues of IoT systems. These control papers had to be present in the set of papers found using the search strings.

After a couple of refinement cycles, a general search string was finally established as

('Integration Testing' AND IoT) OR ('Integration Testing' AND 'Internet of Things') OR ('Interoperability Testing' AND IoT) OR ('Interoperability Testing' AND 'Internet of Things')

where the expression in apostrophes denotes the exact string to be searched at the same time. The general search string has been adopted based on particular notations used by individual databases. The timespan was determined to be from 2009 to 2019.

Journal papers, book chapters, and conference papers were selected for download. In the initial stage, we also downloaded conference posters and popular magazine articles, which were subsequently filtered. The number of initially downloaded papers is presented in Table 1, column *Initial sample size*.

Once the papers were downloaded, they were filtered in several steps. First, we excluded conference posters, papers shorter than two pages, and articles from popular magazines. Subsequently, two members of our research lab independently analyzed the paper title, abstract, and full text to assess whether the downloaded papers were relevant to the examined field. This process was conducted in parallel and the results were compared; in the case of mismatch of results, the relevance of the paper was assessed in a discussion until a consensus was reached. This was the case for 11% of the analyzed studies on average. The number of filtered papers for individual databases is presented in Table 1, column *After filtering*.

In the next step, we followed the snowball sampling process; here, we analyzed other relevant papers and articles found in the references of the filtered papers, which were not already a part of the set of filtered papers. Studies and reports found during this sampling underwent the same filtering and assessment process as the downloaded set of papers; two lab members independently analyzed the title, abstract, and full text of the papers.

The majority of the papers acquired by the snowballing process were obtained from the four major databases employed in this study (IEEE Xplore, ACM Digital Library, Springer Link, and Elsevier ScienceDirect) and two papers have been obtained from other databases. The described filtering process has been applied to the papers acquired by snowballing regardless of their source database.

Those papers that were found relevant were added to the analyzed sample. The number of papers found by individual databases after this step is presented in Table 1, column *After snowball*.

Table 1. Numbers of papers after filtering and snowball sampling.

Source	Initial sample size	After filtering	After snowball
IEEE Xplore	384	45	53
ACM Digital Library	87	10	12
Springer Link	199	32	32
ScienceDirect	133	15	16
Other databases	0	0	2
Total	**803**	**102**	**115**

During the data extraction and analysis phase, extracted data were independently verified by a specialist, who analyzed the set of papers and matched them with extracted metadata. A "two pair of eyes" approach was adopted for paper classification. Two specialists classified the papers independently; in the case of a mismatch, particular cases were discussed, papers were analyzed, and the final decision was made based on the discussion results. During this analysis, 8% of the papers underwent mentioned discussion because of mismatch in the classification. The final set after this phase contained 115 papers.

The narrowed selection of the papers was analyzed by publication year to answer RQ1 and by author names and affiliations to answer RQ2. Publication media were categorized by type (journal article, book chapter, conference paper, and workshop paper) and name to answer RQ3. Then, to answer RQ4, we classified the papers by categories presented in Table 2. Categories were organized in two levels: main category and subcategories. Subsequently, full text and detailed analysis of the paper content were used to answer RQs 5 to 7.

The final set of 115 papers with their metadata including abstract, category, source URL, source library, and BibTex string are available for download at http://still.felk.cvut.cz/iot-integration-testing/. In the folder, the list is available in CSV, OpenOffice spreadsheet, and MS Excel format.

4 Results

This section presents the results of the conducted analyses and answers to the individual RQs. Answers to each RQ are provided in a separate subsection.

4.1 RQ1: Publication Trend in Time

In the recent decade, the number of publications discussing interoperability and integration testing issues of IoT systems has constantly grown, as shown by the data presented in Fig. 2.

Table 2. Categories used in the paper classification

Main category	Category short name	Category description
–	IoT quality discussion	Interoperability/integration testing included in a general IoT quality discussion
Testing methodology	Testing methodology, including	General testing methodology including interoperability/integration testing as its part
	Focused testing methodology	Methodology specially focused on interoperability/integration testing
	Formal techniques	Formal testing/verification techniques for interoperability/integration of IoT systems
	Testing methodology, applicable	General testing methodology applicable to interoperability/integration testing
	Literature review	Literature review related to IoT testing methods, which also includes interoperability and integration aspects
Testing frameworks, tools and testbeds	Testing frameworks, supporting	General testing framework directly supporting interoperability/integration testing
	Test automation framework	Specialized test automation framework directly supporting integration testing
	Testbeds	Report on IoT testbed directly supporting interoperability/integration testing
	Testing framework, applicable	General testing framework applicable to interoperability/integration testing
	Frameworks and tools overview	Overview of testing frameworks and tools applicable to integration testing
Simulation frameworks	Simulation frameworks, applicable	General IoT simulation frameworks applicable to interoperability/integration testing
	Simulation frameworks, supporting	General IoT simulation framework supporting interoperability/integration testing
–	Development frameworks	IoT systems development framework/approach/standard including interoperability/integration testing

A more significant number of publications started to appear since 2014. The growth in publication numbers from 2016 to 2019 is almost constant. When extrapolating the trend, we can expect similar growth of publications discussing interoperability and integration testing of IoT systems in the following years.

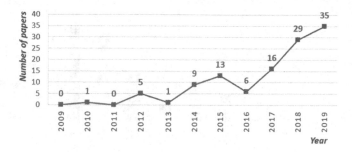

Fig. 2. Number of publications by years

4.2 RQ2: Active Researchers

In the final set of analyzed relevant studies, eight authors emerged to be actively publishing in the field of interoperability and integration testing of IoT systems. They were Brian Pickering (University of Southampton, UK), Bruno Lima (University of Porto, Portugal), Hamza Baqa (Institut Polytechnique Paris, France), Koray Incki (Ozyegin University, Turkey), Mengxuan Zhao (France Telecom), Michael Felderer (University of Innsbruck, Austria), Paul Grace (Aston University, UK), and Thomas Watteyne (Inria, France); they all published three studies.

No author from the analyzed set published more than three studies from 2009 to 2019, 29 authors published two studies, and 431 authors published one study. A total of 468 unique authors were found in the analyzed studies.

This analysis also points out the relative heterogeneity of the research community and absence of research mainstream in this field. However, this is a contemporary situation and might change in the near future.

4.3 RQ3: Publication Media in IoT Integration Testing

During the analysis of the papers, we analyzed four main publication media types: journal article, conference paper, workshop paper, and book chapter. Papers of conference proceedings published in a book series (e.g., LNCS by Springer) were considered as conference papers. Among the analyzed set of papers, several have been published in conferences aggregating parallel workshops; such papers were also considered as conference papers. Most papers were published in conference proceedings (61%), followed by journal articles (22%), workshop papers (9%), and book chapters (9%). Figure 3 presents more details on the publication media type by individual years of the analyzed period.

Among the media types of the published studies on interoperability and integration testing, we will start by analyzing conference papers. The analyzed studies were published in a wide variety of conferences spanning from established conferences in system testing (e.g., IEEE Conference on Software Testing, Validation and Verification (ICST), IFIP International Conference on Testing

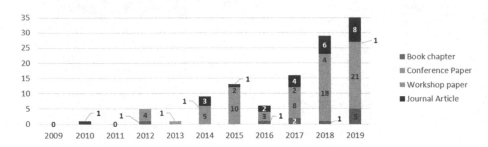

Fig. 3. Venue types by individual years

Software and Systems, and IEEE International Conference on Software Quality, Reliability and Security (QRS)) to various forums related to IoT technology (e.g., IEEE World Forum on Internet of Things (WF-IoT), IEEE International Conference on Future Internet of Things and Cloud Workshops (FiCloudW), and European Conference on Wireless Sensor Networks).

However, the spectrum of the conferences publishing papers focusing on IoT integration and interoperability testing is rather heterogenic, and apart from a few exceptions, we have not found a leading conference publishing more than three papers in the analyzed sample. The IEEE World Forum on Internet of Things (WF-IoT) published three papers, and the Global Internet of Things Summit (GIoTS) published two papers. The remainder of the analyzed papers were published in various unique conferences.

Regarding the journals publishing IoT interoperability and integration testing studies, the situation was found to be similar. Articles were published in a relatively wide spectrum of journals dedicated to computer systems, networks, software testing, and related areas. Three articles were published in IEEE Access and two articles in the International Journal on Software Tools for Technology Transfer. The remaining studies were published in various unique journals. The details can be found in the complete list of analyzed papers available at http:// still.felk.cvut.cz/iot-integration-testing/.

To summarize, publication media for integration and interoperability testing studies are relatively heterogenic. Even though integration and interoperability testing are understood as established discipline in the industrial praxis, in the research world, no major journal or conferences outlies as a venue especially publishing in this specific field. This can be explained by the relative novelty of the field. However, considering that the present industry calls for more effective and systematic methods for interoperability and integration testing, the research community will very likely react to these demands, and the situation will possibly change in the coming years.

4.4 RQ4: Topics and Subproblems Being Addressed

Figure 4 presents the classification of analyzed relevant studies using the categories shown in Table 2. The complete list of individual papers assigned to each category are given in the link above. In the analyzed sample, two major groups were found to be testing methodologies supporting or related to interoperability and integration testing (main category *Testing methodology* with 31 papers in total); and testing frameworks and testing tools, including test automation tools and testbeds constructed for or supporting interoperability and integration testing of IoT systems (main category *Testing frameworks, tools, and testbeds* with 46 papers in total). The analyzed set of papers also includes various IoT simulation frameworks applied to IoT interoperability and integration testing (main category *Simulation frameworks* with 12 papers in total).

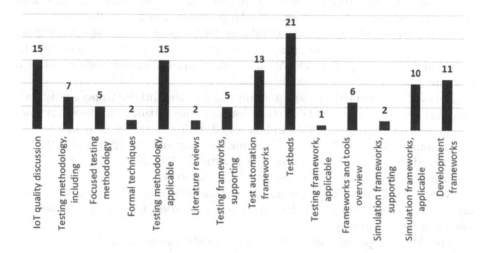

Fig. 4. Classification of analyzed studies

In the detailed categories, the largest number of analyzed studies include discussions on various IoT testbeds supporting integration testing (21 papers), followed by general IoT quality discussions (15 papers), and IoT testing methodologies applicable to integration and interoperability testing (15 papers). Interoperability and integration of IoT systems are discussed in 13 papers dedicated to IoT test automation frameworks. This topic is also the subject of 11 studies presenting various development frameworks for IoT solutions.

On the contrary, the presence of formal methods in the analyzed papers is low; only two papers focus on this topic. Similarly, only five studies present a directly focused integration testing methodology. We analyze the used techniques and approaches in Sect. 4.5.

Two of the analyzed papers were also literature reviews relevant to the scope of this paper: a literature review dedicated to testing methods for embedded systems [23] and a study summarizing general testing methods for the IoT filed [16].

4.5   RQ5: Used Testing Techniques and Approaches

In the studies relevant to interoperability and integration testing of IoT systems, a variety of testing techniques and approaches have been researched and applied, from formal verifications [13] to informal crowdsourcing techniques that can be compared to exploratory testing [22].

In this study, by a testing approach, we mean (1) general approach to test design and test execution, e.g., formal verifications, Model-based Testing or informal testing, and, (2) generic testing approaches based on various test levels as unit testing, integration testing or acceptance testing, for instance. By testing techniques, we mean techniques to create test cases; for instance, combinatorial or constrained interaction testing, path-based testing, and data-flow testing.

Regarding established testing techniques, path-based testing using finite state machines (or analogous structures) as a system under test (SUT) model is discussed in five studies [5,7,20,25,55]. In addition, an SUT model based on a timed state machine has also been employed [35].

Datta et al. presented a prospective approach to semantic interoperability testing of IoT devices or services [17]. In their concept, they distinguish between syntactic and semantic interoperability to be verified during the tests. Semantic testing is also employed in a test automation framework proposed by Kim et al. [32].

Regarding the established test case notations, TTCN-3 standard by ETSI has been employed in six proposals [38,41,46,48,50,55].

Nevertheless, established testing techniques related to IoT integration testing in the studied papers are few. In contrast, general testing approaches are discussed more intensely.

The MBT approach, in general, is explicitly discussed in several studies [1,2,5,9,20,25,29,36], which mostly describe a general concept; particular testing technique, namely path-based testing, is discussed in the studies by Aicherning et al. [5], Estivill-Castro et al. [20], and Grace et al. [25].

Suggestions of formal verifications [13] and runtime verifications [28] do appear; however, for integration and interoperability testing of IoT systems, these have to be further elaborated.

Mutation testing has been used by Lu et al. for verification of RFID devices [37]; this technique can be expected to be used in future works to verify the effectiveness of developed testing techniques.

Other testing approaches include use case testing [51,52], and, practically, exploratory testing and error guessing [22].

Several studies suggest test strategies and approaches for IoT systems that consist of general test levels (e.g., unit testing, integration testing, and acceptance testing) and approaching these test levels informally (e.g., testing of individual sensors, testing or integration, and security testing) [19,21,26,30,39,42–44,47,54,56]. These studies can be used as a basis for setting up a test strategy for an IoT system.

4.6   RQ6: Challenges and Limitations

After the analysis of the current studies in terms of interoperability and integration testing and comparing the state-of-the-art methods with the current industry demand, several conclusions can be drawn and several prospective research directions can be suggested.

The research community in the interoperability and integration testing of IoT systems seems rather heterogenic; from the analyzed studies, there is no clear leading publishing medium or author in this field focusing on this topic. This heterogeneity can be explained by a combination of several factors:

1. The field of IoT testing and quality assurance is relatively novel; despite the active production of innovative IoT solutions in the last five years, research and development of IoT-specific testing methods is currently a developing field.
2. General methods from the field of integration testing might be considered as satisfactory for testing IoT systems; thus, demand for IoT-specific interoperability and integration testing methods is not specially recognized in the research community.
3. In the research community, several research streams and subcommunities have been established, covering path-based testing, combinatorial interaction testing, constrained interaction testing, data-flow testing, and other individual basic testing techniques that can be combined to establish comprehensive integration testing methods. Hence, interoperability and integration testing itself is not considered as a subject of primary research. Instead, the focus is on primary testing approaches that can be employed for the interoperability and integration testing process.

In particular, the second and third points deserve further analysis and discussion. Regarding the second point (hypothetical low necessity to develop IoT-specific interoperability and integration testing methods, because there are general testing methods for these cases already available), it is worthwhile to analyze the situation in the current IoT systems briefly. Compared to standard software systems or relatively isolated proprietary cyber-physical systems not connected to the Internet, the situation in interconnected IoT systems might be different for a number of cases. In these systems, a more extensive set of various protocols on different networks and application levels can be integrated together, and seamless integration has to be maintained. These protocols might span from standardized protocols like WiFi, Bluetooth, IEEE 802.15.4, Z-wave, or ZigBee for low levels of the system; REST, MQTT, CoAP, or LWM2M protocols for higher levels of the system [6]; to various proprietary protocols used by individual vendors. These proprietary protocols might also contain more defects than established standards, and this fact makes smooth interoperability and integration of an IoT system more challenging.

This situation leads to the increased necessity to employ techniques testing correct functionality of integration interfaces and interoperability with different configurations. It also leads us to suggest that the current testing methods shall be revised in the IoT context to increase their potential to detect relevant defects.

The same applies to individual devices, where the level of standardization might be relatively low. Several attempts to standardize IoT devices and allow their interoperability have been made (e.g., ETSI GS CIM 009 or ISO/IEC 21823); however, no major standard is currently established. This is the reason for significant integration and interoperability challenges.

Therefore, the capability of previous interoperability and integration testing techniques should be revised, at the minimum; opportunities to create more effective approaches based on IoT system specifics have to be examined. These opportunities cover Combinatorial and Constrained Interaction Testing [4] as well as path-based testing and data-flow testing [53] techniques for integration testing (typically end-to-end integration tests).

Regarding the third point, the argument that interoperability and integration testing itself might not be understood as a subject of primary research, rather as an application of primary testing approaches, there are two counter-arguments worth mentioning. First, in general system testing research, integration testing is understood as a standalone research topic, as is documented in previous mapping studies [27,49]; in particular, the study by Haser et al. documents the broad extent of studies dedicated to integration testing of software and cyber-physical systems [27]. Moreover, another finding by a recent study conducted by Ahmed et al. [3] should be considered. Even in the discussed primary testing approaches such as path-based testing, combinatorial interaction testing, constrained interaction testing, or data-flow testing, no specific variants of these techniques are published for IoT systems to a large extent.

Hence, to summarize, relative heterogeneity of the IoT interoperability and integration testing approaches might be explained as a result of the relative novelty of the field. Further development of IoT-specific testing techniques to cover these areas is a prospective future research direction. We analyze potential research directions further in Sect. 4.7.

4.7   RQ7: Future Research Directions

Regarding interoperability and integration testing methods for IoT systems, several prospective future research directions can be discussed considering the industrial needs and specifics of IoT systems.

First, specific techniques for integration and interoperability testing of IoT systems have not yet been studied extensively in the literature. The techniques might have been published under different names; for experts in the field, it might be an easy task to get an overall picture. However, for testing practitioners and researchers from other fields, getting such a picture might be more difficult.

The first future research area is handling possible combinatorial explosion problems in integration testing when considering possible configurations to test large-scale IoT systems. When various devices are integrated together in IoT systems, where these devices may vary in versions, many different system configurations can be established; flawless interoperability of devices in these variants need to be tested. The current combinatorial [40] and constrained [4] testing disciplines handle the problem on a general level. However, IoT-specific support regarding the modelling of the problem and application of general combinatorial techniques to IoT and integration testing using specific metadata from an IoT system might represent another perspective direction for future research.

Another relevant field is testing the seamless integration of various devices in an IoT system operating with limited network connectivity. Transmission of data from sensors and between actuators operating in areas with weak network signal coverage might be disrupted during the system run. Hence, in such situations, the overall functionality of an IoT system should be checked for functional correctness and transaction processing of the data, if required. To the best of our knowledge, in the testing of such reliability, current publications focus on lower levels of the system (typically network layer), and systematic methods for such tests on higher levels of an IoT system have yet to be provided.

In addition, to ensure more effective tests and also give the testing practitioners better guidance on how to construct test cases, cross-over techniques between path-based testing [8] and combinatorial interaction testing [40] for testing of close APIs in IoT systems might be researched. Using specific information and metadata from the tested system usually helps focus on the test cases more effectively, and this direction can also be explored in the case of IoT systems.

5 Conclusion

In this study, we focused on the field of integration and interoperability testing of IoT systems. The motivation was twofold: the importance of this field in the current industry and the fact that this specific area has not yet been covered by a focused, systematic literature mapping study.

In the study, we analyzed 803 papers from four major primary databases, namely, IEEE Xplore, ACM Digital Library, Springer Link, and Elsevier ScienceDirect and followed the current established recommendations for conducting mapping studies by Kitchenham and Charters [34]. After a detailed assessment of the papers and quality check, 115 papers were found to be relevant to the field.

Our results suggest that currently there are general testing methods, which can be applied to the field of integration and interoperability testing of IoT systems; therefore, there is a research opportunity to evolve more specific testing methods directly focused on IoT systems, which might work more effectively in the IoT context.

On the other hand, a number of testing and test automation frameworks that support interoperability and integration testing are being created already, and we can also find examples of individual testbeds supporting this field.

There may be several concerns related to the validity of this study. The main concern may be the exclusion of some relevant papers from the list. This possible problem was effectively mitigated by multiple-stage paper filtering and snowballing process, as described in Sect. 3, which also includes a thorough validity check phase.

Another possible concern may be the inclusion of irrelevant papers in the scope, which was also mitigated by the methodology (see Sect. 3) following well-known methods for the selection criteria as well as the "two pairs of eyes" quality check.

A limitation of this mapping study is that it analyzes papers published only in the four primary major databases (IEEE Xplore, ACM Digital Library, Springer Link and Elsevier ScienceDirect) and does not involve other possible sources such as Google Scholar, Scopus, researchgate.net or arxxiv.org, which might contain other relevant studies.

Despite these possible limitations, several prospective research directions were suggested in this study.

Acknowledgement. This research is conducted as a part of the project TACR TH0 2010296 Quality Assurance System for the Internet of Things Technology. The authors acknowledge the support of the OP VVV funded project CZ.02.1.01/0.0/0.0/16_019 /0000765 "Research Center for Informatics".

References

1. Ahmad, A., Bouquet, F., Fourneret, E., Le Gall, F., Legeard, B.: Model-based testing as a service for IoT platforms. In: Margaria, T., Steffen, B. (eds.) ISoLA 2016. LNCS, vol. 9953, pp. 727–742. Springer, Cham (2016). https://doi.org/10. 1007/978-3-319-47169-3_55
2. Ahmad, A., Bouquet, F., Fourneret, E., Legeard, B.: Model-based testing for internet of things systems. In: Advances in Computers, vol. 108, pp. 1–58. Elsevier (2018)
3. Ahmed, B.S., Bures, M., Frajtak, K., Cerny, T.: Aspects of quality in internet of things (IoT) solutions: a systematic mapping study. IEEE Access **7**, 13758–13780 (2019)
4. Ahmed, B.S., Zamli, K.Z., Afzal, W., Bures, M.: Constrained interaction testing: a systematic literature study. IEEE Access **5**, 25706–25730 (2017)
5. Aichernig, B.K., et al.: Learning a behavior model of hybrid systems through combining model-based testing and machine learning. In: Gaston, C., Kosmatov, N., Le Gall, P. (eds.) ICTSS 2019. LNCS, vol. 11812, pp. 3–21. Springer, Cham (2019). https://doi.org/10.1007/978-3-030-31280-0_1
6. Al-Fuqaha, A., Guizani, M., Mohammadi, M., Aledhari, M., Ayyash, M.: Internet of things: a survey on enabling technologies, protocols, and applications. IEEE Commun. Surv. Tutor. **17**(4), 2347–2376 (2015)
7. Amalfitano, D., Amatucci, N., De Simone, V., Riccio, V., Rita, F.A.: Towards a thing-in-the-loop approach for the verification and validation of IoT systems. In: Proceedings of the 1st ACM Workshop on the Internet of Safe Things, SafeThings 2017, pp. 57–63. ACM, New York (2017). https://doi.org/10.1145/ 3137003.3137007
8. Anand, S., et al.: An orchestrated survey of methodologies for automated software test case generation. J. Syst. Softw. **86**(8), 1978–2001 (2013)
9. Arrieta, A., Sagardui, G., Etxeberria, L.: A model-based testing methodology for the systematic validation of highly configurable cyber-physical systems, October 2014

10. Bures, M.: PCTgen: automated generation of test cases for application workflows. In: Rocha, A., Correia, A.M., Costanzo, S., Reis, L.P. (eds.) New Contributions in Information Systems and Technologies. AISC, vol. 353, pp. 789–794. Springer, Cham (2015). https://doi.org/10.1007/978-3-319-16486-1_78

11. Bures, M., Ahmed, B.S.: Employment of multiple algorithms for optimal path-based test selection strategy. Inf. Softw. Technol. **114**, 21–36 (2019)

12. Bures, M., Cerny, T., Ahmed, B.S.: Internet of things: current challenges in the quality assurance and testing methods. In: Kim, K.J., Baek, N. (eds.) ICISA 2018. LNEE, vol. 514, pp. 625–634. Springer, Singapore (2019). https://doi.org/10.1007/978-981-13-1056-0_61

13. Camilli, M., Bellettini, C., Capra, L.: Design-time to run-time verification of microservices based applications. In: Cerone, A., Roveri, M. (eds.) SEFM 2017. LNCS, vol. 10729, pp. 168–173. Springer, Cham (2018). https://doi.org/10.1007/978-3-319-74781-1_12

14. Cavalcante, E., et al.: On the interplay of internet of things and cloud computing: a systematic mapping study. Comput. Commun. **89**, 17–33 (2016)

15. Cortés, M., Saraiva, R., Souza, M., Mello, P., Soares, P.: Adoption of software testing in internet of things: a systematic literature mapping. In: Proceedings of the IV Brazilian Symposium on Systematic and Automated Software Testing, pp. 3–11 (2019)

16. Cortés, M., Saraiva, R., Souza, M., Mello, P., Soares, P.: Adoption of software testing in internet of things: a systematic literature mapping. In: Proceedings of the IV Brazilian Symposium on Systematic and Automated Software Testing, SAST 2019, pp. 3–11. Association for Computing Machinery, New York (2019). https://doi.org/10.1145/3356317.3356326

17. Datta, S.K., Bonnet, C., Baqa, H., Zhao, M., Le-Gall, F.: Approach for semantic interoperability testing in internet of things. In: 2018 Global Internet of Things Summit (GIoTS). IEEE, June 2018. https://doi.org/10.1109/giots.2018.8534582

18. Dias, J.P., Couto, F., Paiva, A.C., Ferreira, H.S.: A brief overview of existing tools for testing the internet-of-things. In: 2018 IEEE International Conference on Software Testing, Verification and Validation Workshops (ICSTW), pp. 104–109. IEEE (2018)

19. Eckhart, M., Meixner, K., Winkler, D., Ekelhart, A.: Securing the testing process for industrial automation software. Comput. Secur. **85**, 156–180 (2019). https://doi.org/10.1016/j.cose.2019.04.016

20. Estivill-Castro, V., Hexel, R., Stover, J.: Modeling, validation, and continuous integration of software behaviours for embedded systems. In: 2015 IEEE European Modelling Symposium (EMS), pp. 89–95, October 2015. https://doi.org/10.1109/EMS.2015.24

21. Felderer, M., Russo, B., Auer, F.: On testing data-intensive software systems. In: Biffl, S., Eckhart, M., Lüder, A., Weippl, E. (eds.) Security and Quality in Cyber-Physical Systems Engineering, pp. 129–148. Springer, Cham (2019). https://doi.org/10.1007/978-3-030-25312-7_6

22. Fernandes, J., et al.: IoT lab: towards co-design and IoT solution testing using the crowd. In: 2015 International Conference on Recent Advances in Internet of Things (RIoT), pp. 1–6, April 2015. https://doi.org/10.1109/RIOT.2015.7104907

23. Garousi, V., Felderer, M., Karapıçak, Ç.M., Yılmaz, U.: Testing embedded software: a survey of the literature. Inf. Softw. Technol. **104**, 14–45 (2018). https://doi.org/10.1016/j.infsof.2018.06.016

24. Giraldo, J., Sarkar, E., Cardenas, A.A., Maniatakos, M., Kantarcioglu, M.: Security and privacy in cyber-physical systems: a survey of surveys. IEEE Des. Test **34**(4), 7–17 (2017)
25. Grace, P., Pickering, B., Surridge, M.: Model-driven interoperability: engineering heterogeneous IoT systems. Ann. Telecommun. **71**(3–4), 141–150 (2015). https://doi.org/10.1007/s12243-015-0487-2
26. Guşeilă, L.G., Bratu, D., Moraru, S.: Continuous testing in the development of IoT applications. In: 2019 International Conference on Sensing and Instrumentation in IoT Era (ISSI), pp. 1–6 (2019)
27. Häser, F., Felderer, M., Breu, R.: Software paradigms, assessment types and non-functional requirements in model-based integration testing: a systematic literature review. In: Proceedings of the 18th International Conference on Evaluation and Assessment in Software Engineering, p. 29. ACM (2014)
28. Incki, K., Ari, I.: Democratization of runtime verification for internet of things. Comput. Electr. Eng. **68**, 570–580 (2018). https://doi.org/10.1016/j.compeleceng.2018.05.007
29. Incki, K., Ari, I.: Observing interoperability of IoT systems through model-based testing. In: Fortino, G., et al. (eds.) InterIoT/SaSeIoT -2017. LNICST, vol. 242, pp. 60–66. Springer, Cham (2018). https://doi.org/10.1007/978-3-319-93797-7_8
30. Kaiser, A., Hackel, S.: Standards-based IoT testing with open-source test equipment. In: 2019 IEEE 19th International Conference on Software Quality, Reliability and Security Companion (QRS-C), pp. 435–441 (2019)
31. Khan, M.A., Salah, K.: IoT security: review, blockchain solutions, and open challenges. Future Gener. Comput. Syst. **82**, 395–411 (2018)
32. Kim, H., et al.: IoT-TaaS: towards a prospective IoT testing framework. IEEE Access **6**, 15480–15493 (2018). https://doi.org/10.1109/access.2018.2802489
33. Kiruthika, J., Khaddaj, S.: Software quality issues and challenges of internet of things. In: 2015 14th International Symposium on Distributed Computing and Applications for Business Engineering and Science (DCABES), pp. 176–179. IEEE (2015)
34. Kitchenham, B., Charters, S.: Guidelines for performing systematic literature reviews in software engineering (2007)
35. Larsen, K.G., Legay, A., Mikučionis, M., Nielsen, B., Nyman, U.: Compositional testing of real-time systems. In: Katoen, J.-P., Langerak, R., Rensink, A. (eds.) ModelEd, TestEd, TrustEd. LNCS, vol. 10500, pp. 107–124. Springer, Cham (2017). https://doi.org/10.1007/978-3-319-68270-9_6
36. Lima, B.: Automated scenario-based integration testing of time-constrained distributed systems. In: 2019 12th IEEE Conference on Software Testing, Validation and Verification (ICST). IEEE, April 2019. https://doi.org/10.1109/icst.2019.00060
37. Lu, A., Fang, W., Xu, C., Cheung, S.C., Liu, Y.: Data-driven testing methodology for RFID systems. Front. Comput. Sci. China **4**(3), 354–364 (2010). https://doi.org/10.1007/s11704-010-0387-6
38. Makedonski, P., et al.: Test descriptions with ETSI TDL. Softw. Qual. J. **27**(2), 885–917 (2018). https://doi.org/10.1007/s11219-018-9423-9
39. Medhat, N., Moussa, S., Badr, N., Tolba, M.F.: Testing techniques in IoT-based systems. In: 2019 Ninth International Conference on Intelligent Computing and Information Systems (ICICIS), pp. 394–401 (2019)
40. Nie, C., Leung, H.: A survey of combinatorial testing. ACM Comput. Surv. (CSUR) **43**(2), 11 (2011)

41. Park, H., Kim, H., Joo, H., Song, J.: Recent advancements in the internet-of-things related standards: a oneM2M perspective. ICT Express **2**(3), 126–129 (2016). https://doi.org/10.1016/j.icte.2016.08.009
42. Pontes, P.M., Lima, B., Faria, J.A.P.: Izinto: a pattern-based IoT testing framework. In: Companion Proceedings for the ISSTA/ECOOP 2018 Workshops, ISSTA 2018, pp. 125–131. ACM, New York (2018). https://doi.org/10.1145/3236454.3236511
43. Pontes, P.M., Lima, B., Faria, J.A.P.: Test patterns for IoT. In: Proceedings of the 9th ACM SIGSOFT International Workshop on Automating TEST Case Design, Selection, and Evaluation, A-TEST 2018, pp. 63–66. ACM, New York (2018). https://doi.org/10.1145/3278186.3278196
44. Popereshnyak, S., Suprun, O., Suprun, O., Wieckowski, T.: IoT application testing features based on the modelling network. In: 2018 XIV-th International Conference on Perspective Technologies and Methods in MEMS Design (MEMSTECH), pp. 127–131, April 2018. https://doi.org/10.1109/MEMSTECH.2018.8365717
45. Jaffar-ur Rehman, M., Jabeen, F., Bertolino, A., Polini, A.: Testing software components for integration: a survey of issues and techniques. Softw. Test. Verif. Reliab. **17**(2), 95–133 (2007)
46. Rings, T., Poglitsch, P., Schulz, S., Serazio, L., Vassiliou-Gioles, T.: A generic interoperability testing framework and a systematic development process for automated interoperability testing. Int. J. Softw. Tools Technol. Transf. **16**(3), 295–313 (2013). https://doi.org/10.1007/s10009-013-0281-2
47. Sand, B.: IoT testing - the big challenge why, what and how. In: Mandler, B., et al. (eds.) IoT360 2015. LNICST, vol. 170, pp. 70–76. Springer, Cham (2016). https://doi.org/10.1007/978-3-319-47075-7_9
48. Schieferdecker, I., Kretzschmann, S., Rennoch, A., Wagner, M.: IoT-testware - an eclipse project. In: 2017 IEEE International Conference on Software Quality, Reliability and Security (QRS). IEEE, July 2017. https://doi.org/10.1109/qrs.2017.59
49. Shashank, S.P., Chakka, P., Kumar, D.V.: A systematic literature survey of integration testing in component-based software engineering. In: 2010 International Conference on Computer and Communication Technology (ICCCT), pp. 562–568. IEEE (2010)
50. Sotiriadis, S., Lehmets, A., Petrakis, E.G.M., Bessis, N.: Testing cloud services using the TestCast tool. In: Latifi, S. (ed.) Information Technology - New Generations. AISC, vol. 558, pp. 819–824. Springer, Cham (2018). https://doi.org/10.1007/978-3-319-54978-1_101
51. de Souza, B.P., Motta, R.C., de O. Costa, D., Travassos, G.H.: An IoT-based scenario description inspection technique. In: Proceedings of the XVIII Brazilian Symposium on Software Quality, SBQS 2019, pp. 20–29. Association for Computing Machinery, New York (2019). https://doi.org/10.1145/3364641.3364644
52. de Souza, B.P., Motta, R.C., Travassos, G.H.: The first version of SCENARIotCHECK: a checklist for IoT based scenarios. In: Proceedings of the XXXIII Brazilian Symposium on Software Engineering, SBES 2019, pp. 219–223. Association for Computing Machinery, New York (2019). https://doi.org/10.1145/3350768.3350796
53. Su, T., et al.: A survey on data-flow testing. ACM Comput. Surv. (CSUR) **50**(1), 1–35 (2017)

54. Tan, T.-B., Cheng, W.-K.: Software testing levels in internet of things (IoT) architecture. In: Chang, C.-Y., Lin, C.-C., Lin, H.-H. (eds.) ICS 2018. CCIS, vol. 1013, pp. 385–390. Springer, Singapore (2019). https://doi.org/10.1007/978-981-13-9190-3_40
55. Tönjes, R., Reetz, E.S., Moessner, K., Barnaghi, P.M.: A test-driven approach for life cycle management of internet of things enabled services. In: 2012 Future Network Mobile Summit (FutureNetw), pp. 1–8, July 2012
56. Walker, M.A., Schmidt, D.C., Dubey, A.: Testing at scale of IOT blockchain applications (chap. 6). In: Kim, S., Deka, G.C., Zhang, P. (eds.) Role of Blockchain Technology in IoT Applications, Advances in Computers, vol. 115, pp. 155–179. Elsevier (2019). https://doi.org/10.1016/bs.adcom.2019.07.008

FRED: Conditional Model Checking via Reducers and Folders

Dirk Beyer[1] and Marie-Christine Jakobs[1,2]

[1] LMU Munich, Munich, Germany
[2] Department of Computer Science, TU Darmstadt,
Darmstadt, Germany

Abstract. There are many hard verification problems that are currently only solvable by applying several verifiers that are based on complementing technologies. Conditional model checking (CMC) is a successful solution for cooperation between verification tools. In CMC, the first verifier outputs a condition describing the state space that it successfully verified. The second verifier uses the condition to focus its verification on the unverified state space. To use arbitrary second verifiers, we recently proposed a reducer-based approach. One can use the reducer-based approach to construct a conditional verifier from a reducer and a (non-conditional) verifier: the reducer translates the condition into a residual program that describes the unverified state space and the verifier can be any off-the-shelf verifier (that does not need to understand conditions). Until now, only one reducer was available. But for a systematic investigation of the reducer concept, we need several reducers. To fill this gap, we developed FRED, a Framework for exploring different REDucers. Given an existing reducer, FRED allows us to derive various new reducers, which differ in their trade-off between size and precision of the residual program. For our experiments, we derived seven different reducers. Our evaluation on the largest and most diverse public collection of verification problems shows that we need all seven reducers to solve hard verification tasks that were not solvable before with the considered verifiers.

1 Introduction

Due to the undecidability of software verification, even after more than 40 years of research on automatic software verification [31], some hard verification tasks cannot be solved by a single verifier alone. To increase the number of solvable tasks, one needs to combine the strengths of distinct verifiers. Several combinations [3,8,9,20,23,25,32,33,37] were proposed in the literature. One promising combination is *conditional model checking* (CMC) [9], which unlike others does not modify the programs nor let the combined techniques know each other.

Replication package available on Zenodo [12].
Funded in part by the Deutsche Forschungsgemeinschaft (DFG) – 418257054 (Coop).

F. de Boer and A. Cerone (Eds.): SEFM 2020, LNCS 12310, pp. 113–132, 2020.
https://doi.org/10.1007/978-3-030-58768-0_7

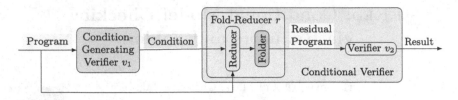

Fig. 1. Reducer-based CMC configuration $(v_2 \circ r) \circ v_1$ with FRED

CMC works as follows: If the first verifier gives up on the verification task, it outputs a condition that describes the state space that it successfully verified. The (conditional) second verifier uses the condition of the first verifier to focus its work on the still-unverified state space. Note that one can easily extend the CMC approach to more than two verifiers by letting all verifiers generate conditions.

To easily construct conditional verifiers (i.e., verifiers that understand conditions) from existing off-the-shelf verifiers, a recent work proposed the concept of reducer-based CMC [13]. Instead of making a verifier aware of conditions, reducer-based CMC constructs a conditional verifier from an existing verifier by plugging a *reducer* in front of the verifier. The reducer is a preprocessor that given the original program and the condition as input, translates the condition into a (residual) program, a format that is understandable by classic verifiers.

The construction of a reducer, especially proving its soundness, is complex and so far there exists only one reducer. However, this reducer's translation is very precise, and therefore, may construct programs that are orders of magnitudes larger than the original program. To solve this problem, and to support systematic experimentation with different reducers, we propose the formal framework FRED, which streamlines and simplifies the construction of new reducers from existing ones. Its underlying idea is to construct a new reducer $r = F \circ R$, a so-called fold reducer, by sequentially composing an existing reducer R with a folder F. A *folder* uses a heuristic that specifies how to modify the program constructed by the existing reducer. More concretely, a folder defines which program locations of the program constructed by the existing reducer are collapsed into a new location and, thus, specifies how to coarsen the program. However, to avoid false alarms, the specified coarsening must not add new program behavior.

New conditional verifiers CV can be constructed with FRED according to the equation $CV = V \circ (F \circ R)$, where $r = (F \circ R)$ is the fold-reducer composed of the existing reducer R and a folder F, V is an arbitrary verifier, and $\circ$ is the sequential composition operator. Figure 1 illustrates this construction in the context of reducer-based CMC. We used this construction to build 49 conditional verifiers, which use the already existing reducer, one of seven folders, and one of seven verifiers. Our large experimental study revealed that using several reducers (with different folders) can make the overall verification more effective.

Contributions. We make the following contributions:

- We introduce FRED, a framework for the composition of new reducers from existing reducers and folding heuristics.

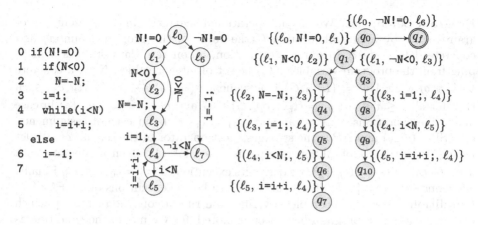

Fig. 2. Example program absPow, its CFA, and a condition for our example absPow with accepting state q_f and assumptions elided (all true)

- We prove that FRED derives valid reducers in case the existing reducer is valid and the folding heuristic adheres to a correctness constraint.
- We use our framework FRED to derive seven new reducers from the existing reducer PARCOMP [13] and use them in various conditional verifiers.
- We experimentally show that the overall effectiveness of reducer-based CMC can be increased using various reducers.
- Our reducers and all experimental data are available for replication and to construct further conditional model checkers (see Sect. 6).

2 Background

Program Representation. Following the literature [8,10], we model a program by a *control-flow automaton* (CFA) $C = (L, \ell_0, G)$ consisting of a set L of locations, an initial location $\ell_0 \in L$, and a set of control-flow edges $G \subseteq L \times Ops \times L$. The set Ops describes all possible operations. In our presentation, we only consider operations on integer variables that are either boolean expressions (so-called assume operations) or assignments. However, our implementation supports C programs. In the following, we use $\mathcal{L}$ for the superset of all location sets and $\mathcal{C}$ for the set of all CFAs. A *CFA* $C = (L, \ell_0, G)$ *is deterministic* (i.e., representable as a C program) if for all control-flow edges $(\ell, op_1, \ell_1), (\ell, op_2, \ell_2) \in G$ either $op_1 = op_2$ and $\ell_1 = \ell_2$, or op_1 and op_2 are assume operations with $op_1 \equiv \neg op_2$.

The left of Fig. 2 shows our example program absPow, which computes $f(N) = 2^{\lceil \log_2 |N| \rceil}$ for $N \neq 0$ and e.g., ensures the property $f(N) \neq 0$. Next to program absPow, its deterministic CFA is shown, which contains one edge per assignment and two edges for each condition of an if- or while-statement. The two edges per if- or while-statement are labeled with the condition and its negation and represent the two evaluations of the condition.

Program Semantics. We use an operational semantics and represent a program's state by a pair of location ℓ (the value of the program counter) and concrete data state c. In our representation, a concrete data state is a mapping from the program variables into the set of integer values. Now, a concrete path π of a CFA $C = (L, \ell_0, G)$ is a sequence $(\ell_0, c_0) \xrightarrow{g_1} \cdots \xrightarrow{g_n} (\ell_n, c_n)$ such that for all $1 \leq i \leq n : g_i = (\ell_{i-1}, op_i, \ell_i) \in G$ and $c_{i-1} \xrightarrow{op_i} c_i$, i.e., (a) in case of assume operations, $c_{i-1} \models op_i$ and $c_{i-1} = c_i$ or (b) in case of assignments, $c_i = \mathrm{SP}_{op_i}(c_{i-1})$ and SP is the strongest-post operator of the semantics. We let $paths(C)$ be the set of all concrete paths of a CFA C. Given a concrete path $\pi = (\ell_0, c_0) \xrightarrow{g_1} \cdots \xrightarrow{g_n} (\ell_n, c_n)$, we derive its execution $ex(\pi) = c_0 c_1 \ldots c_n$. Finally, we define $ex(C) := \{ex(\pi) \mid \pi \in paths(C)\}$ to be the executions of a CFA C.

Condition. After an (incomplete) verification run, a condition sums up which concrete paths of a program have been explored [9]. We model the condition as an automaton describing the syntactical program paths that have been verified and the assumptions that have been made on these paths (i.e., which concrete data states were included). Thus, the condition's edges are labeled by pairs of program edges and assumptions. We model assumptions as state conditions, letting Φ denote the set of all state conditions. Accepting states subsume explored paths, i.e., if a path's prefix is accepted by the condition, the path has been explored. Non-explored paths either end in a non-accepting state or more often have a prefix that ends in a state q from which no further transition is applicable. Typically, the latter means that the verifier did not explore beyond the prefix.

The automaton on the right of Fig. 2 shows a condition for our example program absPow. For the sake of presentation, we left out the assumptions, which are all true. The condition states that the else-branch of the outermost if-statement was explored and that the verifier performed a BFS alike exploration of the if-branch, which split the exploration of the inner if-branch and which is interrupted after one loop unrolling. Formally, a condition is defined as follows.[1]

Definition 1. *A condition $A = (Q, \Sigma, \delta, q_0, F)$ consists of*

- *a finite set Q of states, an initial state $q_0 \in Q$, and accepting states $F \subseteq Q$,*
- *an alphabet $\Sigma \subseteq 2^G \times \Phi$, and*
- *a transition relation $\delta \subseteq Q \times \Sigma \times Q$ with $\neg \exists (q_f, \cdot, q) \in \delta : q_f \in F \wedge q \notin F$.*

We let $\mathcal{A}$ be the set of conditions.

As already said, a condition describes which paths of a program have been looked at. The following definition formalizes this coverage property. Note that we use $c \models \varphi$ to describe that a concrete data state c satisfies a state condition φ.

Definition 2. *A condition $A = (Q, \Sigma, \delta, q_0, F)$ covers a concrete path $\pi = (\ell_0, c_0) \xrightarrow{g_1} \cdots \xrightarrow{g_n} (\ell_n, c_n)$ if there exists a run $\rho = q_0 \xrightarrow{(G_1, \varphi_1)} \cdots \xrightarrow{(G_k, \varphi_k)} q_k$ in A such that (a) $0 \leq k \leq n$, (b) $q_k \in F$, and (c) $\forall 1 \leq i \leq k : g_i \in G_i \wedge (c_i \models \varphi_i)$.*

---

[1] This paper considers only conditions that are represented as automata, while CMC in general [9] is not restricted to a particular representation.

Reducer. The CMC approach suggests that after an incomplete verification run, a second verifier should use the produced condition to explore only the uncovered paths. However, many verifiers do not understand conditions. To overcome this problem, reducer-based CMC [13] suggests to extend verifiers with a preprocessing step that translates the condition into a residual program. A residual program may overapproximate those program paths that are not covered by the condition, but must not introduce additional program behavior. We follow reducer-based CMC [13] and use *reducers* to compute residual programs.

Definition 3. *A reducer is a function* $red : \mathcal{C} \times \mathcal{A} \to \mathcal{C}$ *satisfying the residual property:* $\forall C \in \mathcal{C}, \forall A \in \mathcal{A} : ex(C) \backslash \{ex(\pi) \mid A \text{ covers } \pi\} \subseteq ex(red(C, A)) \subseteq ex(C)$.

First, a reducer for a specific class of conditions was proposed [26]. Then, reducer-based CMC [13] generalized the first approach to use a reducer, named PARCOMP, which supports all kinds of conditions, and showed that it is indeed a reducer [13]. To compute a residual program, the reducer PARCOMP performs a parallel composition of the program and the condition. Starting in the initial location and initial condition state, it matches CFA edges with condition transitions that subsume the respective CFA edge. If no matching condition transition exists, PARCOMP switches to consider CFA edges only. Additionally, it stops exploring states containing a final state $q \in F$ since the condition covers all longer paths.

However, the reducer PARCOMP has one drawback. Verifiers often unfold the program, e.g., unroll loops or inspect branches separately. Due to partially explored paths, some of the unfoldings become part of the condition and will be encoded in the residual program generated by PARCOMP. Thus, the residual program constructed by PARCOMP may become orders of magnitudes larger than the original program resulting in increased parsing costs for the second verifier. Additionally, a verifier v_2 analyzing the residual program generated by PARCOMP is forced to apply the same unfoldings on the non-covered paths as the condition-generating verifier v_1. However, it might be more effective or efficient if verifier v_2 would less often (or never) unfold certain program structures of the original program. To tackle this problem, we present the framework FRED that extends reducers like PARCOMP to let them compute smaller residual programs with fewer unfoldings at the cost of adding more explored paths to the residual program, i.e., computing less precise residual programs.

3 FRED: Fold-Reducers from Reducers

To assist a systematic exploration of the reducer design space, we present the framework FRED. With FRED one can methodically derive new reducers from existing ones, thereby controlling the precision and size of the produced residual programs. One only needs to define how to compress the residual programs computed by the original reducer. Currently, FRED is limited to the class of path-preserving reducers. *Path-preserving reducers* have the advantage that they keep the reference to the original program within the syntactical structure of the residual program, i.e., except for location renaming they encode a subset of the syntactical paths of the original program. This makes it easier to derive new reducers from them. Next, we formally define a path-preserving reducer, where $\mathcal{U}$ is the universe of location markers (e.g., condition states).

Definition 4. *A reducer ppr is* path-preserving *if for any generated residual program $ppr((L, \ell_0, G), A) = (L_r, \ell_{0,r}, G_r)$ it is valid that (a) $L_r \subseteq L \times \mathcal{U}$ for some $\mathcal{U}$, (b) $\ell_{0,r} = (\ell_0, \cdot)$, and (c) $\forall((\ell, u), op, (\ell', u')) \in G_r : \exists(\ell, op, \ell') \in G$.*

Given a path-preserving reducer like PARCOMP, the goal of FRED is to derive new reducers that produce smaller, less precise residual programs. Our idea is that the new reducers aggregate certain similar behavior of the residual program C_r produced by the given path-preserving reducer. So far, the framework FRED supports syntactical aggregations that unite location states of the program C_r. These aggregations can be used to revert loop-unfoldings or separation of branches, the main cause for large residual programs. Additionally, these aggregations are simple to compute. One needs to define only a partitioning of C_r's location states into equivalence classes. However, to get proper reducers, the derived reducers must not introduce new program behavior. Transferred to our aggregations, this means that we must not combine location states of C_r that refer to different locations of the original program. We introduce the concept of a *location-consistent partitioner* that computes partitions respecting this requirement.

Definition 5. *A* location-consistent partitioner *is a function p that maps a set $L_r \subseteq \mathcal{L} \times \mathcal{U}$ to a partition $\{L_1, \ldots, L_n\}$ of L_r s.t. $\forall 1 \le i \le n : |\{\ell \mid (\ell, \cdot) \in L_i\}| = 1$. We use $\mathcal{P}$ for the set of all location-consistent partitioners.*

As examples, we consider the two extreme location-consistent partitioners cfa and sep as defined in the following. Partitioner cfa groups all elements with the same location and sep never groups elements.

$$\mathrm{cfa}(L_r) = \big\{\{(\ell, u) \in L_r \mid \ell = \ell'\} \mid \exists(\ell', \cdot) \in L_r\big\} \quad \mathrm{sep}(L_r) = \big\{\{(\ell, u)\} \mid (\ell, u) \in L_r\big\}$$

All remaining location-consistent partitioners group subsets of elements with same locations. Often, they are context dependent, i.e., they take into account the structure of the original program or the program C_r generated by the path-preserving reducer. For instance, we use the following partitioner that combines locations referring to the same loop head in the original program. The partitioner is parameterized by the loop heads L' of the original program.

$$\mathrm{lh}_{L'}(L_r) = \mathrm{cfa}\big(\{(\ell, u) \in L_r \mid \ell \in L'\}\big) \cup \mathrm{sep}\big(\{(\ell, u) \in L_r \mid \ell \notin L'\}\big)$$

A partioning of the nodes of a graph, e.g., a CFA, induces a coarser graph. Each set of nodes becomes a node of the new graph and there exists an edge between two sets of nodes if there exists an edge between two nodes in the original graph, one in each set. A *folder* applies this principle to compress a residual program computed by a path-preserving reducer. A location-consistent partitioner defines the partitioning of location states. Furthermore, the new initial program location is the set of location states that contains the original initial location. Due to the partitioner's properties, exactly one such set exists.

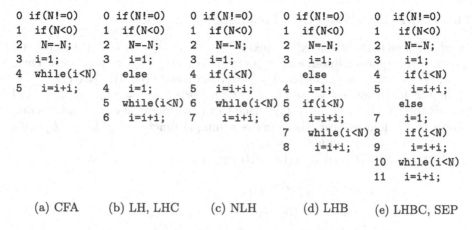

(a) CFA   (b) LH, LHC   (c) NLH   (d) LHB   (e) LHBC, SEP

Fig. 3. Five residual programs with increasing program sizes and varying program structure, constructed by the seven fold-reducers considered in the evaluation

Definition 6. *A folder* $\mathrm{fold} : \mathcal{C} \times \mathcal{P} \rightarrow \mathcal{C}$ *compresses a CFA* $C_r = (L_r, \ell_{0,r}, G_r)$ *with a location-consistent partitioner p such that*

$$\mathrm{fold}((L_r, \ell_{0,r}, G_r), p) = (p(L_r), \ell_{0,p}, G_p) \text{ with}$$

$$\ell_{0,r} \in \ell_{0,p} \text{ and } G_p = \big\{ (\ell_p, op, \ell_p') \mid \ell_p, \ell_p' \in p(L_r) \wedge \exists (\ell, op, \ell') \in G_r : \ell \in \ell_p \wedge \ell' \in \ell_p' \big\}.$$

We use folders to construct so called *fold-reducers* from an existing path-preserving reducer. To this end, we concatenate the path-preserving reducer with a folder.

Definition 7. *Let* p *be a location-consistent partitioner and ppr a path-preserving reducer. The* fold-reducer *for p and ppr is*

$$\mathrm{FOLDRED}_p^{ppr}(C, A) := \mathrm{fold}(ppr(C, A), p).$$

Figure 3 shows five residual programs constructed from program absPow (Fig. 2, left) and the condition for it (Fig. 2, right). The residual programs differ in their program size and structure. They were constructed by the seven different fold-reducers used in the evaluation, all of them using the reducer PARCOMP [13], but we converted them into a better readable form using proper if- and while-statements instead of gotos. Note that for this example, some fold-reducers constructed the same residual program. To construct the residual programs in Figs. 3a and 3e, the partitioners cfa and sep could be used, respectively. For the residual program in Fig. 3b, we used partitioner $\mathrm{lh}_{L'}$ with $L' = \{\ell_4\}$. The partitioner used to construct the program in Fig. 3c undoes unfoldings of if-statements but keeps loop-unfoldings. Finally, the program in Fig. 3d is generated with a partitioner that allows loop-unfoldings up to a given bound of ten and then folds them. However, loop heads of the same iteration are always combined.

Above, we used fold-reducers to compute residual programs. In general, we plan to use fold reducers in the construction of conditional verifiers. Thus, we must show that fold-reducers are reducers. Syntactically, fold-reducers look like reducers. It remains to be shown that fold-reducers fulfill the residual property.

Theorem 1. *Every fold-reducer* FOLDRED_p^{ppr} *is a reducer.*

Proof. We need to show that $\text{ex}(C)\backslash\{\text{ex}(\pi)\,|\,A \text{ covers } \pi\} \subseteq \text{ex}(\text{FOLDRED}_p^{ppr}(C,A))$ $\subseteq \text{ex}(C)$. Since ppr is reducer, $\text{ex}(C)\backslash\{\text{ex}(\pi)\,|\,A \text{ covers } \pi\} \subseteq \text{ex}(ppr(C,A))$. Thus, it suffices to show that $\text{ex}(ppr(C,A)) \subseteq \text{ex}(\text{FOLDRED}_p^{ppr}(C,A)) \subseteq \text{ex}(C)$.

In the following, let $C = (L_o, \ell_{0,o}, G_o)$, $ppr(C,A) = (L_r, \ell_{0,r}, G_r)$, and $\text{FOLDRED}_p^{ppr}(C,A) = (L_f, \ell_{0,f}, G_f)$. Due to the requirements on p and the definition of the fold-reducer, there exists a unique function $h : L_r \to L_f$ with $\forall \ell_r \in L_r : \ell_r \in h(\ell_r)$ and $h(\ell_{0,r}) = \ell_{0,f}$.

Part I) $\text{ex}(ppr(C,A)) \subseteq \text{ex}(\text{FOLDRED}_p^{ppr}(C,A))$:

$$c_0 c_1 \ldots c_n \in \text{ex}(ppr(C,A))$$
$$\Longrightarrow \text{ there exists } \pi_r = (\ell_{0,r}, c_0) \xrightarrow{g_1^r} \cdots \xrightarrow{g_n^r} (\ell_{n,r}, c_n) \text{ s.t.}$$
$$\forall 1 \leq i \leq n : g_i^r = (\ell_{i-1,r}, op_i, \ell_{i,r}) \in G_r \wedge c_{i-1} \xrightarrow{op_i} c_i$$
$$\Longrightarrow \forall 1 \leq i \leq n : \exists g_i^f = (h(\ell_{i-1,r}), op_i, h(\ell_{i,r})) \in G_f$$
$$\Longrightarrow \pi_f = (h(\ell_{0,r}), c_0) \xrightarrow{g_1^f} \cdots \xrightarrow{g_n^f} (h(\ell_{n,r}), c_n) \text{ is a concrete path}$$
$$\text{of } \text{FOLDRED}_p^{ppr}(C,A)$$
$$\Longrightarrow c_0 c_1 \ldots c_n \in \text{ex}(\text{FOLDRED}_p^{ppr}(C,A))$$

Part II) $\text{ex}(\text{FOLDRED}_p^{ppr}(C,A)) \subseteq \text{ex}(C)$:

$$c_0 c_1 \ldots c_n \in \text{ex}(\text{FOLDRED}_p^{ppr}(C,A))$$
$$\Longrightarrow \text{ there exists } \pi_f = (\ell_{0,f}, c_0) \xrightarrow{g_1^f} \cdots \xrightarrow{g_n^f} (\ell_{n,f}, c_n) \text{ s.t.}$$
$$\forall 1 \leq i \leq n : g_i^f = (\ell_{i-1,f}, op_i, \ell_{i,f}) \in G_f \wedge c_{i-1} \xrightarrow{op_i} c_i$$
$$\Longrightarrow \forall 1 \leq i \leq n \text{ there exists } g_i^r = (\ell_{i,r}, op_i, \ell'_{i,r}) \in G_r$$
$$\text{with } \ell_{i,r} \in \ell_{i-1,f} \wedge \ell'_{i,r} \in \ell_{i,f}$$
$$\Longrightarrow \forall 1 \leq i \leq n \text{ there exists } g_{i,o} = (\ell_{i,o}, op_i, \ell'_{i,o}) \in G_o$$
$$\text{with } \ell_{i,r} = (\ell_{i,o}, \cdot) \wedge \ell'_{i,r} = (\ell'_{i,o}, \cdot)$$
$$\Longrightarrow \forall 1 \leq i \leq n : (i = 1 \vee \ell_{i,o} = \ell'_{i-1,o}) \wedge \ell_{1,o} = \ell_{0,o}$$
$$(\text{since } \ell'_{i,r}, \ell_{i+1,r} \in \ell_{i,f}, \ell_{1,r} \in \ell_{0,f}, \text{p location-consistent})$$
$$\Longrightarrow (\ell_{1,o}, c_0) \xrightarrow{g_{1,o}} (\ell'_{1,o}, c_1) \xrightarrow{g_{2,o}} \cdots \xrightarrow{g_{n,o}} (\ell'_{n,o}, c_n) \in path(C)$$
$$\Longrightarrow c_0 c_1 \ldots c_n \in \text{ex}(C)$$

In practice, arbitrary fold-reducers are unsatisfactory since they may produce non-deterministic CFAs, which cannot be translated to C programs. Figure 4 shows an example of a non-deterministic CFA generated by a fold-reducer. In the example, the non-determinism is caused by the partitioner $lh_{\{\ell_4\}}$, which only combines loop heads. Generally, also the condition may cause non-determinism.[2] To solve the non-determinism problem, we transform a fold-reducer into a deterministic fold-reducer that generates deterministic residual programs from deterministic, input programs. The basic idea is to adapt the partitioner to compute a coarser

---

[2] Theoretically, the non-determinism may also be caused by a non-deterministic, original program. However, we assume that the original program is deterministic.

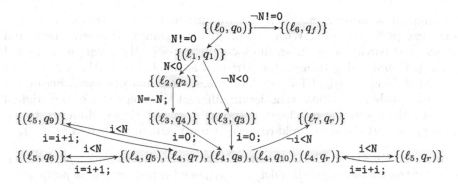

Fig. 4. Nondeterministic residual program built from program `absPow`, the condition from Fig. 2, and a fold-reducer using reducer PARCOMP and partitioner $lh_{\{\ell_4\}}$

Algorithm 1 det

Input: CFA $C_r = (L_r, \ell_{0,r}, G_r)$, p // residual program, location-consistent partitioner

Output: *part*   // location-consistent partition of L_r

1: oldPart:=$\emptyset$; part:=$p(L_r)$;
2: **while** oldPart $\neq$ part **do**
3:     oldPart:=part;
4:     **for each** $(L_i, L_j, L_k) \in$ oldPart $\times$ part $\times$ part **do**
5:         **if** $L_i \in$ part $\wedge L_i \neq L_j \wedge \exists(\ell_k, op, \ell_i), (\ell'_k, op, \ell_j) \in G_r :$
            $\ell_k, \ell'_k \in L_k \wedge \ell_i \in L_i \wedge \ell_j \in L_j$ **then**
6:             part:=$(\text{part}\backslash\{L_i, L_j\}) \cup \{L_i \cup L_j\}$;
7: **return** part

---

partitioning. The coarser partitioning combines all partition elements of the original partition that would cause the residual program to be non-deterministic.

Algorithm 1 shows how to compute such a coarser partitioning from the original partitioning. Starting with the original partitioning, it combines partitions of its current partitioning as long as there exist two CFA edges causing non-determinism, i.e., they consider the same operation and start in the same partition element, but end in different partition elements.

Attentive readers already noticed that Alg. 1 uses the program C_r generated by the path-preserving reducer to adapt the partitioning. Since multiple programs may consider the same set of location states but different control-flow edges, it is impossible to adapt the partitioner without knowledge of C_r. Thus, a deterministic fold-reducer must use different adaptions of the partitioner p. The correct adaption depends on the input program and the path-preserving reducer. We use the following adaption, which depends on the original program and the path-preserving reducer ppr used by the fold-reducer.

$$\text{det}_{ppr(C,A),p}(L) := \begin{cases} \det(ppr(C,A), p) & \text{if } ppr(C,A) = (L, \cdot, \cdot) \wedge C \text{ deterministic} \\ p(L) & \text{else} \end{cases}$$

The adapted partitioner returns the partitioning computed by the original partitioner except for one case. When the original program C is deterministic and the adapted partitioner is given the location states of the program computed by the path-preserving reducer, the partition is adapted with Alg. 1. Note that we neglect to apply Alg. 1 for non-deterministic original programs, because it then may combine partitions considering different location states of the original program, thus, resulting in a location-inconsistent partitioner. However, to use the adapted partitioner in a fold-reducer, it must remain location-consistent.

Lemma 1. *For a given CFA C, condition A, path-preserving reducer ppr, location-consistent partitioner p, function* $\det_{ppr(C,A),p}$ *is a location-consistent partitioner.*

Knowing that the adapted partitioner remains location-consistent, we explain how to derive a *deterministic fold-reducer* from a fold-reducer. The idea is simple. The deterministic fold-reducer uses for each input program a dedicated variant of the original fold-reducer. This dedicated variant uses the prescribed adaption $\det(ppr(C, A), p)$ of the original partitioner to the original program.

Definition 8. *Let* FOLDRED_p^{ppr} *be a fold-reducer. We define the* deterministic fold-reducer *to be* $\text{FOLDRED}_{p,ppr}^{\det} (C, A) := \text{FOLDRED}_{\det_{ppr(C,A),p}}^{ppr} (C, A)$.

We already showed that the proposed adaption of the location-consistent partitioner results in a location-consistent partitioner. Now, we can easily conclude that deterministic fold-reducers guarantee the residual property and, thus, can be used to construct conditional verifiers.

Corollary 1. *Every deterministic fold-reducer* $\text{FOLDRED}_{p,ppr}^{\det}$ *is a reducer.*

While the previous property is mandatory, we build deterministic fold-reducers to produce deterministic programs when given deterministic programs. The subsequent proposition certifies this property of deterministic fold-reducers.

Proposition 1. *Given a deterministic fold-reducer* $\text{FOLDRED}_{p,ppr}^{\det}$*, a deterministic control-flow automaton C, and a condition A, then the residual program* $\text{FOLDRED}_{p,ppr}^{\det} (C, A)$ *is deterministic.*

4   Evaluation

The main goals of our experiments are to systematically investigate different (fold-)reducers and to find out whether fold-reducers can overcome the problem that reducer PARCOMP sometimes generates too large and precise residual programs. Since PARCOMP was the only available reducer our goal was to counteract on its weaknesses (i.e., the sometimes large residual programs), investigating whether one needs to settle for PARCOMP's weakness is beyond the scope of this evaluation. Another goal of our evaluation is to compare CMC with fold-reducers against non-cooperative combinations, especially sequential combinations. This leads us to three research questions:

RQ 1. Do distinct fold-reducers generate different residual programs?

RQ 2. Can fold-reducer be better than reducer PARCOMP and is there a reducer that dominates the others?

RQ 3. Can reducer-based CMC replace non-cooperative verifier combinations?

4.1 Experimental Setup

CMC Configurations. A reducer-based CMC configuration consists of (1) a condition-generating verifier v_1, (2) a reducer r, and (3) a second verifier v_2 (cf. Fig. 1). For components v_1 and r, we use CPAchecker [14] in revision r32965 since it already provides condition-generating verifiers and reducer PARCOMP [13].

As in other works [9,13], we use a predicate analysis [15] and a value analysis [16], both using a time limit of $100\,s^3$, as condition-generating verifiers. If they do not succeed within 100 s, they give up and output a condition. For verifier v_2, we use the three tools CPA-SEQ [29], ESBMC [34], and VeriAbs [30] that performed best on the reachability categories of SV-COMP 2020[4] as well as Symbiotic, which performed best in the SoftwareSystems category of SV-COMP 2020. For all four tools, we use their version submitted to SV-COMP 2020. Additionally, we used three well-maintained analyses, kInduction [7], predicate analysis [15], and value analysis [16], which are part of the award-winning sequential composition of CPAchecker [29]. For them, we also use CPAchecker revision r32965.

We investigated seven fold-reducers r, which we implemented in the FRED plug-in for CPAchecker. All fold-reducers inline functions and typically use the deterministic fold-reducer variant of the reducers described in Sect. 3. Only the CFA and the SEP reducers already generate deterministic, residual programs and do not need to use the deterministic variant. The seven fold-reducers are.

CFA Fold-reducer that uses partitioner cfa, i.e., it combines elements with same location states and, thus, reconstructs those parts of the original CFA that have not been fully explored.

LH Fold-reducer that is based on partitioner $lh_{L'}$ and undoes loop-unfoldings. It combines all elements with the same loop-head location state from L'.

LHC Fold-reducer that also aims at reverting loop-unfoldings, but avoids to combine loop executions started in different contexts, i.e., reached on different syntactical paths ignoring finished loops.

LHB Fold-reducer that limits loop-unfoldings, i.e., keeps loop-unfoldings up to a given bound (we use 10) and afterwards collapse the unfoldings.

LHBC Fold-reducer that like LHB limits loop-unfoldings up to a bound of 10, but additionally separates loop executions with different contexts like LHC.

NLH Fold-reducer that undoes branch- but not loop-unfoldings (keeps different loop iterations separated).

SEP Fold-reducer that never combines elements, uses partitioner sep (same as PARCOMP [13]).

---

[3] We chose a time limit of 100 s because a large proportion of the solvable tasks (>86%) were solved in less than 100 s.

[4] https://sv-comp.sosy-lab.org/2020/systems.php

Combining each fold-reducer r with all second verifiers v_2 we obtain 49 conditional verifiers $v_2 \circ r$. Combining the conditional verifiers with the condition-generating verifier gives us 84 reducer-based CMC configurations.[5]

Tasks. For our evaluation, we considered the well-established benchmark set[6] from the competition on software verification [4]. We focused on the 6 907 tasks of the ReachSafety categories, because all considered analyses can verify the property "no call to function __VERIFIER_error() is reachable". For each condition-generating verifier v_1, we created a task set that excludes all tasks for which all reducers reported an error ($\approx$11%) as well as all easy tasks ($\approx$45%). A task is considered easy if it does not require CMC because it can be solved in 100 s by v_1 or in 1 000 s[7] by all verifiers v_2. Thus, we only look at tasks for which CMC can contribute additional value (2 949 tasks for CMC with $v_1 =$ predicate analysis and 3 046 tasks for CMC with $v_1 =$ value analysis).

Execution Framework. We performed our experiments on machines with 33 GB of memory and an Intel Xeon E3-1230 v5 CPU (8 processing units and a frequency of 3.4 GHz). The machines run a Ubuntu 18.04 operating system (Linux kernel 4.15). We use BenchExec [17] to run our experiments. To ensure that all CMC configurations with the same verifier v_1 use the same conditions, we run the condition-generating verifiers v_1 once with a runtime limit of 100 s[8] and a memory limit of 15 GB. The generated conditions are then used when running the conditional verifiers with a runtime limit of 900 s and a memory limit of 15 GB.

Replication Support. Our experimental data are available online (see Sect. 6).

4.2   Experimental Results

RQ 1 (Different residual programs?) Already our example (Fig. 3) shows that residual programs generated by different reducers can significantly differ in the program size and the branching structure. To further investigate the difference of residual programs, we searched our tasks for programs for which all seven reducers generated residual programs with different numbers of program locations, and selected the program sqrt_Householder_interval.c. Figure 5 shows graph shapes of the CFAs of the residual programs generated by the seven fold-reducers. In a graph shape, the width of line i is proportional to the number of CFA nodes with a shortest path of length i from the initial location. We observe that the graph shapes differ in their height and width. Thus, residual programs differ in their branching structure. Finally, we looked at the size increase of the residual programs, i.e., number of locations of residual program ($|L_{residual}|$) divided by number of locations of original program ($|L_{original}|$). Figure 6 shows boxplots depicting

---

[5] We excluded the 14 combinations in which verifiers v_1 and v_2 are identical because they do not describe a cooperation between different verifiers, but are basically identical to a verification with a single verifier with some additional overhead.

[6] https://github.com/sosy-lab/sv-benchmarks/tree/svcomp20

[7] We grant CMC 1 000 s. We use a a standard time limit of 900 s for the conditional verifier and, as already explained, 100 s for the condition-generating verifier v_1.

[8] To not interrupt condition writing, we applied the limit to the verification algorithm. Imprecise enforcement or condition writing may result in runtimes larger than 100 s.

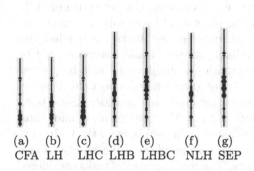

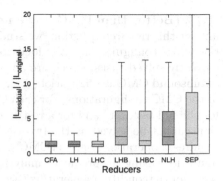

(a) (b) (c) (d) (e) (f) (g)
CFA LH LHC LHB LHBC NLH SEP

Fig. 5. Shape graphs (indicating structure) of residual programs constructed from program `sqrt_Householder_interval.c` by respective fold-reducer

Fig. 6. Boxplot for size increase of residual programs

Table 1. Number of verification tasks solved correctly by each CMC configuration that uses the predicate analysis (upper part) or the value analysis (lower part) for condition generation; last column combines the previous columns

r	+CPASeq		+ESBMC		+Symbiotic		+VeriAbs		+kInd.		+Val.		+All	
	2949	1636	2949	1773	2949	1983	2949	730	2949	1928	2949	2082	2949	433
CFA	946	28	397	165	541	41	**397**	24	762	62	**296**	17	**1342**	38
LH	**951**	**30**	397	165	542	42	391	24	**764**	64	295	17	**1342**	38
LHC	949	**30**	397	165	541	41	395	24	761	63	295	17	1338	37
LHB	700	29	413	189	510	**43**	365	20	624	68	172	17	1129	41
LHBC	699	**30**	412	189	509	**43**	366	20	623	68	169	17	1122	41
NLH	722	27	447	212	508	42	367	22	634	**78**	169	17	1155	41
SEP	662	29	**500**	**226**	**570**	**43**	**397**	22	614	75	132	16	1195	**42**
All	997	41	558	277	609	46	479	26	783	76	298	17	1501	54
ID	1269	0	1003	0	709	0	2166	0	860	0	657	0	2446	0

Verifier v_2

r	+CPASeq		+ESBMC		+Symbiotic		+VeriAbs		+kInd.		+Pred.		+All	
	3046	1713	3046	1800	3046	2112	3046	758	3046	1610	3046	2123	3046	434
CFA	**1018**	**51**	**492**	**178**	**536**	70	**600**	41	**937**	78	697	114	**1452**	**52**
LH	955	49	481	176	515	72	573	41	870	77	682	115	1411	**52**
LHC	940	**51**	481	176	512	72	568	**42**	860	78	683	115	1402	**52**
LHB	822	44	458	143	511	**75**	503	41	761	73	677	**147**	1348	44
LHBC	824	45	458	143	508	**75**	499	41	754	75	674	144	1342	44
NLH	940	**51**	401	90	460	72	549	39	859	**81**	715	146	1310	44
SEP	610	43	488	123	410	**75**	440	36	588	70	509	124	957	35
All	1041	64	650	273	548	75	623	45	944	84	772	177	1525	61
ID	1228	0	1045	0	734	0	2210	0	1121	0	673	0	2482	0

for each reducer the distribution of the size increases of its residual programs. We observe that the boxes differ in size, the median (middle line) and the whiskers, which supports that residual programs from distinct reducers differ.

RQ 2 (Better than PARCOMPand existence of dominating reducer?) To answer this research question, we study the number of tasks solved correctly by the CMC configurations. We focus on correctly solved tasks and exclude incorrectly solved tasks, which are an unreliable source of information caused by an unsound CMC configuration, e.g., due to an unsound verifier or a bug in one of the CMC configurations. For each CMC configuration, we report the numbers for the full task set[9] and for a restricted task set that only considers those tasks that cannot be solved by the two verifiers in the CMC configuration and, thus, requires cooperation, e.g., via CMC. Table 1 shows the numbers for the CMC configurations using the predicate analysis (upper part) and the value analysis (lower part) for the condition-generating verifier v_1. The total number of tasks considered in each column are reported at the top. The CMC configurations are fixed by the reducer (row) and the verifier v_2 (columns). Column '+All' displays the numbers of correctly solved tasks by CMC configurations with any verifier v_2, but excluding tasks that one of the CMC configurations solved incorrectly.[10] Similarly, row 'All' uses any reducer. The last row is discussed later.

Looking at Table 1, we first observe that there exist verifier combinations for which the CMC configurations using the SEP reducer, which is identical to reducer PARCOMP, does not solve the most tasks (bold numbers). We also observe that for some CMC configurations the best reducer differs when considering the full or the restricted task set. Also, the best reducers differ when changing the condition-generating verifier. Hence, the best reducer depends on (1) the task set, and (2) the verifier combination. Additionally, we observe that the numbers in row 'All' are often larger than in the previous rows. Thus, we are more effective when using different reducers. Moreover, our raw data revealed that for all seven reducers there exist tasks that can only be solved by a verifier combination when using this particular reducer. Therefore, we need all seven reducers.

RQ 3 (Replacement for non-cooperative verifier combinations?) To answer this question, we compare CMC with fold-reducers against a combination that executes verifier v_1 and v_2 in sequence using the same program for both verifiers and without exchanging any information. This combination is identical to CMC with the identity reducer ID, which returns the input program. Row ID in Table 1 shows the number of tasks solved correctly by the sequential composition. Obviously, the sequential composition does not solve any task in the restricted task set, which only contains tasks that cannot be solved by v_1 and v_2. To solve these tasks, one needs cooperation approaches like reducer-based CMC. For the full task set, we observe that except for one case row ID solves more tasks than the other rows. Hence, reducer-based CMC should only be used for hard verification tasks that cannot be solved by single verifiers and, thus, need cooperation.

4.3   Threats to Validity

In theory, our reducers fulfill the residual condition. However, in practice our reducer implementation might contain bugs that lead to residual programs that add or miss program behavior, i.e., violate the residual condition. In principle,

---

[9] Remember that the full task set depends on the condition-generating verifier v_1 because we only look at tasks for which CMC can contribute additional value.

[10] For +All, the tasks in the restricted set are neither solved by v_1 nor any verifier v_2.

such bugs can lead to residual programs fulfilling the same property as the original program, but that are easier to verify. Hence, some of the correctly solved tasks might come from such bugs. Furthermore, our results concerning the reducers may not generalize. First, we considered a subset of the SV-COMP tasks and analyses that are run in SV-COMP. The analyses are likely trained on the tasks. However, also CMC configurations that unfold the original program a lot, and thus generate residual programs that look differently from the original program, solved many tasks. We are confident that our results apply to other programs. Second, we used specific time limits for the condition-generating verifier v_1 and the conditional verifier (reducer plus verifier v_2). While we chose common time limits, our results may look differently when using different limits.

5   Related Work

Our work is based on the idea of conditional model checking (CMC) [9], which combines analyses via condition passing. The early conditional model checkers [9] used the condition to directly steer the exploration of the second analysis. Translating the condition into a residual program was first proposed in 2015 [26]. Besides slicing, they construct the residual program from a parallel combination of condition and program. Recently, reducer-based CMC [13] generalized the idea of residual programs and introduced the concept of a reducer. The proposed reducer was similar to the earlier parallel combination [26]. In this paper, we construct multiple, new reducers from the original reducer [13].

Combination of Analyses. One type of combination testifies verification results. These combinations try to confirm alarms [18,25,28,35,44,47] or proofs [1,39,41,45], possibly excluding unconfirmed results. Violation and correctness witnesses [5,6] provide a tool-independent exchange format for alarms and proofs, enabling other tools to check a verifier's result. Further combinations join forces of different analyses. On the one hand, analysis domains are integrated [8,10,23,24,33] to get more precise domains than the pure product. On the other hand, interleavings of analysis algorithms are proposed [3,27,36,37] to benefit from (intermediate) results of other algorithms. A third class of combinations distributes the verification effort among different tools. CMC [9] and reducer-based CMC [13], which we apply, belong to this class. Often, the program parts that could not be verified by the first analyzer are encoded with programs. Sometimes annotations (assertions) are added [19–21,46], while program trimming [32] adds assume statements to the original program. Reducer-based CMC [13] and program partitioning [43] output a new program describing a subset of the original program paths. Abstraction-driven concolic testing [27] interleaves concolic testing and predicate abstraction to construct test cases for test goals. CoVeriTest [11] recently generalized this approach. Conditional static analysis [49] splits the program paths into subsets, runs one dataflow analysis on each subset and finally combines the results of these restricted analyses.

Program Transformation for Verification. Our work uses fold-reducers to transform the original program to remove already-verified paths. Like any reducer, fold-reducers may unfold the structure (execution paths) of the original program. Moreover, fold-reducers use a folder that aims at reverting some of the unfoldings introduced by the existing reducer used in the fold-reducer. Likewise, verification refactoring [53] heuristically undoes compiler optimizations to ease verification. Programs-from-proofs [42] pursues the same goal, but it unfolds the program structure to ease verification. Program partitioning [43] and abstraction-driven concolic testing [27] transform the original program to remove tested or infeasible program paths. Unfolding the program structure is a common approach to remove infeasible paths [2,38,48] or improve the analysis result [40,50,51]. In contrast, folding is used less often. Examples are compiler optimizations like constant propagation [52] and common-subexpression elimination [22].

6   Conclusion

One solution to the problem of verifying complex software systems is to improve verification algorithms and theories. An orthogonal solution is to combine existing techniques. Conditional model checking (CMC) is a promising approach to combine the strengths of different verifiers. To construct new conditional model checkers from existing model checkers in an implementation-less and configurable manner (off-the-shelf, plug-and-play), the concept of reducer-based CMC was recently proposed [13]. Instead of spending developer resources on adapting existing verifiers to make them understand conditions—the information exchange format in CMC—, reducer-based CMC suggests to put reducers in front of existing, off-the-shelf verifiers. The task of a reducer is to convert the condition into a format that the verifier already understands, namely program code. Until now, only one reducer existed. Our experiments revealed that there is a lot of potential for improving the effectiveness by using different kinds of reducers.

Developing new reducers can be a laborious task. One must define how to compute the residual program from the input condition and program. Moreover, one must prove that the reducer fulfills the residual property, a correctness property for the reducer. To systematically study reducers, we developed the framework FRED, which simplifies the development of new reducers. FRED allows us to derive the new reducer from an existing one and a heuristic that describes how to coarsen the residual program generated by the existing reducer. To prove that the derived reducer is indeed a reducer, one only needs to show that the specified heuristic is a location-consistent partitioner, a property much simpler than the residual property. Our experience with FRED is that developing and implementing a new heuristic takes at most a few hours. In the future, algorithm selection could be applied to choose the most suitable reducer for a task.

Data Availability Statement The reducers and all experimental data are publicly available for replication on a web page [11] and as replication package [12].

---

[11] https://www.sosy-lab.org/research/fred/

References

1. Albert, E., Puebla, G., Hermenegildo, M.V.: Abstraction-carrying code. In: Proc. LPAR, LNCS, vol. 3452, pp. 380–397. Springer (2004). https://doi.org/10.1007/978-3-540-32275-7_25
2. Balakrishnan, G., Sankaranarayanan, S., Ivancic, F., Wei, O., Gupta, A.: SLR: Path-sensitive analysis through infeasible-path detection and syntactic language refinement. In: Proc. SAS, LNCS, vol. 5079, pp. pp. 238–254. Springer (2008). https://doi.org/10.1007/978-3-540-69166-2_16
3. Beckman, N., Nori, A.V., Rajamani, S.K., Simmons, R.J.: Proofs from tests. In: Proc. ISSTA, pp. 3–14. ACM (2008). https://doi.org/10.1145/1390630.1390634
4. Beyer, D.: Advances in automatic software verification: SV-COMP 2020. In: Proc. TACAS (2), LNCS, vol. 12079, pp. 347–367. Springer (2020). https://doi.org/10.1007/978-3-030-45237-7_21
5. Beyer, D., Dangl, M., Dietsch, D., Heizmann, M.: Correctness witnesses: Exchanging verification results between verifiers. In: Proc. FSE, pp. 326–337. ACM (2016). https://doi.org/10.1145/2950290.2950351
6. Beyer, D., Dangl, M., Dietsch, D., Heizmann, M., Stahlbauer, A.: Witness validation and stepwise testification across software verifiers. In: Proc. FSE, pp. 721–733. ACM (2015). https://doi.org/10.1145/2786805.2786867
7. Beyer, D., Dangl, M., Wendler, P.: Boosting k-induction with continuously-refined invariants. In: Proc. CAV, LNCS, vol. 9206, pp. 622–640. Springer (2015). https://doi.org/10.1007/978-3-319-21690-4_42
8. Beyer, D., Gulwani, S., Schmidt, D.: Combining model checking and data-flow analysis. In: Handbook of Model Checking, pp. 493–540. Springer (2018). https://doi.org/10.1007/978-3-319-10575-8_16
9. Beyer, D., Henzinger, T.A., Keremoglu, M.E., Wendler, P.: Conditional model checking: A technique to pass information between verifiers. In: Proc. FSE. ACM (2012). https://doi.org/10.1145/2393596.2393664
10. Beyer, D., Henzinger, T.A., Théoduloz, G.: Program analysis with dynamic precision adjustment. In: Proc. ASE, pp. 29–38. IEEE (2008). https://doi.org/10.1109/ASE.2008.13
11. Beyer, D., Jakobs, M.C.: CoVeriTest: Cooperative verifier-based testing. In: Proc. FASE, LNCS, vol. 11424, pp. 389–408. Springer (2019). https://doi.org/10.1007/978-3-030-16722-6_23
12. Beyer, D., Jakobs, M.C.: Replication package for article 'FRED: Conditional model checking via reducers and folders' in: Proc. SEFM 2020 (2020). https://doi.org/10.5281/zenodo.3953565
13. Beyer, D., Jakobs, M.C., Lemberger, T., Wehrheim, H.: Reducer-based construction of conditional verifiers. In: Proc. ICSE, pp. 1182–1193. ACM (2018). https://doi.org/10.1145/3180155.3180259
14. Beyer, D., Keremoglu, M.E.: CPACHECKER: A tool for configurable software verification. In: Proc. CAV, LNCS, vol. 6806, pp. 184–190. Springer (2011). https://doi.org/10.1007/978-3-642-22110-1_16
15. Beyer, D., Keremoglu, M.E., Wendler, P.: Predicate abstraction with adjustable-block encoding. In: Proc. FMCAD, pp. 189–197. FMCAD (2010)
16. Beyer, D., Löwe, S.: Explicit-state software model checking based on CEGAR and interpolation. In: Proc. FASE, LNCS, vol. 7793, pp. 146–162. Springer (2013). https://doi.org/10.1007/978-3-642-37057-1_11

17. Beyer, D., Löwe, S., Wendler, P.: Reliable benchmarking: Requirements and solutions. Int. J. Softw. Tools Technol. Transfer **21**(1), 1–29 (2017). https://doi.org/10.1007/s10009-017-0469-y

18. Chebaro, O., Kosmatov, N., Giorgetti, A., Julliand, J.: Program slicing enhances a verification technique combining static and dynamic analysis. In: Proc. SAC, pp. 1284–1291. ACM (2012). https://doi.org/10.1145/2245276.2231980

19. Christakis, M., Müller, P., Wüstholz, V.: Collaborative verification and testing with explicit assumptions. In: Proc. FM, LNCS, vol. 7436, pp. 132–146. Springer (2012). https://doi.org/10.1007/978-3-642-32759-9_13

20. Christakis, M., Müller, P., Wüstholz, V.: Guiding dynamic symbolic execution toward unverified program executions. In: Proc. ICSE, pp. 144–155. ACM (2016). https://doi.org/10.1145/2884781.2884843

21. Christakis, M., Wüstholz, V.: Bounded abstract interpretation. In: Proc. SAS, LNCS, vol. 9837, pp. 105–125. Springer (2016). https://doi.org/10.1007/978-3-662-53413-7_6

22. Cocke, J.: Global common subexpression elimination. In: Proc. Symposium on Compiler Optimization, pp. 20–24. ACM (1970). https://doi.org/10.1145/800028.808480

23. Cousot, P., Cousot, R.: Systematic design of program-analysis frameworks. In: Proc. POPL, pp. 269–282. ACM (1979). https://doi.org/10.1145/567752.567778

24. Cousot, P., Cousot, R., Feret, J., Mauborgne, L., Miné, A., Monniaux, D., Rival, X.: Combination of abstractions in the ASTRÉE static analyzer. In: Proc. ASIAN'06, LNCS, vol. 4435, pp. 272–300. Springer (2008). https://doi.org/10.1007/978-3-540-77505-8_23

25. Csallner, C., Smaragdakis, Y.: Check 'n' Crash: Combining static checking and testing. In: Proc. ICSE, pp. 422–431. ACM (2005). https://doi.org/10.1145/1062455.1062533

26. Czech, M., Jakobs, M., Wehrheim, H.: Just test what you cannot verify! In: Proc. FASE, LNCS, vol. 9033, pp. 100–114. Springer (2015). https://doi.org/10.1007/978-3-662-46675-9_7

27. Daca, P., Gupta, A., Henzinger, T.A.: Abstraction-driven concolic testing. In: Proc. VMCAI, LNCS, vol. 9583, pp. 328–347. Springer (2016). https://doi.org/10.1007/978-3-662-49122-5_16

28. Dams, D., Namjoshi, K.S.: Orion: High-precision methods for static error analysis of C and C++ programs. In: Proc. FMCO, LNCS, vol. 4111, pp. 138–160. Springer (2005). https://doi.org/10.1007/11804192_7

29. Dangl, M., Löwe, S., Wendler, P.: CPACHECKER with support for recursive programs and floating-point arithmetic (competition contribution). In: Proc. TACAS, LNCS, vol. 9035, pp. 423–425. Springer (2015). https://doi.org/10.1007/978-3-662-46681-0_34

30. Darke, P., Prabhu, S., Chimdyalwar, B., Chauhan, A., Kumar, S., Chowdhury, A.B., Venkatesh, R., Datar, A., Medicherla, R.K.: VeriAbs: Verification by abstraction and test generation (competition contribution). In: Proc. TACAS, LNCS, vol. 10806, pp. 457–462. Springer (2018). https://doi.org/10.1007/978-3-319-89963-3_32

31. D'Silva, V., Kröning, D., Weissenbacher, G.: A survey of automated techniques for formal software verification. IEEE Trans. CAD Integr. Circ. Syst. **27**(7), 1165–1178 (2008). https://doi.org/10.1109/TCAD.2008.923410

32. Ferles, K., Wüstholz, V., Christakis, M., Dillig, I.: Failure-directed program trimming. In: Proc. ESEC/FSE, pp. 174–185. ACM (2017). https://doi.org/10.1145/3106237.3106249

33. Fischer, J., Jhala, R., Majumdar, R.: Joining data flow with predicates. In: Proc. FSE, pp. 227–236. ACM (2005). https://doi.org/10.1145/1081706.1081742
34. Gadelha, M.Y.R., Monteiro, F.R., Cordeiro, L.C., Nicole, D.A.: ESBMC v6.0: Verifying C programs using k-induction and invariant inference (competition contribution). In: Proc. TACAS (3), LNCS, vol. 11429, pp. 209–213. Springer (2019). https://doi.org/10.1007/978-3-030-17502-3_15
35. Ge, X., Taneja, K., Xie, T., Tillmann, N.: DyTa: Dynamic symbolic execution guided with static verification results. In: Proc. ICSE, pp. 992–994. ACM (2011). https://doi.org/10.1145/1985793.1985971
36. Godefroid, P., Nori, A.V., Rajamani, S.K., Tetali, S.: Compositional may-must program analysis: Unleashing the power of alternation. In: Proc. POPL, pp. 43–56. ACM (2010). https://doi.org/10.1145/1706299.1706307
37. Gulavani, B.S., Henzinger, T.A., Kannan, Y., Nori, A.V., Rajamani, S.K.: SYNERGY: A new algorithm for property checking. In: Proc. FSE, pp. 117–127. ACM (2006). https://doi.org/10.1145/1181775.1181790
38. Gulwani, S., Jain, S., Koskinen, E.: Control-flow refinement and progress invariants for bound analysis. In: Proc. PLDI, pp. 375–385. ACM (2009). https://doi.org/10.1145/1542476.1542518
39. Henzinger, T.A., Jhala, R., Majumdar, R., Necula, G.C., Sutre, G., Weimer, W.: Temporal-safety proofs for systems code. In: Proc. CAV, LNCS, vol. 2404, pp. 526–538. Springer (2002). https://doi.org/10.1007/3-540-45657-0_45
40. Holley, L.H., Rosen, B.K.: Qualified data-flow problems. In: Proc. POPL, pp. 68–82. ACM (1980). https://doi.org/10.1145/567446.567454
41. Jakobs, M.C., Wehrheim, H.: Certification for configurable program analysis. In: Proc. SPIN, pp. 30–39. ACM (2014). https://doi.org/10.1145/2632362.2632372
42. Jakobs, M.C., Wehrheim, H.: Programs from proofs: A framework for the safe execution of untrusted software. ACM Trans. Program. Lang. Syst. 39(2), 7:1–7:56 (2017). https://doi.org/10.1145/3014427
43. Jalote, P., Vangala, V., Singh, T., Jain, P.: Program partitioning: A framework for combining static and dynamic analysis. In: Proc. WODA, pp. 11–16. ACM (2006). https://doi.org/10.1145/1138912.1138916
44. Li, K., Reichenbach, C., Csallner, C., Smaragdakis, Y.: Residual investigation: predictive and precise bug detection. In: Proc. ISSTA, pp. 298–308. ACM (2012). https://doi.org/10.1145/2338965.2336789
45. Necula, G.C.: Proof-carrying code. In: Proc. POPL, pp. 106–119. ACM (1997). https://doi.org/10.1145/263699.263712
46. Necula, G.C., McPeak, S., Weimer, W.: CCURED: Type-safe retrofitting of legacy code. In: Proc. POPL, pp. 128–139. ACM (2002). https://doi.org/10.1145/503272.503286
47. Post, H., Sinz, C., Kaiser, A., Gorges, T.: Reducing false positives by combining abstract interpretation and bounded model checking. In: Proc. ASE, pp. 188–197. IEEE (2008). https://doi.org/10.1109/ASE.2008.29
48. Sharma, R., Dillig, I., Dillig, T., Aiken, A.: Simplifying loop-invariant generation using splitter predicates. In: Proc. CAV, LNCS, vol. 6806, pp. 703–719. Springer (2011). https://doi.org/10.1007/978-3-642-22110-1_57
49. Sherman, E., Dwyer, M.B.: Structurally defined conditional data-flow static analysis. In: Proc. TACAS (2), LNCS, vol. 10806, pp. 249–265. Springer (2018). https://doi.org/10.1007/978-3-319-89963-3_15
50. Steffen, B.: Property-oriented expansion. In: Proc. SAS, LNCS, vol. 1145, pp. 22–41. Springer (1006). https://doi.org/10.1007/3-540-61739-0_01

51. Thakur, A.V., Govindarajan, R.: Comprehensive path-sensitive data-flow analysis. In: Proc. CGO, pp. 55–63. ACM (2008). https://doi.org/10.1145/1356058.1356066
52. Wegman, M.N., Zadeck, F.K.: Constant propagation with conditional branches. In: Proc. POPL, pp. 291–299. ACM (1985). https://doi.org/10.1145/318593.318659
53. Yin, X., Knight, J.C., Weimer, W.: Exploiting refactoring in formal verification. In: Proc. DSN, pp. 53–62. IEEE (2009). https://doi.org/10.1109/DSN.2009.5270355

Difference Verification with Conditions

Dirk Beyer[1], Marie-Christine Jakobs[1,2],
and Thomas Lemberger[1]

[1] LMU Munich, Munich, Germany
[2] Department of Computer Science, TU Darmstadt, Darmstadt, Germany

Abstract. Modern software-verification tools need to support development processes that involve frequent changes. Existing approaches for incremental verification hard-code specific verification techniques. Some of the approaches must be tightly intertwined with the development process. To solve this open problem, we present the concept of *difference verification with conditions*. Difference verification with conditions is independent from any specific verification technique and can be integrated in software projects at any time. It first applies a change analysis that detects which parts of a software were changed between revisions and encodes that information in a condition. Based on this condition, an off-the-shelf verifier is used to verify only those parts of the software that are influenced by the changes. As a proof of concept, we propose a simple, syntax-based change analysis and use difference verification with conditions with three off-the-shelf verifiers. An extensive evaluation shows the competitiveness of difference verification with conditions.

1 Introduction

Software changes frequently during its life-cycle: developers fix bugs, adapt existing features, or add new features. In agile development, software construction is an intrinsically incremental process. Every change to a working system holds a risk to introduce a new defect. Since software failures are often costly and may even endanger human lives, it is an integral part of software development to find potential failures and ensure their absence.

However, running a full verification after each change is inadequate: Changes rarely affect the complete program behavior. For example, consider program absSum (Fig. 1, middle). If the assignment of program variable r is changed in the else-branch at location 5 ($absSum^{mod}$, Fig. 1, right), only program executions that take that else-branch show different behavior. Program executions that take the if-branch (highlighted in gray) are not affected by the change. This is typical for program changes: A modified program P' exhibits some new or changed program executions compared to an original program P, but some executions also stay the same (Fig. 1, left). To ensure the safety of P', it is sufficient to inspect only the changed behavior $ex(P') \setminus ex(P)$.

Replication package available on Zenodo [12].
Funded in part by the Deutsche Forschungsgemeinschaft (DFG) – 418257054 (Coop) and 378803395 (GRK ConVeY).

F. de Boer and A. Cerone (Eds.): SEFM 2020, LNCS 12310, pp. 133–154, 2020.
https://doi.org/10.1007/978-3-030-58768-0_8

134   D. Beyer, M.-C. Jakobs, and T. Lemberger

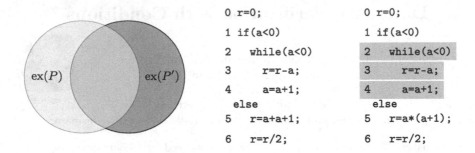

```
0 r=0;              0 r=0;
1 if(a<0)           1 if(a<0)
2   while(a<0)      2   while(a<0)
3     r=r-a;        3     r=r-a;
4     a=a+1;        4     a=a+1;
  else                else
5   r=a+a+1;        5   r=a*(a+1);
6 r=r/2;            6 r=r/2;
```

Fig. 1. Relation between program executions of original and modified program (left) and an example: Program absSum (middle) and its modified version absSum^{mod} (right). The modification at location 5 is shown in blue. Program parts unaffected by the modification are highlighted in gray.

Many incremental verification approaches [39,40] use this insight: Regression-test selection [62] tries to only execute those tests in a test suite that are relevant w.r.t. the change, and incremental formal verification techniques adapt existing proofs [33,49,53,54], reuse intermediate results [16,59], or skip the exploration of unchanged behavior [21,47,60,61]. However, they (a) all focus on one fixed verification approach, (b) require a strong coupling between the original verification approach and the incremental technique, and (c) require an initial, full verification run. Often, this inflexibility makes an approach prohibitive.

As an alternative, we define the concept of *difference verification with conditions*: Given the original and the changed software, difference verification with conditions first identifies all executions that are affected by changes and encodes them in a condition, an exchange format already known from conditional model checking [10]—we call this first part DIFFCOND. Then, a conditional verifier uses that condition to verify only the changed program behavior. For this step, any existing off-the-shelf verifier can be turned into a conditional verifier with the reducer-based approach [13].

Difference verification with conditions allows us to (a) use varying verification approaches for incremental verification, (b) automatically turn any existing verifier into an incremental verifier, and (c) skip an initial, costly verification run.
Contributions. We make the following contributions:

- We propose *difference verification with conditions*, which is an incremental verification approach that combines existing tools and approaches.
- We provide the algorithm DIFFCOND, an integral part of difference verification with conditions, which outputs a description of the modified execution paths in an exchangeable condition format. We also prove its correctness.
- We implemented DIFFCOND in the verification framework CPACHECKER and combined it with existing verifiers to construct difference verifiers.
- To study the effectiveness and efficiency of difference verification with conditions, we performed an extensive evaluation on more than 10 000 C programs.
- DIFFCOND and all our data are available for replication and to construct further difference verifiers (see Sect. 7).

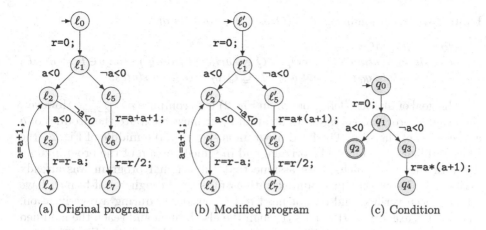

(a) Original program   (b) Modified program   (c) Condition

Fig. 2. CFA of absSum (Fig. 1), CFA of absSum^{mod}, and a condition that describes the common executions of both programs, as created by our approach

2 Background

Programs. For ease of presentation, we consider imperative programs with deterministic control-flow, which execute statements from a set *Ops*. Our implementation supports C programs. Following literature [8,9,30], we model programs as control-flow automata.

Definition 1. *A* control-flow automaton *(CFA)* $P = (L, \ell_0, G)$ *consists of*

– *a set L of program locations with initial location $\ell_0 \in L$, and*
– *a set $G \subseteq L \times Ops \times L$ of control-flow edges.*

CFA P is deterministic *if* $(\ell, op, \ell'), (\ell, op, \ell'') \in G \Rightarrow \ell' = \ell''$.

Figure 2 shows the CFA of the example program absSum from Fig. 1. A sequence $\ell_0 \xrightarrow{op_1} \ell_1 \cdots \xrightarrow{op_n} \ell_n$ is a *syntactical path* through CFA $P = (L, \ell_0, G)$, if $\forall i \in [1, n] : (\ell_{i-1}, op_i, \ell_i) \in G$. We rely on standard operational semantics and model a program state by a pair of (1) the program counter, whose value refers to a program location in the CFA, and (2) a concrete data state c, whose shape we do not further specify [8]. We denote the set of all concrete data states as C. The function $sp_{op} : C \to 2^C$ describes the possible effects of operation $op \in Ops$ on concrete data state $c \in C$. Based on this, a sequence $(\ell_0, c_0) \xrightarrow{op_1} (\ell_1, c_1) \cdots \xrightarrow{op_n} (\ell_n, c_n)$ is a *program path* through CFA $P = (L, \ell_0, G)$, if $\ell_0 \xrightarrow{op_1} \ell_1 \cdots \xrightarrow{op_n} \ell_n$ is a syntactical path through P and $\forall i \in [1, n] : c_i \in sp_{op_i}(c_{i-1})$. We denote the set of all program paths by paths(P). *Program executions* are derived from program paths. If $p = (\ell_0, c_0) \xrightarrow{op_1} (\ell_1, c_1) \cdots \xrightarrow{op_n} (\ell_n, c_n)$ is a program path, then ex(p) $= c_0 \xrightarrow{op_1} c_1 \cdots \xrightarrow{op_n} c_n$ is a program execution. The executions of a program P are defined as ex(P) := $\{ex(p) \mid p \in \text{paths}(P)\}$.

Conditions. A condition describes which program executions were already verified, e.g., in a previous verification run. We use automata to represent conditions and use accepting states to identify already verified executions [13].

Definition 2. *A condition $A = (Q, \delta, q_0, F)$ consists of:*

- *a finite set Q of states,*
- *a transition relation $\delta \subseteq Q \times Ops \times Q$ ensuring $\forall (q, op, q') \in \delta : q \in F \Rightarrow q' \in F$,*
- *the initial state $q_0 \in Q$, and a set $F \subseteq Q$ of accepting states.*[1]

The goal of `absSum` (left program in Fig. 2) is to compute $r = \sum_{i=0}^{|a|}$. However, the original program is buggy: In location ℓ_5, it must compute the product of a and $a + 1$, not the sum. The fixed program is shown in the middle of Fig. 2—the fix is highlighted in blue. The original and modified version of the program only differ in the else-branch. If we assume that the original program was already verified, we know that program executions passing through the if-branch have already been verified and do not need to be considered during a reverification. In contrast, executions that pass through the else-branch and reach the modified statement must be verified. The condition shown on the right of Fig. 2 encodes this insight. Program executions that pass through the if-branch ($a < 0$) lead to the accepting state q_2—we say they are covered by the condition. In contrast, program executions that pass the else-branch ($\neg a < 0$) never reach q_2 —they are not covered by the condition, and must be analyzed.

Definition 3. *A condition $A = (Q, \delta, q_0, F)$ covers an execution $\pi = c_0 \xrightarrow{op_1} c_1 \cdots \xrightarrow{op_n} c_n$ if there exists an index $k \in [0, n]$ and a run $\rho = q_0 \xrightarrow{op_1} q_2 \cdots \xrightarrow{op_k} q_k$, s.t. $q_k \in F$ and $\forall i \in [1, k] : (q_{i-1}, op_i, q_i) \in \delta$.*

Next, we introduce a simple and efficient way to systematically compute a condition that covers the common executions of an original and a modified program.

3   Component DIFFCOND for Modular Construction

The ultimate goal of difference verification with conditions is to speed up reverification of modified programs. To achieve this goal, we aim at ignoring unmodified program behavior during verification. Conditions are a well-fitting format to describe the unmodified program behavior. However, to benefit from difference verification with conditions, the construction of such conditions must be efficient, i.e., consume only a small portion of the overall execution time of the verification. Therefore, we use a syntactic approach to compute the condition, DIFFCOND (Alg. 1), which is linear in time regarding the size of the modified program.

DIFFCOND gets as input the original program P and the modified program P'. In lines 1 to 11, DIFFCOND traverses the modified and the original program in parallel, stops traversal if the original and the modified program differ, and remembers the edge that differs in the modified program.

It uses three data structures: Set $E \subseteq L \times L' \times Ops \times L \times L'$ stores all compared edges (ℓ_1, op, ℓ_2) and (ℓ'_1, op, ℓ'_2) that are equal in both programs. These are

---

[1] In general [10,13] the transition relation of a condition also specifies assumptions on the program states. Since difference verification with conditions requires no assumptions on the program states, we omit this additional characteristic.

Algorithm 1 DIFFCOND(P, P')

Input: CFA $P = (L, \ell_0, G)$ // original program
Input: CFA $P' = (L', \ell_0', G')$ // modified program
Output: $A = (Q, \delta, q_0, F)$ // difference condition
Variables: Set $E \subseteq L \times L' \times Ops \times L \times L'$ of composite CFA edges equal in the original and the modified program, set $D \subseteq L \times L' \times Ops \times L'$ of CFA edges that differ in the modified program, set $waitlist \subseteq L \times L'$ of program locations in original and modified program for which to compare outgoing edges.

    ▷ *Change detection*
1: $E := \emptyset; \; D := \emptyset$
2: $waitlist := \{(\ell_0, \ell_0')\}$
3: **while** $waitlist \neq \emptyset$ **do**
4:     pop (ℓ_1, ℓ_1') from $waitlist$
5:     **for each** $(\ell_1', op, \ell_2') \in G'$ **do**
6:        **if** $\neg \exists \ell_2 \in L : (\ell_1, op, \ell_2) \in G$ **then**
7:           $D := D \cup \{((\ell_1, \ell_1'), op, \ell_2')\}$
8:        **else**
9:           $E := E \cup \{((\ell_1, \ell_1'), op, (\ell_2, \ell_2'))\}$
10:          **if** $(\cdot, \cdot, (\ell_2, \ell_2')) \notin E$ **then**
11:             $waitlist := waitlist \cup \{(\ell_2, \ell_2')\}$

    ▷ *Condition Generation*
12: $Q := \{q \mid \exists (\cdot, \cdot, q) \in D\}$
13: $waitlist := Q$
14: **while** $waitlist \neq \emptyset$ **do**
15:     pop q' from $waitlist$
16:     **for each** $(q, op, q') \in E \cup D$ with $q \notin Q$ **do**
17:        $Q := Q \cup \{q\}$
18:        $waitlist := waitlist \cup \{q\}$
19: **if** $Q = \emptyset$ **then**
20:     ▷ *No difference edges, automaton always accepts*
21:     **return** $(\{(\ell_0, \ell_0')\}, \emptyset, (\ell_0, \ell_0'), \{(\ell_0, \ell_0')\})$
22: **else**
23:     $F := \{q' \mid \exists (q, op, q') \in E \wedge q \in Q \wedge q' \notin Q\}$
24:     $Q := Q \cup F$
25:     $\delta := \{(q, op, q') \in E \cup D \mid q, q' \in Q \wedge q \notin F\}$
26:
27:     **return** $(Q, \delta, (\ell_0, \ell_0'), F)$

---

called *standard edges*. They are stored in the composite form $((\ell_1, \ell_1'), op, (\ell_2, \ell_2'))$. Set $D \subseteq L \times L' \times Ops \times L'$ stores all edges (ℓ_1', op, ℓ_2') of the modified program P' that represent a change from the original program P at ℓ_1, called *difference edges*. They are stored in the form $((\ell_1, \ell_1'), op, \ell_2')$. Set $waitlist \subseteq L \times L'$ stores all pairs of program locations (ℓ_1, ℓ_1') for which a program path with the same syntactic structure exist in P and P', and for which no outgoing edges have been considered yet. Initially, E and D are empty—no edges were checked so far, and the algorithm

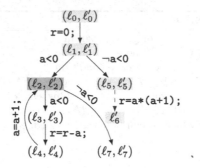

Fig. 3. Parallel composition of absSum and absSum^{mod} as computed by DIFFCOND

starts at the two initial program locations, i.e., $waitlist = \{(\ell_0, \ell'_0)\}$ (lines 1 and 2). As long as $waitlist$ contains program locations, the algorithm picks one of them, here depicted as (ℓ_1, ℓ'_1) (line 4). It considers all outgoing edges (ℓ'_1, op, ℓ'_2) of ℓ'_1 in the modified program. If the same operation op does not exist at any outgoing edge of ℓ_1, it is considered to be changed and the difference edge $((\ell_1, \ell'_1), op, \ell'_2)$ is stored in D before continuing with the next state in $waitlist$. However, if the same operation op exists at an outgoing edge (ℓ_1, op, ℓ_2), it is considered to be equal and the standard edge $((\ell_1, \ell'_1), op, (\ell_2, \ell'_2))$ is stored in E before continuing with the next state in $waitlist$. To this end, DIFFCOND explores the syntactical composition of the original and modified program. In addition, if the tuple (ℓ_2, ℓ'_2) of locations has not been detected before (line 10), it is added to the waitlist for further exploration. Figure 3 shows the graph built from edges E (black) and D (blue and dashed) when executing DIFFCOND on absSum and absSum^{mod}.

To compute the condition, we first determine the condition's states. Lines 12 to 18 compute all nodes that can reach a successor of a difference edge. Figure 3 highlights these nodes in green. Nodes that are not discovered in lines 12–18 cannot lead to a difference edge and, thus, not to different program behavior. Consequently, undiscovered nodes that are successors of nodes discovered in lines 12–18 become final states (line 23). Figure 3 highlights these nodes in gray (only node (ℓ_2, ℓ'_2)). The union of discovered and final states become our condition states. To complete the construction, we use the pair of initial program locations as the initial state (ℓ_0, ℓ'_0) and add to the transition relation all transitions from E and D that connect condition states. Figure 2c shows the condition created from Fig. 3.

Finally, note that lines 19–21 handle the special case that the set D of difference edges is empty, thus resulting in $Q = \emptyset$ in line 19. The set D is empty if the original and the modified program only differ in the names of their program locations[2] or if the modified program is empty $((\ell'_0, \cdot, \cdot) \notin G')$. In both cases, all executions of the modified program are covered by the executions of the original program. As a result, the condition covers all executions: its only state is both initial and accepting state, and the condition has no transitions.

The purpose of algorithm DIFFCOND is to compute a condition that supports skipping unchanged behavior during reverification of a modified program.

---

[2] In practice, this can happen if empty lines are added or removed from the program.

To still have a sound reverification, the produced condition must not cover executions that do not occur in the original program. The following theorem states this property of algorithm DIFFCOND.

Theorem 1. *Let* $P = (L, \ell_0, G)$ *and* $P' = (L', \ell'_0, G')$ *be two CFAs.* DIFFCOND(P, P') *does not cover any execution from* $\mathrm{ex}(P') \setminus \mathrm{ex}(P)$.

Proof. Assume $\mathrm{ex}(P') \setminus \mathrm{ex}(P) \neq \emptyset$. Hence, DIFFCOND$(P, P') = (Q, \delta, q_0, F)$ is returned in line 27. Let $(Q, \delta, q_0, F) = A$, let $\pi = c_0 \xrightarrow{op_1} c_1 \cdots \xrightarrow{op_n} c_n \in \mathrm{ex}(P') \setminus \mathrm{ex}(P)$, and let $\rho = q_0 \xrightarrow{op_1} q_1 \cdots \xrightarrow{op_k} q_k$ be a run through A, s.t. $0 \leq k \leq n$ and $\forall 1 \leq i \leq k : (q_{i-1}, op_i, q_i) \in \delta$. By construction, (1) $q_0 \notin F$, (2) $\forall 1 \leq i < k :$ $(q_{i-1}, op_i, q_i) \in E \wedge q_i \notin F$, and (3) $(q_{k-1}, op_k, q_k) \in E \cup D$. We need to show that $q_k \notin F$. Case $k = 0$ follows from (1).

Next, consider the case $k = n$. If $(q_{k-1}, op_k, q_k) \in E$, by construction there exists syntactical path $sp = \ell_0 \xrightarrow{op_1} \ell_2 \cdots \xrightarrow{op_n} \ell_n$ in P and due to program semantics, $\pi \in \mathrm{ex}(P)$. Since $\pi \in \mathrm{ex}(P') \setminus \mathrm{ex}(P)$, we infer $(q_{k-1}, op_k, q_k) \in D$ and thus $q_k \notin F$.

Finally, consider the case $k < n$. If $(q_{k-1}, op_k, q_k) \in D$, we infer $q_k \notin F$. Assume $(q_{k-1}, op_k, q_k) \in E$. By construction, there exists a syntactical path $sp = \ell_0 \xrightarrow{op_1} \ell_2 \cdots \xrightarrow{op_k} \ell_k$ in program P and a syntactical path $sp' = \ell'_0 \xrightarrow{op_1} \ell'_2 \cdots \xrightarrow{op_k} \ell'_k$ in program P', s.t. $\forall 0 \leq i \leq k : q_i = (\ell_i, \ell'_i)$. Let $\ell_0 \xrightarrow{op_1} \ell_2 \cdots \xrightarrow{op_k} \ell_k \xrightarrow{op_{k+1}} \ell_{k+1} \cdots \xrightarrow{op_m} \ell_m$ be an extension of the syntactical path sp s.t. $m = n$ or $(\ell_m, op_{m+1}, \cdot) \notin G$. Due to program semantics and $\pi \in \mathrm{ex}(P') \setminus \mathrm{ex}(P)$, we conclude $k \leq m < n$. Due to program semantics, P' being deterministic, and $\pi \in \mathrm{ex}(P')$, there exists an extension $\ell'_0 \xrightarrow{op_1} \ell'_2 \cdots \xrightarrow{op_k} \ell'_k \xrightarrow{op_{k+1}} \ell'_{k+1} \cdots \xrightarrow{op_m} \ell'_m$ of the syntactical path sp'. By construction, $\forall 1 \leq i \leq m : ((\ell_{i-1}, \ell'_{i-1}), op_i, (\ell_i, \ell'_i)) \in E$ and there exists $((\ell_m, \ell'_m), op_{m+1}, \cdot) \in D$. Hence, $\forall 0 \leq i \leq m : (\ell_{i-1}, \ell'_{i-1}) \in Q \setminus F$. Since $q_k = (\ell_k, \ell'_k)$ and $k \leq m$, $q_k \notin F$.

Theoretical Limitations. The effectiveness of difference verification with conditions depends on the amount of program code potentially affected by a change, which is determined by the DIFFCOND component. DIFFCOND only excludes program parts that cannot be syntactically reached from a program change. Therefore, difference verification is ineffective if some initial variable assignments at the very beginning of the program or some global declarations change. Moreover, the structure of a program strongly influences the effectiveness of difference verification. For example, programs like absSum$^\infty$ (Fig. 4) that mainly consist of a loop are problematic. Program absSum$^\infty$ (Fig. 4) is similar to absSum, but has an additional, outer loop that dominates the program. So when location ℓ_7 is changed in absSum$^\infty$, difference verification with conditions can only exclude the if-branch for the very first iteration of the outer loop. Thereafter, the change in location ℓ_7 may propagate into the if-branch.

In contrast, difference verification with conditions can be effective on programs that allow the exclusion of program parts, e.g., if the program is modular and, thus, consists of multiple, loosely coupled parts. Examples for modularity are the *strategy* design pattern, object-oriented software, or software applications with multiple program features.

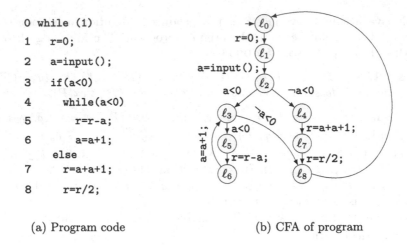

(a) Program code   (b) CFA of program

Fig. 4. Example program absSum$^\infty$ with loop dominating the whole program

When designing our experiments, we will consider these limitations of difference verification with conditions. Before we get to our experiments, we must describe the modular composition of the DIFFCOND component with a verifier, which specifies the difference verifier.

4   Modular Combinations with Existing Verifiers

The DIFFCOND algorithm can be combined with any off-the-shelf conditional verifier [10] to produce a difference verifier in a modular way. The goal of a difference verifier is to verify only modified program paths. To this end, it first uses DIFFCOND to discover potentially modified program paths and then runs a conditional verifier to explore only those paths identified by DIFFCOND. Figure 5 shows the construction template for difference verification with conditions. DIFF-COND gets the original and modified program as input and encodes the modified paths in a condition. The constructed condition is forwarded to a conditional verifier, which uses the condition to restrict its analysis of the modified program to those paths that are not covered by the condition (i.e., the modified paths). Based on this template, we can construct difference verifiers from arbitrary conditional verifiers. Moreover, we can construct difference verifiers from non-conditional verifiers by using the concept of reducer-based conditional verifiers [13]. The idea of a reducer-based conditional verifier is shown on the right of Fig. 5. To turn an arbitrary verifier into a conditional one, a reducer-based conditional verifier puts a preprocessor (called reducer) in front of the verifier. The reducer gets a program and a condition and outputs a new, residual program that represents the program paths not covered by the condition. A full verification

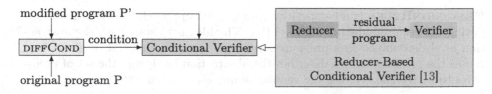

Fig. 5. DIFFCOND + conditional verifier = difference verifier

of this residual program is then equivalent to a conditional verification of the original program with the produced condition. However, note that the existing reducers are designed for model checkers and do not necessarily work with other verification technologies like deductive verifiers.

In this paper, we transform three verifiers into difference verifiers: CPA-SEQ, UAUTOMIZER, and PREDICATE. The first two are the best verifiers from SV-COMP 2020 [5], and the third is a predicate-abstraction approach. We use the off-the-shelf verifiers CPA-SEQ and UAUTOMIZER as non-conditional verifiers and thus add a reducer, while we use PREDICATE as conditional verifier. Since a difference verifier can now be built from any off-the-shelf verifier, we can also combine difference verification with other incremental verification techniques. As an example, we can use precision reuse [16]. This technique is implemented in CPACHECKER [16] and UAUTOMIZER [49] and can be used with the previously mentioned approaches. Next we explain the technologies of the selected verifiers.

CPA-SEQ uses several different strategies from the CPACHECKER verification framework [6,11,14]. CPA-SEQ first analyzes different features of the program under verification. The program features considered are: recursion, concurrency, occurrence of loops, and occurrence of complex data types like pointers and structs. Based on these features, CPA-SEQ uses one of five different verification techniques (cf. [6]). For non-recursive, non-concurrent programs with a non-trivial control flow, CPA-SEQ uses a sequential combination of four different analyses: It uses value analysis with and without Counterexample-guided Abstraction Refinement (CEGAR) [24], a predicate analysis similar to PREDICATE, and k-induction with invariant generation [7]. Invariants are generated by numerical and predicate analyses and are forwarded to the k-induction analysis.

UAUTOMIZER is the automata-based approach from the ULTIMATE verification framework [29,31]. It uses a CEGAR approach to successively refine an over-approximation of the error paths, which is given in form of automata. In each refinement step, a generalization of an infeasible error path is excluded from the over-approximation. The generalization of the error path is described by a Floyd-Hoare automaton [31], which assigns Boolean formulas over predicates to its states. The predicates are obtained via interpolation along the infeasible error path [43].

PREDICATE is the predicate-abstraction approach from the CPACHECKER framework [14] with adjustable-block encoding (ABE) [15]. ABE is instructed to abstract at loop heads only. CEGAR together with lazy refinement [34] and interpolation [32] determines the necessary set of predicates.

PRECISIONREUSE is a competitive incremental approach that avoids recomputing the required abstraction level [16]. The idea is to start with the abstraction level determined in a previous verification run. To this end, it stores and reuses the precision, which describes the abstraction level, e.g., the set of predicates to be tracked. We use the version as implemented in CPACHECKER.

5   Evaluation

We systematically evaluate our proposed approach along the following claims:

Claim 1. Difference verification with conditions can be more effective than a full verification. *Evaluation Plan:* For all verifiers, we compare the number of tasks solved by difference verification with conditions and by the pure verifier.

Claim 2. Difference verification with conditions is more effective when using multiple verifiers. *Evaluation Plan:* We compare the number of tasks solved by each difference verifier with the union of tasks solved by all difference verifiers.

Claim 3. Difference verification with conditions can be more efficient than a full verification. *Evaluation Plan:* For all verifiers, we compare the run time of difference verification with conditions and of the pure verifier.

Claim 4. The run time of difference verification with conditions is dominated by the run time of the verifier. *Evaluation Plan:* We relate the time for verification to the time required by the DIFFCOND algorithm and the reducer.

Claim 5. Difference verification with conditions can complement existing incremental verification approaches. *Evaluation Plan:* We compare the results of difference verification with conditions with the results of precision reuse [16], a competitive incremental verification approach.

Claim 6. Combining difference verification with conditions with existing incremental verification approaches can be beneficial. *Evaluation Plan:* We compare the results of difference verification with the results of a combination of difference verification with conditions and precision reuse.

5.1   Experiment Setup

Computing Environment. We performed all experiments on machines with an Intel Xeon E3-1230 v5 CPU, 3.4 GHz, with 8 cores each, and 33 GB of memory, running Ubuntu 18.04 with Linux kernel 4.15. We limited each analysis run to 15 GB of memory, a time limit of 900 s, and 4 CPU cores. To enforce these limits, we ran our experiments with BENCHEXEC [17], version 2.3.

Verifiers. For our experiments, we use the software verifiers CPA-SEQ[3] [6,14] and UAUTOMIZER[4] [29,31] as submitted for SV-COMP 2020, and CPACHECKER [14,15]

---
[3] https://gitlab.com/sosy-lab/sv-comp/archives-2020/-/raw/master/2020/cpa-seq.zip
[4] https://gitlab.com/sosy-lab/sv-comp/archives-2020/-/raw/master/2020/uautomizer.zip

in revision 32864[5]. CPA-SEQ and UAUTOMIZER are used as verifiers. CPACHECKER provides the verifier PREDICATE, but also the new DIFFCOND component and the REDUCER component for reducer-based conditional verification. The difference verifier based on PREDICATE is realized as a single run. In contrast, the difference verifiers based on CPA-SEQ and UAUTOMIZER are realized as composition of two separate runs. The first run executes the DIFFCOND algorithm followed by the reducer to generate the residual program. It is only executed once per task, i.e., the same residual programs are given to CPA-SEQ and UAUTOMIZER. In a second run, CPA-SEQ and UAUTOMIZER, respectively, verify the residual program. To deal with residual programs, we increased the Java stack size for CPA-SEQ and UAUTOMIZER.

Existing Incremental Verifier. We use PREDICATE with precision reuse [16].

Verification Tasks. We use verification tasks from the public repository sv-benchmarks (tag svcomp20)[6], which is the most diverse, largest, and well-established collection of verification tasks. Since difference verification with conditions is an incremental verification approach, we require different program versions. We searched the benchmark repository for programs that come with multiple versions and for which at least one version is hard to solve, i.e., at least one of the three considered verifiers takes more than 100 s for verification of that version, but is successful. From these programs, we arbitrarily picked the following: eca05 and eca12 (event-condition-action systems, both have 10 versions each), gcd (greatest common divisor computation, has 4 versions), newton (approximation of sine, has 24 versions), pals (leader election, has 26 versions), sfifo (second-chance FIFO replacement, has 5 versions), softflt (a software implementation of floats, has 5 versions), square (square-root computation, has 8 versions), and token (a communication protocol, has 28 versions). Unfortunately, all of these programs are specialized implementations with a single purpose. Thus, their implementation is strongly coupled and any reasonable program change affects the complete program. As explained before, this prohibits effective difference verification with conditions.

To get benchmark tasks that instead contain independent program parts, we create new combinations from the selected programs. We choose two programs, e.g., eca05 and token. We then combine these two programs according to the following scheme: We create a new program with all declarations and definitions of both original programs, but a new main function. This new main function randomly calls the main function of one of the two original programs. Name clashes are resolved via renaming. Figure 6 shows the conceptual structure of each program created through this combination. For our experiments, we consider the following combinations of programs: (1) eca05+token, (2) gcd+newton, (3) pals+eca12, (4) sfifo+token, (5) square+softflt. To create different versions of our combinations, we replace one of the two program parts with a different version of that part. For example, to get a different

---

[5] https://gitlab.com/sosy-lab/software/cpachecker/-/tree/230d2ca5
[6] https://github.com/sosy-lab/sv-benchmarks/tree/svcomp20

```
 0 extern int __VERIFIER_nondet_int();
 1 int main1() { /* main method of task 1 ... */ }
 2 /* other definitions of task 1 ... */
 3 int main2() { /* main method of task 2 ... */ }
 4 /* other definitions of task 2 ... */
 5 int main() {
 6   if (__VERIFIER_nondet_int())
 7     main1();
 8   else
 9     main2();
10 }
```

Fig. 6. Conceptual example of combination of verification tasks

version of the original program eca05+token, we change the version of the eca05 part or the token part, but never both.

With this procedure, we get a large amount of different versions of our program combinations. For our evaluation, we consider each pair (O, N) of versions O and N of program combinations that fulfills the following two conditions: (1) N reflects a change, i.e., the two programs are different. (2) Version O, version N, or both versions are bug-free. This ensures that verification and difference verification can only find the same bugs. With this construction of benchmark tasks for incremental verification we get a total of 10 426 tasks that we use in our experiments.

5.2   Experimental Results

Claim 1 (Difference verification with conditions more effective).
Table 1 gives an overview of our experimental results. Each column represents one task set. The rows refer to verifiers, i.e., pure verifiers (X) and difference verifiers (X^Δ). The last two rows are the union of the results of all three verifiers. For each task set and verifier, the table provides the number of tasks for which the verifier finds a proof ($\checkmark$), finds a bug (!), and only the difference verifier gives a conclusive answer ($\star$). It also shows the number of tasks ($\blacklozenge$) that cannot be solved. Neither the pure nor the difference verifiers reported incorrect results.

The table shows that for each verifier there exist task sets on which the number of solved correct tasks ($\checkmark$) is higher for the difference verifier. Looking at columns $\star$, we observe that typically there exist tasks that only the difference verifier can solve. Thus, this shows that our new difference verification with conditions can be more effective.

Difference verification with conditions is not always more effective. Especially, CPA-SEQ$^\Delta$ and UAUTOMIZER$^\Delta$ sometimes perform worse. For example, CPA-SEQ$^\Delta$ finds significantly less bugs than CPA-SEQ for eca05+token. The reason for this is the residual program constructed by the reducer, which is necessary to turn

Table 1. Experimental results for PREDICATE, CPA-SEQ and UAUTOMIZER, as pure verifiers (X) and difference verifiers (X^Δ) showing how many correct tasks ($\checkmark$) and tasks with a bug (!) are solved, how many tasks are only solved by the difference verifier ($\star$) and which are too hard to solve ($\blacklozenge$)

	eca05+token (3 640)				gcd+newton (1 924)				pals+eca12 (2 750)				sfifo+token (1 872)				square+softflt (240)			
	$\checkmark$	!	$\star$	$\blacklozenge$	$\checkmark$	!	$\star$	$\blacklozenge$	$\checkmark$	!	$\star$	$\blacklozenge$	$\checkmark$	!	$\star$	$\blacklozenge$	$\checkmark$	!	$\star$	$\blacklozenge$
PREDICATE$^\Delta$	1447	999	451	1194	48	572	48	1304	15	55	20	2680	655	494	98	723	81	75	70	84
PREDICATE	1080	944		1616	0	572		1352	0	50		2700	558	507		807	33	53		154
CPA-SEQ$^\Delta$	966	671	350	2003	48	572	48	1304	183	50	233	2517	480	390	108	1002	61	69	61	110
CPA-SEQ	755	1268		1617	0	572		1352	0	0		2750	372	619		881	0	75		165
UAUTOMIZER$^\Delta$	270	260	270	3110	16	0	16	1908	0	0	0	2750	349	234	112	1289	61	45	49	134
UAUTOMIZER	0	325		3315	0	520		1404	0	48		2702	341	258		1273	44	57		139
All$^\Delta$	1527	999	448	1114	48	572	48	1304	183	95	228	2472	655	494	98	723	81	75	40	84
All	1080	1295		1265	0	572		1352	0	50		2700	558	626		688	55	75		110

CPA-SEQ into the required conditional verifier. The created residual programs, on which the off-the-shelf verifiers run, have a different structure than the original program. They make heavy use of goto statements and deeply nested branching structures. While semantically equivalent, this can have unexpected effects on analyses: In the case of the tasks in `eca05+token`, CPA-SEQ was not able to detect required information about loops and thus aborts its verification. Note that this is not a direct issue of difference verification with conditions, but an orthogonal issue. To fix the problem, verification tools must be improved to better deal with the generated residual programs or the structure of the residual program must be improved. Despite of the problem with residual programs, difference verification can solve many tasks that a full verification run cannot solve.

Since PREDICATE is already a conditional model checker, PREDICATE$^\Delta$ does not suffer from the residual program problem. Thus, the effectiveness of difference verification with conditions becomes even more obvious when comparing PREDICATE with PREDICATE$^\Delta$. For the first three task sets, PREDICATE$^\Delta$ solves all tasks that PREDICATE solves plus a significant amount of additional tasks that PREDICATE cannot solve. For the last two task sets PREDICATE$^\Delta$ fails to solve a few tasks that PREDICATE can solve. However, PREDICATE$^\Delta$ still solves more tasks in total. One reason for this is that the predicate abstraction used by PREDICATE may compute different predicates (due to a slightly different exploration of the state space), which may result in a more expensive abstraction, if the explored state-space looks different. For some tasks, these different predicates may be less suited to solve the task and thus require more time, which results in the analysis hitting the time limit. Typically, we observe this phenomenon when PREDICATE is expensive already (in our experiments, when it takes at least 700 s). While for complicated tasks with large changes, difference verification may produce worse results, PREDICATE$^\Delta$ is still more effective than PREDICATE in all categories.

Claim 2 (Better with several verifiers). To study the usefulness of using several verifiers in difference verification, we look at the tasks solved by the three difference verifiers together. We observe that PREDICATE$^\Delta$ solves the most tasks in all task sets except for `pals+eca12`, in which CPA-SEQ$^\Delta$ is better. Moreover,

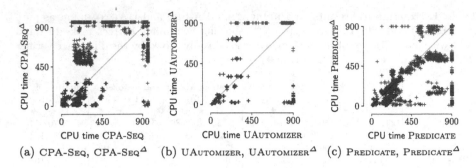

(a) CPA-SEQ, CPA-SEQ$^\Delta$ (b) UAUTOMIZER, UAUTOMIZER$^\Delta$ (c) PREDICATE, PREDICATE$^\Delta$

Fig. 7. CPU time (in s) of full verification vs. difference verification, per task

when looking at All$^\Delta$, which takes the union of all results, we observe that for
`eca05+token` multiple tasks without a property violation exist that cannot be
solved by the best difference verifier of this task set (PREDICATE$^\Delta$). Thus, the
difference verification is more effective when using several verifiers.

Claim 3 (Difference verification with conditions more efficient). We
compare the run times of the verifiers with the run times of the difference
verifiers. For all three verifiers, the scatter plots in Fig. 7 show the CPU time
required to check a task without (x-axis) and with difference verification (y-axis).
If a task was not solved, because the verifier either runs out of resources or
encountered an error, we assume the maximum CPU time of 900 s. Figures 7a
and 7b compare the two non-conditional verifiers CPA-SEQ and UAUTOMIZER,
for which we use the reducer-based conditional verifier approach. For a significant number of tasks (below diagonal), the difference verifier is faster than
the respective verifier CPA-SEQ and UAUTOMIZER, and the tasks on the right
edge can only be solved by the difference verifier. There are tasks for which
difference verification is slower (above diagonal). Note that the problem is the
residual program, not our approach. For example, many tasks located at the
upper edge do not represent timeouts of the difference verification, but failures of
the verifier caused by the structure of the residual program. Figure 7c compares
the conditional verifier PREDICATE. For the majority of tasks, the CPU time
required by PREDICATE$^\Delta$ is equal to or less than the time required by PREDICATE
(tasks below the line). Moreover, there are only few tasks for which PREDICATE$^\Delta$
is slower than PREDICATE (tasks above the line). The reason for this slow-down
is most likely the computation of worse predicates (see Claim 1). To sum up,
difference verification with conditions can successfully increase efficiency.

Claim 4 (Verifier dominates run time). We aim to show that the DIFF-
COND component and the residual program construction (in the reducer-based
approach to construct conditional verifiers) require a negligible run time compared to the complete verification run time. We show in Fig. 8a for each task
verified with CPA-SEQ$^\Delta$ and UAUTOMIZER$^\Delta$, the CPU time required by the full
verification run (x-axis) and the CPU time of that run spent for DIFFCOND plus
the reducer (y-axis). The time required by DIFFCOND + reducer does not depend
on the run time of the verifier, and it is below 60 s for all tasks.

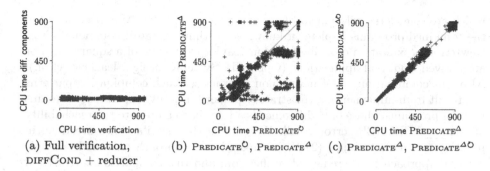

(a) Full verification,   (b) PREDICATE$^{\circlearrowleft}$, PREDICATE$^{\triangle}$ (c) PREDICATE$^{\triangle}$, PREDICATE$^{\triangle\circlearrowleft}$
DIFFCOND + reducer

Fig. 8. CPU time (in s) of (a) full difference-verification runs and the time spent for the two diff. components DIFFCOND + reducer, (b) PREDICATE with precision reuse (PREDICATE$^{\circlearrowleft}$) vs. PREDICATE with difference verification (PREDICATE$^{\triangle}$), and (c) PREDICATE$^{\triangle}$ vs. PREDICATE$^{\triangle}$ with precision reuse (PREDICATE$^{\triangle\circlearrowleft}$)

Claim 5 (Difference verification with conditions complementary). To show that difference verification with conditions complements existing incremental verification, we need to compare difference verification with conditions against an existing incremental approach. Looking at existing approaches that are (1) available as replication artifact and (b) able to run on verification tasks from sv-benchmarks, we identified two: both based on precision reuse, one implemented in CPAchecker [16] and one in Ultimate [49]. We use the one in CPAchecker. Figure 8b shows the CPU time of precision reuse with PREDICATE, called PREDICATE$^{\circlearrowleft}$ (x-axis) against our difference verification with PREDICATE, called PREDICATE$^{\triangle}$ (y-axis). Many tasks are solved efficiently by both techniques (large cluster in lower left). For the remaining hard tasks, difference verification is often faster than precision reuse, or precision reuse cannot even solve the task (points below the diagonal and on right edge). This shows that difference verification with conditions can improve on precision reuse for a significant number of tasks. It can thus complement existing incremental techniques.

Claim 6 (Combinations sometimes beneficial). We combined difference verification with conditions with precision reuse, called PREDICATE$^{\triangle\circlearrowleft}$. Figure 8c shows that this combination rarely becomes faster than difference verification PREDICATE$^{\triangle}$ alone. In the worst case, the combination even slows down because precision reuse tracks previously used predicates from the beginning while difference verification would only detect the necessary ones lazily. This more precise abstraction leads to more, sometimes unnecessary computations. Nevertheless, the combination can solve 29 tasks that neither PREDICATE, its difference verifier, nor precision reuse can solve alone. Thus, while a combination of the two incremental techniques is not beneficial in general, it can be.

5.3 Threats to Validity

External Validity. (1) Our benchmark tasks might not represent real program changes, and thus, our results might not transfer to reality. However, we built our tasks from a well-established collection of software-verification problems, which are considered relevant in the verification community. Moreover, many of the combined programs implement known algorithms (greatest common divisor, Newton approximation of a sine function, Taylor expansion of a square root) or are derived from real applications (OpenSSL, SystemC design, leader election). Also, our combination is not uncommon in practice. Such combination patterns e.g. result from implementing the strategy pattern. Finally, our task set contains pairs of programs whose only difference is a bug fix to eliminate the reachability of the __VERIFIER_error() call. We believe that similar fixes are done in practice to eliminate bugs. (2) We compared our approach only with a single existing approach for incremental verification, and this comparison is restricted to a single verifier. Our observations may not apply to different incremental verification approaches or different verifiers. The same holds for the combination of difference verification with orthogonal, incremental verification approaches. *Internal Validity.* (3) The implementation of the DIFFCOND algorithm may contain bugs, and thus, produces conditions that also exclude modified paths. We would expect that such a bug also excludes error paths. Since we never observed false proofs, we assume this is unlikely. (4) Difference verification with CPA-SEQ and UAUTOMIZER could appear improved simply because we separated verification from the execution of DIFFCOND + REDUCER and granted both runs a limit of 900 s. But the sum of the two times are always below 900 s for all correctly solved tasks.

6   Related Work

Equivalence Checking. Regression verification [27,28,55,56], SYMDIFF [23], UC-Klee [48], and other approaches [4,26] check whether the input-output behavior of the original and modified method or program is the same. Differential assertion checking [38] inspects whether the original and modified program trigger the same assertions when given the same inputs. Equivalence checking does not need to be restricted to a simple yes or no answer. Semantic Diff [35] reports all dependencies between variables and input values that occur either in the original or modified program. Conditional equivalence [37] infers under which input assumption the original and modified program produce the same output. Over-approximation of the differences between the original and modified program was also investigated [45]. Differential symbolic execution [46] compares function summaries and constructs a delta that describes the input values on which the summaries are unequal. Partition-based regression verification [19] splits the program input space into inputs on which original and modified program behave equivalently and those on which the two programs are unequal. Equivalence checking is not directly tailored to property verification, but determining when the original and modified programs may behave differently is similar to the goal of the DIFFCOND algorithm.

Result Adaption. Incremental data-flow analysis [51], Reviser [3], and IncA [57,58] adapt the existing data-flow solution to program modifications. Similarly, incremental abstract interpretation [52] adapts the solution of the abstract interpreter. Incremental model checking in the modal-μ calculus [54] adapts a previous fixed point and restarts the fixed-point iteration. Other approaches [18,20] model data-flow analysis and verification as computation of attributed parse trees. A change results in an update of the attributed parse tree. Extreme model checking [33] reuses valid parts of the abstract reachability graph (ARG) and resumes the state-space exploration from those nodes with invalid successors. Incremental state-space exploration [41] reuses a previous state-space graph to prune the current exploration. HiFrog [1] and eVolCheck [25] implement an approach that reuses function summaries and recomputes invalid summaries [53]. UAUTOMIZER adapts a previous trace abstraction [49], a set of Floyd-Hoare automata that describe infeasible error paths, to reuse it on the modified program. While result adaption uses the same verification technique for original and modified program, our approach may use different techniques.

Reusing Intermediate Results. Green [59], GreenTrie [36], and Recal [2] support the reuse of constraint proofs. Similarly, iSaturn [44] supports the reuse of SAT results of Boolean constraints that are identical. Precision reuse [16] reuses the precision of an abstraction, e.g., which variables or predicates to track, from a previous verification run. These approaches are orthogonal to our approach. In the experiments, we even combined precision reuse [16] with our approach.

Skipping Unaffected Verification Steps. Regression model checking [60] stops exploration of a state as soon as no program change can be reached from that state. Directed incremental [47,50] and memoized [61] symbolic execution restrict the exploration to paths that may be affected by the program change. Additionally, memoized symbolic execution does not check constraints as long as the path prefix is unchanged. The Dafny verifier rechecks methods affected by a change reusing unchanged verification conditions [42]. iCoq [21,22] detects and only rechecks those Coq proofs that are affected by a change in the Coq project. These ideas are similar to ours but are tailored to specific techniques.

7   Conclusion

Software is frequently changed during development. Verification techniques must deal with repeatedly verifying nearly the same software again and again. To be able to construct efficient incremental verifiers from off-the-shelf components, we introduce *difference verification with conditions*, which steers an arbitrary existing verifier to reverify only the changed parts. Compared to existing techniques, our approach is tool-agnostic and can be used with arbitrary algorithms for change analysis. We provide an implementation of a change analysis as reusable component, which we combined with three existing verifiers. In a thorough evaluation on more than 10 000 tasks, we showed the effectiveness and efficiency of difference verification with conditions.

Data Availability Statement. DIFFCOND and all our data are available for replication and to construct further difference verifiers on our supplementary web page[7] and in a replication package on Zenodo [12].

---

7 httpoi//www.sosy lab.org/research/difference/

References

1. Alt, L., Asadi, S., Chockler, H., Even-Mendoza, K., Fedyukovich, G., Hyvärinen, A.E.J., Sharygina, N.: HiFrog: SMT-based function summarization for software verification. In: Proc. TACAS, LNCS, vol. 10206, pp. 207–213. Springer (2017). https://doi.org/10.1007/978-3-662-54580-5_12
2. Aquino, A., Bianchi, F.A., Chen, M., Denaro, G., Pezzè, M.: Reusing constraint proofs in program analysis. In: Proc. ISSTA, pp. 305–315. ACM (2015). https://doi.org/10.1145/2771783.2771802
3. Arzt, S., Bodden, E.: Reviser: Efficiently updating IDE-/IFDS-based data-flow analyses in response to incremental program changes. In: Proc. ICSE, pp. 288–298. ACM (2014). https://doi.org/10.1145/2568225.2568243
4. Backes, J., Person, S., Rungta, N., Tkachuk, O.: Regression verification using impact summaries. In: Proc. SPIN, LNCS, vol. 7976, pp. 99–116. Springer (2013). https://doi.org/10.1007/978-3-642-39176-7_7
5. Beyer, D.: Advances in automatic software verification: SV-COMP 2020. In: Proc. TACAS (2), LNCS, vol. 12079, pp. 347–367. Springer (2020). https://doi.org/10.1007/978-3-030-45237-7_21
6. Beyer, D., Dangl, M.: Strategy selection for software verification based on Boolean features: A simple but effective approach. In: Proc. ISoLA, LNCS, vol. 11245, pp. 144–159. Springer (2018). https://doi.org/10.1007/978-3-030-03421-4_11
7. Beyer, D., Dangl, M., Wendler, P.: Boosting k-induction with continuously-refined invariants. In: Proc. CAV, LNCS, vol. 9206, pp. 622–640. Springer (2015). https://doi.org/10.1007/978-3-319-21690-4_42
8. Beyer, D., Gulwani, S., Schmidt, D.: Combining model checking and data-flow analysis. In: Handbook of Model Checking, pp. 493–540. Springer (2018). https://doi.org/10.1007/978-3-319-10575-8_16
9. Beyer, D., Henzinger, T.A., Jhala, R., Majumdar, R.: The software model checker BLAST. Int. J. Softw. Tools Technol. Transfer 9(5–6), 505–525 (2007). https://doi.org/10.1007/s10009-007-0044-z
10. Beyer, D., Henzinger, T.A., Keremoglu, M.E., Wendler, P.: Conditional model checking: A technique to pass information between verifiers. In: Proc. FSE. ACM (2012). https://doi.org/10.1145/2393596.2393664
11. Beyer, D., Henzinger, T.A., Théoduloz, G.: Configurable software verification: Concretizing the convergence of model checking and program analysis. In: Proc. CAV, LNCS, vol. 4590, pp. 504–518. Springer (2007). https://doi.org/10.1007/978-3-540-73368-3_51
12. Beyer, D., Jakobs, M.C., Lemberger, T.: Replication package for article 'Difference verification with conditions'. Zenodo (2020). https://doi.org/10.5281/zenodo.3954933
13. Beyer, D., Jakobs, M.C., Lemberger, T., Wehrheim, H.: Reducer-based construction of conditional verifiers. In: Proc. ICSE, pp. 1182–1193. ACM (2018). https://doi.org/10.1145/3180155.3180259
14. Beyer, D., Keremoglu, M.E.: CPACHECKER: A tool for configurable software verification. In: Proc. CAV, LNCS, vol. 6806, pp. 184–190. Springer (2011). https://doi.org/10.1007/978-3-642-22110-1_16
15. Beyer, D., Keremoglu, M.E., Wendler, P.: Predicate abstraction with adjustable-block encoding. In: Proc. FMCAD, pp. 189–197. FMCAD (2010)
16. Beyer, D., Löwe, S., Novikov, E., Stahlbauer, A., Wendler, P.: Precision reuse for efficient regression verification. In: Proc. FSE, pp. 389–399. ACM (2013). https://doi.org/10.1145/2491411.2491429

17. Beyer, D., Löwe, S., Wendler, P.: Benchmarking and resource measurement. In: Proc. SPIN, LNCS, vol. 9232, pp. 160–178. Springer (2015). https://doi.org/10. 1007/978-3-319-23404-5_12

18. Bianculli, D., Filieri, A., Ghezzi, C., Mandrioli, D.: Syntactic-semantic incrementality for agile verification. SCICO **97**, 47–54 (2015). https://doi.org/10.1016/j. scico.2013.11.026

19. Böhme, M., Oliveira, B.C.d.S., Roychoudhury, A.: Partition-based regression verification. In: Proc. ICSE, pp. 302–311. IEEE (2013). https://doi.org/10.1109/ICSE. 2013.6606576

20. Carroll, M.D., Ryder, B.G.: Incremental data-flow analysis via dominator and attribute updates. In: Proc. POPL, pp. 274–284. ACM (1988). https://doi.org/ 10.1145/73560.73584

21. Çelik, A., Palmskog, K., Gligoric, M.: iCoq: Regression proof selection for large-scale verification projects. In: Proc. ASE, pp. 171–182. IEEE (2017). https://doi. org/10.1109/ASE.2017.8115630

22. Çelik, A., Palmskog, K., Gligoric, M.: A regression proof selection tool for Coq. In: Proc. ICSE (Companion Volume), pp. 117–120. ACM (2018). https://doi.org/ 10.1145/3183440.3183493

23. Chaki, S., Gurfinkel, A., Strichman, O.: Regression verification for multi-threaded programs (with extensions to locks and dynamic thread creation). FMSD **47**(3), 287–301 (2015). https://doi.org/10.1007/s10703-015-0237-0

24. Clarke, E.M., Grumberg, O., Jha, S., Lu, Y., Veith, H.: Counterexample-guided abstraction refinement for symbolic model checking. J. ACM **50**(5), 752–794 (2003). https://doi.org/10.1145/876638.876643

25. Fedyukovich, G., Sery, O., Sharygina, N.: eVolCheck: Incremental upgrade checker for C. In: Proc. TACAS, LNCS, vol. 7795, pp. 292–307. Springer (2013). https:// doi.org/10.1007/978-3-642-36742-7_21

26. Felsing, D., Grebing, S., Klebanov, V., Rümmer, P., Ulbrich, M.: Automating regression verification. In: Proc. ASE, pp. 349–360. ACM (2014). https://doi.org/ 10.1145/2642937.2642987

27. Godlin, B., Strichman, O.: Regression verification. In: Proc. DAC, pp. 466–471. ACM (2009). https://doi.org/10.1145/1629911.1630034

28. Godlin, B., Strichman, O.: Regression verification: Proving the equivalence of similar programs. Softw. Test. Verif. Reliab. **23**(3), 241–258 (2013). https://doi.org/ 10.1002/stvr.1472

29. Heizmann, M., Chen, Y.F., Dietsch, D., Greitschus, M., Hoenicke, J., Li, Y., Nutz, A., Musa, B., Schilling, C., Schindler, T., Podelski, A.: ULTIMATE AUTOMIZER and the search for perfect interpolants (competition contribution). In: Proc. TACAS (2), LNCS, vol. 10806, pp. 447–451. Springer (2018). https://doi.org/10.1007/978-3-319-89963-3_30

30. Heizmann, M., Hoenicke, J., Podelski, A.: Refinement of trace abstraction. In: Proc. SAS, LNCS, vol. 5673, pp. 69–85. Springer (2009). https://doi.org/10.1007/ 978-3-642-03237-0_7

31. Heizmann, M., Hoenicke, J., Podelski, A.: Software model checking for people who love automata. In: Proc. CAV, LNCS, vol. 8044, pp. 36–52. Springer (2013). https://doi.org/10.1007/978-3-642-39799-8_2

32. Henzinger, T.A., Jhala, R., Majumdar, R., McMillan, K.L.: Abstractions from proofs. In: Proc. POPL, pp. 232–244. ACM (2004). https://doi.org/10.1145/ 964001.964021

33. Henzinger, T.A., Jhala, R., Majumdar, R., Sanvido, M.A.A.: Extreme model checking. In: Verification: Theory and Practice, LNCS, vol. 2772, pp. 332–358 (2003). https://doi.org/10.1007/978-3-540-39910-0_16
34. Henzinger, T.A., Jhala, R., Majumdar, R., Sutre, G.: Lazy abstraction. In: Proc. POPL, pp. 58–70. ACM (2002). https://doi.org/10.1145/503272.503279
35. Jackson, D., Ladd, D.A.: Semantic Diff: A tool for summarizing the effects of modifications. In: Proc. ICSM, pp. 243–252. IEEE (1994). https://doi.org/10.1109/ICSM.1994.336770
36. Jia, X., Ghezzi, C., Ying, S.: Enhancing reuse of constraint solutions to improve symbolic execution. In: Proc. ISSTA, pp. 177–187. ACM (2015). https://doi.org/10.1145/2771783.2771806
37. Kawaguchi, M., Lahiri, S., Rebelo, H.: Conditional equivalence. Tech. rep., Microsoft Research (2010)
38. Lahiri, S.K., McMillan, K.L., Sharma, R., Hawblitzel, C.: Differential assertion checking. In: Proc. FSE, pp. 345–355. ACM (2013). https://doi.org/10.1145/2491411.2491452
39. Lahiri, S.K., Murawski, A., Strichman, O., Ulbrich, M.: Program Equivalence (Dagstuhl Seminar 18151). Dagstuhl Reports 8(4), 1–19 (2018). https://doi.org/10.4230/DagRep.8.4.1
40. Lahiri, S.K., Vaswani, K., Hoare, C.A.R.: Differential static analysis: Opportunities, applications, and challenges. In: Proc. FoSER, pp. 201–204. ACM (2010). https://doi.org/10.1145/1882362.1882405
41. Lauterburg, S., Sobeih, A., Marinov, D., Viswanathan, M.: Incremental state-space exploration for programs with dynamically allocated data. In: Proc. ICSE, pp. 291–300. ACM (2008). https://doi.org/10.1145/1368088.1368128
42. Leino, K.R.M., Wüstholz, V.: Fine-grained caching of verification results. In: Proc. CAV, LNCS, vol. 9206, pp. 380–397. Springer (2015). https://doi.org/10.1007/978-3-319-21690-4_22
43. McMillan, K.L.: Interpolation and SAT-based model checking. In: Proc. CAV, LNCS, vol. 2725, pp. 1–13. Springer (2003). https://doi.org/10.1007/978-3-540-45069-6_1
44. Mudduluru, R., Ramanathan, M.K.: Efficient incremental static analysis using path abstraction. In: Proc. FASE, LNCS, vol. 8411, pp. 125–139. Springer (2014). https://doi.org/10.1007/978-3-642-54804-8_9
45. Partush, N., Yahav, E.: Abstract semantic differencing for numerical programs. In: Proc. SAS, LNCS, vol. 7935, pp. 238–258. Springer (2013). https://doi.org/10.1007/978-3-642-38856-9_14
46. Person, S., Dwyer, M.B., Elbaum, S.G., Păsăreanu, C.S.: Differential symbolic execution. In: Proc. FSE, pp. 226–237. ACM (2008). https://doi.org/10.1145/1453101.1453131
47. Person, S., Yang, G., Rungta, N., Khurshid, S.: Directed incremental symbolic execution. In: Proc. PLDI, pp. 504–515. ACM (2011). https://doi.org/10.1145/1993498.1993558
48. Ramos, D.A., Engler, D.R.: Practical, low-effort equivalence verification of real code. In: Proc. CAV, LNCS, vol. 6806, pp. 669–685. Springer (2011). https://doi.org/10.1007/978-3-642-22110-1_55
49. Rothenberg, B., Dietsch, D., Heizmann, M.: Incremental verification using trace abstraction. In: Proc. SAS, LNCS, vol. 11002, pp. 364–382. Springer (2018). https://doi.org/10.1007/978-3-319-99725-4_22

50. Rungta, N., Person, S., Branchaud, J.: A change impact analysis to characterize evolving program behaviors. In: Proc. ICSM, pp. 109–118. IEEE (2012). https://doi.org/10.1109/ICSM.2012.6405261
51. Ryder, B.G.: Incremental data-flow analysis. In: Proc. POPL, pp. 167–176. ACM (1983). https://doi.org/10.1145/567067.567084
52. Seidl, H., Erhard, J., Vogler, R.: Incremental abstract interpretation. In: From Lambda Calculus to Cybersecurity Through Program Analysis - Essays Dedicated to Chris Hankin on the Occasion of His Retirement, LNCS, vol. 12065, pp. 132–148. Springer (2020). https://doi.org/10.1007/978-3-030-41103-9_5
53. Sery, O., Fedyukovich, G., Sharygina, N.: Incremental upgrade checking by means of interpolation-based function summaries. In: Proc. FMCAD, pp. 114–121. FMCAD Inc. (2012)
54. Sokolsky, O.V., Smolka, S.A.: Incremental model checking in the modal mu-calculus. In: Proc. CAV, LNCS, vol. 818, pp. 351–363. Springer (1994). https://doi.org/10.1007/3-540-58179-0_67
55. Strichman, O., Godlin, B.: Regression verification – a practical way to verify programs. In: Proc. VSTTE, LNCS, vol. 4171, pp. 496–501. Springer (2008). https://doi.org/10.1007/978-3-540-69149-5_54
56. Strichman, O., Veitsman, M.: Regression verification for unbalanced recursive functions. In: Proc. FM, LNCS, vol. 9995, pp. 645–658 (2016). https://doi.org/10.1007/978-3-319-48989-6_39
57. Szabó, T., Bergmann, G., Erdweg, S., Voelter, M.: Incrementalizing lattice-based program analyses in DATALOG. PACMPL 2(OOPSLA), 139:1–139:29 (2018). https://doi.org/10.1145/3276509
58. Szabó, T., Erdweg, S., Voelter, M.: IncA: A DSL for the definition of incremental program analyses. In: Proc. ASE, pp. 320–331. ACM (2016). https://doi.org/10.1145/2970276.2970298
59. Visser, W., Geldenhuys, J., Dwyer, M.B.: GREEN: Reducing, reusing, and recycling constraints in program analysis. In: Proc. FSE, pp. 58:1–58:11. ACM (2012). https://doi.org/10.1145/2393596.2393665
60. Yang, G., Dwyer, M.B., Rothermel, G.: Regression model checking. In: Proc. ICSM, pp. 115–124. IEEE (2009). https://doi.org/10.1109/ICSM.2009.5306334
61. Yang, G., Păsăreanu, C.S., Khurshid, S.: Memoized symbolic execution. In: Proc. ISSTA, pp. 144–154. ACM (2012). https://doi.org/10.1145/2338965.2336771
62. Yoo, S., Harman, M.: Regression testing minimization, selection, and prioritization: A survey. STVR 22(2), 67–120 (2012). https://onlinelibrary.wiley.com/doi/abs/10.1002/stvr.430

A Formal Modeling Approach
for Portable Low-Level OS Functionality

Renata Martins Gomes$^{(\boxtimes)}$, Bernhard Aichernig, and Marcel Baunach

Graz University of Technology, Graz, Austria
{renata.gomes,baunach}@tugraz.at, aichernig@ist.tugraz.at

Abstract. The increasing dependability requirements and hardware diversity of the Internet of Things (IoT) pose a challenge to developers. New approaches for software development that guarantee correct implementations will become indispensable. Specially for Real Time Operating Systems (RTOSs), automatic porting for all current and future devices will also be required. As part of our framework for embedded RTOS portability, based on formal methods and code generation, we present our approach to formally model low-level operating-system functionality using Event-B. We show the part of our RTOS model where the switch into the kernel and back to a task happens, and prove that the model is correct according to the specification. Hardware details are only introduced in late refinements, which allows us to reuse most of the RTOS model and proofs for several target platforms. As a proof of concept, we refine the generic model to two different architectures and prove safety and liveness properties of the models.

Keywords: Event-B · RTOS · Portability · Refinement · Verification

1 Introduction

The amount of devices in the Internet of Things (IoT) (e.g. autonomous vehicles, smart infrastructures, automated homes and production facilities), is expected to increase exponentially, along with the diversity on both the hardware and the software side [15,20]. Operating System (OS) developers, who currently focus on just a couple of different computing platforms, will face a huge variety of devices, ranging from simple single-core to more complex multi or many-core systems, including specialized ASIC or even reconfigurable FPGA components [12,18].

While high-level code can more easily be compiled for another hardware, low-level functionality (i.e. context switches, system initialization routines, interrupt handling) are still handwritten for each architecture. To support a new Instruction Set Architecture (ISA), for example, an OS must have many low-level parts completely rewritten, which requires in-depth knowledge of both software and

This work is partially supported by the TU Graz LEAD project "Dependable Internet of Things in Adverse Environments".

F. de Boer and A. Cerone (Eds.): SEFM 2020, LNCS 12310, pp. 155–174, 2020.
https://doi.org/10.1007/978-3-030-58768-0_9

hardware, including a deep understanding of their interaction. From our own experience and industry cooperations, supporting additional MCU families or just variants is not straightforward, even if there are only a few differences to existing ports. This increases the development time, often limiting OS support to a low number of devices. Even though the code base of many OSs is modular, there are noticeably often just a few complete and directly usable ports available. Especially when developed under time pressure, wrong implementations, new bugs, and security breaches are common. Besides, changes in the logic of low-level software must be manually introduced to all implementations, which also hinders or slows down important improvements of the OS. Since dependability is key for the IoT [4,15,36], we propose an approach to improve the portability of embedded Real Time Operating Systems (RTOSs) based on formal models, refinement, and code generation to target-specific code.

We report on the first part of the approach: the modeling and verification of low-level functionality. Parts of the model of an RTOS are presented that focus on the switch into the kernel and back to a task, detailing the operations that happen in these transitions. We chose the context switch as demonstrating example, because it is architecture-specific, requires reimplementation for each architecture, and its correctness is crucial: corrupted task contexts, resulting from incorrect implementations, may produce errors that are hard to find and compromise the OS's ability to properly interleave concurrently running tasks.

First, we model the OS execution flow and functionality incrementally through formal refinements. Then, as a proof of concept, we further refine the generic OS model to two different architectures: an MSP430 and a RISC-V. In order to verify safety (something bad must *not* happen) and liveness (something good *should* eventually happen) properties [25], we (1) prove that our RTOS models do not corrupt any task's context by properly saving and loading them, even though the process for saving and restoring a context differs for different MCU architectures; (2) prove that the kernel runs in the appropriate CPU state and changes it as specified for task execution; (3) prove that the kernel executes in the correct order and finishes execution. Since we only introduce hardware details in late refinements, most of those proofs need only be done once, on the generic RTOS model. The refinement to each architecture, as well as their proofs follow and become much simpler, as we will show.

Contributions. To the best of our knowledge, this is the first time that OS low-level functionality is formally modeled with focus on its portability. Our main contributions in this paper are: (1) we decouple low-level functionality from hardware specifics; (2) a generic formal RTOS model with context switches; (3) safety and liveness verification of two instantiations of the generic model via interactive theorem proving and model checking.

Structure. Section 2 discusses related work and Sect. 3 provides background on the tools and the two target HW architectures. Section 4 presents the requirements and the modeled RTOS. Section 5 introduces the general idea of the modeling process and our refinement strategy, while the model itself is detailed in Sect. 6. Section 7 discusses verification. We conclude in Sect. 8.

2   Related Work

Many works investigate how to formally model and verify OSs. Brandenburg [6] introduces a new concept to develop RTOSs with time predictability. Craig [8,9] specifies an OS using formal models, also showing it can be refined to executable code. However, he either assumes several HW details or leaves further refinements to be done, conceding that "the hardware specification poses a slight problem". Novikov and Zakharov [29] verify Linux to detect faults in the entire mono-lithic kernel. Alkhammash *et al.* present modeling guidelines of FreeRTOS [2], and Cheng *et al.* model FreeRTOS' task model [7]. Stoddart *et al.* [33] model an interrupt driven scheduler in B. Danmin *et al.* [11] also use B to model an OS. Su *et al.* [34] design an RTOS memory manager in Event-B. With correct-ness proofs from abstract kernel function specification down to the binary file, seL4 [16] does not model the direct hardware instructions, assuming correct-ness of hardware-specific code, such as handwritten assembly code, boot code, etc [24]. Syeda and Klein [35] tackle the modeling of low-level cached address translation, whose correctness is usually left as an assumption, aiming to even-tually integrate their model into seL4's verification. Baumann *et al.* [3] develop a method to model the underlying hardware of embedded systems such that the detailed modeling of each hardware component can be delayed, while still allowing the verification of high level security properties. OpenComRTOS [37], was designed with TLA+ and has been ported to several targets, however code is always handwritten.

Others tried to generate code from models: Hu *et al.* [21] report on problems found when trying to synthesize an OS. Fathabadi *et al.* [14] design a platform-independent formal model of an OS module that interacts with the HW and automatically generates C code. Dalvandi *et al.* [10] generate verifiable code from formal models. Popp *et al.* [31] generate information about device properties and addresses. Méry [28] presents formal modeling design patterns later translated to software. The generated software in these works is semantically dependent on the HW, but the syntax is pure C, not solving the problem of generating low-level OS code, that must, at least partially, be handwritten in assembly. Wright [40,41] formally specifies an entire ISA in Event-B and automatically generates a virtual machine capable of simulating it. Borghorst *et al.* [5] generate code for low-level OS functions using abstract assembly to describe the software and a HW architecture description to generate code, but without formal methods.

These works advance the state of the art in model-based OS development either by modeling and proving properties of high-level parts of the kernel (such as scheduling, task management, or resource management), or assuming HW characteristics that render the model HW-specific. Some code can often be gen-erated for different programming languages, but the low-level code remains to be ported manually, and the models are not usable for different HW platforms. Our work aims at covering this gap on low-level software, providing an approach for its modeling and automatic code generation.

3   Background

Model Checking and ProB. Temporal logic [27,30] is a logic system that formally describes properties of time. Linear Temporal Logic (LTL) is the most popular and widely used temporal logic in computer science to specify and verify the correct behavior of reactive and concurrent programs [19]. It is particularly useful for expressing properties such as *safety* (given a precondition, then undesirable states that violate the safety condition will never occur), *liveness* (given a precondition, then a desirable state will eventually be reached), and *fairness* (involves combinations of temporal patterns of the form a predicate holds "infinitely often" or "eventually always"). ProB is an animator, constraint solver, and model checker for the B-Method [26] that integrates as a plugin-in Rodin and can be easily used for LTL model checking of our RTOS models.

Event-B and Rodin. Event-B is a formal method for system-level modeling and analysis [1,13]. The Rodin Platform [23], an Event-BIDE based on Eclipse, supports the development and refinement of models with automatic generation and partial discharging of mathematical Proof Obligations (POs). Event-B is based on set theory and state transitions. The two top elements of a model are *contexts* and *machines*. The term *context* is overloaded in the domains of OSs and formal methods. Hence, we will always refer to a context in Event-B as *Event-B context*. Event-B contexts describe all static information

```
1 SETS // sets block
2 S
3 VARIABLES // variables block
4 x ⊆ S
5 f ∈ S ⇸ DATA // f is a partial
    function
6 b ∈ S ⤖ DATA // b is a bijective
    function
7 eventName // event block
8 ANY // parameter block
9 p ⊆ x
10 WHERE // guards block
11 p ≠ ∅
12 x ⩤ b = x ⩤ f // b and f are equal
    for all domain elements not in x (
    domain subtraction ⩤)
13 THEN // actions block.
14 f := f ⩤ (p ◁ b) // f is
    overwritten (⩤) by the pairs in b
    whose first element is in p (domain
    restriction ◁)
15 x := x \ p // set subtraction
```

Fig. 1. Event-B notation

about the system. They are composed by carrier sets, constants, and axioms. Dynamic information is represented by the machines, which are composed of variables, invariants, and events. Event-B machines can *see* Event-B contexts, such that the machine can use their constants and axioms to relate static and dynamic information as well as to discharge POs. Considering machine states as sets of the variables' values, each event represents a state transition. Events are enabled if the state satisfies the corresponding *guard* condition and modify the current state according to their *actions*, which are executed in parallel when the event is enabled. When a machine refines another one, it must refine (or keep) its events, adding details or more variables; POs are automatically generated by Rodin to e.g. guarantee that invariants always hold and that refined events do not contradict the abstract ones. In order to ease the understanding for readers not familiar with Event-B, Fig. 1 presents a summary of the Event-B notation used in our models. We assume the reader is familiar with basic set theory notation.

Next, we present the main characteristics of the two HW architectures we use as examples for the architecture-specific instantiations of our model in Sect. 6.

MSP430. The TI MSP430 [22] family of MCUs comprises a range of ultra-low power devices featuring 16 and 20-bit RISC architectures with a large variation of on-chip peripherals, depending on the model. Among its 16 registers are general purpose registers, the program counter PC, the stack pointer SP, and the status register SR, which stores status flags, such as interrupt enabled, overflow, etc. The MSP430 offers a very simple architecture with only one execution mode and a fully orthogonal instruction set. There is no privileged mode, nor any memory protection or memory management unit. Once an interrupt occurs, the PC and SR registers are pushed onto the stack. Then, further interrupt requests (IRQs) are disabled and the PC is overwritten with the address of the first instruction of the corresponding interrupt handler. The return from interrupt instruction, i.e., RETI, restores SR and PC from the stack and finally continues where the handler has interrupted the regular execution flow.

RISC-V. The open RISC-V instruction set architecture [32] was originally developed by UC Berkeley and is meanwhile supported by a highly active community of software and hardware innovators with more than 100 members from industry and academia. The RISC-V is a load-store architecture, and its specification [39] defines privilege levels used to provide protection between different components of the software stack. We refer to an implementation that supports user and machine modes, with 32-bit integer and multiplication/division instructions (RV32IM) [38]. There are 32 registers available in all modes, including a zero register and the program counter pc. The calling convention specification assigns meanings to the other registers, such as a stack pointer sp, function arguments and return values. Additionally, Control and Status Registers (CSRs) with special access instructions are available for e.g. managing the CPU or accessing on-chip peripherals in defined privilege levels. An IRQ switches the CPU into a higher privilege level, while software can issue an ECALL instruction for that. In both cases, returning to user level is done by the instruction URET.

4   Requirements

We modeled the *MCSmartOS* [17], an RTOS we have developed and used for many years. This section presents its architecture and requirements. An important concept to understand is the *context* (not in the sense of Event-B, but in the sense of operating systems): A *context* is a set of information and configuration of a CPU or a CPU core that is required to control the execution flow of software, i.e. code sequences. Depending on the CPU state and external events, cores can usually switch between different code sequences by loading their respective context. To be able to continue an earlier code sequence from the interrupted instruction, its context is saved before the switch. The actual switching process as well as the composition of the contexts is defined by the interrupt concept of the CPU; in any case, the hardware automatically saves and loads the contexts. If, in addition to interrupts of the hardware, an OS supports preemptive, i.e. interleaved executable tasks (or threads or processes), the *context* is extended. In order to switch between tasks, this extended information is saved (previous task) and loaded (next task) by the kernel. Next, we describe our assumptions about the computing platform and present *MCSmartOS*'s requirements.

4.1   Hardware Assumptions

Even though we aim on keeping the OS model initially independent from the hardware, a target architecture must have certain features in order to be capable of running an operating system. Focusing only on the relevant aspects for our RTOS model, we define data storage and interrupt handling features as environmental assumptions, numbering and labeling them ENV. Different OSs might require other features, but that does not affect our general concept.

ENV1 The CPU provides means to store/load data to/from referable locations. These locations can be, e.g., registers or memory addresses.

ENV2 The context is a well-defined subset of locations and their stored values that the CPU requires for execution of a code sequence. It must be saved when the code sequence is interrupted, so that it can later be resumed from the same point.

ENV3 The CPU has an interrupt enabled flag. Interrupts will only be accepted if the interrupt enabled flag is set.

ENV4 When an interrupt is accepted, the values of the context or a part of it are automatically copied into other locations defined by the architecture.

ENV5 The CPU offers a "return from interrupt" instruction that automatically loads the context with the values automatically saved when the interrupt was accepted (ENV4).

ENV6 The saving process (ENV4) is allowed to modify the context values before they are saved, according to a well-defined and CPU-specific function.

ENV7 The restoring process (ENV5) must reverse the modification of ENV6.

4.2   Software Specification

MCSmartOS provides, among many other features, a preemptive and priority-based scheduler for concurrent tasks. The kernel is invoked when an interrupt occurs or a syscall is called, and is divided into three parts: (1) the *kernel entry* is responsible for stack management and context saving. It unites both entry points, enters kernel mode, and continues to (2) the *kernel body* which handles the actual interrupt or syscall request and runs the scheduler that selects the task to be executed next. Finally, (3) the *kernel exit* executes a context switch by loading the selected task's context and returning to task mode.

In this work, we only model the context switches in *kernel entry* and *exit*, and the conditions required by the OS to execute its other functions. High-level kernel functionality, such as scheduling, task management, etc. is out of scope. The requirements for correct context switches and kernel execution (os) are:

os1 (A) A task executes on the context defined in ENV2. When not running, the values of its context are stored in locations reserved for context saving. (B) Each element of the context has its correspondent in the saved context.

os2 (A) Once the kernel is invoked, *kernel entry* saves the old task's context. (B) On *kernel exit* the next task's context is loaded into the CPU.

os3 (A) Each task has dedicated locations for context saving. (B) These locations with their stored values are the task's saved context, where contexts are saved to and loaded from (os2).

os4 The scheduler chooses the new task and is implemented in *kernel body*.

os5 The cause for kernel invocation, unambiguously identifying which interrupt or syscall has occurred, must be recorded for use within *kernel body*.

os6 (A) The *kernel body* always runs in kernel mode, with interrupts disabled, and on the OS stack. (B) Each task runs on its own stack, with the interrupt flag the same as it was when that task was running last, and never on kernel mode.

os7 A part of *kernel entry* context saving and CPU preparation is automatically executed by the hardware (ENV4). The rest must be executed in software after the automatic part.

os8 The kernel is exited with a return from interrupt instruction (ENV5). The task selected by the scheduler shall continue execution and where it was preempted before.

os9 A part of *kernel exit* context loading and CPU preparation is automatically executed by the return from interrupt instruction (ENV5, os8). The rest must be executed in software before the automatic part.

os10 (A) If the values copied on interrupt (ENV4) are copied into task-specific locations, these locations and their data are considered a part of the saved context. (B) Otherwise, it is the OS's responsibility to save those values into the task's save context, and to copy them back where the CPU expects them to be when returning from an interrupt (ENV5).

os11 If the architecture provides a privileged mode, *kernel body* runs in it, while tasks run in less privileged modes. Switching the mode must be done on *kernel entry* and *kernel exit*.

5 Refinement Strategy: From Abstraction to Detailed Specification

The model has several refinements and showing all would be too cumbersome. So, we divide it into 6 levels of abstraction (referred to as *Level*). Each Level is composed of several refinements and addresses a new set of requirements (Table 1). [1] Up to Level 4, the model remains generic, only requiring the generic

---

[1] Model artifact at https://figshare.com/s/0f262342284eada236f5. The relationship between refinements and levels can be found in the README file. Model elements are referenced as [component.label].

hardware features described in Sect. 4.1. We only introduce further hardware details in Level 5, where we instantiate the model for specific target architectures. This section introduces the general idea of each Level, while Sect. 6 details how each level was modeled. This model focuses on the interface between hardware and software in order to model the kernel's interleaved execution of concurrently running tasks. The goal is to prove that the kernel does not corrupt any task's context by properly saving and loading them, as well as to guarantee that tasks and *kernel body* run in the appropriate conditions described by the requirements from Sect. 4.

Table 1. Model and requirements.

Level	ENV	OS
0	ENV1, ENV2	os1
1	–	os2
2	ENV6, ENV7	os3, os4
3	ENV3	os5, os6
4	ENV4, ENV5	os7, os8, os9, os10
5	Target-specific	os11

The state of an Event-B machine is the set of its variables' values, and state transitions are represented by the machine's events. In our model, these events represent the different parts of the kernel, building a state machine that starts with the switch into the kernel and finishes with the switch back to a task. The events, therefore, are modeled such that their order is well-defined, in the order the kernel parts must run: *kernel entry* executes first, then *body*, and finally *exit*; and the automatic part of *entry* executes before the manual part that must be executed in software (os7), and in *exit* manual executes before automatic (os9).

Level 0 In this initial abstraction, we only present the expected result of the OS execution, i.e., that an old context is saved and a new one is loaded, without modeling how this will be achieved. We also define the basic Event-B sets and their relations, used along the refinements.

Level 1 In the first refinements, we define the entry and exit parts of the kernel simply as two context copies: one in *kernel entry* for saving a context, and another one in *kernel exit* for loading a context. At this level, we do not yet define where those contexts are copied from or to, nor do we have any notion of tasks or conditions for proper task and *kernel body* execution.

Level 2 Next, we introduce tasks, their saved contexts, and *kernel body*. This level also defines where the context is saved to and loaded from.

Level 3 Then, we introduce and set up the variables that control the conditions for proper task and *kernel body* execution (interrupts disabled, kernel mode, running on its own stack, and cause for the kernel execution).

Level 4 Refines the model to a generic hardware that automatically saves and loads a subset of the context, and the software that complements the switches.

Level 5 Finally, we refine the model into architecture-specific models from which OS code can be generated (code generation is not in the scope of this paper).

6   Kernel Model

This section details the levels from Sect. 5. Please, refer to Fig. 1 for the Event-B notation used in the following listings.

Level 0. First, we define the carrier set LOCATION (Fig. 2a), an abstract representation of memory addresses and registers. In combination with DATA, a subset of $\mathbb{Z}$, memory and registers can be represented according to ENV1. Two non-overlapping subsets with the same cardinality, CONTEXT and SAVEDCTX represent the subset of locations that compose the context (ENV2) and the subset of locations of a saved context (OS1.A), respectively. The bijective function ctx2saved $\in$ CONTEXT$\rightarrowtail$SAVEDCTX relates each context location to where it is saved, while saved2ctx is its inverse (OS1.B). The context is defined as a relation from CONTEXT to DATA, while a saved context is a relation from SAVEDCTX to DATA.

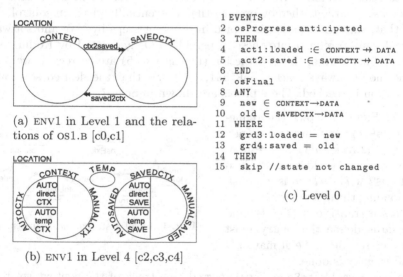

(a) ENV1 in Level 1 and the relations of OS1.B [c0,c1]

(b) ENV1 in Level 4 [c2,c3,c4]

```
 1 EVENTS
 2  osProgress anticipated
 3  THEN
 4     act1:loaded :∈ CONTEXT ⇸ DATA
 5     act2:saved  :∈ SAVEDCTX ⇸ DATA
 6  END
 7  osFinal
 8  ANY
 9     new ∈ CONTEXT→DATA
10     old ∈ SAVEDCTX→DATA
11  WHERE
12     grd3:loaded = new
13     grd4:saved = old
14  THEN
15     skip //state not changed
```

(c) Level 0

Fig. 2. Diagrams of LOCATION and initial abstraction

The initial abstraction (Fig. 2c), sees the context switches as two context copies: one copies old context to saved $\in$ SAVEDCTX $⇸$ DATA, and the other loads new context to loaded $\in$ CONTEXT $⇸$ DATA. The old and new contexts that are copied are simply event parameters, that will later be refined into the actual contexts that are copied. The OS is modeled in the event osProgress. The event osFinal is not a part of the OS, but is only introduced to model the state where the OS has successfully executed. This event is composed only of guards, that is, it is enabled once the state represented in its guards is reached but does not change it anymore. The event osProgress, that represents the OS kernel, is allowed to change the variables saved and loaded, but does not yet describe

```
1 osEntry REFINES osProgress          1 osExit REFINES osProgress
2 ANY                                 2 ANY
3 saveSet ⊆ toSave                    3 loadSet ⊆ toLoad
4 old ∈ SAVEDCTX⇸DATA                 4 new ∈ CONTEXT⇸DATA
5 WHERE                               5 WHERE
6 saveSet ≠ ∅                         6 loadSet ≠ ∅
7 saved = toSave ◁ old                7 loaded = toLoad ◁ new
8 loaded = ∅ //load not started       8 toSave = ∅ //save complete
9 THEN                                9 THEN
10 saved := saved ∪ (saveSet ◁ old)  10 loaded := loaded ∪ (loadSet ◁ new)
11 toSave := toSave\saveSet          11 toLoad := toLoad\loadSet
```

(a) Kernel entry   (b) Kernel exit

Fig. 3. Level 1

how the copies are made. It is made *anticipated*, which, in Event-B, means that it may execute several times, but must eventually give up control and allow the model to reach `osFinal`. Refinements of an anticipated event must *converge*, i.e., decrease a variant, thereby proving that it eventually gives up control. The idea is that, since the context is copied in different steps by HW and software, this event can be refined into these steps. The POs generated by Rodin verify that the refinements of this abstraction (Levels 1 to 5) are correct. If we prove that the model always reaches `osFinal`, we prove that the desired state after OS execution is reached. These proofs are shown in Sect. 7.

Level 1. Figure 3 shows the refinement of `osProgress` into two events: `osEntry` (OS2.A: *kernel entry* responsible for saving the old context), and `osExit` (OS2.B: *kernel exit* is responsible for loading the new context). They model state transitions (Fig. 4), and their guards define that entry must happen before exit, and exit may only start after entry is done.

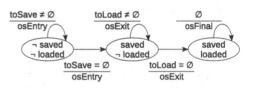

Fig. 4. Level 1 states and transitions

The new variable `toSave ⊆` SAVEDCTX keeps track of the context yet to be saved, while the parameter `saveSet` defines the context subset saved in each run of `osEntry`. The event is made convergent on the variant `toSave`, and `saveSet` is subtracted from `toSave` in each run (Fig. 3a, Line 11). This guarantees that, eventually, the save process will complete and we move to a *saved* state. Similarly, the new variable `toLoad ⊆` CONTEXT represents the context yet to be loaded, while `loadSet` defines the context subset loaded in each run of `osExit`. The event is made convergent on the variant `toLoad`, and `loadSet` is subtracted from `toLoad` on each run (Fig. 3b, Line 11), allowing the event to eventually reach the *loaded* state. Event `osFinal` remains unchanged.

Level 2. Next, we define the input constants `oldTask ∈` TASKS and `oldCtx ∈` CONTEXT → DATA that represent the old task and its context when the kernel was requested. The saving operation in `osEntry` must save `oldCtx` into `oldTask`'s

```
1 osEntry REFINES osEntry
2 ANY
3  saveSet ⊆ toSave
4 WHERE
5  saveSet ≠ ∅
6  toSave ◁ t_saved(runningTask) =
     toSave ◁ transform(oldCtx)
7  loaded = ∅ // load not started
8 THEN
9  t_saved(runningTask) := t_saved(
     runningTask) ⩤ (saveSet ◁
     transform(oldCtx))
10  toSave := toSave\saveSet
```

(a) Kernel entry

```
1 osExit REFINES osExit
2 ANY
3  loadSet ⊆ toLoad
4 WHERE
5  loadSet ≠ ∅
6  loaded = toLoad ◁ invTransform(
     t_saved(runningTask))
7  toSave = ∅ //save complete
8 THEN
9  loaded := loaded ∪ (loadSet ◁
     invTransform(t_saved(runningTask)))
10  toLoad := toLoad\loadSet
```

(b) Kernel exit

Fig. 5. Level 2

save space. In order to save the context, we must map it to a saved context. Additionally, the context might be modified during the saving process (ENV6), e.g. the stack pointer is changed before it is saved when the architecture automatically pushes some registers onto the stack. We must account for this modification, since what is finally saved is the transformed version of the values, and not the original input values. Thus, we define the functions ctxTransform ∈ CONTEXT→(DATA⇸DATA) and transform ∈ (CONTEXT→DATA)⇸(SAVEDCTX→ DATA). The architecture-specific function ctxTransform is only declared at this level, and represents the modification of each value in the context. The function itself is only fully specified in Level 5. The function transform converts a context into a saved context according to ctx2saved, modifying the values stored in each location according to ctxTransform. This is modeled by the axiom.

```
c1.axm7: ∀ ctx,el · ctx ∈ CONTEXT→DATA ∧ el ∈ CONTEXT ⇒
transform(ctx)(ctx2saved(el)) = ctxTransform(el)(ctx(el))
```

With these definitions in Event-B contexts, we also refine the machine variables and events (Fig. 5). To represent the saved contexts of all tasks (OS3.A), saved

```
1 osFinal (guards)
2  loaded = invTransform(t_saved(runningTask))
3  t_saved(oldTask) = transform(oldCtx)
4  toSave = ∅
```

Fig. 6. Level 2: osFinal

is refined into t_saved ∈ TASKS→(SAVEDCTX → DATA), with glue invariant saved = toSave ◁ t_saved(oldTask). The new variable runningTask ∈ TASKS is equal to the constant oldTask before *kernel body* is run, and represents the new scheduled task after the scheduler has run. While osFinal always uses oldTask to check if the context has been correctly saved, osEntry refers to runningTask to save the context. This way, all three kernel parts (*entry*, *body*, and *exit*) deal with the same variable, simplifying code generation. We can finally replace the abstract save action in Fig. 3a (Line 10) by the action in Fig. 5a (Line 9).

The context to be loaded during *kernel exit* actually comes from the saved context of `runningTask`, thus we replace the abstract load from Fig. 3b (Line 10) by the load in Fig. 5b (Line 9). The functions `ctxTransform` and `transform` used for saving a context have their inverses, used for the load process, defined as ctxInvTransform $\in$ SAVEDCTX$\rightarrow$(DATA $\rightarrowtail$ DATA) and `invTransform` $\in$ (SAVEDCTX $\rightarrow$ DATA)$\rightarrowtail$(CONTEXT $\rightarrow$ DATA), related with the axiom

```
c1.axm8: ∀ sctx,el · sctx ∈ SAVEDCTX→DATA ∧ el ∈ SAVEDCTX ⇒
invTransform(sctx)(saved2ctx(el)) = ctxInvTransform(el)(sctx(el))
```

Now, we can refine the `old` and `new` parameters to reflect the real source and destination of the context copies (OS3.B) in Level 2 (Fig. 5a, 5b, and 6).

Finally, the new event `osBody` models *kernel body* (Fig. 7), abstractly representing the scheduler (OS4). We do not model *kernel body* in more detail in this work, but will refine it to guarantee its execution according to the OS requirements.

```
1 osBody
2 WHERE
3   toSave = ∅
4   toLoad = CONTEXT
5 THEN
6   runningTask :∈ TASKS
```

Fig. 7. Level 2: osBody

Level 3. Though we do not model *kernel body*, we want to guarantee that *kernel entry* prepares the CPU to start its execution. Analogously, we do not model tasks, but want to guarantee that *kernel exit* prepares the CPU to run them. Thus, we introduce the variables that control the conditions for proper task and *kernel body* execution (OS5, OS6): `kernelMode` is a flag that indicates when the kernel has been entered. `osBody` can only be enabled if it is true, and `osFinal` if it is false; `kernelCause` records why the kernel has been invoked. It unambiguously identifies each interrupt and syscall, and must be valid within `osBody`; `interruptEnable` is the interrupt enabled flag (ENV3). It must be false in `osBody`, and loaded from the next task's saved context during *kernel exit*; `currStack` indicates the stack currently in use, abstractly representing a kernel or a task stack. `osBody` is enabled if `currStack` indicates kernel stack, while `osFinal` requires it to indicate task stack. We strengthen `osBody` and `osFinal` guards to fulfill OS5 and OS6. Modification of these variables in *kernel entry* and *exit* remain nondeterministic, since they are highly hardware-dependent. Figure 8 shows the new sets, variables, and guards. We also create the event `entryNothingToSave`, that mimics `osEntry` and is explained in Level 4.

Level 4. Now, *kernel entry* and *exit* are divided in two parts: one models what is *automatically* done by the hardware, via an interrupt acceptance or a return from interrupt instruction (ENV4, ENV5). This may save some registers, turn off the interrupt enabled flag, switch the CPU mode, etc. The remaining actions of *kernel entry* (OS7) and *exit* (OS8, OS9) are fulfilled by their *manual* parts.

This Level still does not refer to specific details of a potential target architecture. Therefore, the model must support different behaviors: the hardware might, on interrupt, copy a set of its registers into another set of registers designed for that (OS10.B), or it might copy them to memory, for example pushing them onto the stack (OS10.A). In the first case, we call this a temporary save, since

```
1 SETS (new)
2 STACKS
3 KERNELCAUSES
4 VARIABLES (new)
5 kernelMode ∈ BOOL
6 kernelCause ∈ KERNELCAUSES
7 interruptEnable ∈ BOOL
8 currStack ∈ STACKS
```

(a) New carrier sets and variables

```
1 AXIOMS (new)
2 partition(STACKS,KERNELSTACK,TASKSTACKS)
3 partition(KERNELCAUSES,{kCause_invalid},
      KCAUSE_SYSCALLS,KCAUSE_FLOWINTS)
```

(b) New axioms

```
1 osBody (new guards)
2 kernelMode = TRUE
3 kernelCause ≠ kCause_invalid
4 interruptEnable = FALSE
5 currStack ∈ KERNELSTACK
```

(c) New guards in body

Fig. 8. Level 3: Additions to model

the destination is the same for all tasks and must, therefore, still be made permanent by copying it to the task's saved context in *kernel entry*. To model this, we partition CONTEXT and SAVEDCTX in three sections, as shown in Fig. 2b: sections MANUALCTX and MANUALSAVED for the locations only manipulated in the manual part, and two others for those automatically handled by the hardware. AUTODIRECTCTX and AUTODIRECTSAVE for those locations permanently saved by the hardware, and AUTOTEMPCTX and AUTOTEMPSAVE for those first copied to/from a TEMP location. TEMP is another subset of LOCATION, created in this level.

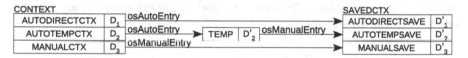

Fig. 9. *Kernel entry* context save. $D_x \subset$ DATA and $D'_x =$ ctxTransform(D_x)

We refine the events osEntry and osExit by splitting each in two, and refining their parameters (saveSet and loadSet in Fig. 5) to differentiate the partitions in CONTEXT and SAVEDCTX. The transform and invTransform functions are also refined to reflect the refinements of this level and the separation of the different levels of context copy. The events are refined according to Fig. 9: osAutoEntry saves values from AUTODIRECTCTX into AUTODIRECTSAVE and copies from AUTOTEMPCTX to the new variable temp ∈ TEMP → DATA. For architectures that only copy part of the context to temporary locations, not saving anything, we refine entryNothingToSave into tempSave, adding a copy to temp and making it convergent on the variant TEMP \ dom(temp) (must add elements to temp). We also keep entryNothingToSave only modifying variables from Level 3. Then, osManualEntry saves MANUALCTX into MANUALSAVED and copies temp into the AUTOTEMPSAVE location, completing the saving of the temporary part of the context. The inverse operation is modeled in *kernel exit*: First, osManualExit loads from MANUALSAVED into MANUALCTX and copies from AUTOTEMPSAVE into temp, then osAutoExit loads all AUTODTX from temp and AUTODIRECTSAVE.

Level 5 - Architecture-Specific Instantiations. Having intentionally modeled the OS independent from the hardware so far, we finally introduce hardware details in a new refinement level per target architecture. For each, we extend the Event-B context and define, within LOCATION, all registers available in the architecture. At the same time, we also define which of them are part of CONTEXT (and to which subset), TEMP, etc. We also define the locations for saved contexts and the CPU-specific functions ctxTransform and ctx2saved. For each target, one Event-B machine refines the last Level 4 machine, *see* the correspondent Event-B context, and the architecture-specific actions from Level 3 are made deterministic. On interrupt, RISC-V copies some registers into temp, not saving anything directly, therefore osAutoEntry is never enabled and we can remove it. tempSave is refined into interrupt and ecall, which are very similar: both switch into kernel (machine) mode, disable interrupts and copy data into temp. Additionally, interrupt registers the interrupt ID (kernelCause). For a syscall, we need to do this before ecall, so we refine entryNothingToSave into __syscall. We can refine kernelMode to the privilege levels, adding an invariant that relates kernelMode = TRUE to machine mode and kernelMode = FALSE to user mode (os11). On MSP430, registers are pushed onto the task's stack, and there are no temporarily saved registers, so tempSave is removed. Without privileged modes, kernelMode is a variable, which is set to TRUE in osManualEntry and to FALSE in osManualExit. osAutoEntry is refined into interrupt and __syscall. The latter imitates the former, additionally registering which syscall triggered the kernel. Since the interrupt can not do this automatically, entryNothingToSave is refined to interruptHandler, which is enabled after the interrupt.

7   Proofs and Model Checking

This section shows the properties we verified via theorem proving in Rodin and LTL model checking. From the requirements, we elaborate safety properties to be proved: (**S1**) Contexts are never corrupted by the kernel (os2), (**S2**) osBody always runs in the specified conditions for its execution and osFinal is reached with the specified conditions for task execution (os5, os6). And liveness properties guarantee the model reaches the intended states: (**L1**) The kernel executes in the correct order, and (**L2**) always finishes execution (always reaches osFinal).

7.1   Theorem Proving

All refinements in our model must correspond to their abstraction, which is proved with discharging the POs generated by Rodin. The initial abstraction, Level 0, defines the state (osFinal guards) we want to achieve after OS execution, namely that an old context is saved and a new context is loaded. This state must be reached by osProgress, which models the OS. Event osProgress is refined into the three main parts of the kernel (entry, body, and exit). Entry and exit are responsible, respectively, for saving the old task's context and loading the new task into the CPU. The first abstraction is modeled such that `osProgress` can not run forever. The idea is that it must change the state until it finally enables `osFinal`, i.e. the desired terminal state. Through the refinements, we model how exactly this happens, splitting `osProgress` into several events, and creating invariants and actions that model the OS requirements.

Some of the discharged POs guarantee that the events refining `osProgress` also give up control, and in Sect. 7.2 we prove they indeed modify the state such that it eventually reaches `osFinal`. Other POs prove that actions always respect the invariants (INV POs), or that a concrete event's actions do simulate the abstract correspondents (SIM POs). There are several other rules for PO generation, which we do not detail here. Table 2 summarizes the number of POs generated in each level of abstraction, and shows how many of them were automatically or manually discharged. The manually discharged ones are differentiated according to their discharging complexity: *simple* POs only required a few steps to be discharged, while the *complex* POs required more experience with the proving system and the PO's breakdown in several proving steps.

In Level 2, two invariants to guarantee that the save and load processes do save `oldCtx` and load the `runningTask`'s saved context:

```
m05.inv2:toSave = ∅ ⇔ saved = transform(oldCtx)
m07.inv4:toLoad = ∅ ⇔ loaded = invTransform(t_saved(runningTask))
```

Discharging the related INV POs proves that, for every refinement, when our model considers the old context as saved and the new context as loaded, they indeed are. Those INV POs were always automatically discharged, except in few refinements, where they were manually discharged in a few steps.

Table 2. Number of POs discharged

Level	#POs	Auto	Simple	Complex
0	8	8	0	0
1	17	15	2	0
2	63	52	11	0
3	14	14	0	0
4	83	39	35	9
5	70	58	6	6
Total	255	186	54	15
	100%	73%	21%	6%

The SIM POs involving save and load actions, however, were rather complex, especially in Level 4. In particular for events `osManualEntry` and `osAutoExit`, we had to create a new parameter and a theorem in order to discharge the SIM POs. We detail here the proof strategy for the save action SIM PO in `osManualEntry`. The same strategy was applied to `osAutoExit`. We must prove that the action modeling the `osManualEntry` arrows in Fig. 9 as described in Level 4, simulates its abstract correspondent in Fig. 5a (Line 9):

```
m12.osManualEntry.act2: t_saved(runningTask) := t_saved(runningTask) ⊲- (
  autoSaveSet ◁ autoTempTEMPSVDtransform(temp)) ⊲-(manualSaveSet ◁
  manualTransform(MANUALCTX ◁ oldCtx))
```

We replace the automatic save part of the action by the parameter aux = autoSaveSet ◁ autoTempTEMPSVDtransform(temp) and add to the event's guards the theorem aux = autoSaveSet ◁ autoTempTransform(AUTOTEMPCTX ◁ oldCtx). After proving the theorem, the SIM PO is much easier to discharge.

7.2 LTL Model Checking

For the liveness verification, we encode a set of LTL formulas that guarantee the specified execution order and that osFinal is eventually enabled. The model shall (1) eventually reach osFinal, staying there forever, (2) not reach a state where all events are disabled, (3) always have exactly one event enabled, and (4) implement the specified execution order: first, *entry*, then *body*, and finally *exit*, and manual save after auto save (OS7) and manual load before auto load (OS9).

Since the model's axioms are rather complex, we need to create a minimal set of CONTEXT and SAVEDCTX elements to represent the locations that compose contexts and saved contexts, otherwise the state space explodes and ProB cannot run. For this, we extend the Event-B contexts with the constant instantiations, and refine the machines we want to check. These machines are not modified any further, except for the model checks of Level 3 and 4, where the nondeterministic actions introduced in Level 3 would cause the checks to fail, since paths would exist in which osBody and osFinal could not be reached. As our intention is to leave this determinism to the architecture-specific models, the actions are modified to enforce the correct execution path. In Level 5, all actions are left unmodified, and we can check if the variables have been correctly set.

One error was found in Level 2: LTL finds a counterexample for reachability, so the model may never reach osFinal. An infinite loop is possible, because osBody does not decrease any variant and does not modify any variables that affect its guards. Thus, we introduce a new boolean variable osBodyRun, initialize it with FALSE, and add the guard osBodyRun = FALSE and an action osBodyRun := TRUE. A similar error was found when entryNothingToSave was introduced, prompting us to make it convergent and create a variant as explained in Level 4.

Model checking Level 4 also revealed that the execution order of events as not as intended: one formula fails because we forgot to strengthen osManualEntry's guards to require it to only be enabled after all AUTODIRECTSAVE elements have been saved, as required by OS7. The new guard AUTODIRECTSAVE ∩ toSave = ∅ forces this order. Similarly, osAutoExit may only execute after all MANUALCTX is loaded (OS9), thus the new guard MANUALCTX ∩ toLoad = ∅ was introduced.

With these modifications to the models and the discharging of all proofs, we prove that the requirements are fulfilled and the model is correct.

8 Conclusion and Future Work

We have presented the first step in our approach towards portability of embedded RTOS based on formal methods and code generation. We have shown a generic formal RTOS model in Event-B with context switches that decouples low-level functionality from hardware specifics. This allows us to reuse the model and its proofs for several architectures. Then, we instantiated the model for two architectures and verified them via interactive theorem proving and model checking. The safety and liveness verification of the models (1) proved that the generic model and its instantiations do not corrupt task contexts by having them properly saved and loaded; (2) proved that the kernel and the tasks run in the appropriate CPU states and privilege levels by having them properly changed; (3) proved that the kernel executes in the correct order and finishes execution.

To the best of our knowledge, this is the first time that OS low-level functionality is formally modeled for portability and verification. With the target-specific models, we can already generate significant parts of the OS assembly code for the MSP430 and RISC-V architectures, however this is still an ongoing work. Besides the code generation and automatic porting of low-level code, we are also working on the modeling and verification of additional aspects in the OS, such as security, timing, and energy consumption.

There is still much to do to make automatic porting a reality: Among other issues, the effort of modeling is not negligible, specially for the average software developer, who often lacks a background in formal methods. Besides, the correctness proofs can only be as good as the model itself, so the modeling process must be thorough. Additionally, modeling and verifying an entire OS, including all its low-level components, will require considerable effort. Nevertheless, it has been proved that formal modeling in software improves its quality and can reduce costs. Furthermore, architectures with completely different concepts would require the model to be adapted. While the effort must still be investigated, the hardware requirements of our current model should be fulfilled by most modern architectures. For maintainability, specially for porting, we expect that it will not only be beneficial, but also crucial within the IoT. The effort invested in modeling can be mitigated by increasing the number of ports and partially replacing testing by verification for guaranteed dependability during the development process. Another issue we must mention is the time and computation power required for model checking. The axioms in the presented model already cause state explosion in ProB if all registers available in the target architectures are included, which prompted us to create a minimal set for model checking. With bigger and more complex models, even a minimal set will eventually not avoid state explosion. We hope that advances in formal methods will eventually solve this problem. Other methods, such as TLA+, Isabelle/HOL, and HOL4 are potentially suitable for the model presented in this work, and should be investigated in future works.

References

1. Abrial, J.R.: Modeling in Event-B: System and Software Engineering, 1st edn. Cambridge University Press, New York (2010)
2. Alkhammash, E.H., Butler, M.J., Cristea, C.: Modeling guidelines of FreeRTOS in Event-B. In: International Conference on Communication, Management and Information Technology, pp. 453–462. CRC Press (2017)
3. Baumann, C., Schwarz, O., Dam, M.: Compositional verification of security properties for embedded execution platforms. In: Kühne, U., Danger, J.L., Guilley, S. (eds.) 6th International Workshop on Security Proofs for Embedded Systems, PROOFS 2017. EPiC Series in Computing, vol. 49, pp. 1–16. EasyChair (2017). https://doi.org/10.29007/h4rv. https://easychair.org/publications/paper/wkp9

4. Boano, C.A., Römer, K., Bloem, R., Witrisal, K., Baunach, M., Horn, M.: Dependability for the Internet of Things–from dependable networking in harsh environments to a holistic view on dependability. e & i Elektrotechnik und Informationstechnik **133**(7), 304–309 (2016). https://doi.org/10.1007/s00502-016-0436-4
5. Borghorst, H., Bieling, K., Spinkczyk, O.: Towards versatile models for contemporary hardware platforms. In: 12th Annual Workshop on Operating Systems Platforms for Embedded Real-Time Applications, OSPERT 2016, pp. 7–9, July 2016
6. Brandenburg, B.B.: The case of an opinionated, theory-oriented real-time operating system. In: NGOSCPS 2019, April 2019
7. Cheng, S., Woodcock, J., D'Souza, D.: Using formal reasoning on a model of tasks for FreeRTOS. Formal Aspects Comput. **27**(1), 167–192 (2014). https://doi.org/10.1007/s00165-014-0308-9
8. Craig, I.D.: Formal Refinement for Operating System Kernels. Springer, London (2007). https://doi.org/10.1007/978-1-84628-967-5
9. Craig, I.D.: Formal Models of Operating System Kernels, 1st edn. Springer, London (2010). https://doi.org/10.1007/978-1-84628-718-3
10. Dalvandi, M., Butler, M., Rezazadeh, A., Salehi Fathabadi, A.: Verifiable code generation from scheduled Event-B models. In: Butler, M., Raschke, A., Hoang, T.S., Reichl, K. (eds.) ABZ 2018. LNCS, vol. 10817, pp. 234–248. Springer, Cham (2018). https://doi.org/10.1007/978-3-319-91271-4_16
11. Danmin, C., Yue, S., Zhiguo, C.: A formal specification in B of an operating system. Open Cybern. Syst. J. **9**(1) (2015)
12. Dhote, S., Charjan, P., Phansekar, A., Hegde, A., Joshi, S., Joshi, J.: Using FPGA-SoC interface for low cost IoT based image processing. In: 2016 International Conference on Advances in Computing, Communications and Informatics (ICACCI), pp. 1963–1968, September 2016. https://doi.org/10.1109/ICACCI.2016.7732339
13. Event-B: Event-B and the Rodin Platform. www.event-b.org
14. Fathabadi, A.S., et al.: A model-based framework for software portability and verification in embedded power management systems. J. Syst. Archit. **82**, 12–23 (2018). https://doi.org/10.1016/j.sysarc.2017.12.001. http://www.sciencedirect.com/science/article/pii/S1383762117305234
15. Frühwirth, T., Krammer, L., Kastner, W.: Dependability demands and state of the art in the internet of things. In: 2015 IEEE 20th Conference on Emerging Technologies Factory Automation (ETFA), pp. 1–4, September 2015. https://doi.org/10.1109/ETFA.2015.7301592
16. General Dynamics C4 Systems: The seL4 microkernel (2016). https://sel4.systems/. Accessed 05 Feb 2020
17. Gomes, R.M., Baunach, M., Malenko, M., Ribeiro, L.B., Mauroner, F.: A co-designed RTOS and MCU concept for dynamically composed embedded systems. In: OSPERT 2017 (2017)
18. Gomes, T., Pinto, S., Gomes, T., Tavares, A., Cabral, J.: Towards an FPGA-based edge device for the Internet of Things. In: 2015 IEEE 20th Conference on Emerging Technologies Factory Automation (ETFA), pp. 1–4, September 2015. https://doi.org/10.1109/ETFA.2015.7301601
19. Goranko, V., Galton, A.: Temporal logic. In: Zalta, E.N. (ed.) The Stanford Encyclopedia of Philosophy. Metaphysics Research Lab, Stanford University, winter 2015 edn. (2015). https://plato.stanford.edu/archives/win2015/entries/logic-temporal/
20. Hahm, O., Baccelli, E., Petersen, H., Tsiftes, N.: Operating systems for low-end devices in the Internet of Things: a survey. IEEE Internet Things J. **3**(5), 720–734 (2016). https://doi.org/10.1109/JIOT.2015.2505901

21. Hu, J., Lu, E., Holland, D.A., Kawaguchi, M., Chong, S., Seltzer, M.I.: Trials and tribulations in synthesizing operating systems. In: Proceedings of the 10th Workshop on Programming Languages and Operating Systems, PLOS 2019, pp. 67–73. Association for Computing Machinery, New York (2019). https://doi.org/10.1145/3365137.3365401
22. Texas Instruments: MSP430 ultra-low-power sensing and measurement MCUs (2019). http://www.ti.com/microcontrollers/msp430-ultra-low-power-mcus/overview/overview.html
23. Jastram, M., Butler, P.M.: Rodin User's Handbook: Covers Rodin vol. 2.8, USA (2014)
24. Klein, G., et al.: Comprehensive formal verification of an OS microkernel. ACM Trans. Comput. Syst. **32**(1) (2014). https://doi.org/10.1145/2560537
25. Lamport, L.: Proving the correctness of multiprocess programs. IEEE Trans. Softw. Eng. **SE-3**(2), 125–143 (1977). https://doi.org/10.1109/TSE.1977.229904
26. Leuschel, M., Butler, M.: ProB: an automated analysis toolset for the B method. Int. J. Softw. Tools Technol. Transf. **10**(2), 185–203 (2008). https://doi.org/10.1007/s10009-007-0063-9
27. Manna, Z., Pnueli, A.: The Temporal Logic of Reactive and Concurrent Systems: Specification. Springer, New York (2012). https://doi.org/10.1007/978-1-4612-0931-7
28. Méry, D.: Modelling by patterns for correct-by-construction process. In: Margaria, T., Steffen, B. (eds.) ISoLA 2018. LNCS, vol. 11244, pp. 399–423. Springer, Cham (2018). https://doi.org/10.1007/978-3-030-03418-4_24
29. Novikov, E., Zakharov, I.: Verification of operating system monolithic kernels without extensions. In: Margaria, T., Steffen, B. (eds.) ISoLA 2018. LNCS, vol. 11247, pp. 230–248. Springer, Cham (2018). https://doi.org/10.1007/978-3-030-03427-6_19
30. Pnueli, A.: The temporal logic of programs. In: 18th Annual Symposium on Foundations of Computer Science, SFCS 1977, pp. 46–57, October 1977. https://doi.org/10.1109/SFCS.1977.32
31. Popp, M., Moreira, O., Yedema, W., Lindwer, M.: Automatic HAL generation for embedded multiprocessor systems. In: Proceedings of the 13th International Conference on Embedded Software, EMSOFT 2016, ACM, New York (2016). https://doi.org/10.1145/2968478.2968493
32. RISC-V Foundation: RISC-V. https://riscv.org/
33. Stoddart, B., Cansell, D., Zeyda, F.: Modelling and proof analysis of interrupt driven scheduling. In: Julliand, J., Kouchnarenko, O. (eds.) B 2007. LNCS, vol. 4355, pp. 155–170. Springer, Heidelberg (2006). https://doi.org/10.1007/11955757_14
34. Su, W., Abrial, J.R., Pu, G., Fang, B.: Formal development of a real-time operating system memory manager. In: 2015 20th International Conference on Engineering of Complex Computer Systems (ICECCS). IEEE, December 2015. https://doi.org/10.1109/iceccs.2015.24
35. Syeda, H.T., Klein, G.: Formal reasoning under cached address translation. J. Autom. Reason. **64**, 911–945 (2020). https://doi.org/10.1007/s10817-019-09539-7
36. Taivalsaari, A., Mikkonen, T.: A roadmap to the programmable world: software challenges in the IoT era. IEEE Softw. **34**(1), 72–80 (2017). https://doi.org/10.1109/MS.2017.26
37. Verhulst, E., Boute, R.T., Faria, J.M.S., Sputh, B., Mezhuyev, V.: Formal Development of a Network-Centric RTOS. Springer, Boston (2011). https://doi.org/10.1007/978-1-4419-9736-4

38. Waterman, A., Asanović, K.: The RISC-V instruction set manual volume I: user-level ISA version 2.2, May 2017. https://riscv.org/specifications
39. Waterman, A., Lee, Y., Avizienis, R., Patterson, D.A., Asanović, K.: The RISC-V instruction set manual volume II: privileged architecture version 1.7. Technical report UCB/EECS-2015-49, EECS Department, University of California, Berkeley, May 2015. http://www2.eecs.berkeley.edu/Pubs/TechRpts/2015/EECS-2015-49.html
40. Wright, S.: Formal construction of instruction set architectures. Ph.D. thesis, University of Bristol (2009). http://www.cs.bris.ac.uk/Publications/Papers/2001121.pdf
41. Wright, S.: Automatic generation of C from Event-B. In: Workshop on Integration of Model-Based Formal Methods and Tools, p. 14 (2009)

Model-Based Testing Under Parametric Variability of Uncertain Beliefs

Matteo Camilli$^{(\boxtimes)}$ (iD) and Barbara Russo (iD)

Faculty of Computer Science, Free University of Bozen-Bolzano, Bolzano, Italy
{mcamilli,brusso}@unibz.it

Abstract. Modern software systems operate in complex and changing environments and are exposed to multiple sources of uncertainty. Considering uncertainty as a first-class concern in software testing is currently on an uptrend. This paper introduces a novel methodology to deal with testing under uncertainty. Our proposal combines the usage of parametric model checking at design-time and online model-based testing algorithms to gather runtime evidence and detect requirements violations. As modeling formalism, we adopt parametric Markov Decision Processes where transition probabilities are not fixed, but are possibly given as a set of uncertain parameters. The design-time phase aims at analyzing the parameter space to identify the constraints for requirements satisfaction. Then, the testing activity applies a Bayesian inference process to identify violations of pre-computed constraints. An extensive empirical evaluation shows that the proposed technique is effective in discovering violations and is cheaper than existing testing under uncertainty methods.

Keywords: Model-based Testing · Parametric Markov Decision Processes · Uncertainty analysis · Bayesian inference

1 Introduction

Modern software-intensive systems are often situated in complex ecosystems that can be hard or even impossible to fully understand and precisely describe at design-time. Nevertheless, unreliable or unpredictable software behavior cannot be tolerated as society increasingly depends on it. For this reason, there exists the increasing need for systematic approaches to deal with incomplete knowledge and sources of uncertainty while engineering complex systems. Endowing conventional software engineering methodologies with techniques and practices able to model, quantify, and mitigate uncertainty is becoming increasingly crucial [1]. In particular, research effort in techniques that explicitly consider uncertain expected behavior in software testing is currently on an evident uptrend (e.g., see [2–5]).

This paper introduces a novel methodology to deal with uncertainty quantification by combining parametric model checking [6] at design-time and online (or on-the-fly) Model-based Testing (MBT) algorithms [7,8]. MBT is a software

© Springer Nature Switzerland AG 2020
F. de Boer and A. Cerone (Eds.): SEFM 2020, LNCS 12310, pp. 175–192, 2020.
https://doi.org/10.1007/978-3-030-58768-0_10

testing technique where run-time behavior of a software System Under Test (SUT) is checked against a formal model describing the system's behavior [7]. Our MBT approach allows the design-time probabilistic model to be underspecified. Namely, the modeler can explicitly represent partial knowledge on the SUT by means of uncertain model parameters in a Markov Decision Process (MDP). Parametric model checking is used to verify design-time requirements under variability of uncertain model parameters. The outcome of this stage is a mapping from regions of these parameters to truth values encoding the verification conditions to be evaluated at runtime. Thus, our MBT approach leverages these conditions to drive the testing activity by maximizing the probability to hit the uncertain components of the SUT multiple times. The objective of the MBT phase is to gather runtime evidence over uncertain model parameters using a Bayesian inference approach [9]. Thus, the MBT spots requirements violations by comparing the incremental posterior knowledge and the pre-computed verification conditions on uncertain parameters. The whole methodology is supported by a software toolchain whose core component is a MBT module which integrates test case generation, execution and evaluation. The MBT module makes use of fine grained characteristics of the uncertain model parameters to reduce the effort required by testing. The design-time analysis of the region space of uncertain parameters (i.e., the outcome of the parametric model checker) is leveraged to detect requirements violations and decide over termination.

To illustrate our approach we make use of an existing open-source case study called SafeHome. It represents an exemplar of Cyber Physical Systems (CPSs) borrowed from [5]. We conducted an empirical evaluation to study the cost-effectiveness of our testing method by varying the number of uncertain parameters and the distance between actual values and verification conditions. We also compared our approach with selected existing MBT methods, pointing out advantages and threats to validity.

The major contribution of this paper can be summarized as follows:

i. description of our methodology to MBT under parametric variability of uncertain beliefs;
ii. extensive evaluation to assess the cost-effectiveness of our approach and comparison with existing testing methods.

Our empirical evaluation shows that the whole methodology is effective to spot requirements violations with bounded effort. Furthermore, the developed MBT method outperforms existing MBT strategies.

The remainder of this article is structured as follows. Section 2 introduces a preview of our methodology. Section 3 recalls the necessary background concepts. Section 4 presents a running example (i.e., the SafeHome system), used throughout the article to illustrate the main phases of the methodology. Section 5 introduces a formal treatment of our approach. Section 6 reports our evaluation and discusses threats to validity. Section 7 describes related work. Section 8 concludes the paper.

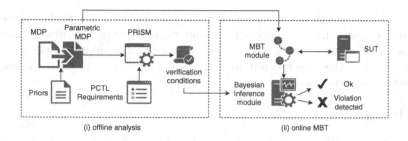

Fig. 1. High-level schema of our approach.

2 Preview of the Approach

In this work we focus on systems modeled as MDPs and quantitative requirements expressed using Probabilistic Computation Tree Logic (PCTL) [10]. MDPs represent a widely accepted formalism to model and verify software system dependability (e.g., reliability, availability, safety) [11]. Recent research activities show also the effective usage of MDPs in testing probabilistic systems [2]. As described in [12], models developed at design-time are often subject to sources of uncertainty. Namely, certain behaviors of the system itself and the surrounding environment are hard to predict. For instance, the success probability of a software task, or the failure rate of a hardware device (represented by transitions in the MDP) may be hard to specify in a complete and accurate way. So, to deal with uncertainty, our approach gives the modeler the ability of representing partial knowledge (i.e., beliefs) on transition probabilities by means of Prior probability density functions [9], or simply Priors. On top of these assumptions, we informally introduce here the two main phases of the approach (see Fig. 1): (*i*) offline analysis; and (*ii*) online MBT.

The offline analysis (or pre-computation) aims at studying the parameter space. We leverage the parametric model checking functionality of PRISM [6] to analyze how parameters affect the satisfaction of PCTL requirements. The Prior density functions are used to mechanically build a parametric MDP model and the search space of each individual uncertain parameter. The result of the model checker is a mapping from regions of these parameters to truth values (i.e., either true or false with respect to requirements satisfaction). It is worth noting that model checking is computationally expensive and requires exhaustive exploration of the model's state space to analyze arbitrarily complex properties [13]. Since the computational cost of model-checking may be prohibitive for online usage, we keep this pre-computation separated as an offline phase, where we can execute demanding activities without interfering with the system operation. The outcome of the pre-computation encodes verification conditions to be satisfied to meet the requirements. Thus, the online MBT phase performs a controlled exploration of the SUT by using an uncertainty-aware test case generation strategy. Such a strategy leverages the structural characteristics of the model to direct the effort towards transitions associated with uncertain parameters. In other words, we aim at concentrating on those components of the SUT whose behavior is subject to sources of uncertainty. The MBT feeds a Bayesian inference process that computes the actual value of uncertain model parameters based on the evidence gathered during testing. The actual values are then checked against the (pre-computed) verification conditions to detect violations of design-time requirements.

3   Background

This section recalls required background notions to understand the formal aspects of the approach we developed. In the following we briefly revisit parametric MDPs, the quantitative temporal logic PCTL, and Bayesian Inference. For a complete treatment we let the reader refer to [9,11,14].

3.1   Parametric Markov Decision Processes

Let θ be a finite set of variables. Let $\mathbb{Q}[\theta]$ denote the set of all rational-coefficient polynomial functions (i.e., a sum of terms, where each term is given by a coefficient and a monomial). A parametric Markov Decision Process (pMDP) $\mathcal{M}$ is a tuple $(S, \theta, A, s_0, \delta, AP, L)$ where S is a (finite) set of states, θ is a finite set of parameters, A is an alphabet of actions, $s_0 \in S$ is the initial state, and $\delta : S \times A \times S \to \mathbb{Q}[\theta] \cup [0,1]$ is the partial probabilistic transition function, AP is a set of atomic propositions, $L : S \to 2^{AP}$ is a labeling function that associates to each state the set of atomic propositions that are true in that state. State transitions occur in two steps: a nondeterministic choice among available actions; and a stochastic choice of the successor state according to δ. In the rest of the paper, the notation $p_{i,j}^a$ will be used as short form for $\delta(s_i, a, s_j)$. The function $A(s_i)$ is used to denote the actions in A available from the state s_i.

Note that a parameter-free pMDP coincides with standard MDP, as defined in [11]. A MDP can be obtained from a pMDP by simply assigning values to parameters. Formally, we need to create an *instantiation val* : $\theta \to \mathbb{R}$ s.t. the δ function is well-defined, i.e., $\sum_{s_j \in S} p_{i,j}^a = 1$ for all $s_i \in S$ and $a \in A(s_i)$. In the following we use $\mathcal{M}[val]$ to denote the MDP obtained from the pMDP $\mathcal{M}$ with instantiation *val*.

Both MDP and pMDP models can be augmented with *rewards* to quantify a benefit (or loss) due to the occurrence of a certain transitions. A reward usually represents non-functional aspects such as average execution time, power consumption or usability. Rewards are formally specified by using the notion of *reward structure*, i.e., a function $r : S \times A \times S \to \mathbb{R}$. Given a standard MDP and a reward structure r, a deterministic policy π specifies for each state s_i the action $\pi(s_i) \in A(s_i)$ chosen by a decision maker to solve nondeterminism. The notion of *best policy* π^* refers to the policy able to maximize the expected cumulated reward over a potentially infinite horizon. The best policy can be computed solving the following Bellman's Eq. 1 using dynamic programming approaches as reported in [11].

$$\pi^*(s_i) = \arg\max_{a \in A(s_i)} \sum_j p_{i,j}^a \cdot (r_{i,j}^a + \gamma V^*(s_j)) \tag{1}$$

where $V^*(s_j)$ represents the expected cumulated reward when starting from s_j and acting optimally along a infinite horizon; $\gamma \in [0,1]$ is a discount factor that alleviates the contribution of future rewards in favor of present rewards.

3.2   Probabilistic Computation Tree Logic

To specify requirements of interest we consider here the logic PCTL. The syntax supports the definition of state formulas ϕ and path formulas ψ, which are evaluated over states and paths, respectively. Formally, a formula is defined as follows:

$$\phi ::= \text{true} \mid a \mid \phi \wedge \phi \mid \neg\phi \mid \mathcal{P}{\bowtie}p[\psi], \quad \psi ::= \mathtt{X}\phi \mid \phi \ \mathtt{U} \ \phi, \tag{2}$$

where $a \in AP$ and a path formula ψ is used as the parameter of the *probabilistic path operator* $\mathcal{P}{\bowtie}p[\psi]$, such that ${\bowtie} \in \{\leq, <, \geq, >\}$ and $p \in [0,1]$ is a probability bound. The symbol $\mathtt{X}$ represents the *next* operator, $\mathtt{U}$ is the *until* operator. The operators $\mathtt{G}$ (i.e., *globally*) and $\mathtt{F}$ (i.e., *eventually*) can be derived from the previous ones as for CTL. A state $s \in S$ satisfies $\mathcal{P}{\bowtie}p[\psi]$ if, under any nondeterministic choice, the probability of taking a path from s satisfying ψ is in the interval specified by ${\bowtie}p$.

Parametric model checking [14] is a verification technique able to analyze the parametric variability of a pMDP model $\mathcal{M}$ and determine how such a variability affects the satisfaction of a set of target PCTL properties. Formally, the outcome of the model checker is a mapping between *hyper-rectangles* and truth values, where an hyper-rectangle is a multidimensional rectangle $h = \bigtimes_{x \in \theta}[l_x, u_x]$ with $l_x, u_x \in \mathbb{R}$ lower- and upper-bound for parameter x, respectively. Intuitively, for each *true* hyper-rectangle h, the model $\mathcal{M}[val]$ satisfies the properties iff $val(x) \in [l_x, u_x]$ for all $x \in \theta$.

3.3   Bayesian Inference

Bayesian inference [15] really comes into its own in domains where uncertainty must be taken into account. The main goal is to learn about one or more uncertain/unknown parameters θ affecting the behavior of a stochastic phenomenon of interest. The Prior knowledge (i.e., initial hypothesis or belief) of θ is incrementally updated based on a collected data sample $y = (y_1, y_2, \ldots, y_n)$ describing the actual behavior of the target phenomenon. By using Bayes' theorem we obtain the Posterior distribution $f(\theta|y)$, describing the best knowledge of θ, given the evidence y.

$$f(\theta|y) \propto f(\theta) \cdot f(y|\theta) \tag{3}$$

The density $f(y|\theta)$ is usually referred to as the likelihood function and represents the compatibility of the data with the hypothesis. The hypothesis is often available from external sources such as expert information based on past experience or previous studies. This information is encoded by the Prior distribution $f(\theta)$. The posterior distribution can be used in turn to perform point and interval estimation. Point estimation is typically addressed in the multivariate case,

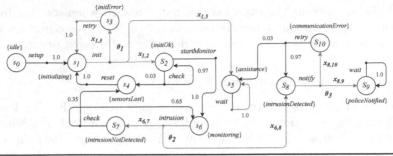

Fig. 2. MDP model of the SafeHome system.

by summarizing the distribution through the Posterior mean $E[f(\theta|y)]$ and the (95%) Highest Density Region $\text{HDR}[f(\theta|y)]$, defined as follows.

$$E[f(\theta|y)] = \int \theta \cdot f(\theta|y)d\theta, \quad \text{HDR}[f(\theta|y)] = \{\theta : f(\theta|y) \geq 0.95\} \quad (4)$$

The magnitude of the HDR region yields the highest possible accuracy in the estimation of the true value of θ and is usually adopted as a measure of the confidence gained after the inference process. In Bayesian statistics, it represents the credible region within which parameter values fall with probability 0.95.

4 A Running Example: The SafeHome System

The SafeHome security system represents an open-source benchmarking example in charge of controlling and configuring alarms and related sensors that implement a number of security and safety features such as intrusion detection. For the sake of readability, here we use an extract of the whole SafeHome by emphasizing the relevant characteristics for our problem domain. We let the reader refer to [5] for a comprehensive description.

Figure 2 shows the high-level behavior of the system through a pMDP model. The system behavior exhibits three main phases: *initialization, monitoring* and *alarm*, in charge of sensor initialization, detection, and alarm handling, respectively. From state s_2 the SafeHome system tries to initialize all the available sensors by executing the action *init*. If the task succeeds, the sensors are correctly registered and the action *startMonitoring* can be executed to proceed towards the *monitoring* and then *alarm* phase. According to [4], sources of uncertainty in CPSs affect the behavior of the SUT at different levels: *application* level, due to events/data originating from software components running upon physical units of the CPS; *infrastructure* level, due to data transmission through networking

Table 1. PCTL requirement examples for the SafeHome system.

Id	Type	Description	PCTL definition
R_1	Global reliability	The probability of reaching a state where assistance is required is less than 0.05	$P_{<0.05}$ [F $assistance$]
R_2	Sensors availability	The probability of observing operable sensors without failures is greater than 0.9	$P_{>0.9}$ [!$sensorsLost$ U $sensorsOk$]
R_3	Network reliability	If sensors are operable, the probability of eventually notifying the emergency unit is greater than 0.98	$sensorsOk \rightarrow P_{>0.98}$ [F $policeNotified$]

and/or cloud infrastructure; *integration* level, due to interactions among physical units at either application level or infrastructure levels. For instance, consider the following common scenario in our target system. When the system is in state s_6 (i.e., *monitoring* holds), sensors can send the *intrusion* trigger to the security system that eventually causes a notification to be sent to an external emergency service (i.e., *policeNotified* state). However, the intrusion detection is affected by uncertainty at integration level. In fact, this capability is conditioned by the way sensors interact and their individual ability of correctly sensing the physical environment. Thus, the action *intrusion* leads to either state s_8 (i.e., the intrusion has been sensed) or state s_7 (i.e., the intrusion has not been sensed) with a substantial degree of uncertainty. This uncertain outcome is explicitly represented by uncertain parameters (i.e., $x_{6,8}$ and $x_{6,7}$, respectively). The uncertain parameters associated with a state-action pair is called *uncertain region* and we denote it as θ_i. The disjoint union of all θ_i is θ (i.e., the set of uncertain parameters). Figure 2 lists all the uncertain regions in SafeHome and affected levels.

Table 1 lists some requirements for our example, formally specified using PCTL. It is worth noting that the ability of satisfying these requirements depends on the actual value of model parameters. Figure 2 contains initial (uncertain) beliefs on these parameters.

5 The Testing Framework

This section illustrates the whole testing framework. The presentation is partitioned into two main fragments, reflecting the two main phases of our proposal.

5.1 Offline Analysis

The tester specifies the SUT behavior through a pMDP model (e.g., the Safe-Home model in Fig. 2). The uncertain values of each region θ_i are formally defined by a k-dimensional *categorical* distribution [9], with k the number of target states from the state-action (s, a) identified by θ_i. For instance, the region θ_1

is defined by the density function $Cat(x_{1,2}, x_{1,3}, x_{1,5})$, describing the distribution of transition probabilities from s_1 to s_2, s_3, and s_5, respectively, when the action *init* is chosen. As described in [9], the natural conjugate Prior of a categorical distribution is the *Dirichlet* distribution (i.e., a multivariate generalization of the *Beta*). For instance, the mdoeler specifies the Prior knowledge of θ_1 by using either a non-informative Prior $Dir(1, 1, 1)$, or a informative one, such as:

$$f(\theta_1) = Dir(47, 2, 1) \tag{5}$$

when past experience is available. In this latter case, the Prior has been built based on 50 past observations as follows: $47 \cdot s_2$, $2 \cdot s_3$, and $1 \cdot s_5$.

The Prior knowledge specification provides the baseline for further offline and online analysis. The initial guess for the uncertain parameters (e.g., values assigned to parameters in Fig. 2) is automatically extracted by summarizing the Priors through the mean values. The 95% HDR is used instead of computing the range of possible values for each parameter in θ. Thus, we leverage this information to limit the search space only to those values that are credible with respect to the given beliefs. For instance, given the informative Prior defined in Eq. 5, the HDR sets the following bounds.

$$HDR[f(\theta_1)] = x_{1,2} \in [0.87, 0.99], x_{1,3} \in [0.00, 0.09], x_{1,5} \in [0.00, 0.05] \tag{6}$$

Since the Dirichlet is multivariate, the HDR is composed of a number of intervals, one for each parameter.

It is worth noting that the HDR of each marginal distribution of a Dirichlet (i.e., univariate Beta distribution) is instead a single interval defining the bounds of each individual parameter. In the rest of the paper we will use $HDR[f_x(\cdot)]$ to denote the HDR of the marginalized $f(\cdot)$ by retaining the variable x. For instance, considering the Prior of θ_1 introduced in Eq. 5, the following holds.

$$HDR[Dir_{x_{1,2}}(\cdot)] = [0.87, 0.99] \tag{7}$$

After computing the HDR of each Prior, we execute the parametric model checking functionality of PRISM to obtain the hyper-rectangles that meet the desired PCTL requirements (e.g., SafeHome properties in Table 1). In our running example, the outcome of this activity is a set of *true* hyper-rectangles $\{h_1, \ldots, h_n\}$ encoding verification condition for the SafeHome. Each element h_i is composed of a number of closed intervals, one for each uncertain parameter.

5.2 Online Model-Based Testing

As anticipated in Sect. 5, the online phase takes as input the model and the hyper-rectangles to carry out the testing activity. The online MBT aims at exploring the SUT in a controlled way by directing the effort towards the uncertain model regions.

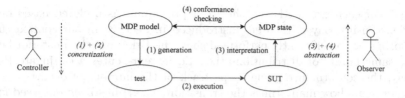

Fig. 3. Conformance game iteration.

Conformance Game. Figure 3 shows the main steps of the whole iterative approach. The idea originally introduced in [7] is to view the SUT as a black box and distinguish between *controllable* behavior from the tester (i.e., inputs or more in general external stimuli from the environment) and *observable* behavior from the running software system (i.e., outputs or more in general an observable stimulus'response). The Controller and the Observer components execute a *conformance game* [2,7] until the *termination condition* is met. The game starts from the initial state of the MDP model and, for each step, the controller chooses an available action in $A(s)$ from the current state s, depending on the adopted test case generation strategy. The generation step (1) translates the action to a controllable behavior to reach the same level of abstraction of the SUT. Intuitively, the chosen action maps to a valid input provided by using a service exposed by the SUT APIs. At this point, the external stimulus is provided to the SUT (2) that reacts in turn by exposing an observable outcome. Thus, the observer evaluates (3) the outcome and interprets it to determine the target model state s' in order to reach again the level of abstraction of the MDP. Here the evaluation is conducted by means of a post-condition function mapping to model states. This way, we can determine the target state s' s.t. the post-condition, evaluated on the observed outcome, holds. The last step is the conformance checking (4) that verifies whether the obtained outcome is feasible in the sense of the formal specification. Formally, the above steps are used to verify the existence of a *conformance relation* between the model and the SUT. The conformance relation is formalized in turn by leveraging the notions of *probabilistic alternating simulation* and *refinement*, as described in [16]. A comprehensive theoretical discussion of these aspects is not part of the contribution of this paper, so we let the reader refer to [16] for further details.

Bayesian Inference Module. Besides the conformance game, the Observer component feeds a Bayesian inference process (see Sect. 3) to calibrate the uncertain model parameters based on the gathered evidence by testing. An overview on the statistical machinery used to perform this activity follows. Formally, we let the parameters of the categorical distribution describing θ_i be defined by a Dirichlet Prior as follows:

$$(x_{i,j}, \ldots, x_{i,k}) \sim Dir(\alpha_i), \text{ with } \alpha_i = (\alpha_{i,j}, \ldots, \alpha_{i,k}) \tag{8}$$

Values in α_i are the hyper-parameters of the Prior. Based on this formulation, we can learn the uncertain parameters by belief monitoring during the testing process. For each executed test, the Prior probability is updated based on the experience using Bayes' theorem instroduced in Sect. 3. In our context, belief monitoring can be efficiently performed since the Prior and the Posterior belong to the same family of distributions (i.e., Eq. 8 representes a conjugate Prior). Namely, the conformance game keeps track of the number of occurrences $n_{i,j}$ that represents how many times the transition (s_i, s_j) has been observed for all θ_i and uncertain parameter $x_{i,j}$. Thus, given a sequence of observations y (i.e., the runtime evidence), the Posterior is defined as follows.

$$(x_{i,j}, \ldots, x_{i,k})|y \sim Dir(\alpha_i'), \text{ with } \alpha_i' = (\alpha_{i,j} + n_{i,j}, \ldots, \alpha_{i,k} + n_{i,k}) \quad (9)$$

For instance, considering the SafeHome system, we can compute the Posterior of θ_1 by updating the hyper-parameters $\alpha_1' = (47 + 93, 2 + 2, 1 + 5)$ if we observe: $93 \cdot s_2$, $2 \cdot s_3$, and $5 \cdot s_5$, as outcome of 100 invocations of the action *init* from state s_1. By summarizing the Posterior with the HDR we obtain the following updated bounds.

$$
\begin{aligned}
HDR[f(\theta_1)] &= x_{1,2} \in [0.87, 0.99], x_{1,3} \in [0.00, 0.09], x_{1,5} \in [0.00, 0.05] \\
HDR[f(\theta_1|y)] &= x_{1,2} \in [0.89, 0.97], x_{1,3} \in [0.00, 0.05], x_{1,5} \in [0.01, 0.07]
\end{aligned}
\quad (10)
$$

Uncertainty-Aware Test Case Generation. We introduce here the test case generation strategy used by our online MBT algorithm. This strategy leverages the notion of *uncertainty-aware* reward structure, motivated by the practical need of identifying those actions that increase the likelihood of testing uncertain regions (i.e., transitions annotated with uncertain parameters). In fact, our goal is to equip MBT with the ability of stressing the uncertain components of the SUT. The uncertainty-aware reward structure is formally defined as follows.

Definition 1 (uncertainty-aware reward structure). *Given a pMDP model* $\mathcal{M}$, *an uncertain region* θ_i, *and two numeric values* $r_h, r_l \in \mathbb{N}_{>0}$ *s.t.* $r_h \gg r_l$, *the* uncertainty-*aware reward structure* u *is defined as follows:*

$$
u_{i,j}^a = \begin{cases} r_h & p_{i,j}^a > 0 \text{ and } \exists \theta_i \text{ for } (s_i, a) \\ r_l & otherwise \end{cases}
$$

The rationale is to assign a high reward r_h to transitions associated to uncertain parameters and a low reward r_l elsewhere. Then we use the *uncertainty-aware* reward structure to automatically compute the best exploration policy (Eq. 1) that maximizes the expected cumulated uncertainty-aware rewards. Intuitively, given θ_i, the best policy π_i^* drives a decision maker optimally towards the uncertain model region θ_i.

Indeed, multiple uncertain regions determine alternative testing scenarios targeting different portions of the model. The way we sample from available choices (i.e., actions provided by alternative best policies) determines the whole test case generation strategy. Our strategy provides control over test scenarios during MBT based on a probabilistic function as defined below.

Definition 2 (HDR-aware strategy). *Given a pMDP model $\mathcal{M}$ a set of uncertain regions $\theta_1, \ldots, \theta_k$ and related best policies $\pi_1^*, \ldots, \pi_k^*$, the HDR-aware test case generation strategy is defined by the following partial probabilistic function:*

$$P(a|s) = \begin{cases} 0 & \omega(s, a') = 0 \\ \omega(s, a) / \sum_{a' \in A(s)} \omega(s, a') & otherwise \end{cases} \quad (11)$$

where ω represents a per-state weight function that maps a state and an action to a value in $\mathbb{R}_{\geq 0}$ such that:

$$\omega(s, a) = \max_{i:\pi_i^*(s)=a} \|HDR[f(\theta_i|y)]\| \quad (12)$$

Intuitively, the weight function selectively increases or decreases the probability of certain actions based on the magnitude of the Posteriors associated with uncertain regions. As anticipated in Sect. 3, Bayesian statistics uses the magnitude of the HDR as a measure of the degree of confidence in the inference process: the smaller the magnitude, the higher the confidence. Thus, here we leverage this measure to selectively increase the probability of actions that drive testing towards regions associated with a lower degree of confidence.

Termination Condition. Our approach uses the ability of detecting violation of requirements to build the termination condition for the online MBT algorithm. In particular, since the testing activity incrementally builds the Posterior knowledge of each θ_i, we can iteratively compare the summarization of the Posteriors and the (pre-computed) hyper-rectangles encoding verification conditions. Thus, the termination of the MBT can be formalized by means of the following two alternative cases.

Definition 3 (Successful run). *Given a pMDP $\mathcal{M}$, a set of hyper-rectangles H, and the Posterior $f(\theta_i|y)$ for all i, we say that the MBT is succesful iff there exists $h \in H$, $[l_x, u_x] \in h$ s.t. $[l_x, u_x] \supseteq HDR[f_x(\theta_i|y)]$ for all i and $x \in \theta_i$.*

Definition 4 (Failing run). *Given a pMDP $\mathcal{M}$, a set of hyper-rectangles H, and the Posterior $f(\theta_i|y)$ for all i, we say that the MBT is failing iff for all $h \in H$ there exists i, $x \in \theta_i$ s.t. $[l_x, h_x] \cap HDR[f_x(\theta_i|y)] = \emptyset$, with $[l_x, h_x] \in h$.*

The intuitive meaning of these two cases follows. The testing activity can terminate by either confirming that requirements are met (i.e., successful run) or identifying violated requirements (i.e., failing run) based on the observed evidence. In the first case, the Posterior knowledge tells that the model $\mathcal{M}[val]$ satisfies requirements for all instantiation val constructed by using the Posteriors' HDR. In fact, all the values that can be drawn from the HDRs meet the pre-computed verification conditions. In the latter case, the verification conditions cannot be satisfied because the HDR identifies disjoint intervals with respect to pre-computed hyper-rectangles.

It is worth noting that Definition 3 and Definition 4 identify two disjoint conditions. Furthermore, termination by satisfying one of the two conditions is always guaranteed because of the asymptotic behavior of the Posterior in the limit of infinite observations. Loosely, if consistent estimates are available, then Bayesian inference is consistent [17]. Moreover, the Posterior converges to a distribution independent of the initial Prior if the random variable in consideration has a finite probability space [18].

6   Empirical Evaluation

We introduce our research questions and design of the evaluation in Sect. 6.1; we present the results in Sect. 6.2; we finally discuss threats to validity in Sect. 6.3.

6.1   Research Questions and Design

The main goal of the evaluation is to investigate the cost-effectiveness of our testing method. The cost (or effort) refers to the number of tests required to achieve termination. The effectiveness here represents the ability of identifying requirements violations. Thus, we aim at answering three research questions:

RQ1: Is the approach able to detect requirements violations?
RQ2: What is the cost required by our testing method to achieve termination?
RQ3: How does our approach compare with existing MBT methods in terms of cost-effectiveness?

We addressed these questions by conducting an extensive testing campaign using different versions of the SafeHome as SUT. In particular, we considered variations taking control over two main factors of interest: *degree of uncertainty* in terms of percentage of uncertain model parameters (varying from 25% to 100%); and *distance* between actual values of model parameters and verification conditions given by hyper-rectangles (varying from 0.01 to 0.16). We have tested each version of the SUT by using the approach presented in this paper and we compared its cost-effectiveness with a traditional *Random* MBT approach [19], and also an existing *uncertainty*-aware MBT method called *Flat* [16].

For all experiments, we measured the number of tests spent for each uncertain region (i.e., the cost) and the failure detection capability (i.e., the effectiveness). Hereafter we discuss the most relevant results and we refer the reader to our implementation and dataset for the replicability of the experiments[1].

6.2   Results

Results for RQ1. We addressed this question by assessing the ability of exhibiting failing runs when the actual values of uncertain parameters fall outside the boundaries of the hyper-rectangles. Thus, we took control over actual values and hyper-rectangles and then we executed the HDR-aware MBT 100 times for each

---

[1] The MBT module is open source software publicly available at https://github.com/SELab-unimi/mbt-module. A replication package of the experiments is available at https://github.com/SELab-unimi/sefm2020-replication-package.

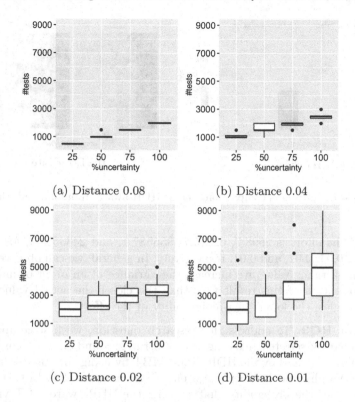

(a) Distance 0.08

(b) Distance 0.04

(c) Distance 0.02

(d) Distance 0.01

Fig. 4. Effort by varying the distance and the degree of uncertainty.

combination of degree of uncertainty, distance, and truth value (i.e., either true or false w.r.t. requirements violation). From the results, we observe that, in all cases, the process effectively returns the expected outcome with bounded effort. Namely, the MBT process terminated with no more than 9000 tests, representing the effort value measured in the worst case (i.e., 100% uncertainty and 0.01 distance). Further details on the evaluation of the effort follow.

Results for RQ2. Figure 4 shows the effort required by the HDR-aware MBT. Each box-plot has been built considering 100 runs for each degree of uncertainty and a specific distance value. Since the case "0.16 distance" is comparable to the 0.08 one, it has been omitted. From the data reported by each individual plot, we observe that the effort increases linearly with the degree of uncertainty. Namely, for each distance value we assessed the existence of a linear dependency between degree of uncertainty and number of tests with correlation value greater than 0.5. The slope of the estimated lines varies from 16.4 to 37.5. The shorter the distance the steeper the growth. This means that parameters close to hyper-rectangle borders are likely to increase the effort when the number of uncertain parameters increases. Furthermore, we observe that the variability of the effort values increases when reducing the distance value. The average

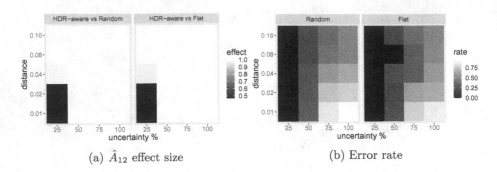

(a) $\hat{A}_{12}$ effect size   (b) Error rate

Fig. 5. Effectiveness comparison among HDR-aware, Random, and Flat.

variance of the effort is 2998.7, 62815.7, 355587.1, and 2433554.3, for distance values 0.08, 0.04, 0.02, and 0.01, respectively. In general, we can observe that by halving the distance value, we increase the variance of an order of magnitude. The interpretation of this result tells that the closer the actual values to the hyper-rectangles, the lower the predictability of the effort.

Results for RQ3. To address this research question, we first computed the effort required by selected (existing) MBT strategies and then we compared it with the effort required by the HDR-aware MBT by using the standardized non-parametric Vargha and Delaney's $\hat{A}_{12}$ effect size measure [20]. In this context, the $\hat{A}_{12}$ encodes the probability that running the HDR-aware MBT yields less effort than the Random and the Flat MBT strategies. Figure 5a shows a heat map of the effect size by varying uncertainty and distance factors. The two plots refer to the pairwise comparisons: HDR-aware versus Random (left); and HDR-aware versus Flat (right). Data shows that Random and Flat are similar, i.e., the $\hat{A}_{12}$ effect size values are comparable. In general, the probability of observing less effort when adopting the HDR-aware MBT is high. It represents the certain event for almost all cases. We observe outliers when the degree of uncertainty is low (25%) and the distance is short (less than 0.04). In this settings, all the strategies (HDR-aware, Random, and Flat) are likely to exhibit the same effort.

The effectiveness has been assessed by executing all the selected strategies by assuming the same total amount of effort. Namely, we fixed the limit according to the maximum effort required by the HDR-aware method. The rationale is to execute both Random and Flat by using an effort value that ensures termination of the HDR-aware method with the correct outcome. At the end of each execution we summarized the Posteriors to determine whether the run succeeded or failed with respect to pre-computed hyper-rectangles. Thus, we counted the number of wrong outcomes to measure the verification error rate when using either Random or Flat instead of HDR-aware. Figure 5b shows a heat map of the error rate by varying uncertainty and distance factors. The two plots refer to the errors obtained by using: Random (left); and Flat (right). Data shows that both approaches are likely to terminate by exhibiting a wrong outcome. Thus, the effectiveness of both Random and Flat is lower w.r.t. the HDR-aware method. The two plots show a comparable pattern: the error rate increases when the distance decreases and the uncertain parameters increase. In both cases we observe the worst effectiveness values with distance equal to 0.01 and uncertainty equal to 100%. In this setting, the error rate values are 0.96 and 0.90 for Random and Flat methods, respectively.

6.3   Threats to Validity

To limit threats to *external validity* we conducted a testing campaign on several versions of the SafeHome by taking control and detailing the important factors of interest (i.e., uncertain regions, uncertainty degree, and distance) for all executed experiments. Further generalization of our findings to different application domains and model sizes requires additional experiments. We dealt with *internal validity* threats in the empirical study by directly manipulating independent variables. Namely, we have direct assess to both actual values of uncertain parameters and design-time beliefs expressed by Priors. It is worth noting that direct manipulation of these factors has been crucial to assess cause-effect between them and the cost-effectiveness of our approach. Such a fine grained access to independent variables allows the internal validity to be increased with respect to conclusions based on an association observed without manipulation. Direct manipulation permits the creation of the same experimental conditions within repeated runs. We addressed threats to *conclusion validity* by reducing the possibility of obtaining results by chance. We repeated experiments 100 for each SUT variant and for each testing method. Then, we followed the guidelines introduced in [20] to detect statistical difference. Namely, we conducted a pairwise comparison among testing methods using the Mann-Whitney U test to calculate the p-value with significance level $\alpha = 0.05$. We also detected a *practical value* using the standardized Vargha and Delaney's $\hat{A}_{12}$ non-parametric effect size measure. We handled major threats to *construct validity* by assessing the validity of the metrics adopted in our experiments. In particular, the cost has been assessed by considering the number of tests required to achieve termination. This represents a traditional metric in assessing randomized testing algorithms [20]. The effectiveness has been measured by verifying the ability of identifying failures (i.e., requirements violation in our context). In search-based testing, this represents a traditional measure to assess the effectiveness.

7   Related Work

A taxonomy of potential sources of uncertainty affecting the development of software systems is presented in [21]. Uncertainty is categorized at different stages such as requirements, design, and production. Testing in this work is almost neglected. Further effort in categorizing and guiding software engineers in recognizing different types of uncertainty has been presented in [22]. Probabilistic models have been adopted extensively to model and analyze uncertainties in the context of self-adaptive systems. The approach introduced in [23] continuously updates transition probabilities of discrete time Markov models using efficient runtime monitoring. Another approach, introduced in [12], describes runtime quantitative verification and sensitivity analysis to support adaptation in order to achieve perpetual meeting of nonfunctional requirements. Queueing networks have been adopted and extended in [24] with adaptation knobs to dynamically fulfill performance goals. All these lines of research aim at modifying probabilistic models to react to uncertain changes during operation. In [25] MDPs are extended by attaching confidence intervals to transition probabilities in order to compute Pareto optimal policies. Our approach does not apply multi-objective optimization but uses uncertainty to drive MBT.

Recent research activities show increasing effort in delivering approaches and techniques that jointly consider testing and uncertainty quantification methods. Uncertainty sampling has been introduced in [26] to generate suitable test data. Namely, a "Query Strategy Framework" is adopted to infer a behavioral model and then select those tests on which the behavior of the system is uncertain. This approach outperforms conventional and adaptive random testing at exposing faults. A so called uncertainty-wise UML-based modeling framework has been introduced in [4] with the aim of creating models that can be executed to test CPSs. A offline MBT approach that leverages on the uncertainty-wise modeling framework has been presented in [5]. The approach generates test cases in a cost-effective way by minimizing the number of tests but maintain coverage of models. The approach presented in [2,16] incorporates uncertainty mitigation into an online MBT framework. Nevertheless, requirements are neglected during the testing process which is guided by coarse information of uncertain components.

To summarize, the methodology introduced in this paper differs from the state-of-the-art since it combines offline analysis of parametric variability of uncertain model beliefs and online MBT to detect requirements violations.

8   Conclusion

This paper introduces a novel approach to online model-based testing under uncertainty encoded as parameters of a Markov Decision process. We use design-time parametric model checking and then online testing algorithms to gather runtime evidence and detect requirements violations. The design-time phase analyzes the parameter space to pre-compute the constraints for requirements satisfaction. The online testing activity feeds a Bayesian inference process able to detect violations of pre-computed constraints. We provided a theoretical discussion of the approach and the description of an empirical evaluation aiming at assessing its cost-effectiveness. During the evaluation we conducted a large testing campaign using a number of variations of the SafeHome case study. The experience collected during our experiments suggests that the approach is able to spot requirements violations with bounded effort. The HDR-aware method outperforms both the Random and the Flat strategies considered in our quantitative comparison. Our testing framework has been released publicly to encourage adoption and repetition of experiments.

References

1. Esfahani, N., Malek, S.: Uncertainty in self-adaptive software systems. In: de Lemos, R., Giese, H., Müller, H.A., Shaw, M. (eds.) Software Engineering for Self-Adaptive Systems II. LNCS, vol. 7475, pp. 214–238. Springer, Heidelberg (2013). https://doi.org/10.1007/978-3-642-35813-5_9
2. Camilli, M., Bellettini, C., Gargantini, A., Scandurra, P.: Online model-based testing under uncertainty. In: 2018 IEEE 29th International Symposium on Software Reliability Engineering (ISSRE), pp. 36–46, October 2018
3. Camilli, M., Gargantini, A., Madaudo, R., Scandurra, P.: HYPPOTEST: hypothesis testing toolkit for uncertain service-based web applications. In: Ahrendt, W., Tapia Tarifa, S.L. (eds.) IFM 2019. LNCS, vol. 11918, pp. 495–503. Springer, Cham (2019). https://doi.org/10.1007/978-3-030-34968-4_27
4. Zhang, M., Ali, S., Yue, T., Norgren, R., Okariz, O.: Uncertainty-wise cyber-physical system test modeling. Softw. Syst. Model. (2017). https://doi.org/10.1007/s10270-017-0609-6
5. Zhang, M., Ali, S., Yue, T.: Uncertainty-wise test case generation and minimization for cyber-physical systems. J. Syst. Softw. **153**, 1–21 (2019). https://doi.org/10.1016/j.jss.2019.03.011
6. Hahn, E.M., Hermanns, H., Wachter, B., Zhang, L.: PARAM: a model checker for parametric Markov models. In: Touili, T., Cook, B., Jackson, P. (eds.) CAV 2010. LNCS, vol. 6174, pp. 660–664. Springer, Heidelberg (2010). https://doi.org/10.1007/978-3-642-14295-6_56
7. Broy, M., Jonsson, B., Katoen, J.-P., Leucker, M., Pretschner, A. (eds.): Model-Based Testing of Reactive Systems: Advanced Lectures. LNCS, vol. 3472. Springer, Heidelberg (2005). https://doi.org/10.1007/b137241
8. Camilli, M., Gargantini, A., Scandurra, P., Bellettini, C.: Towards inverse uncertainty quantification in software development (short paper). In: Cimatti, A., Sirjani, M. (eds.) SEFM 2017. LNCS, vol. 10469, pp. 375–381. Springer, Cham (2017). https://doi.org/10.1007/978-3-319-66197-1_24
9. Robert, C.P.: The Bayesian Choice: From Decision-Theoretic Foundations to Computational Implementation, 2nd edn. Springer, New York (2007). https://doi.org/10.1007/0-387-71599-1
10. Forejt, V., Kwiatkowska, M., Norman, G., Parker, D.: Automated verification techniques for probabilistic systems. In: Bernardo, M., Issarny, V. (eds.) SFM 2011. LNCS, vol. 6659, pp. 53–113. Springer, Heidelberg (2011). https://doi.org/10.1007/978-3-642-21455-4_3
11. Puterman, M.L.: Markov Decision Processes: Discrete Stochastic Dynamic Programming, 1st edn. Wiley, New York (1994)
12. Filieri, A., Tamburrelli, G., Ghezzi, C.: Supporting self-adaptation via quantitative verification and sensitivity analysis at run time. IEEE Trans. Software Eng. **42**(1), 75–99 (2016)
13. Courcoubetis, C., Yannakakis, M.: The complexity of probabilistic verification. J. ACM (JACM) **42**(4), 857–907 (1995). https://doi.org/10.1145/210332.210339
14. Hahn, E.M., Han, T., Zhang, L.: Synthesis for PCTL in parametric Markov decision processes. In: Bobaru, M., Havelund, K., Holzmann, G.J., Joshi, R. (eds.) NFM 2011. LNCS, vol. 6617, pp. 146–161. Springer, Heidelberg (2011). https://doi.org/10.1007/978-3-642-20398-5_12
15. Berger, J.: Statistical Decision Theory and Bayesian Analysis. Springer Series in Statistics. Springer, New York (1985). https://doi.org/10.1007/978-1-4757-4286-2

16. Camilli, M., Gargantini, A., Scandurra, P.: Model-based hypothesis testing of uncertain software systems. Softw. Test. Verif. Reliab. **30**(2), e1730 (2020)
17. Doob, J.L.: Application of the theory of martingales. In: Actes du Colloque International Le Calcul des Probabilités et ses applications, pp. 23–27 (1949)
18. Freedman, D.A.: On the asymptotic behavior of Bayes estimates in the discrete case II. Ann. Math. Stat. **36**(2), 454–456 (1965)
19. Veanes, M., Campbell, C., Schulte, W., Tillmann, N.: Online testing with model programs. In: Proceedings of the 10th European Software Engineering Conference/13th ACM International Symposium on Foundations of Software Engineering, pp. 273–282 (2005)
20. Arcuri, A., Briand, L.: A practical guide for using statistical tests to assess randomized algorithms in software engineering. In: Proceedings of the 33rd International Conference on Software Engineering, ser. ICSE 2011, pp. 1–10. Association for Computing Machinery, New York (2011). https://doi.org/10.1145/1985793.1985795
21. Ramirez, A.J., Jensen, A.C., Cheng, B.H.C.: A taxonomy of uncertainty for dynamically adaptive systems. In: Proceedings of the 7th International Symposium on Software Engineering for Adaptive and Self-Managing Systems, ser. SEAMS 2012, pp. 99–108. IEEE Press, Piscataway (2012). http://dl.acm.org/citation.cfm?id=2666795.2666812
22. Perez-Palacin, D., Mirandola, R.: Uncertainties in the modeling of self-adaptive systems: a taxonomy and an example of availability evaluation. In: Proceedings of the 5th ACM/SPEC International Conference on Performance Engineering, ser. ICPE 2014, pp. 3–14. ACM, New York (2014). http://doi.acm.org/10.1145/2568088.2568095
23. Filieri, A., Grunske, L., Leva, A.: Lightweight adaptive filtering for efficient learning and updating of probabilistic models. In: Proceedings of the 37th International Conference on Software Engineering - Volume 1, ser. ICSE 2015, pp. 200–211. IEEE Press, Piscataway (2015). http://dl.acm.org/citation.cfm?id=2818754.2818781
24. Incerto, E., Tribastone, M., Trubiani, C.: Software performance self-adaptation through efficient model predictive control. In: International Conference on Automated Software Engineering, pp. 485–496 (2017)
25. Scheftelowitsch, D., Buchholz, P., Hashemi, V., Hermanns, H.: Multi-objective approaches to Markov decision processes with uncertain transition parameters. In: International Conference on Performance Evaluation Methodologies and Tools, pp. 44–51 (2017)
26. Walkinshaw, N., Fraser, G.: Uncertainty-driven black-box test data generation. In: 2017 IEEE International Conference on Software Testing, Verification and Validation (ICST), pp. 253–263, March 2017

Hoare-Style Logic for Unstructured Programs

Didrik Lundberg[1,2](✉)[iD], Roberto Guanciale[1][iD], Andreas Lindner[1][iD], and Mads Dam[1][iD]

[1] KTH Royal Institute of Technology, Lindstedtsvägen 5, 100 44 Stockholm, Sweden
{didrikl,robertog,andili,mfd}@kth.se
[2] Saab AB, Nettovägen 6, 175 41 Järfälla, Sweden

Abstract. Enabling Hoare-style reasoning for low-level code is attractive since it opens the way to regain structure and modularity in a domain where structure is essentially absent. The field, however, has not yet arrived at a fully satisfactory solution, in the sense of avoiding restrictions on control flow (important for compiler optimization), controlling access to intermediate program points (important for modularity), and supporting total correctness. Proposals in the literature support some of these properties, but a solution that meets them all is yet to be found. We introduce the novel Hoare-style program logic $\mathcal{L}_A$, which interprets postconditions relative to program points when these are first encountered. The logic can support both partial and total correctness, derive contracts for arbitrary control flow, and allows one to freely choose decomposition strategy during verification while avoiding step-indexed approximations and global invariants. The logic can be instantiated for a variety of concrete instruction set architectures and intermediate languages. The rules of $\mathcal{L}_A$ have been verified in the interactive theorem prover HOL4 and integrated with the toolbox HolBA for semi-automated program verification, making it applicable to the ARMv6 and ARMv8 instruction sets.

Keywords: Program logics · Formal verification · Theorem proving · Binary analysis · Hoare logic

1 Introduction

Many scenarios require verification of machine code: in microkernels [19,34], the manipulation of processor contexts and hardware configurations have side effects that are not captured by the semantics of high-level languages; in cryptographic routines, resilience to side-channel attacks may require to analyse the

---

This work has been supported by the TrustFull project financed by the Swedish Foundation for Strategic Research and the KTH CERCES Center for Resilient Critical Infrastructures financed by the Swedish Civil Contingencies Agency.

F. de Boer and A. Cerone (Eds.): SEFM 2020, LNCS 12310, pp. 193–213, 2020.
https://doi.org/10.1007/978-3-030-58768-0_11

exact sequence of memory accesses performed by software [8]; in critical software components, to minimise the trusted computing base the compiler can be designated as untrusted; in software fault isolation techniques [59], it may be required to analyse the binary of closed source software.

One of the main difficulties in verifying machine code is the unstructured and dynamic control flow. This makes it difficult, or in the case of highly optimized code impossible, to adapt logics for high-level languages by mapping binary fragments to high-level statements: the code may be re-ordered by compilation, and one high-level statements may be implemented by multiple overlapping fragments and share fragments with other statements. A number of authors have explored the possibility of regaining Hoare-style reasoning also for the unstructured case [2,10,18,21,28,35,44,51,53,55]. However, we argue that there is still room for progress. In order to provide the formal basis for a binary verification toolkit, it is desirable that a Hoare-style logic for unstructured programs has the following properties:

1. ability to express and verify both partial and total correctness;
2. support for verification of programs with arbitrary unstructured control flow, including irreducible loops, i.e., loops with multiple entry points;
3. support for verification of programs with dynamic control flow, e.g., function abstraction and exception handling;
4. freedom to decompose the verification using several strategies, e.g., splitting the program into two fragments which may overlap;

We motivate these requirements in Sect. 2 via two simple but illustrative examples. Our main contribution is the novel logic $\mathcal{L}_A$ that meets these requirements, which is presented in Sect. 3. In order to provide a general verification framework that supports programs in arbitrary machine and intermediate languages, the logic abstracts from the axiomatization of primitive state transitions. We show that the logic is sound and complete, and we present a definitional extension that simplifies the verification of binary programs. The logical framework is demonstrated in Sect. 4, where we verify the two running examples. Finally, $\mathcal{L}_A$ has been formalised in the HOL4 interactive theorem prover, integrated into the HOL4 binary analysis framework HolBA [38][1], and instantiated for two machine models: the ARMv8 ISA and the HolBA intermediate language, which is called BIR. This is described in Sect. 5. In Sect. 6, $\mathcal{L}_A$ is compared with related work, in particular, it is argued how existing solutions do not meet all of the requirements listed above. The paper ends with some concluding remarks in Sect. 7.

2   Two Motivating Examples

We introduce two small programs and their intended properties. Despite their size, the programs present some important challenges for binary verification.

---

[1] The HolBA Github repository is located at https://github.com/kth-step/HolBA and our $\mathcal{L}_A$ implementation for this paper is available at the commit tagged SEFM2020 in the directory `src/theory/abstract_hoare_logic`.

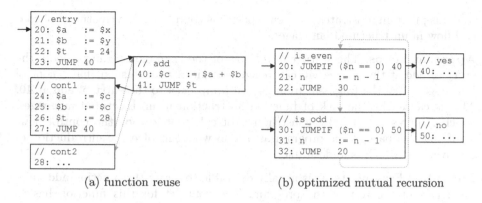

(a) function reuse   (b) optimized mutual recursion

Fig. 1. Example code and control flow graph.

They are expressed in an assembly-like pseudolanguage, which represents an abstract unstructured programming language.

2.1 Example: Function Reuse

The first program consists of a function to add two integers as well as a main program that calls this function twice. Figure 1a presents the program code with its static control flow graph using program fragments as nodes. Each fragment consists of multiple statements with unique address labels. For example, the statement 40: $c := $a + $b is located at address 40 and is part of the fragment representing the function add. It evaluates $a + $b, assigns the result to the variable $c, and gives control to the next statement. In this case, the next statement is the indirect jump to the value in the variable $t, representing the return from add.

The main program consists of three fragments and takes the two parameters $x and $y. It computes $2 * (\$x + \$y)$ by calling add twice and assigning the result to $c. The fragments for entry and cont1 prepare the parameters of the function, as well as the return address, and call add using direct jumps. The ellipses in fragment cont2 represent the code that follows afterwards.

The program satisfies the following contract:

$$[\$x = v_1 \wedge \$y = v_2]\ 20 \rightarrow \{28\}\ [\$c = 2 * (v_1 + v_2)] \tag{1}$$

It states that whenever an execution reaches the entry point at address 20 and the precondition $\$x = v_1 \wedge \$y = v_2$ holds, then, execution reaches the exit point at address 28 and there the desired postcondition $\$c = 2 * (v_1 + v_2)$ holds.

The control flow edges for the first and second calls are represented by solid black and dashed grey arrows, respectively. Notice that the static control flow contains two edges from add to the two return targets, while the dynamic control flow only uses one return edge per call context, i.e., the first call always returns to cont1 and the second call returns to cont2.

This program illustrates how reuse patterns complicate the treatment of control flow in unstructured languages.

Apparent Loops. The static control flow of the example contains a loop: the entry of add at the address 40 can reach the exit of add; this exit has a control flow edge to 24; the fragment from 24 can jump back to the entry of add at 40. This is caused by the lack of function abstraction in unstructured languages, which requires a form of reconstruction of call contexts for the control flow. Verifying this part of the program as a loop would involve the introduction of an invariant, which is undesirable.

Individual Fragments. It is usually desirable to verify the function add independently of the rest of the program. The contract for this function has to capture the initial values of $a, $b and $t when starting execution from address 40:

$$[\$a = v_1 \wedge \$b = v_2 \wedge \$t = v_3]\, 40 \rightarrow \{v_3\}\, [\$c = v_1 + v_2] \tag{2}$$

The initial value of $t represents the return address of the function. In the state where execution reaches this address, the variable $c must be the sum of the initial parameter values. Notice how the precondition ties the return address to the exit point of the contract with the free variable v_3. This allows expressing properties of reusable fragments in terms of generic contracts that can be instantiated per call.

Overlapping Fragments. A natural strategy to verify the whole program is to sequentially compose the following two contracts, which capture the two steps of the main program:

$$[\$x = v_1 \wedge \$y = v_2]\, 20 \rightarrow \{24\}\, [\$c = v_1 + v_2]$$

$$[\$c = v_1]\, 24 \rightarrow \{28\}\, [\$c = 2 * v_1]$$

The two contracts concern overlapping fragments of the program because the fragment of each contract contains one invocation of the function add: the invocation of the first contract ends in 24, and the other one ends in 28.

2.2   Example: Optimized Mutual Recursion

Figure 1b presents a program that uses mutual recursion between two functions to determine the parity of a given integer. The function is_even ends in address 40 if the input is even, otherwise in 50. Likewise, is_odd ends in 40 if the input is odd, otherwise in 50. The example does not use a stack, which could be the result of an optimized compilation.

Upon entry to either of the two functions, the control flow has a loop (whose control flow edges are represented by dashed grey arrows) with two exit points yes and no. Considering the entry point is_even, the program meets the following contract:

$$[\$n = v_1]\, 20 \rightarrow \{40, 50\}\, [(\$pc = 40 \wedge v_1 \% 2 = 0) \vee (\$pc = 50 \wedge v_1 \% 2 = 1)] \tag{3}$$

Here $pc represents the program counter, and it is used in the postcondition to specify that the exit point reached depends on the input parity. For example, execution reaches 40 and not 50 if the initial value of $n modulo 2 is 0. The program satisfies an analogous contract for entry point is_odd.

Multiple Exit Points. The given example consists of two fragments that, both individually and combined, have two exit points each. To capture this specific case as well as arbitrary branch structures in a natural way, it is necessary to express and compose contracts with multiple exit points.

Irreducible Loops. The loop of the example is irreducible because it has multiple entry points, which is not uncommon for optimized code. For this reason, verification of unstructured programs requires the ability to deal with these types of loops.

3 The Program Logic $\mathcal{L}_A$

We assume a machine model consisting of a deterministic transition system. Let Σ be the set of machine states ranged over by s. The execution of a single machine instruction is modeled by the partial function $\mathbf{nxt} : \Sigma \hookrightarrow \Sigma$ with $\mathbf{nxt}^n$ as its nth iteration. The partiality of the transition relation allows one to model failing executions. We assume a function $\mathbf{lbl} : \Sigma \to \Lambda$ from states to a set of control states Λ. This function can be used to retrieve the label or address of the next instruction executed from a state and can be thought of as accessing the program counter. The generality of $\mathbf{lbl}$ allows it to also include stack pointers and other parts of concrete machine states.

We use the notion of entry/exit points, or labels, to identify program fragments. The weak transition relation $\mathbf{weak}(s, L, s')$ relates an initial state s to the final state s' that is reached when executing the fragment whose entry point is $\mathbf{lbl}(s)$ and exit points are L.

Definition 1 (Weak transition relation)

$$\mathbf{weak}(s, L, s') = \exists n.\, n > 0 \wedge \mathbf{nxt}^n(s) = s' \wedge \mathbf{lbl}(s') \in L \wedge$$
$$\forall n' : 0 < n' < n.\, \mathbf{lbl}(\mathbf{nxt}^{n'}(s)) \notin L$$

The weak transition relation is deterministic, partial (since a program may never reach L from s), and guarantees that no intermediate state has $\mathbf{lbl}$ in L. That is, when $\mathbf{weak}(s, L, s')$ then s' represents the first encounter of a state with label in L after s.

The Hoare-style judgment of $\mathcal{L}_A$, $[P]\, l \to L\, [Q]$, states total correctness in terms of pre- and postconditions P and Q, entry point l, and set of possible exit points L. In the following, we abstract from the assertion language used for pre- and postconditions.

Definition 2 (Judgment of $\mathcal{L}_A$). *The judgment $[P]\, l \to L\, [Q]$ is valid iff*

$$\forall s.\ \mathbf{lbl}(s) = l \wedge P(s) \implies \exists s'.\, \mathbf{weak}(s, L, s') \wedge Q(s').$$

$$\frac{[P \wedge C]\, l \to L\,[Q] \quad [P \wedge \neg C]\, l \to L\,[Q]}{[P]\, l \to L\,[Q]} \; \text{CASE}$$

$$\left(\begin{array}{l} \vDash (\mathbf{lbl} = l) \wedge P_2 \implies P_1 \\ \vDash (\mathbf{lbl} \in L) \wedge Q_1 \implies Q_2 \end{array} \right) \frac{[P_1]\, l \to L\,[Q_1]}{[P_2]\, l \to L\,[Q_2]} \; \text{CONSEQ}$$

$$\frac{[P]\, l \to L_1 \cup L_2\,[Q] \quad [Q]\, L_1 \to L_2\,[Q]}{[P]\, l \to L_2\,[Q]} \; \text{SEQ}$$

$$(\vDash l \notin L) \; \frac{\begin{array}{c} [I \wedge C \wedge V = x]\, l \to \{l\} \cup L\,[\mathbf{lbl} = l \wedge I \wedge V < x] \\ [I \wedge \neg C]\, l \to L\,[Q] \end{array}}{[I]\, l \to L\,[Q]} \; \text{LOOP}$$

Fig. 2. Inference rules for $\mathcal{L}_A$

Notice that due to Definition 1, we call this a *first-encounter judgment*. A partial-correctness version can be obtained by exchanging the conjunction in the conclusion to an implication. In the following, we use $\mathbf{lbl} = l$ and $\mathbf{lbl} \in L$ for the predicates that constrain the label of a state. Since commonly a program fragment must guarantee different properties for different exit points, we use the notation $l \mapsto Q$ for $(\mathbf{lbl} = l) \wedge Q$. For instance, the following contract describes the effects of the first statement of the program in Fig. 1a:

$$C_1 = [\top]\, 20 \to \{21, 22\}\, [21 \mapsto \$x = \$a] \tag{4}$$

Notice that the postcondition of C_1 is equivalent to $\mathbf{lbl} = 21 \wedge \$x = \$a$, therefore the contract implicitly guarantees that execution starting from 20 reaches the address 21 without encountering the address 22.

Since unstructured code can have multiple entry points, many program logics feature multiple-entry judgments [10,26,44,51,53]. These are actually equivalent to conjuncts of multiple judgments. In a slight abuse of notation, we use $[P]\, L_1 \to L_2\,[Q]$ to refer to the set of all $[P]\, l \to L_2\,[Q]$ such that $l \in L_1$, interpreted conjunctively. Multiple-exit judgments cannot be so reduced. Consider the example of a conditional jump with targets l_1 and l_2: if it is required that the contract states that l_1 is not visited before l_2, this cannot be phrased using single-exit judgments only.

3.1   Inference Rules

Figure 2 shows the inference rules of $\mathcal{L}_A$. Note that there are no rules for primitive transitions (execution of only one transition) - these are added when the inference system is instantiated for a specific ISA (see Sect. 5), for example, contract C_1 of Eq. 4 is obtained in this fashion.

The CASE rule allows for combining judgments on different paths of execution (split by a condition C on the initial state) that both end up in states with program counters in L. This is useful when verifying branching structures.

The CONSEQ rule can strengthen the precondition and weaken the postcondition. Note that in contrast to the standard Consequence rule [31], CONSEQ only requires that the implications hold for states in the entry and exit points (l and in L, respectively). For instance, contract C_1 of Eq. 4 can be weakened to $[\top]\, 20 \rightarrow \{21, 22\}\, [(21 \mapsto \$x = \$a) \vee (23 \mapsto \top)]$ (since 23 is not in the exit label set).

The SEQ rule allows for sequential composition of two fragments, with the label set L_1 designating the midpoints. As an example, consider the two first statements of the **entry** function in Fig. 1a. The contract C_1 of Eq. 4 holds for the first statement. Similarly for the second statement, the contract

$$C_2 = [21 \mapsto \$x = \$a]\, 21 \rightarrow \{22\}\, [22 \mapsto \$x = \$a \wedge \$y = \$b]$$

holds. In order to sequentially compose these two contracts, the precondition of C_2 and the postcondition of both C_1 and C_2 has to be identical. Just like for the composition rule in Hoare logic, it is required the same predicate on the point(s) of composition holds. Let Q be $(21 \mapsto \$x = \$a) \vee (22 \mapsto \$x = \$a \wedge \$y = \$b)$. Since $21 \mapsto \$x = \$a$ implies Q, the contract C_1 can be weakened to $[\top]\, 20 \rightarrow \{21, 22\}\, [Q]$. In fact, since C_1 guarantees that 22 is not encountered between 20 and 21, we can enforce any property in the (impossible) case of ending the fragment in 22. Also, since 22 is not the entry point and 21 is not an exit point of C_2, the CONSEQ rule can be used to weaken C_2 to $[Q]\, 21 \rightarrow \{22\}\, [Q]$. This enables to use SEQ rule to infer $[\top]\, 20 \rightarrow \{22\}\, [Q]$ and CONSEQ rule to obtain $[\top]\, 20 \rightarrow \{22\}\, [\$x = \$a \wedge \$y = \$b]$. Note the shape of the premises of SEQ, which are due to unstructured control flows: the fragment starting from l may reach the endpoints L_2 without encountering the midpoints L_1, for instance if the first fragment contains the compilation of a **break** statement. For this reason the rule requires that the first fragment directly establishes Q if it reaches the endpoints L_2 before L_1.

The premises of LOOP are contracts for the loop body and loop exit. For the loop body, the invariant I and the condition C entail that execution starting from l does not reach any of the exit points in L before returning to l, preserves the invariant, and strictly decreases the variant. For the loop exit, the invariant I and the negation of the condition C guarantee that execution starting from l reaches the exit points L and establishes Q. The side condition $l \notin L$ ensures that execution with entry point l and exit points L establishes Q on the first encounter of L also in the case when C holds. Also, notice that if $l \in L$ then the fragment associated with $[I]\, l \rightarrow L\, [Q]$ corresponds to the loop body, since the weak transition does not loop through l.

The version for partial correctness simply disregards the variant. Note that unlike similar rules for structured loops [39], the LOOP rule must take into account possible side effects of exiting the loop as well as multiple exit points. For this reason, the postcondition in the conclusion is Q and not $I \wedge \neg C$. Multiple loop entry points can also be handled by formulating one invariant and

variant per entry point, allowing for analysis of irreducible loops. Moreover, the
condition C is not syntactically extracted from the program.

The following rule is not necessary for completeness, but is used to unify
contracts stating different properties on the final states:

$$\frac{[P]\,l \to L\,[Q_1] \qquad [P]\,l \to L\,[Q_2]}{[P]\,l \to L\,[Q_1 \wedge Q_2]} \text{ CONJ}$$

Theorem 1 (Soundness). *If $[P]\,l \to L\,[Q]$ can be derived from valid assumptions using the inference rules of $\mathcal{L}_A$, then $[P]\,l \to L\,[Q]$ is valid.*

Proof. By structural induction over the individual rules.

3.2   Completeness of $\mathcal{L}_A$

Note that since $\mathcal{L}_A$ is agnostic with regard to the concepts of programs, statements and instructions, the completeness theorem is formulated relative to a
sound and complete oracle for primitive transitions.

Theorem 2 (Completeness of $\mathcal{L}_A$). *Given that the logic used for stating pre-
and postconditions is sufficiently expressive to state invariants, variants, weakest
preconditions and strongest postconditions, and that there exists a sound and
complete oracle for contracts of primitive transitions, the first-order theory of the
underlying program and the theory of well-founded orders, then $\vdash [P]\,l \to L\,[Q]$
if $[P]\,l \to L\,[Q]$ is valid.*

Proof. To prove completeness of $\mathcal{L}_A$, the following definition is introduced for
the control-flow graph of $[P]\,l \to L\,[Q]$:

$$CFG(P, l, L) = \left\{ (\mathbf{lbl}(\mathbf{nxt}^n(s)),\ \mathbf{lbl}(\mathbf{nxt}^{n+1}(s))) \ \middle| \ \begin{array}{l} P(s) \wedge \mathbf{lbl}(s) = l \wedge n \geq 0 \wedge \\ \forall 0 < n' \leq n.\,\mathbf{lbl}(\mathbf{nxt}^{n'}(s)) \notin L \end{array} \right\}$$

The edges of the control-flow graph $CFG(P, l, L)$ are the possible transitions
starting from the state with label l for which the precondition P holds, up to
and including edges into the exit label set L.

The proof is then by induction over set inclusion on $CFG(P, l, L)$.

For the base case, only one edge exists. This means that every state that
satisfies P and whose $\mathbf{lbl}$ is l immediately reaches L in one transition. The
contract describing this is derivable directly from contracts for the primitive
transitions.

For the inductive case, the induction hypothesis is that if $CFG(P', l', L')$ is
a strict subgraph of $CFG(P, l, L)$, then $[P']\,l' \to L'\,[Q'] \implies \vdash [P']\,l' \to L'\,[Q']$.

First, consider the case where all edges in $CFG(P, l, L)$ go directly from l to L.
Then, $\vdash [P]\,l \to L\,[Q]$ follows directly from the rules for primitive transitions and
the CASE rule. In the case where not all edges go directly to L from l, consider

the case for which the labels of $CFG(P, l, L) \setminus (\Lambda \times L)$ can be partitioned into *sequential sets* L_a, L_b such that

$$(CFG(P, l, L) \setminus (\Lambda \times L)) \cap (L_b \times L_a) = \emptyset.$$

Let C_b be the predicate on states in l identifying all states from which execution reaches L_b before L (this is provided by the oracle in the assumptions of the theorem). Furthermore, let L_{mid} be the subset of L_b which has incoming edges from L_a. Then, $\vdash [P \wedge C_b] \, l \to L_{mid} \cup L [R_1]$ follows from the inductive hypothesis for some strongest postcondition R_1 provided by the oracle in the assumptions (note that this contract will not visit L by definition of C_b). $\vdash [R_2] \, L_{mid} \to L [Q]$ follows for similar reasons, where R_2 is some weakest precondition provided by the oracle. After unifying the midcondition using the CONSEQ rule (by precondition strengthening), then the two contracts can be composed using the SEQ rule to obtain $\vdash [P \wedge C_a] \, l \to L [Q]$. If $C_b = \top$, then this derives the complete contract $[P] \, l \to L [Q]$. If not, then $[P \wedge \neg C_b] \, l \to L [Q]$ must be valid, and derivable since it is a strict subgraph of $CFG(P, l, L)$. $[P] \, l \to L [Q]$ is then derivable by the CASE rule.

In case the partition into sequential sets is not possible, then l is in the transitive closure for every label except those in L, and since no edges go directly from l to L, then $l \notin L$. Let C_l be the predicate on states in l identifying all states such that execution from l goes back to l before reaching L:

$$C_l = \left\{ \begin{matrix} s. \, \mathbf{I}(s) \wedge \exists n. \, n > 0 \wedge \mathbf{nxt}^n(s) = s' \wedge \mathbf{lbl}(s) = l \wedge \\ \forall n'. \, n' < n \wedge \mathbf{nxt}^{n'}(s) = s' \implies s' \notin L \end{matrix} \right\}$$

I is the predicate identifying all possible states in l:

$$I = \left\{ \begin{matrix} s'. \, \exists s, n. \, P(s) \wedge \mathbf{lbl}(s) = l \wedge n \geq 0 \wedge \\ \mathbf{nxt}^n(s) = s' \wedge \mathbf{lbl}(s') = l \wedge \forall n'. \, n' < n \\ \mathbf{nxt}^{n'}(s) = s'' \implies s'' \notin L \end{matrix} \right\}$$

and V is a loop variant (which must exist, due to the total-correctness judgment in the antecedent of the proof obligation). Then the contract for the loop body $[I \wedge C_l \wedge V = x] \, l \to \{l\} \cup L [\mathbf{lbl} = l \wedge I \wedge V < x]$ must be valid, and derivable since it lacks any edge to L. Also, $[I \wedge \neg C_l] \, l \to L [Q]$ will be valid by definition of C_l, and lack all edges going back to l, and accordingly be derivable. Since $P \implies I$ (the invariant also holds by definition in the very initial state) then the two contracts can be used with the LOOP rule to obtain $[P] \, l \to L [Q]$, which was to be proved, completing the proof.

3.3 $\mathcal{L}_{AS}$ - Definitional Extension of $\mathcal{L}_A$

There are some common strategies that simplify verification via $\mathcal{L}_A$. First, for sequential composition it is useful to clearly identify which labels in the exit label set are not encountered by execution in the first contract, since it is required to prove the exit label set of the first contract must include the exit points of the second contract. Secondly, while analysing concrete binary code it is usually necessary to demonstrate preservation of invariants, such as the code being in memory, the stack pointer being outside the code memory, and so on.

For these reasons we introduce a definitional extension of $\mathcal{L}_A$. The judgment for $\mathcal{L}_{AS}$ $[P]\, l \xrightarrow{I} \langle L_W \mid L_B \rangle\, [Q]$ adds an invariant I, which must hold in the initial and final states of execution, and two disjoint exit label sets L_W and L_B. The sets L_W and L_B are referred to as *whitelist* and *blacklist* respectively: the labels in L_B must not be encountered before reaching exit points in L_W.

Definition 3 (Judgment of $\mathcal{L}_{AS}$). *Given that the* whitelist *and* blacklist *satisfy $L_W \cap L_B = \emptyset$ and $L_W \neq \emptyset$, the judgment $[P]\, l \xrightarrow{I} \langle L_W \mid L_B \rangle\, [Q]$ is defined as $[P \wedge I]\, l \to L_W \cup L_B\, [(\mathbf{lbl} \notin L_B) \wedge Q \wedge I]$.*

The set of rules for $\mathcal{L}_{AS}$ are derived from $\mathcal{L}_A$ and for brevity we just introduce them with short comments. It is possible to weaken a contract by freely dropping labels from the blacklist or moving them to the whitelist:

$$\frac{[P]\, l \xrightarrow{I} \langle L_W \mid L_B \rangle\, [Q]}{[P]\, l \xrightarrow{I} \langle L_W \mid L_B \setminus L \rangle\, [Q]}\ \text{BL-Subset}$$

$$(\vDash L \subseteq L_B)\ \frac{[P]\, l \xrightarrow{I} \langle L_W \mid L_B \rangle\, [Q]}{[P]\, l \xrightarrow{I} \langle L_W \cup L \mid L_B \setminus L \rangle\, [Q]}\ \text{BL-to-WL}$$

On the contrary, to move a label from the whitelist to the blacklist, the postcondition must entail that the label is not encountered:

$$\left(\begin{array}{c} \vDash L \subset L_W \\ \vDash Q \implies \mathbf{lbl} \notin L \end{array}\right)\ \frac{[P]\, l \xrightarrow{I} \langle L_W \mid L_B \rangle\, [Q]}{[P]\, l \xrightarrow{I} \langle L_W \setminus L \mid L_B \cup L \rangle\, [Q]}\ \text{WL-to-BL}$$

Finally, a simplified and more conventional sequential composition is possible when (i) the whitelist of the second fragment is included in this blacklist of the first one and (ii) the midpoints L_W do not overlap with the final endpoints L'_W:

$$\left(\begin{array}{c} \vDash L'_W \subseteq L_B \\ \vDash L_W \cap L'_W = \emptyset \end{array}\right)\ \frac{[P]\, l \xrightarrow{I} \langle L_W \mid L_B \rangle\, [R] \qquad [R]\, L_W \xrightarrow{I} \langle L'_W \mid L'_B \rangle\, [Q]}{[P]\, l \xrightarrow{I} \langle L'_W \mid L_B \cap L'_B \rangle\, [Q]}\ \text{S-Seq}$$

In contrast to $\mathcal{L}_A$, the consequence rule has been split up into the two separate rules to remove the need for unnecessary computation in the implementation of proof procedures. The rule PRE-STR is for precondition strengthening and POST-WEAK for postcondition weakening.

$$(\vDash (\mathbf{lbl} = l) \wedge P_2 \implies P_1)\ \frac{[P_1]\, l \xrightarrow{I} \langle L_W \mid L_B \rangle\, [Q]}{[P_2]\, l \xrightarrow{I} \langle L_W \mid L_B \rangle\, [Q]}\ \text{Pre-Str}$$

$$(\vDash (\mathbf{lbl} \in L_W) \wedge Q_1 \implies Q_2)\ \frac{[P]\, l \xrightarrow{I} \langle L_W \mid L_B \rangle\, [Q_1]}{[P]\, l \xrightarrow{I} \langle L_W \mid L_B \rangle\, [Q_2]}\ \text{Post-Weak}$$

Table 1. Function reuse formulas.

Abbr.	Formula
P_{add}	$40 \mapsto \$a = v_1 \wedge \$b = v_2 \wedge \$t = v_3$
R_{add}	$41 \mapsto \$c = v_1 + v_2 \wedge \$t = v_3$
Q_{add}	$v_3 \mapsto \$c = v_1 + v_2$
P_{main_1}	$20 \mapsto \$x = x \wedge \$y = y$
R_{main_1}	$40 \mapsto \$a = x \wedge \$b = y \wedge \$t = 24$
S_{main_1}	$24 \mapsto \$c = x + y$
P_{main_2}	S_{main_1}
R_{main_2}	$40 \mapsto \$a = \$b = x + y \wedge \$t = 28$
S_{main_2}	$28 \mapsto \$c = (x + y) + (x + y)$
Q_{main}	$28 \mapsto \$c = 2 * (x + y)$

Table 2. Mutual recursion formulas.

Abbr.	Formula
cond	$1 < \$n$
var	$\$n$
inv	$v_1 \% 2 = \$n \% 2$
P_{loop_b}	inv $\wedge$ cond $\wedge$ var $= v_2$
Q_{loop_b}	inv $\wedge$ var $< v_2$
P_{loop_e}	inv $\wedge \neg$cond
Q_{loop_e}	$(40 \mapsto v_1 \% 2 = 0) \vee (50 \mapsto v_1 \% 2 = 1)$
R_{loop}	inv
Q_{loop}	Q_{loop_e}
P_{loop}	$\$n = v_1$

The loop rule S-LOOP is very similar to LOOP of $\mathcal{L}_A$. Here the loop invariant uses the place of the $\mathcal{L}_{AS}$ invariant, and the side condition accounts for the split of the end labels into whitelist and blacklist.

$$\left(\begin{array}{c} \vDash l \notin L_W \\ \vDash l \notin L_B \end{array} \right) \frac{[C \wedge V = x] \, l \xrightarrow{I} \langle \{l\} \cup L_W \mid L_B \rangle \, [\mathbf{lbl} = l \wedge V < x]}{[I] \, l \xrightarrow{\top} \langle L_W \mid L_B \rangle \, [Q]} \quad \text{S-LOOP}$$

$$[\neg C \wedge I] \, l \xrightarrow{\top} \langle L_W \mid L_B \rangle \, [Q]$$

4 Verification of the Examples

To exemplify the usage of our logic, we verify the programs from Sect. 2.

4.1 Function Reuse

We first establish a generic contract for the function add that is then instantiated for the two function invocations. Figure 3 visualizes the verification flow and Table 1 collects the predicates for this example. In the following, we simply omit the blacklists if they are empty. The contract add generic corresponds to Eq. 2 and it is generic in terms of the function arguments v_1 and v_2 as well as the return label v_3. For simplicity, we set the blacklist as the set $\{20 \dots 28\} \setminus \{v_3\}$, which are all the addresses of the example outside of add, except the return address. In a more general use case, the blacklist is a variable set, where the return label v_3 and all function labels except the entry cannot be included.

The contract add return refers to a single primitive transition; hence it is not derived from the inference rules of $\mathcal{L}_A$. Instead, it is established using the semantics of the single indirect jump at program address 41, which guarantees $[R_{add}] \, 41 \to \langle \{20 \dots 28, v_3\} \mid \rangle \, [Q_{add}]$. This contract is weakened to add

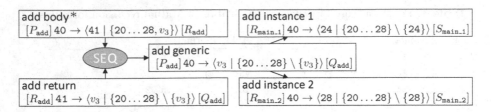

Fig. 3. Verification workflow for function **add** with the state predicates from Table 1.

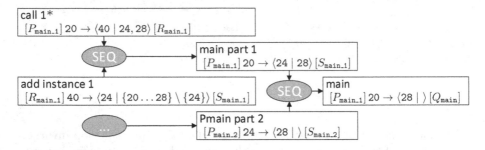

Fig. 4. Verification workflow for main program with the state predicates from Table 1.

return with the rule WL-TO-BL. Similarly, **add body** is derived from the semantics of the single assignment at program address 40, which guarantees $[P_{add}]\ 40 \to \langle\{20,\ldots,28,41,v_3\} \mid \rangle [R_{add}]$. Here, we need to impose the side condition $v_3 \neq 41$ in order to use the rule WL-TO-BL to obtain **add body**. The label v_3 is included into the blacklist to allow subsequent sequential composition with **add return** to **add body**.

This contract is instantiated twice for the two function invocations, where concrete values are substituted for the return address v_3 and the function arguments v_1 and v_2. For the first function call (i.e. **add instance 1**) $v_1 = x$, $v_2 = y$, $v_3 = 24$ and for the second function call (i.e. **add instance 2**) $v_1 = v_2 = x + y$, $v_3 = 28$. Figure 4 shows the flow to verify the main program. For brevity, it omits the source contracts of the second function invocation. The verification consists of several sequential compositions, where the whitelists of subsequent contracts have to be included in blacklists of preceding contracts. For example, **main part 1** has 28 in the blacklist so that we can compose it with **main part 2**, where 28 is in the whitelist. Finally, we use weakening to obtain the overall contract **main**, which corresponds to Eq. 1.

4.2   Mutual Recursion

The verification steps of the two recursion entry points is_even and is_odd are virtually equivalent. Hence, we only present the steps for is_even as shown in Fig. 5. Because the control flow is a loop, we start by identifying the condition to stay in the loop cond as well as loop variant var and loop invariant inv, which are

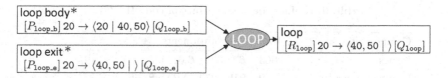

Fig. 5. Verification workflow for the recursive function is_even with the state predicates from Table 2.

defined together with the state predicates in Table 2. These predicates allow us to establish the contracts **loop body** and **loop exit** using sequential reasoning, as for the previous example. These contracts are then combined using the loop composition rule. Finally, precondition strengthening allows us to obtain the desired contract corresponding to Eq. 3 from **loop** because $P_{\texttt{loop}}$ implies $R_{\texttt{loop}}$.

5 Implementation

We implemented our logic and verified its soundness in HOL4. We also instantiated the logic for two transition systems: the formal model of ARMv8 and the machine-independent intermediate language, BIR, of the binary analysis framework HolBA [38].

HolBA supports the following verification workflow: first, the HolBA transpiler translates ARMv8 (among other ISAs) binary code to BIR together with a bisimulation proof. The bisimulation relation guarantees correspondence of ARMv8 state components with BIR variable assignments and the BIR program counter. Second, the BIR program can be verified to meet contracts - for these examples, this has been done using a weakest precondition generator and prover. Third, the contracts are transferred to the ARMv8 model using the bisimulation. Transpilation to and from BIR as well as proving contracts for acyclic program fragments is fully automated, meaning the verification code consists of specification as well as fitting together contracts for acyclic program fragments, where applying one rule typically takes one LOC. The integration of our logic in HolBA allows composing ARMv8 contracts either directly, or indirectly by composing BIR contracts and transferring the result to ARMv8.

The ARMv8 instantiation uses the L3-based machine model [29]. An ARMv8 machine state consists of registers, processor flags and memory. The program counter is one of the registers and indicates which memory location contains the next instruction to execute. Consequently, for this model, **lbl** retrieves the program counter from the state and Λ are all memory addresses. The state transition function **NextStateARM8** represents the execution of a single instruction and corresponds to **nxt**. Because the program is stored in memory, it may change by memory operations. The invariant of $\mathcal{L}_{\text{AS}}$ can be used to fix the program under analysis and exclude self-modifying code, by requiring that the program binary is loaded in system memory.

Table 3. HOL4 code sizes in lines of code (LOC).

Component	Total	Subcomponents
Logics	863	$\mathcal{L}_A$: 372, $\mathcal{L}_{AS}$: 491
Instantiations	1040	BIR: 974, ARMv8: 66
BIR composition tools	742	
Examples	1180	Function reuse: 428, Mutual recursion: 382, ARMv8: 370

The BIR instantiation uses the model defined in HolBA. BIR is designed to have as few language primitives as possible, to simplify the construction of analysis tools. In fact, it is very similar to the pseudolanguage used in Sect. 2. A BIR state consists of a map of variable names to values, a program counter, and execution status flags to indicate whether the program is running or is in an exceptional state. The variable map is used to represent both register and memory assignments. In BIR, the program is not part of the state like in ARMv8 — a program is in system memory. It can therefore change only due to an explicit jump statement. For this model, **lbl** extracts the program counter of the BIR state and **nxt** is the execution of the sequence of BIR statements that simulate a single machine instruction. The transition function **nxt** is only defined for transitions to non-exceptional states.

We chose to use boolean BIR expressions as state predicates in order to reuse the existing automation of HolBA. Because BIR expressions can only refer to variable assignments, but not to the program counter, this choice restricts the expressiveness of pre- and postconditions. For this reason, BIR judgments are defined as a specialisation of $\mathcal{L}_{AS}$ where the postconditions are maps from labels to BIR expressions following the syntax of $\mapsto$ from Sect. 3. We also proved in HOL4 a program composition rule for BIR, i.e., contracts of subprograms can be applied to larger programs.

We extended HolBA to support our specialized BIR judgments in the existing verification infrastructure. Specifically, we modified the weakest precondition tool of HolBA to enable automatic proofs of contracts for non-looping BIR statement sequences without indirect jumps by using the existing SMT solver integration and contract entailment. This allowed us, for example, to establish the contracts marked with ∗ in Figs. 3, 4 and 5. We created a library to automate the application of composition rules and used it to verify the two example programs according to the workflows presented in Sect. 4. This was also used together with the HolBA transpiler to verify an ARMv8 program that has been compiled from C code.

Table 3 shows the code sizes (calculated using `cloc` [20]) for our verification of the logics, their instantiations, the supporting HOL4 tools to semi-automate contract composition, and the verification of the examples. Each example of this paper amounts to about 10 BIR statements and can be verified in less than 10 s

Table 4. Summary of features of existing logics for unstructured programs.

Logic	Total correctness	Partial correctness	First encounter	Overlapping fragments	Completeness
Myreen, Gordon [44]	■	□	□	■	□
ISCAP [56]	□	■	Only function ret.	□	□
Saabas, Uustalu [7,51]	■	■	■	□	■
Tan, Appel [53]	□	■	■	■	■
Benton [10]	□	■	■	■	□

on an Intel i7-4800MQ with our proof-of-concept implementations. The ARMv8 example consists of 48 BIR statements and takes less than 40 s for transpilation and verification.

6   Related Work

When Tony Hoare introduced the formal system that later became known as *Hoare logic* in 1969, he did not initially treat arbitrary jumps and noted that these likely present a problem with complex solutions [31]. The following years, several extensions of Hoare logic were proposed to deal with unstructured code [2,17,18,35] which were shown to be unsound [2,3,50].

In 1976, Wang [55] proposed a program logic for total correctness of unstructured Algol-like programs, introducing multi-exit postconditions with different postconditions depending on exit label. However, in this logic, the judgments do not guarantee that the postcondition is met at the initial encounter of an associated label, unless this happens to entail exiting the program segment. In 1981, de Bruin [21] introduced a logic for partial correctness of unstructured programs. This logic is dependent on a list of global label invariants, which must hold every time the corresponding label is reached. This could be cumbersome to handle during practical verification.

Years later, in the early 2000s, computational resources had made program verification possible on a larger scale, facilitating the extension of the scope of analysis from idealized high-level languages to machine code. In particular, typed assembly languages [41] and proof-carrying code [1,48] originated a renewal of interest in the logical foundations for reasoning about programs. Table 4 contains a summary of recently proposed unstructured program logics.

Starting in 2002, the FLINT project began working on the CAP family of unstructured languages and their program logics [15,16,28,49,56,57]. Various dialects of these logics have been formalized in Coq [22,23], instantiated for x86 and SPARCv8 ISAs [58], and used to verify simplified OS kernels [27]. The initial CAP logics are written in continuation-passing style (in order to support first-class code pointers easily) and incorporate separation logic. In 2011, they presented ISCAP, a direct-style logic that supports a partial-correctness judgment only for entire functions [56]. The CAP family does not include any logic for total correctness like $\mathcal{L}_A$.

In 2005, Benton [10] proposed a program logic for partial correctness with multiple entry points and multiple exit points. Benton formalised a version of his logic in Coq [11] and used it for proofs of type safety in a certified compiler between two languages [12,13]. Benton uses continuation-passing style reasoning with step-indexed approximations to provide the partial-correctness judgment. This has some limitations; for example, a label continuation can never be both in the pre- and postcondition. Also, the logic has global label invariants, similar to those of de Bruin.

Tan and Appel introduced a program logic for partial correctness similar to Benton's, basing it on continuation-passing style reasoning with step-indexed approximations [53]. This logic was used in the Foundational Proof-Carrying Code project for type-safety proofs of SPARC machine code. No total-correctness version of this logic is known to exist by the authors.

In 2006, Saabas and Uustalu [51] constructed a program logic for partial correctness. Bartels et al. [5–7,32,33] used a derived logic with totally correct judgment formalised in Isabelle/HOL to reason about communicating unstructured code. Marti et al. [40] used another formalisation in Coq to reason about MIPS assembly in a minimal OS. In contrast to $\mathcal{L}_A$, these logics are compositional only over non-overlapping code fragments.

Another program logic for unstructured code with totally correct judgment was suggested in 2007 by Myreen and Gordon [44], most famously used in the CakeML verified compiler [36]. In the implementation of the logic, the axiomatization of single instructions is done via *decompilation into logic* [42,45–47] and the logic has been used to verify a bignum implementation [43], validate the compilation of seL4 [52], verify device drivers [24,25], and provide machine-checkable proofs of security properties of realistic executables [54]. Unlike $\mathcal{L}_A$, the judgments of this logic do not guarantee that the postcondition is met at the first encounter of the exit labels, which is equivalent to relaxing the condition $\forall n' : 0 < n' < n.\ \mathbf{lbl}(\mathbf{nxt}^{n'}(s)) \notin L$ in the weak transition relation. For this reason, the judgment of the logic cannot express contracts such as C_1 in Eq. 4, which disallow intermediate visits to certain labels. Also, a counterpart to the CONJ rule of $\mathcal{L}_A$ is not possible in this type of logic, since it is not possible to guarantee that if two contracts with the same entry and exit labels hold, then the program establishes both postconditions at the same time. Having a stronger judgment comes with other benefits of clarity as well. For example, with first-encounter judgments stating loop variants and invariants (meaning $\{l\} = L$), it is always known that the invariant holds on every iteration of the loop, whereas this is impossible in the other case, where invariants could hold only every nth loop.

Several authors [4,9,14,37] have proposed mechanisms for semi-automatic verification of contracts for unstructured programs. These approaches use different variations of the weakest precondition calculus to generate verification conditions in the same style that we followed in Sect. 5 to verify loop-free BIR fragments. However, these works do not introduce a general program logic to enable the composition of contracts that have been established using different verification methods.

7   Conclusion

We have presented a Hoare-style program logic $\mathcal{L}_A$ which combines total correctness and postconditions stated on the first encounter of the endpoints. This program logic been defined inside the ITP HOL4, and integrated with the HolBA toolbox to perform semi-automated verification of binary programs. We also prove relative completeness of $\mathcal{L}_A$. In practical verification, the drawback of a first-encounter judgment is that the exit points of the final contract to be derived need to form a subset of the exit labels in every sub-contract. Usually, this is handled by generously populating the blacklist, for example with the complement of the labels touched by execution in the contract.

The verification procedures we integrated into the toolbox HolBA are unoptimized prototypes to exemplify the usage of the logic and do not present a complete verification tool yet. Because of this, a significant amount of code in the verification examples consists of ad-hoc procedures for special cases and should be properly factored out into the toolbox. We are currently working on improving our tool to enable the verification of small and critical low-level components like, for example, microkernels and cryptographic routines.

In this work, we assume a deterministic transition relation. However, we believe that a partial correctness version of $\mathcal{L}_A$ can be straightforwardly extended to non-deterministic systems. However, the completeness proof might require changes to the assumption on primitive transitions, since these can be nondeterministic. Extending the total correctness version of the logic to deal with non-determinism would likely be more complicated since the contract will have to reason about execution traces.

Our work abstracts from the assertion language of $\mathcal{L}_A$, which is typically restricted when the logic is instantiated. For instance, in our implementation for BIR, we restricted the assertion language to use BIR boolean expressions. Other possibilities for the assertion language can be the assertion language of separation logic for enabling a frame rule, and rely-guarantee for reasoning about concurrency. However, these restrictions of the assertion language do not, in general, allow to directly transfer the completeness proof.

We are currently extending $\mathcal{L}_A$ with *strong invariants* in the sense of Hähnle and Mostowski [30]. This would allow stating properties at every execution step, as opposed to the existing invariants of $\mathcal{L}_{AS}$ which only hold at the initial and final states. Adding such invariants would allow expressing continuous integrity of shared memory sections.

References

1. Appel, A.W.: Foundational proof-carrying code. In: Proceedings 16th Annual IEEE Symposium on Logic in Computer Science, pp. 247–256. IEEE (2001)
2. Arbib, M.A., Alagić, S.: Proof rules for gotos. Acta Informatica **11**(2), 139–148 (1979). https://doi.org/10.1007/BF00264021
3. Ashcroft, E., Hoare, C.A.R., et al.: Remarks on "program proving: jumps and functions" by M. Clint and C.A.R. Hoare. Acta Informatica·**6**, 317–318 (1976)

4. Barnett, M., Leino, K.R.M.: Weakest-precondition of unstructured programs. In: Proceedings of the 6th ACM SIGPLAN-SIGSOFT Workshop on Program Analysis for Software Tools and Engineering, pp. 82–87 (2005)
5. Bartels, B.: A mechanized verification environment for real-time process algebras and low-level programming languages. Ph.D. thesis, Technical University of Berlin (2014)
6. Bartels, B., Glesner, S.: Verification of distributed embedded real-time systems and their low-level implementations using timed CSP. In: 2011 18th Asia-Pacific Software Engineering Conference, pp. 195–202. IEEE (2011)
7. Bartels, B., Jähnig, N.: Mechanized, compositional verification of low-level code. In: Badger, J.M., Rozier, K.Y. (eds.) NFM 2014. LNCS, vol. 8430, pp. 98–112. Springer, Cham (2014). https://doi.org/10.1007/978-3-319-06200-6_8
8. Barthe, G., Grégoire, B., Laporte, V.: Secure compilation of side-channel countermeasures: the case of cryptographic "constant-time". In: 2018 IEEE 31st Computer Security Foundations Symposium (CSF), pp. 328–343. IEEE (2018)
9. Barthe, G., Rezk, T., Saabas, A.: Proof obligations preserving compilation. In: Dimitrakos, T., Martinelli, F., Ryan, P.Y.A., Schneider, S. (eds.) FAST 2005. LNCS, vol. 3866, pp. 112–126. Springer, Heidelberg (2006). https://doi.org/10.1007/11679219_9
10. Benton, N.: A typed, compositional logic for a stack-based abstract machine. In: Yi, K. (ed.) APLAS 2005. LNCS, vol. 3780, pp. 364–380. Springer, Heidelberg (2005). https://doi.org/10.1007/11575467_24
11. Benton, N.: Abstracting allocation. In: Ésik, Z. (ed.) CSL 2006. LNCS, vol. 4207, pp. 182–196. Springer, Heidelberg (2006). https://doi.org/10.1007/11874683_12
12. Benton, N., Zarfaty, U.: Formalizing and verifying semantic type soundness for a simple compiler (preliminary report). Technical report, Technical Report MSR-TR-2007-31, Microsoft Research (2007)
13. Benton, N., Zarfaty, U.: Formalizing and verifying semantic type soundness of a simple compiler. In: Proceedings of the 9th ACM SIGPLAN International Conference on Principles and Practice of Declarative Programming, pp. 1–12 (2007)
14. Burdy, L., Pavlova, M.: Java bytecode specification and verification. In: Proceedings of the 2006 ACM Symposium on Applied Computing, pp. 1835–1839 (2006)
15. Chlipala, A.: Mostly-automated verification of low-level programs in computational separation logic. In: Proceedings of the 32nd ACM SIGPLAN Conference on Programming Language Design and Implementation, pp. 234–245 (2011)
16. Chlipala, A.: The bedrock structured programming system: combining generative metaprogramming and Hoare logic in an extensible program verifier. In: Proceedings of the 18th ACM SIGPLAN International Conference on Functional Programming, pp. 391–402 (2013)
17. Clint, M.: Program proving: coroutines. Acta Informatica $2(1)$, 50–63 (1973). https://doi.org/10.1007/BF00571463
18. Clint, M., Hoare, C.A.R.: Program proving: jumps and functions. Acta Informatica $1(3)$, 214–224 (1972)
19. Dam, M., Guanciale, R., Nemati, H.: Machine code verification of a tiny Arm hypervisor. In: Proceedings of the 3rd International Workshop on Trustworthy Embedded Devices, pp. 3–12 (2013)
20. Danial, A.: Count Lines of Code (CLOC) (2020). https://github.com/AlDanial/cloc. version 1.86
21. De Bruin, A.: Goto statements: semantics and deduction systems. Acta Informatica $15(4)$, 385–424 (1981). https://doi.org/10.1007/BF00264536

22. Dong, Y., Ren, K., Wang, S., Zhang, S.: Certify once, trust anywhere: modular certification of bytecode programs for certified virtual machine. In: Hu, Z. (ed.) APLAS 2009. LNCS, vol. 5904, pp. 275–293. Springer, Heidelberg (2009). https://doi.org/10.1007/978-3-642-10672-9_20

23. Dong, Y., Wang, S., Zhang, L., Yang, P.: Modular certification of low-level intermediate representation programs. In: 2009 33rd Annual IEEE International Computer Software and Applications Conference, vol. 1, pp. 563–570. IEEE (2009)

24. Duan, J.: Formal verification of device drivers in embedded systems. Ph.D. thesis, The University of Utah (2013)

25. Duan, J., Regehr, J.: Correctness proofs for device drivers in embedded systems. In: SSV (2010)

26. Feng, X., Ni, Z., Shao, Z., Guo, Y.: An open framework for foundational proof-carrying code. In: Proceedings of the 2007 ACM SIGPLAN International Workshop on Types in Languages Design and Implementation, pp. 67–78 (2007)

27. Feng, X., Shao, Z., Guo, Y., Dong, Y.: Combining domain-specific and foundational logics to verify complete software systems. In: Shankar, N., Woodcock, J. (eds.) VSTTE 2008. LNCS, vol. 5295, pp. 54–69. Springer, Heidelberg (2008). https://doi.org/10.1007/978-3-540-87873-5_8

28. Feng, X., Shao, Z., Vaynberg, A., Xiang, S., Ni, Z.: Modular verification of assembly code with stack-based control abstractions. ACM SIGPLAN Not. **41**(6), 401–414 (2006)

29. Fox, A.: Directions in ISA specification. In: Beringer, L., Felty, A. (eds.) ITP 2012. LNCS, vol. 7406, pp. 338–344. Springer, Heidelberg (2012). https://doi.org/10.1007/978-3-642-32347-8_23

30. Hähnle, R., Mostowski, W.: Verification of safety properties in the presence of transactions. In: Barthe, G., Burdy, L., Huisman, M., Lanet, J.-L., Muntean, T. (eds.) CASSIS 2004. LNCS, vol. 3362, pp. 151–171. Springer, Heidelberg (2005). https://doi.org/10.1007/978-3-540-30569-9_8

31. Hoare, C.A.R.: An axiomatic basis for computer programming. Commun. ACM **12**(10), 576–580 (1969)

32. Jähnig, N., Göthel, T., Glesner, S.: A denotational semantics for communicating unstructured code. arXiv preprint arXiv:1503.04913 (2015)

33. Jähnig, N., Göthel, T., Glesner, S.: Refinement-based verification of communicating unstructured code. In: De Nicola, R., Kühn, E. (eds.) SEFM 2016. LNCS, vol. 9763, pp. 61–75. Springer, Cham (2016). https://doi.org/10.1007/978-3-319-41591-8_5

34. Klein, G., et al.: seL4: formal verification of an OS kernel. In: Proceedings of the ACM SIGOPS 22nd Symposium on Operating Systems Principles, pp. 207–220 (2009)

35. Kowaltowski, T.: Axiomatic approach to side effects and general jumps. Acta Informatica **7**(4), 357–360 (1977). https://doi.org/10.1007/BF00289468

36. Kumar, R., Myreen, M.O., Norrish, M., Owens, S.: CakeML: a verified implementation of ML. ACM SIGPLAN Not. **49**(1), 179–191 (2014)

37. Lehner, H., Müller, P.: Formal translation of bytecode into BoogiePL. Electron. Not. Theor. Comput. Sci. **190**(1), 35–50 (2007)

38. Lindner, A., Guanciale, R., Metere, R.: TrABin: trustworthy analyses of binaries. Sci. Comput. Program. **174**, 72–89 (2019)

39. Manna, Z., Pnueli, A.: Axiomatic approach to total correctness of programs. Acta Informatica **3**(3), 243–263 (1974). https://doi.org/10.1007/BF00288637

40. Marti, N.: Formal verification of low-level software. Ph.D. thesis, University of Tokyo (2008)

41. Morrisett, G., Walker, D., Crary, K., Glew, N.: From system F to typed assembly language. ACM Trans. Program. Lang. Syst. (TOPLAS) **21**(3), 527–568 (1999)
42. Myreen, M.O.: Formal verification of machine-code programs. Technical report. University of Cambridge, Computer Laboratory (2009)
43. Myreen, M.O., Curello, G.: Proof pearl: a verified bignum implementation in x86-64 machine code. In: Gonthier, G., Norrish, M. (eds.) CPP 2013. LNCS, vol. 8307, pp. 66–81. Springer, Cham (2013). https://doi.org/10.1007/978-3-319-03545-1_5
44. Myreen, M.O., Gordon, M.J.C.: Hoare logic for realistically modelled machine code. In: Grumberg, O., Huth, M. (eds.) TACAS 2007. LNCS, vol. 4424, pp. 568–582. Springer, Heidelberg (2007). https://doi.org/10.1007/978-3-540-71209-1_44
45. Myreen, M.O., Gordon, M.J.: Verification of machine code implementations of arithmetic functions for cryptography. In: Theorem Proving in Higher Order Logics: Emerging Trends Proceedings. Department of Computer Science, University of Kaiserslautern (2007)
46. Myreen, M.O., Gordon, M.J., Slind, K.: Machine-code verification for multiple architectures-an application of decompilation into logic. In: 2008 Formal Methods in Computer-Aided Design, pp. 1–8. IEEE (2008)
47. Myreen, M.O., Gordon, M.J., Slind, K.: Decompilation into logic-improved. In: 2012 Formal Methods in Computer-Aided Design (FMCAD), pp. 78–81. IEEE (2012)
48. Necula, G.C.: Proof-carrying code. In: Proceedings of the 24th ACM SIGPLAN-SIGACT Symposium on Principles of Programming Languages, pp. 106–119 (1997)
49. Ni, Z., Shao, Z.: Certified assembly programming with embedded code pointers. In: Conference record of the 33rd ACM SIGPLAN-SIGACT Symposium on Principles of Programming Languages, pp. 320–333 (2006)
50. O'Donnell, M.J.: A critique of the foundations of Hoare style programming logics. Commun. ACM **25**(12), 927–935 (1982)
51. Saabas, A., Uustalu, T.: A compositional natural semantics and Hoare logic for low-level languages. Electron. Notes Theor. Comput. Sci. **156**(1), 151–168 (2006). http://www.sciencedirect.com/science/article/pii/S1571066106002222
52. Sewell, T.A.L., Myreen, M.O., Klein, G.: Translation validation for a verified OS kernel. In: Proceedings of the 34th ACM SIGPLAN Conference on Programming Language Design and Implementation, pp. 471–482 (2013)
53. Tan, G., Appel, A.W.: A compositional logic for control flow. In: Emerson, E.A., Namjoshi, K.S. (eds.) VMCAI 2006. LNCS, vol. 3855, pp. 80–94. Springer, Heidelberg (2005). https://doi.org/10.1007/11609773_6
54. Tan, J., Tay, H.J., Gandhi, R., Narasimhan, P.: AUSPICE: automatic safety property verification for unmodified executables. In: Gurfinkel, A., Seshia, S.A. (eds.) VSTTE 2015. LNCS, vol. 9593, pp. 202–222. Springer, Cham (2016). https://doi.org/10.1007/978-3-319-29613-5_12
55. Wang, A.: An axiomatic basis for proving total correctness of goto-programs. BIT Numer. Math. **16**(1), 88–102 (1976). https://doi.org/10.1007/BF01940782
56. Wang, W., Shao, Z., Jiang, X., Guo, Y.: A simple model for certifying assembly programs with first-class function pointers. In: 2011 Fifth International Conference on Theoretical Aspects of Software Engineering, pp. 125–132. IEEE (2011)
57. Yu, D., Hamid, N.A., Shao, Z.: Building certified libraries for PCC: dynamic storage allocation. In: Degano, P. (ed.) ESOP 2003. LNCS, vol. 2618, pp. 363–379. Springer, Heidelberg (2003). https://doi.org/10.1007/3-540-36575-3_25

58. Zha, J., Feng, X., Qiao, L.: Modular verification of SPARCv8 code. In: Ryu, S. (ed.) APLAS 2018. LNCS, vol. 11275, pp. 245–263. Springer, Cham (2018). https://doi.org/10.1007/978-3-030-02768-1_14
59. Zhao, L., Li, G., De Sutter, B., Regehr, J.: ARMor: fully verified software fault isolation. In: Proceedings of the Ninth ACM International Conference on Embedded Software, pp. 289–298 (2011)

Synthesis of P-Stable Abstractions

Anna Becchi[1], Alessandro Cimatti[1], and Enea Zaffanella[2(✉)]

[1] Fondazione Bruno Kessler, Trento, Italy
{abecchi,cimatti}@fbk.eu
[2] University of Parma, Parma, Italy
enea.zaffanella@unipr.it

Abstract. Stability is a fundamental requirement of dynamical systems. Most of the works concentrate on verifying stability for a given stability region. In this paper we tackle the problem of *synthesizing* $\mathbb{P}$-*stable abstractions*. Intuitively, the $\mathbb{P}$-stable abstraction of an open dynamical system characterizes the transitions between stability regions in response to external inputs. The stability regions are not given - rather, they are synthesized as the tightest representation with respect to a given set of relevant predicates $\mathbb{P}$. A $\mathbb{P}$-stable abstraction is enriched by timing information derived from the duration of stabilization.

We implement a synthesis algorithm in the framework of Abstract Interpretation, that allows different degrees of approximation. We show the representational power of $\mathbb{P}$-stable abstractions, that provide a high-level account of the behavior of the system with respect to stability, and we experimentally evaluate the effectiveness of a compositional approach, that allows synthesizing $\mathbb{P}$-stable abstractions for significant systems.

1 Introduction

Context. Reactive systems are often designed to operate in some stable condition (in absence of external stimuli), and to reach a possibly different stable condition (in response to some external stimulus). Stability may be reached after variable amounts of time, possibly depending on the physical dynamics being controlled. Notable examples are HVAC systems and relay-based circuits, built out of electromechanical components, pervasively adopted in the railways domain for the control of stations.

System stability is hard to assess. Stability is not to be confused with a completely still situation (i.e. a zero-derivative point) and partly oscillating or limit behaviors may be considered stable. Furthermore, a system may exhibit a large number of stable conditions, which may be difficult to characterize by inspection, especially for legacy systems. Finally, the intended discrete logical behavior depends crucially on the physical status: a light may be on or off depending on the current in a lamp resistor; an engine may be powered or not depending on whether the magnetic field induced by a coil is sufficient to close a switch.

In the context of analyzing legacy systems, one is interested in characterizing the specification of a set of controlling actions in terms of their effects on the

© Springer Nature Switzerland AG 2020
F. de Boer and A. Cerone (Eds.): SEFM 2020, LNCS 12310, pp. 214–230, 2020.
https://doi.org/10.1007/978-3-030-58768-0_12

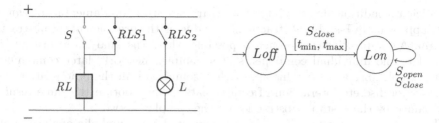

Fig. 1. A circuit regulating a lamp L, based on a switch S and a relay RL, and an automaton that describes the effects of the external actions on the lamp state.

system state. These inputs may trigger a sequence of complex internal changes, both *discrete* (like relay interactions) and *continuous* (like the charging process of a capacitor) before reaching the next stable state. The duration of these evolutions is also important: after an action, it may be necessary to wait some time before evaluating the state of the system or before accepting a new input.

As an example, consider the simple circuit represented on the left-hand side of Fig. 1. It receives external inputs corresponding to actions on the switch S: when the delayed relay RL receives enough current (i.e., if the switch stays closed for a sufficient time for its charging process) it closes the corresponding switches RLS_1 and RLS_2. We consider the problem of extracting the relation between some evaluations of interest, e.g., the lamp L being on or off, and the sequence of performed actions, in a formalism that allows formal verification.

Contribution. In this paper we investigate the problem of characterizing the effects of events on a hybrid system by analyzing where the triggered behaviors stabilize. We define the notion of $\mathbb{P}$-*stable abstraction* as the automaton that captures the essence of stabilization following each external input.

The granularity of the abstraction is induced by a given set of relevant predicates $\mathbb{P}$. Intuitively, an (abstract) state is associated to predicate valuations, and identifies the (concrete) states that are stable in the corresponding region. The transitions between abstract states describe the stabilization process of the concrete system when responding to an external stimulus. The abstraction is made accurate by requiring the stability regions to be *minimal*: the stability of a trajectory is defined in terms of the smallest $\mathbb{P}$-representable region in which the trajectory eventually converges. The synthesis of $\mathbb{P}$-stable abstractions directly results in a set of temporal properties that are satisfied by the concrete system, and can therefore be used in reverse-engineering and migrating to new technology. In order to capture the duration of stabilizations, a $\mathbb{P}$-stable abstraction is enriched with timing information characterizing the time spent in unstable states. This information can be used to synthesize the correct value to impose a slow-switching hypothesis on the external environment of the system [17].

Second, we prove that the problem can be recast in the framework of Abstract Interpretation (AI) [14] and propose a synthesis algorithm based on the exploration of the abstract state space. At the core of the algorithm is the computation of sufficient conditions for stability. The AI framework is fundamental to seamlessly approximate P-stable abstractions by reducing the precision of the abstract domain. A compositional approach is possible where the analysis algorithm is applied to the individual components of a complex network, later combining their P-stable abstractions. This approach is sound and, in the practically relevant case of discrete interaction of components, it may obtain the same result as obtained by the P-stable abstraction to the complex network.

The proposed algorithm has been implemented in a symbolic analysis tool leveraging the PPLite library [5] for convex polyhedra. An experimental evaluation, focusing on a set of parametric benchmarks representing circuits with run-to-completion behaviors, shows that the proposed techniques can obtain abstractions of rather complex hybrid systems, also providing evidence for the need of adopting the compositional analysis approach in order to improve on scalability.

Structure of the Paper. In Sect. 2 we discuss related work. In Sect. 3 we introduce some background. In Sect. 4 we introduce P-stable abstraction. In Sect. 5 we cast the problem in the AI framework. In Sect. 6 we discuss the implementation, and we experimentally evaluate the approach. In Sect. 7 we draw some conclusions and outline directions for future work.

2 Related Works

State of the Art. Stability is an important property of dynamical and hybrid systems which has been widely studied from different perspectives. Classic stability is defined by requiring that all the trajectories are asymptotically attracted by an equilibrium point x_e [9,17]. Since classical asymptotic stability excludes oscillating behaviors, *region stability* [21,22] requires that the trajectories eventually remain inside a given invariant region, intuitively corresponding to the temporal property AFAGR, for a given region R, even if no single equilibrium point exists. The alternative notion of *strong attractor* also requires that all the trajectories of the system never leave the region once entered, i.e $A\neg RUAGR$.

The problem is typically to verify the global stability of a given system, i.e. proving that every trajectory satisfies the required stability criterion (be it asymptotic or region stability). When global stability does not hold, an additional task is to compute the region of attraction, i.e. the set of states whose outgoing trajectories are stable.

Asymptotic stability can be proven by providing a Lyapunov function as a certificate that the energy of the system is decreasing (in its domain) until the equilibrium point is reached. Several methods have been proposed to this aim, with different levels of automation, soundness and scalability [10,16,20,24]. Region stability verification cannot be directly tackled as a reachability problem. It is proved by reduction to liveness checking with combinations of reachability and SMT solving, or based on the use of (cartesian) predicate abstraction [21,22].

Interestingly, in the case of switching systems, stability of the whole system is not implied by the stability of each modality. Some works (e.g. [6,23]) aim at finding conditions on switching sequences in order to ensure the stability of the composed system. Another approach to achieve global stability is to impose a *slow-switching* condition, i.e. there must be a sufficiently high time interval between subsequent inputs. [8,19] prove the adequacy of such a time interval by analyzing the *average dwell time* of the system.

Novelty. This work differs from the works mentioned above in several ways. First, in contrast to verifying stability with respect to a given region, we *synthesize* a P-stable abstraction that characterizes all the system behaviors with respect to stabilization. Notice that we do not rely on a single convergence region being given. We explore the space of possible convergence regions induced by the set P of predicates, and find the tightest representations. Second, the synthesized region is not a simple invariant of the system: rather, it is *possibly, eventually* invariant only for the trajectories triggered by the event under consideration. Hence we simulate hybrid evolutions with a relation of possible attraction between two stable conditions: we want to express the existence of an eventually convergent trajectory (intuitively corresponding to an EFAGR property, for a given region R), rather than requiring stabilization for all paths (as in AFAGR). Another key difference is that the aforementioned approaches are mainly related to purely dynamical or closed hybrid systems. We adopt a more expressive framework, considering switched systems, open to autonomous events. Specifically, our aim is to analyze the stabilization effects for external inputs, by considering the "closed" dynamic of the system. Finally, we take into account timing information.

This work is also quite distinct from predicate abstraction for hybrid systems [1,2]. The main difference is that predicates are not evaluated in transient states, i.e., "abstract" transitions will connect predicates evaluated only in stable conditions. Consider, for example, that the length of the traces is not retained.

In terms of techniques, this is the first work exploiting the Abstract Interpretation framework [14,15] in the field of stability analysis. We trade precision for efficiency and propose an approximated analysis that can be implemented using known techniques.

3 Background

We write $\mathbb{R}_{\geq}$ for the set of non-negative reals. Given a sequence σ and an index $i \in \mathbb{N}$, let $\sigma[i]$ denote the i-th element of σ. We adopt a logic notation derived by SMT, using a fragment of first-order logic and the theory of Linear Real Arithmetic (LRA). Given a set of Boolean variables L, let $\Psi(L)$ define the set of boolean combinations over L. Given a set of real-valued variables V, let LPred$_V$ define finite conjunctions of LRA predicates with free variables in V. We write $\Psi(L, V)$ to denote SMT(LRA) formulae obtained by boolean combinations of Boolean variables in L and linear predicates over V.

Finite and Timed Automata. A *finite state automaton* is a tuple $\langle Q, Q_0, A, R \rangle$ where Q is a finite set of states, $Q_0 \subseteq Q$ is the set of initial states, A is a finite set of labels and $R \subseteq (Q \times A \times Q)$ is the labeled transition relation between states. A *timed automaton* [3] $\langle Q, Q_0, C, A, \text{inv}, R \rangle$ is an automaton equipped with a finite set of clocks C, with state invariants inv: $Q \to \text{LPred}_C$ associating each state $q \in Q$ with its clock constraints $\text{inv}(q)^1$ and with $R \subseteq (Q \times A \times \text{LPred}_C \times \wp(C) \times A)$, where: edge $(q, a, g, r, q') \in R$ represents the transition from state q to q', labeled with a and guarded by clock constraints g; the set $r \subseteq C$ gives the set of clocks to be reset with this transition. We adopt notation $q \xrightarrow{a,g,r} q'$.

In a timed automaton with a single clock variable c, whenever a state q is involved only in the untimed transitions $q_i \xrightarrow{a,c:=0} q \xrightarrow{\varepsilon, c \geq m} q_j$ and $\text{inv}(q) = (c \leq M)$, we omit it from the set of states in the tuple and write $q_i \xrightarrow{a,[m,M]} q_j$, meaning that q_i reaches q_j with a transition labeled with a in a time between m and M. When clear from context we also omit the 'inv' component from the tuple.

Hybrid Systems. Let $\dot{v}$ denote the time derivative dv/dt. A *linear hybrid system with piecewise affine dynamics* is a tuple $\mathcal{H} = \langle Loc, Var, A, \text{inv}, \text{init}, \text{flow}, \text{disc} \rangle$ where [25] Loc is a finite set of locations; $Var = \{v_1, \ldots, v_n\}$ is a finite set of continuous state variables; A is a finite set of synchronization labels; init: $Loc \to \text{LPred}_{Var}$ defines initial conditions for each location; inv: $Loc \to \text{LPred}_{Var}$ defines invariant conditions for each location; flow: $Loc \to \text{LPred}_{Var \cup \dot{Var}}$ defines the continuous transition relation; disc $\subseteq (Loc \times A \times Loc \times \text{LPred}_{Var \cup Var'})$ defines the labeled discrete transition relation. A *state* of a hybrid system $\mathcal{H}$ is a tuple $\langle \ell, \boldsymbol{x} \rangle$ where $\ell \in Loc$ and $\boldsymbol{x} \in \mathbb{R}^n$. Let Σ denote the state space of $\mathcal{H}$ and $\text{init}(\mathcal{H})$ denote the set of states $s = \langle \ell, \boldsymbol{x} \rangle$ such that $\boldsymbol{x} \models (\text{inv}(\ell) \wedge \text{init}(\ell))$. A *run* of hybrid system $\mathcal{H}$ is a path $\rho = (s_0 \xrightarrow{\delta_1} s_1 \xrightarrow{a_2} s_2 \xrightarrow{\delta_3} s_3 \xrightarrow{a_4} \ldots)$ where $\delta_i \in \mathbb{R}_{\geq}$, $a_i \in A$, $s_i = \langle \ell_i, \boldsymbol{x}_i \rangle \in \Sigma$, $s_0 \in \text{init}(\mathcal{H})$ and each step corresponds to either a continuous transition

$$\frac{\delta \in \mathbb{R}_{\geq} \quad f: [0, \delta] \to \mathbb{R}^n \quad \dot{f}: (0, \delta) \to \mathbb{R}^n \quad f(0) = \boldsymbol{x} \quad f(\delta) = \boldsymbol{x}' }{\langle \ell, \boldsymbol{x} \rangle \xrightarrow{\delta} \langle \ell, \boldsymbol{x}' \rangle}$$
$$\forall \epsilon \in [0, \delta]: f(\epsilon) \models \text{inv}(\ell) \quad \forall \epsilon \in (0, \delta): (f(\epsilon), \dot{f}(\epsilon)) \models \text{flow}(\ell)$$

or a discrete transition

$$\frac{(\ell, a, \ell', \mu) \in \text{disc} \quad (\boldsymbol{x}, \boldsymbol{x}') \models \mu \quad \boldsymbol{x}' \models \text{inv}(\ell')}{\langle \ell, \boldsymbol{x} \rangle \xrightarrow{a} \langle \ell', \boldsymbol{x}' \rangle}.$$

We write $\text{Run}(\mathcal{H})$ for the set of all runs of $\mathcal{H}$. A run ρ diverges if ρ is infinite and the sum $\sum_{i \geq 0} \delta_i$ diverges.[2] We consider systems without Zeno behaviors, i.e.,

---

[1] A clock predicate is a linear predicate over a clock variable c of the form $c \bowtie k$, where k is constant. A clock constraint is a finite conjunction of clock predicates.

[2] We let $\delta_i = 0$ whenever the i-th transition is a discrete one.

every finite run of $\mathcal{H}$ is a prefix of some divergent run of $\mathcal{H}$. If $\mathrm{Run}(\mathcal{H}) \subseteq \mathrm{Run}(\mathcal{H}')$, then $\mathcal{H}'$ is a *relaxation* of $\mathcal{H}$ and $\mathcal{H}$ is a *refinement* of $\mathcal{H}'$ [8].

In hybrid automata, as well as in a switched systems [17], discrete behaviors can be distinguished between controlled (internal) events, for logic-based mechanism, and autonomous (external) events, modeling unpredictable environmental influences. The set of labels for discrete interaction of $\mathcal{H}$ is therefore partitioned in $A = I \cup E$, denoting internal and external events respectively. Given a hybrid automaton $\mathcal{H} = \langle Loc, Var, A, \mathrm{inv}, \mathrm{init}, \mathrm{flow}, \mathrm{disc} \rangle$, we denote with $\mathcal{H}^c$ the corresponding *closed system*, i.e., $\mathcal{H}^c \doteq \langle Loc, Var, I, \mathrm{inv}, \mathrm{init}, \mathrm{flow}, \mathrm{disc}^c \rangle$ with $\mathrm{disc}^c = \{(\ell, i, \ell', \mu) \in \mathrm{disc} \mid i \in I\}$. Let '$\overset{c}{\leadsto}$' denote the reflexive and transitive closure of the transition relation of $\mathcal{H}^c$. When clear from the context, we also use '$s \overset{c}{\leadsto} s'$' to denote the corresponding run from s to s' in the closed system.

Time of a Run and Slow Switching. For each run $\rho = (s_0 \overset{\delta_1}{\longrightarrow} s_1 \overset{a_2}{\longrightarrow} s_2 \dots)$ and index m, the time spent to complete the prefix of length m of ρ is $\tau_m(\rho) \doteq \sum_{i=1}^m \delta_i$. For a finite run of length n, $\tau(\rho)$ is a shortcut for $\tau_n(\rho)$. Let ε be the ordered sequence of indices for the external events of ρ. The sequence of *external switching time points* of ρ is a sequence t of elements in $\mathbb{R}_{\geq}$ such that $t[0] = 0$ and $t[i] = \tau_{\varepsilon[i]}(\rho)$ for all i. For each hybrid automaton $\mathcal{H}$ and time $d \in \mathbb{R}_{\geq}$, $\mathcal{H}_d$ is a refinement of $\mathcal{H}$ such that every run of $\mathcal{H}_d$ is associated with a sequence t of external switching time points satisfying $(t[i+1] - t[i]) > d$ for all i.

Abstract Interpretation. We assume some familiarity with the basic notions of lattice theory [7] and Abstract Interpretation [14,15]. Given a poset $(L, \preceq)$ and a set $S \subseteq L$, its *downward closure* is $\downarrow S \doteq \{x \in L \mid \exists s \in S \,.\, x \preceq s\}$; the set $S \subseteq L$ is downward closed if $S = \downarrow S$. The notation for *upward closure* is similar. Given two posets $(L, \preceq)$ and $(L^\sharp, \preceq^\sharp)$ and two monotonic functions $\alpha \colon L \to L^\sharp$ and $\gamma \colon L^\sharp \to L$, the pair (α, γ) is a *Galois connection* [14], denoted $L \underset{\alpha}{\overset{\gamma}{\rightleftharpoons}} L^\sharp$, if for all $x \in L$, $x^\sharp \in L^\sharp$ it holds that $\alpha(x) \preceq^\sharp x^\sharp$ if and only if $x \preceq \gamma(x^\sharp)$. For each concrete function $F \colon L \to L$, its most precise sound abstraction in $L^\sharp$ according to this Galois connection is $F^\sharp \doteq \alpha \circ F \circ \gamma$.

Temporal Logic. In the rest of this paper, we adopt a notation inspired to model checking for specific patterns of computation-tree logic formulae. In particular, $\mathcal{H}, s \models \mathrm{AG}\phi$ means that for all $\rho \in \mathrm{Run}(\mathcal{H})$ outgoing from s (i.e. such that $\rho[0] = s$), for all $i \in \mathbb{N}$, $\rho[i] \models \phi$. Similarly $\mathcal{H}, s \models \mathrm{EFAG}\phi$ means that there exists a run $\rho \in \mathrm{Run}(\mathcal{H})$ outgoing from s, and a $j \in \mathbb{N}$ such that $\rho[j] \models \mathrm{AG}\phi$.

4   P-stable Abstraction

In this section we characterize the stabilizing executions of a closed hybrid system with respect to the truth values of a given set of predicates. Namely, we build an abstract timed automaton whose transitions simulate the stabilizing runs of the closed system following the occurrence of an external event.

4.1   Region Stability

Given a hybrid system $\mathcal{H} = \langle Loc, Var, A, \text{inv}, \text{init}, \text{flow}, \text{disc}\rangle$, where the discrete interactions A are partitioned into the sets of the internal and external events, we call *closed evolution* (for short evolution) of a state $s \in \Sigma$ a hybrid run of the closed system $\mathcal{H}^c$ starting from s. Given a region $R \subseteq \Sigma$ of the state space, we say that a state $s \in \Sigma$ is *internally stable in R* (for short, stable in R) if and only if R is invariant for all closed evolutions of s; state s is said to be *possibly attracted by R* (for short, attracted by R) if there exists a closed evolution of s reaching a state internally stable in R. More formally:

Definition 1 (Stability and attraction). *For each $s \in \Sigma$ and $R \subseteq \Sigma$,*

$$\text{STABLE}(s, R) \iff (s \models^c \text{AG}R);$$
$$\text{ATTR}(s, R) \implies (s \models^c \text{EFAG}R).$$

Different definitions can be provided for relation 'ATTR': for instance, one could impose the stronger constraint that the trajectory does not oscillate inside and outside R before stabilizing, hence $\text{ATTR}(s, R) \doteq (s \models^c \text{E}(\neg R \text{UAG}R))$.[3] Nonetheless, the results stated in the following will also hold for the weaker definition $\text{ATTR}(s, R) \doteq (s \models^c \text{EFAG}R)$.

The "run-to-completion" closed evolutions of a state $s \in \Sigma$ are described by the regions that possibly attract it: due to the non-determinism of the closed system, taken into account by the existential path quantification, this can be a set of different regions, each of them representing a possible future stable condition. The most precise characterization of these behaviors could be given by the set of *minimal* regions for which $\text{ATTR}(s, R)$ holds. The synthesis of such a set presents us with the problem of minimality. In fact, it is common to find trajectories that exhibit asymptotic behaviors to an equilibrium condition: for instance, the discharging process of a capacitor is described by an exponential flow that, ideally, never reaches a null charge, so that a minimal region of convergence does not exists. Nonetheless, under a certain threshold the capacitor can be assumed to be discharged and the following decay of voltage has no impact on its behavior in the circuit. In other words, within a certain stable region of interest, the exact trajectories may not be relevant for the analysis of the system. This suggests to fix a priori a finite set of predicates $\mathbb{P}$ representing the properties we want to observe: hence, the run-to-completion behaviors will be described as the minimal attracting areas chosen from the (finite) set of regions induced by $\mathbb{P}$.

4.2   Untimed $\mathbb{P}$-stable Abstraction

Given a finite set of predicates $\mathbb{P} \subseteq \Psi(Loc, Var)$ we denote with $\Phi_{\mathbb{P}}$ the set of their (finite) boolean combinations, omitting the subscript when clear from context. We say that $\mathbb{P}$ induces a grid in the state space, since every formula $\phi \in \Phi$ defines a $\mathbb{P}$-expressible region as the set of its models in Σ. Both relations

---

[3] This can be seen as the "existential" version of the *strong attractor* definition [21].

'STABLE' and 'ATTR' defined in Sect. 4.1 can be evaluated on such regions. Note that, given a state s, the set of formulae in Φ such that STABLE(s, ϕ) holds is upward closed (i.e., for all $\phi, \phi' \in \Phi$ such that $\phi \Rightarrow \phi'$, if STABLE(s, ϕ) then STABLE(s, ϕ')). Having fixed a finite set of P-representable regions, we can now define the minimal version of relations STABLE and ATTR.

Definition 2 (Minimal P-stability). *For each $s \in \Sigma$ and $\phi \in \Phi$, let*

$$\text{NO\_STRONGER\_ATTR}(s, \phi) \doteq \nexists \phi' \in \Phi \,.\, ((\phi' \Rightarrow \phi) \wedge (\phi' \neq \phi) \wedge \text{ATTR}(s, \phi'));$$
$$\text{STABLE}_{\min}(s, \phi) \doteq \text{STABLE}(s, \phi) \wedge \text{NO\_STRONGER\_ATTR}(s, \phi);$$
$$\text{ATTR}_{\min}(s, \phi) \doteq \text{ATTR}(s, \phi) \wedge \text{NO\_STRONGER\_ATTR}(s, \phi).$$

Namely, relation 'STABLE$_{\min}$' links a state $s \in \Sigma$ with a formula $\phi \in \Phi$ if ϕ is invariant for the evolutions of s in the closed system and if there are no smaller P-representable regions in which s can converge. If such a ϕ exists, it is unique (modulo logical equivalence) and state s is said to be *minimally P-stable* (or simply stable). If a state has no formula in Φ such that 'STABLE$_{\min}$' holds, then it is said to be *transient*, since there exists an evolution attracted by a smaller P-region that does not contain it. In the following we use the notation TRANSIENT(s). Observe that, by definition, the relation 'ATTR$_{\min}$' is a subset of relation 'ATTR' and, like the latter, it is non-deterministic: 'ATTR$_{\min}$' links a state with the minimal regions in which one of its closed evolution stabilizes.

We say that a system $\mathcal{H}$ has a *well-defined run-to-completion semantics* for the set of predicates P, written WD-RTC$(\mathcal{H}, \mathbb{P})$ for short, if a state of $\mathcal{H}$ cannot delay indefinitely its reaching a P-stable condition. In other words, if ATTR$_{\min}(s, \phi)$, not only there exists a path $s \stackrel{c}{\leadsto} s'$ with STABLE$_{\min}(s', \phi)$, but also, there is no path that satisfies G TRANSIENT. This requirement expresses that the system reaction to an event must be reliable and there must exist a finite time after which the system has completed the process.

As an example, consider an automaton with states $Q = \{q_0, q_1, q_2\}$ and transition relation $R(q_0, q_1)$, $R(q_1, q_1)$, $R(q_1, q_2)$, $R(q_2, q_2)$. The runs starting from q_0 are attracted by predicate $\{q_2\}$, but are allowed to stay in the transient state q_1 for an unbounded number of steps before reaching q_2. Hence, the stabilization process with respect to $\{q_2\}$ is not well-defined. Nevertheless, for the same system WD-RTC holds with predicate $\{q_1 \vee q_2\}$.

Definition 3 (P-stable abstraction). *Let $\mathcal{H} = \langle Loc, Var, A, \text{inv}, \text{init}, \text{flow}, \text{disc} \rangle$ be a hybrid automaton, and $E \subseteq A$ a set of external events. Let $\mathbb{P} \subseteq \Psi(Loc, Var)$ be a set of predicates. The (untimed) P-stable abstraction of $\mathcal{H}$ is the finite state automaton $\mathcal{A} \doteq \langle \Phi, \Phi_0, E, \hookrightarrow \rangle$, where*

$$\Phi_0 = \{ \phi \in \Phi \mid \exists s_0 \in \text{init}(\mathcal{H}), s \in \Sigma \,.\, s_0 \stackrel{c}{\leadsto} s \wedge \text{STABLE}_{\min}(s, \phi) \}$$

and $\phi \stackrel{e}{\hookrightarrow} \phi'$ if and only if there exist $s, s_1, s' \in \Sigma$ such that

$$\text{STABLE}_{\min}(s, \phi), \quad s \stackrel{e}{\longrightarrow} s_1 \stackrel{c}{\leadsto} s', \quad \text{STABLE}_{\min}(s', \phi').$$

Intuitively, the runs of $\mathcal{A}$ represent the evolution of the truth values of the predicates in $\mathbb{P}$ in response to external events once stabilization is reached, upon "absorption" of the transient states. Notice that initial states Φ_0 are defined following the same intuition, and represent the possible initial $\mathbb{P}$-stable regions, since $\mathcal{H}$ may start in a transient condition.

The definition of $\mathbb{P}$-stable abstraction captures the fact that we are studying the effects of the external inputs when $\mathcal{H}$ is *in a stable condition*: we disregard runs where external inputs are received in transient states. This "stable-switching" paradigm can be intuitively thought of as the qualitative counterpart of the slow-switching hypothesis used as sufficient condition for reasoning about global stability in switched systems [17]. We informally define the restriction of $\mathcal{H}$ under stable switching as the hybrid automaton $\mathcal{H}_{ss}$ obtained by applying the guard ¬TRANSIENT to every external transition of $\mathcal{H}$.

The $\mathbb{P}$-stable abstraction of $\mathcal{H}$ is a weak simulation [18] of $\mathcal{H}_{ss}$. The precision depends on the choice of $\mathbb{P}$. In fact, two states that are stable in the same region ϕ are not necessarily connected by a concrete run: when distinct areas of attraction are represented with the same formula, spurious behaviors may be introduced.

We compare the definition of $\mathbb{P}$-stable abstraction with "classic" predicate abstraction [1,2]. In our setting, the concretization of an abstract state ϕ is the set of states in Σ that are stable in ϕ. Similarly, the abstract transitions represent concrete transitions of the form $s \xrightarrow{e} s_1 \xrightarrow{c} s'$, i.e., a single external event possibly followed by internal transitions. Thus, differently from predicate abstraction, a path in the abstraction may be significantly shorter than the corresponding concrete ones.

For each $\phi \xrightarrow{e} \phi'$ in $\mathcal{A}$, let $\Gamma(\phi \xrightarrow{e} \phi')$ be the set of the simulated hybrid runs:

$$\Gamma(\phi \xrightarrow{e} \phi') \doteq \left\{ s \xrightarrow{e} s_1 \xrightarrow{c} s' \; \middle| \; \text{STABLE}_{\min}(s, \phi), \; \text{STABLE}_{\min}(s', \phi') \right\}.$$

The Γ operator is naturally extended to runs of $\mathcal{A}^4$ by concatenation of its applications to single transitions, and to set of runs.

Proposition 1. *If* WD-RTC$(\mathcal{H}, \mathbb{P})$ *holds, the stable-switching runs of $\mathcal{H}$ are simulated by the runs of $\mathcal{A}$, i.e.,* $\text{Run}(\mathcal{H}_{ss}) \subseteq \Gamma(\text{Run}(\mathcal{A}))$.

Example 1. Consider the circuit on the left-hand side of Fig. 1, where external events include the opening/closing of switch S and the property of interest is the condition of lamp L: letting i_L (resp., i_{RL}) denote the intensity of the current passing through the lamp (resp., the relay), we choose $\mathbb{P} = \{(-c \leq i_L \leq c)\}$, so that the state space is partitioned into $Loff \doteq (-c \leq i_L \leq c)$ and $Lon \doteq \neg Loff$. Initially all the switches are open and neither the relay coil RL nor the lamp L receives current. Hence, the system is (internally) stable in $Loff$.

Starting from a condition stable in $Loff$ (Fig. 2), if the external event S_{close} is received, i_{RL} increases with a continuous dynamics implementing the delay of

---

[4] For each $\phi_0 \in \Phi_0$ operator Γ applies to initial transitions as $\Gamma(\hookrightarrow \phi_0) \doteq \{s \xrightarrow{c} s' \mid s \in \text{init}(\mathcal{H}), \text{STABLE}_{\min}(s', \phi_0)\}$.

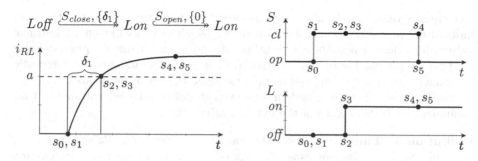

Fig. 2. States of trace $s_0 \xrightarrow{S_{close}} s_1 \xrightarrow{\delta_1} s_2 \xrightarrow{i} s_3 \xrightarrow{\delta_3} s_4 \xrightarrow{S_{open}} s_5$ projected on i_{RL}, the state of the switch S and of lamp L with respect to time t.

its activation. After δ_1 time, i_{RL} reaches the activation threshold a (state s_2) and it closes the corresponding switches with an *internal* discrete transition (labeled i). The closing of RLS_2 turns on the lamp L. The system is now stable in Lon. The hybrid system run $s_0 \xrightarrow{S_{close}} s_1 \xrightarrow{\delta_1} s_2 \xrightarrow{i} s_3$ (with $\text{STABLE}_{min}(s_0, Loff)$, $\text{ATTR}_{min}(s_1, Lon)$, $\text{ATTR}_{min}(s_2, Lon)$ and $\text{STABLE}_{min}(s_3, Lon)$) corresponds to a single transition $Loff \xhookrightarrow{S_{close}} Lon$ in the $\mathbb{P}$-stable abstraction.

Since RLS_1 has been closed, RL receives current even if the switch S gets opened. It follows that when later receiving the external event S_{open} in state s_4 (with $\text{STABLE}_{min}(s_4, Lon)$), the system switches to state s_5 and the lamp stays on (namely, $\text{STABLE}_{min}(s_5, Lon)$). In the $\mathbb{P}$-stable abstraction we will have the transition $Lon \xhookrightarrow{S_{open}} Lon$.

4.3   Timed $\mathbb{P}$-stable Abstraction

We now characterize the time needed to reach a stable condition after receiving an external input.

Definition 4 (Convergence time of $\phi \xhookrightarrow{e} \phi'$). *For each abstract transition* $\phi \xhookrightarrow{e} \phi'$ *its convergence time is the interval in* $\mathbb{R}_{\geq}$ $ct(\phi \xhookrightarrow{e} \phi') \doteq [lb, ub]$, *where*

$$lb = \inf\{\, \tau(\rho) \mid \rho \in \Gamma(\phi \xhookrightarrow{e} \phi') \,\},$$

$$ub = \sup\{\, \tau_m(\rho) \mid \rho \in \Gamma(\phi \xhookrightarrow{e} \phi'), \neg\text{STABLE}_{min}(\rho[m], \phi') \,\}.$$

The convergence time represents the time spent in the transient states. If the system is stable in ϕ and an external event e is received, after $\max ct(\phi \xhookrightarrow{e} \phi')$ time the system will certainly be stable in ϕ'; before $\min ct(\phi \xhookrightarrow{e} \phi')$, the system is certainly still in a transient state so that it is not safe to evaluate the truth value of the predicates. Similar considerations apply to initial conditions: each $\phi \in \Phi_0$ is associated with a convergence time $ct(\hookrightarrow \phi)$, that represents the time needed to stabilize at start up.

Note that, since we are assuming WD-RTC$(\mathcal{H}, \mathbb{P})$, the convergence time of Definition 4 is always bounded from above (i.e., $ub < +\infty$). An unbounded convergence time would imply the existence of a path starting from ϕ that can indefinitely postpone its stabilization in ϕ', which is probably an undesirable system behavior. Hence, the computation of convergence time is a practical way to detect the violation of the WD-RTC$(\mathcal{H}, \mathbb{P})$ hypothesis, and obtain diagnostic information to either debug the model or change the set of predicates $\mathbb{P}$.

On the basis of these considerations, we can define a timed automaton that simulates the $\mathbb{P}$-stable runs of the hybrid system $\mathcal{H}$.

Definition 5 (Timed $\mathbb{P}$-stable abstraction). *Given a $\mathbb{P}$-stable abstraction $\mathcal{A} = \langle \Phi, \Phi_0, E, \hookrightarrow \rangle$ the corresponding timed abstraction is a timed automaton having as initial state an additional state $\star$ and having*

- *transition $\star \xleftarrow{\varepsilon, [m,M]} \phi$, for each $\phi \in \Phi_0$, with $[m, M] = ct(\hookrightarrow \phi)$;*
- *transition $\phi \xleftarrow{e, [m,M]} \phi'$, for each $\phi \xleftarrow{e} \phi'$, with $[m, M] = ct(\phi \xleftarrow{e} \phi')$.*

Starting from the additional state $\star$, each path reaches the first stable condition ϕ in the corresponding initialization time $ct(\hookrightarrow \phi)$. Then, after an external event e, it non-deterministically jumps to the next stable condition within the interval imposed by the associated convergence time.

The convergence time information can be used to define the runs we are abstracting with a *slow*-switching characterization, rather than a (possibly uncomputable) stable-switching one. Let $ct = \max\{ M \mid \phi \xrightarrow{e, [m,M]} \phi' \text{ in } \mathcal{A} \}$; then the refinement $\mathcal{H}_{ct}$ (see Sect. 3), allowing external inputs with a delay of (at least) ct, ensures that the system has always sufficient time to reach stability. It follows that $\mathrm{Run}(\mathcal{H}_{ct}) \subseteq \mathrm{Run}(\mathcal{H}_{ss})$, hence, $\mathcal{H}_{ct}$ defines a concrete semantics compliant with $\mathcal{A}$.

Example 2. Reconsider the circuit of Fig. 1, whose $\mathbb{P}$-stable abstraction has been analyzed in Example 1. We can compute the timing information of the stabilization processes, obtaining $ct(Loff \xrightarrow{S_{close}} Lon) = [\delta_1, \delta_1]$; the other abstract transitions are instantaneous (i.e., their convergence time is 0, as they have no transient states). By waiting δ_1 after each external event, the system $\mathcal{H}_{\delta_1}$ follows the behaviors described by the $\mathbb{P}$-stable abstraction: namely, we know how long switch S must stay closed in order to turn on (and keep on) the lamp.

5 $\mathbb{P}$-stable Abstraction via Abstract Interpretation

The simulation presented in Sect. 4 may not be computable when dealing with complex hybrid systems. In this section we formulate the same concepts in an Abstract Interpretation framework: this provides a formal setting to search for a balance between precision and efficiency.

In order to abstract the semantics of $\mathcal{H}_{ss}$ (i.e, the stable switching semantics of $\mathcal{H}$), we consider as concrete domain the powerset of hybrid states $(\wp(\Sigma), \subseteq)$ and as concrete function the post-image operator of an external event subject to a stability constraint: $\mathrm{post}_{ss}(S, e) \doteq \{s' \in \Sigma \mid \exists s \in S . \neg \mathrm{TRANSIENT}(s) \wedge s \xrightarrow{e} s'\}$.

$\mathbb{P}$-*stable abstraction as Galois connection.* The simulation of Definition 3 can be seen as the abstraction of function post_{ss}. Consider functions (α_1, γ_1), with $\alpha_1(S) \doteq \{\phi \in \Phi \mid \exists s \in S . \; \mathrm{ATTR_{min}}(s, \phi)\}$ for each $S \subseteq \Sigma$, and $\gamma_1(F) \doteq \{s \in \Sigma \mid \forall \phi \in \Phi : \mathrm{ATTR_{min}}(s, \phi) \implies \phi \in F\}$ for each $F \subseteq \Phi$: this couple forms the Galois connection $(\wp(\Sigma), \subseteq) \xleftrightarrow[\alpha_1]{\gamma_1} (\wp(\Phi), \subseteq)$. The use of the powerset of formulae Φ as abstract domain allows for representing a disjunction of regions and describe precisely the non deterministic behavior of the concrete function. The following proposition states that this abstraction defines exactly the same relation introduced in Definition 3.

Proposition 2. *Let $\mathcal{A}$ be the $\mathbb{P}$-stable abstraction of $\mathcal{H}$. For $\phi, \phi' \in \Phi$ and $e \in E$, $\phi \xrightarrow{e} \phi'$ in $\mathcal{A}$ if and only if $\phi' \in \alpha_1(\mathrm{post}_{ss}(\gamma_1(\{\phi\}), e))$; also, $\Phi_0 = \alpha_1(\mathrm{init}(\mathcal{H}))$.*

Approximating the $\mathbb{P}$-stable abstraction. A first simplification step can be to overapproximate disjunctive stable regions with their join: this lets us obtain a deterministic abstract system based on a conservative abstraction of all the possible behaviors of the concrete system. To this aim, we can consider Φ instead of its powerset. In addition, we can further approximate this domain using its cartesian relaxation.

We denote with $(\mathbb{K}, \sqsubseteq)$ the cartesian abstraction [4] of $(\Phi, \Rightarrow)$. This can be formally defined considering the lattice of knowledge values for each predicate $P_i \in \mathbb{P}$, namely $\mathcal{P}_i = (\{\perp_i, p_i, \overline{p}_i, \top_i\}, \sqsubseteq_i)$ with $\perp_i \sqsubseteq_i p_i \sqsubseteq_i \top_i$ and $\perp_i \sqsubseteq_i \overline{p}_i \sqsubseteq_i \top_i$; then, $(\mathbb{K}, \sqsubseteq) = (\otimes_{P_i \in \mathbb{P}} \mathcal{P}_i)$, where '$\otimes$' denotes the smash product operator. Hence, every $k \in \mathbb{K}$, with $k \neq \perp$, is a vector $(k_1, \ldots, k_p)$, with $k_i \in \{p_i, \overline{p}_i, \top_i\}$. Every $k \in \mathbb{K}$ represents a formula in Φ: while $\perp$ is 'false', $(k_1, \ldots, k_p)$ is $(\bigwedge_{k_i = p_i} P_i \wedge \bigwedge_{k_i = \overline{p}_i} \neg P_i)$. We will use $k \in \mathbb{K}$ meaning the corresponding formula in Φ. Note that $(\mathbb{K}, \sqsubseteq)$ is a meet sublattice of $(\Phi, \Rightarrow)$: joins are not preserved since the cartesian abstraction cannot express precisely disjunctions between predicates.

We build an abstraction as composition of Galois connections:

$$(\wp(\Sigma), \subseteq) \xleftrightarrow[\alpha_1]{\gamma_1} (\wp(\Phi), \subseteq) \xleftrightarrow[\alpha_2]{\gamma_2} (\Phi, \Rightarrow) \xleftrightarrow[\alpha_3]{\gamma_3} (\mathbb{K}, \sqsubseteq),$$

where α_2 is the join operator on Φ, i.e., $\alpha_2(F) \doteq \vee(F)$, γ_2 is the downward closure, i.e., $\gamma_2(\phi) \doteq \mathop{\downarrow}\{\phi\}$, and (α_3, γ_3) is the cartesian abstraction, i.e., $\alpha_3(\phi) \doteq \sqcap\{k \in \mathbb{K} \mid \phi \Rightarrow k\}$ and $\gamma_3(k) = k$. Let $\alpha \doteq \alpha_3 \circ \alpha_2 \circ \alpha_1$, and $\gamma \doteq \gamma_1 \circ \gamma_2 \circ \gamma_3$.

Definition 6 (Approximated $\mathbb{P}$-stable abstraction). *The approximated $\mathbb{P}$-stable abstraction of hybrid system $\mathcal{H}$ with external events E is the finite state automaton $\mathcal{A}^\sharp \doteq \langle \mathbb{K}, \{k_0\}, E, \hookrightarrow \rangle$, with initial state $k_0 \doteq \alpha(\mathrm{init}(\mathcal{H}))$ and $k \xhookrightarrow{e} k'$ if and only if $k' = \alpha(\mathrm{post}_{ss}(\gamma(k), e))$.*

In other words, in the *approximated* $\mathbb{P}$-stable abstraction we have transition $k \xhookrightarrow{e} k'$ if *every* trajectory starting from a state that is stable in k with the external event e will eventually have k' as invariant, provided that no other external events are accepted meanwhile.

By definition, $\gamma \circ \alpha$ is an approximation of $\gamma_1 \circ \alpha_1$: since all the concrete functions we are dealing with are monotone, $\mathcal{A}^\sharp$ of Definition 6 is a sound overapproximation of the $\mathbb{P}$-stable abstraction $\mathcal{A}$ of Definition 3. Spurious behaviors can be introduced mainly because non deterministic trajectories are conservatively abstracted with a single transition. Function 'α' loses the ability to distinguish between states that are stable in a region with the ones that are stable in a greater one, therefore losing part of the minimality of the stable predicates. As an example, given two formulae $\phi_1, \phi_2 \in \Phi$, for Definition 3 the set of states that are considered stable in $\phi_1 \vee \phi_2$, are disjoint from the states that are stable in ϕ_1 or in ϕ_2, because minimality is required. Instead, using 'α_2', we consider stable in $\phi_1 \vee \phi_2$ also all the states that are stable in smaller regions, therefore recovering the monotonicity of the concretization function.

Finally, the use of the cartesian structure $\mathbb{K}$ overapproximates disjunctions.

Extending the same reasoning done in Sect. 4.2, for each $k \overset{e}{\hookrightarrow} k'$ in $\mathcal{A}^\sharp$, let $\Gamma^\sharp(k \overset{e}{\hookrightarrow} k')$ be the set of runs abstracted by it:

$$\Gamma^\sharp(k \overset{e}{\hookrightarrow} k') \doteq \left\{ s \overset{e}{\longrightarrow} s_1 \overset{c}{\rightsquigarrow} s' \mid \text{STABLE}(s, k), \text{STABLE}(s', k') \right\}.$$

Since the stabilization criterion is more slack, $\Gamma(\text{Run}(A)) \subseteq \Gamma^\sharp(\text{Run}(\mathcal{A}^\sharp))$. The computation of convergence time information can be extended as well: the time needed by the approximated system to stabilize after an external input will be lower than the one computed for $\mathcal{A}$. Letting $ct^\sharp = \max\{M \mid k \overset{e,[m,M]}{\longrightarrow} k' \text{ in } \mathcal{A}^\sharp\}$, we have that $\mathcal{H}_{ct^\sharp}$ is a *relaxation* of $\mathcal{H}_{ct}$ and $\text{Run}(\mathcal{H}_{ct^\sharp}) \subseteq \Gamma^\sharp(\text{Run}(\mathcal{A}^\sharp))$. Namely, $\mathcal{H}_{ct^\sharp}$ defines a new concrete semantics that is compliant with $\mathcal{A}^\sharp$. Moreover, for each $t \geq ct^\sharp$, we know that the abstraction soundly analyzes the evolution of predicates along the runs of $\mathcal{H}_t$.

6   Implementation and Experimental Evaluation

A possible approach for the computation of the approximation $\mathcal{A}^\sharp$ of the abstract system $\mathcal{A}$ is outlined in Pseudocode 1. Here, a reachability driven fixpoint computation incrementally adds ($\mathbb{P}$-stable) states and transitions to $\mathcal{A}^\sharp$; to this end, each abstract state $k \in \mathbb{K}$ being processed is paired with a corresponding reached set of states S, such that $\text{STABLE}(s, k)$ holds for every $s \in S$.

The procedure abstracts the initial state and then enters the main loop. Function 'post$_\mathcal{H}$' computes the image of an external discrete transition. The key processing step is the computation of a conservative evolution of a source set S in the closed system, which is performed within $\text{INTERNAL\_EVOLVE}_\mathcal{H}(S, \mathbb{P})$. Here, we exploit the cartesian approximation to build the vector k' with a linear number of calls to a *region-stability check*: for each $P_i \in \mathbb{P}$ we test whether the evolution of S is eventually invariant in it or in its negation. The stabilization check is based on the search of abstract lasso-shaped traces, disregarding divergent variables like the global clock. Finally, the addition of abstract locations may call a widening operator, possibly incurring further overapproximations but ensuring the convergence of the procedure.

Pseudocode 1. Build the $\mathbb{P}$-stable abstraction of $\mathcal{H}$.

```
1: function BUILD_ABSTRACTION(H, P)
2:     ⟨A♯, waiting⟩ ← ⟨∅, ∅⟩;
3:     ⟨k₀, S₀, ct₀⟩ ← INTERNAL_EVOLVE_H(init(H), P);
4:     ⟨A♯, waiting⟩ ← add_init_state(A♯, ⟨k₀, S₀⟩, ct₀, waiting);
5:     while waiting ≠ ∅ do
6:         ⟨k, S⟩ ← pop(waiting);
7:         for all e ∈ E such that e enabled in S do
8:             Sₑ ← post_H(S, e);
9:             ⟨k', S', ct⟩ ← INTERNAL_EVOLVE_H(Sₑ, P);
10:            ⟨A♯, waiting⟩ ← add_state(A♯, ⟨k', S'⟩, waiting);
11:            ⟨A♯, waiting⟩ ← add_trans(A♯, ⟨k, e, ct, k'⟩, waiting);
       return A♯;
```

We implemented the abstraction with a symbolic LRA-BDD based approach, built on the PPLite library for convex polyhedra [5], and evaluated it on a set of benchmarks representing circuits, shown in Table 1. External events close or open switches and trigger a run-to-completion process given by the activation of relays. Delayed elements are modeled either with their pragmatic approximation in timed components or by following the continuous dynamics of the internal process of charge/discharge. The predicates of interest focus on the state of some lamps. The abstraction is able to highlight the stabilization process of the signal in a still situation as well as in an oscillating one, e.g., in the periodic flashing of some lamps. The temporal properties extracted from the resulting abstract automata have been checked with the NUXMV model checker [11,13].

Table 1. $\mathbb{P}$-stable abstraction of models with run-to-completion behaviors.

test	$\mathcal{H}$ locs	vars	#E	#P	$\mathcal{A}^\sharp$ locs	trans	time	test	$\mathcal{H}$ locs	vars	#E	#P	$\mathcal{A}^\sharp$ locs	trans	time
s3	512	21	2	6	2	4	0.152	s1	8	7	2	2	2	4	0.001
s4	4096	28	2	8	2	4	2.708	2×s1	64	14	4	4	4	16	0.061
s5	32768	35	2	10	2	4	67.570	3×s1	512	21	6	6	8	48	1.448
r3	1024	29	6	6	7	42	2.060	4×s1	4096	28	8	8	16	128	115.886
s1_1	128	18	2	1	2	4	0.042	5×s1	32768	35	10	10	32	320	–
s1_2	2048	25	2	1	2	4	0.374	s2	64	14	2	4	2	4	0.013
s1_3	24576	32	2	1	2	4	5.444	2×s2	4096	28	4	8	4	16	13.784
s1_4	262144	39	2	1	2	4	99.190	3×s2	262144	42	6	12	8	48	–
s2_1	1024	25	2	3	2	4	0.356	r2	128	18	4	4	4	16	0.073
s2_2	16384	32	2	3	2	4	4.983	2×r2	16384	36	8	8	8	64	–
s2_3	196608	39	2	3	2	4	96.412	h2	4	16	2	2	2	4	0.037
s3_1	8192	32	2	5	2	4	4.743	2×h2	16	32	4	4	4	16	13.581
s3_2	131072	39	2	5	2	4	96.528	3×h2	64	48	6	6	8	48	–
s4_1	65536	39	2	7	2	4	101.797	h3	8	24	2	2	2	4	2.582
r2_1	512	29	4	3	4	16	1.662	2×h3	64	48	4	4	4	16	–
r2_2	2048	36	4	3	4	16	24.502	of	16	24	4	1	2	0	0.501
r3_1	4096	40	6	5	7	42	62.653	2×of	256	48	8	2	4	24	–

Compositional Reasoning. The current implementation is based on the exploration of a single, monolithic automaton, which may result in reduced scalability. When the concrete system is the composition of multiple subsystems having no practical discrete interaction between them (or when the predicates in $\mathbb{P}$ are influenced only by details that are local to the subsystems), then the $\mathbb{P}$-stable abstraction can be approached compositionally. The right-hand side of Table 1 shows an exponential growth in computation time for the analysis of the parallel composition of several independent, identical circuits. In all the tests whose analysis completes without incurring the timeout threshold (150 s), the abstract automaton for the composed system is exactly the cartesian product of the abstraction of its components, so it corresponds – without loss of precision – to the composition of the single abstractions. Hence, the analysis of the overall system can be factorized into the analysis of the subsystems, whose computation and composition are much more efficient. Clearly, in more general cases the predicates may involve relational constraints on the variables of different subsystems, or their internal interaction may have impact on their stability. Hence, the composition of the single abstractions is generally expected to be less precise than the abstraction of the network (but still guaranteed to be an overapproximation). When precision is not enough to verify the target property, a refinement step can be applied, based for example on considering larger subsystems, doing some compositions at the concrete level and hence reducing spurious behaviors.

7 Conclusions

In this paper we tackled the problem of synthesizing an abstract representation of the stabilizing behavior of hybrid automata. We defined $\mathbb{P}$-stable abstractions that have two key distinguishing features: first, they provide the most precise account – with respect to the given set of predicates – of the evolution between stable conditions in response to external events; second, they include timing information derived from the duration of the stabilization process, which provides suitable values for slow-switching control. We proved that the problem of synthesizing $\mathbb{P}$-stable abstractions can be cast in the framework of Abstract Interpretation, and presented a general synthesis algorithm which allows approximating $\mathbb{P}$-stable abstractions with precision depending on the abstract domain being adopted. We show that $\mathbb{P}$-stable abstractions are very informative from a representational standpoint. The experimental evaluation demonstrates that substantial performance improvements can be obtained by a compositional approach, leveraging the structure of hybrid automata networks.

In the future, we will investigate the use of symbolic techniques such as SMT to complement Abstract Interpretation and further improve the scalability and the precision of the engine. On the application side, the synthesis of $\mathbb{P}$-stable abstraction is currently being integrated within a industrial tool chain of the Italian Railway Network [12]. Specifically, the aim is to reverse-engineer legacy relay-based railways interlocking systems, using the $\mathbb{P}$-stable abstraction as reference specification for a computed-based equivalent solution.

References

1. Alur, R., Dang, T., Ivančić, F.: Reachability analysis of hybrid systems via predicate abstraction. In: Tomlin, C.J., Greenstreet, M.R. (eds.) HSCC 2002. LNCS, vol. 2289, pp. 35–48. Springer, Heidelberg (2002). https://doi.org/10.1007/3-540-45873-5_6
2. Alur, R., Dang, T., Ivančić, F.: Counter-example guided predicate abstraction of hybrid systems. In: Garavel, H., Hatcliff, J. (eds.) TACAS 2003. LNCS, vol. 2619, pp. 208–223. Springer, Heidelberg (2003). https://doi.org/10.1007/3-540-36577-X_15
3. Alur, R., Dill, D.L.: A theory of timed automata. Theor. Comput. Sci. **126**(2), 183–235 (1994)
4. Ball, T., Podelski, A., Rajamani, S.K.: Boolean and cartesian abstraction for model checking C programs. Int. J. Softw. Tools Technol. Transf. **5**(1), 49–58 (2003)
5. Becchi, A., Zaffanella, E.: An efficient abstract domain for not necessarily closed polyhedra. In: Podelski, A. (ed.) SAS 2018. LNCS, vol. 11002, pp. 146–165. Springer, Cham (2018). https://doi.org/10.1007/978-3-319-99725-4_11
6. Benerecetti, M., Faella, M., Minopoli, S.: Automatic synthesis of switching controllers for linear hybrid systems: safety control. Theor. Comput. Sci. **493**, 116–138 (2013)
7. Birkhoff, G.: Lattice Theory, Colloquium Publications, vol. XXV, 3rd edn. American Mathematical Society, Providence (1967)
8. Bogomolov, S., Mitrohin, C., Podelski, A.: Composing reachability analyses of hybrid systems for safety and stability. In: Bouajjani, A., Chin, W.-N. (eds.) ATVA 2010. LNCS, vol. 6252, pp. 67–81. Springer, Heidelberg (2010). https://doi.org/10.1007/978-3-642-15643-4_7
9. Branicky, M.: Stability of Hybrid Systems: State of the Art, vol. 1, pp. 120–125 (1998)
10. Brayton, R., Tong, C.: Stability of dynamical systems: a constructive approach. IEEE Trans. Circ. Syst. **CAS–26**, 224–234 (1979)
11. Cavada, R., et al.: The NUXMV symbolic model checker. In: Biere, A., Bloem, R. (eds.) CAV 2014. LNCS, vol. 8559, pp. 334–342. Springer, Cham (2014). https://doi.org/10.1007/978-3-319-08867-9_22
12. Cavada, R., Cimatti, A., Mover, S., Sessa, M., Cadavero, G., Scaglione, G.: Analysis of relay interlocking systems via SMT-based model checking of switched multidomain Kirchhoff networks. In: Bjørner, N., Gurfinkel, A. (eds.) 2018 Formal Methods in Computer Aided Design, FMCAD 2018, Austin, TX, USA, 30 October-2 November 2018, pp. 1–9. IEEE (2018)
13. Cimatti, A., Griggio, A., Magnago, E., Roveri, M., Tonetta, S.: Extending NUXMV with timed transition systems and timed temporal properties. In: Dillig, I., Tasiran, S. (eds.) CAV 2019. LNCS, vol. 11561, pp. 376–386. Springer, Cham (2019). https://doi.org/10.1007/978-3-030-25540-4_21
14. Cousot, P., Cousot, R.: Abstract interpretation: a unified lattice model for static analysis of programs by construction or approximation of fixpoints. In: Graham, R.M., Harrison, M.A., Sethi, R. (eds.) Conference Record of the Fourth ACM Symposium on Principles of Programming Languages, Los Angeles, California, USA, January 1977, pp. 238–252. ACM (1977)
15. Cousot, P., Cousot, R.: Refining model checking by abstract interpretation. Autom. Softw. Eng. **6**(1), 69–95 (1999)

16. Giesl, P., Hafstein, S.F.: Computation and verification of Lyapunov functions. SIAM J. Appl. Dyn. Syst. **14**(4), 1663–1698 (2015)
17. Liberzon, D.: Switching in Systems and Control. Systems & Control: Foundations & Applications. Birkhäuser (2003)
18. Milner, R.: Communication and Concurrency. PHI Series in Computer Science. Prentice Hall, Upper Saddle River (1989)
19. Mitra , S., Liberzon, D.: Stability of hybrid automata with average dwell time: an invariant approach, vol. 2, pp. 1394–1399 (2005)
20. Papachristodoulou, A., Prajna, S.: On the construction of Lapunov functions using the sum of squares decomposition, vol. 3, pp. 3482–3487 (2003)
21. Podelski, A., Wagner, S.: Model checking of hybrid systems: from reachability towards stability. In: Hespanha, J.P., Tiwari, A. (eds.) HSCC 2006. LNCS, vol. 3927, pp. 507–521. Springer, Heidelberg (2006). https://doi.org/10.1007/11730637_38
22. Podelski, A., Wagner, S.: Region stability proofs for hybrid systems. In: Raskin, J.-F., Thiagarajan, P.S. (eds.) FORMATS 2007. LNCS, vol. 4763, pp. 320–335. Springer, Heidelberg (2007). https://doi.org/10.1007/978-3-540-75454-1_23
23. Ravanbakhsh, H., Sankaranarayanan, S.: Counter-example guided synthesis of control Lyapunov functions for switched systems. In: 54th IEEE Conference on Decision and Control, CDC 2015, Osaka, Japan, December 15–18, 2015, pp. 4232–4239. IEEE (2015)
24. Sankaranarayanan, S., Chen, X., Ábrahám, E.: Lyapunov function synthesis using Handelman representations. In: Tarbouriech, S., Krstic, M., (eds.) 9th IFAC Symposium on Nonlinear Control Systems, NOLCOS 2013, Toulouse, France, September 4–6, 2013, pp. 576–581. International Federation of Automatic Control (2013)
25. Schupp, S., et al.: Current challenges in the verification of hybrid systems. In: Berger, C., Mousavi, M.R. (eds.) CyPhy 2015. LNCS, vol. 9361, pp. 8–24. Springer, Cham (2015). https://doi.org/10.1007/978-3-319-25141-7_2

Runtime Verification of Contracts
with Themulus

Alberto Aranda García[1], María-Emilia Cambronero[1], Christian Colombo[3],
Luis Llana[2(✉)], and Gordon J. Pace[3]

[1] University of Castilla-La Mancha, Albacete, Spain
[2] University Complutense of Madrid, Madrid, Spain
llana@ucm.es
[3] University of Malta, Msida, Malta

Abstract. Contracts regulating the behaviour of multiple interacting parties go beyond the notion of pure properties, but allow one to document and analyse the ideal behaviour. In this paper we build upon a real-time deontic logic allowing the description of such contracts and present a runtime verification tool for monitoring of such contracts. We present a verification algorithm used to monitor contracts written in this logic and an airport agreement is used as a case study to illustrate how such agreements and contracts can be monitored using our tool with reasonable processing costs.

Keywords: Deontic logic · Formal methods · Runtime verification · LARVA

1 Introduction

With the rise of multi-party systems and services, the formal notion of contracts or regulated interaction between participating parties has increased in importance. For many such situations, viewing a contract as a logical property which is not to be violated is sufficient—whether it is for the verification, monitoring or enforcement of the communication between parties. However, another view is that the notion of contracts should be first-class objects which speak about ideal behaviour but also cover the possibility that the actual behaviour does not match the ideal one and its consequences. Deontic logics [10] address precisely this aspect, typically using ideal-behaviour modalities such as obligations, permissions and prohibitions. Consider a multi-party system in which, whenever a file is downloaded, then the user should pay. From a deontic perspective, we would see an obligation to perform a *pay* action whenever we see a *download* action. Within the deontic logic, one can also express reparation clauses e.g. an

---

Research partially supported by the Spanish MINECO/FEDER projects DArDOS (TIN2015-65845-C3-1-R) and FAME (RTI2018-093608-B-C31) and the Comunidad de Madrid project FORTE-CM (S2018/TCS-4314) co-funded by EIE Funds of the European Union.

F. de Boer and A. Cerone (Eds.): SEFM 2020, LNCS 12310, pp. 231–246, 2020.
https://doi.org/10.1007/978-3-030-58768-0_13

obligation to pay a fine is added if the obligation to pay is not satisfied. Various approaches have been proposed in the literature for the formal reasoning about such deontic concepts e.g. defeasible logic in [11], event calculus-based in [12], dynamic logic style in $\mathcal{CL}$ [15] and automata-based in [13]. The common theme across these and other related approaches is looking at contracts as first-class entities which can be analysed and transformed independently of the systems they regulate enabling analysis such as conflict analysis or contract bias evaluation.

One recurring challenge across these approaches, beyond the deontic one, is that of addressing temporal issues [14], however, there has been limited work on deontic logic allowing reasoning about continuous time contracts, and no tools we are aware of. Recently, we have proposed Themulus [2], a real-time deontic calculus to reason about contracts over continuous time. From a practical perspective, the use of the calculus for actual verification of system behaviour with respect to a contract raises challenges, particularly due to the real-time nature of the calculus. In this paper, we present some results proving the soundness of a runtime verification algorithm of contracts written in Themulus. We have implemented this algorithm on top of the runtime verification tool Larva [6] in order to enable real-world agreements to be monitored.

(O1)	$\mathcal{O}_k(a)[d] \xrightarrow{a,k} \top$	(F1)	$\mathcal{F}_k(a)[d] \xrightarrow{a,k} \bot$	
(O2)	$\mathcal{O}_k(a)[d] \xrightarrow{\overline{(a,k)}} \top$	(F2)	$\mathcal{F}_k(a)[d] \xrightarrow{\overline{(a,k)}} \bot$	
(O3)	$\mathcal{O}_k(a)[d] \xrightarrow{b,l} \mathcal{O}_k(a)[d],$ $(a,k) \neq (b,l)$	(F3)	$\mathcal{F}_k(a)[d] \xrightarrow{b,l} \mathcal{F}_k(a)[d],$ $(b,l) \neq (a,k)$	
(O4)	$\mathcal{O}_k(a)[d] \xrightarrow{\overline{(b,l)}} \mathcal{O}_k(a)[d],$ $(a,k) \neq (b,l)$	(F4)	$\mathcal{F}_k(a)[d] \xrightarrow{\overline{(b,l)}} \mathcal{F}_k(a)[d],$ $(b,l) \neq (a,k)$	
(O5)	$\mathcal{O}_k(a)[d] \overset{d'}{\rightsquigarrow} \mathcal{O}_k(a)[d-d'],$ $0 < d' \leqslant d$	(F5)	$\mathcal{F}_k(a)[d] \overset{d'}{\rightsquigarrow} \mathcal{F}_k(a)[d-d'],$ $0 < d' \leqslant d$	
(P1)	$\mathcal{P}_k(a)[d] \xrightarrow{a,k} \top$	(C1)	$\text{cond}_k(a)[d](\varphi,\psi) \xrightarrow{a,k} \varphi$	
(P2)	$\mathcal{P}_k(a)[d] \xrightarrow{b,l} \mathcal{P}_k(a)[d],$ $(a,k) \neq (b,l)$	(C2)	$\text{cond}_k(a)[d](\varphi,\psi) \xrightarrow{\overline{(a,k)}} \varphi$	
(P3)	$\mathcal{P}_k(a)[d] \xrightarrow{\overline{(a,k)}} \bot$	(C3)	$\text{cond}_k(a)[d](\varphi,\psi) \xrightarrow{b,l} \psi,$ $(b,l) \neq (a,k)$	
(P4)	$\mathcal{P}_k(a)[d] \xrightarrow{\overline{(b,l)}} \mathcal{P}_k(a)[d],$ $(a,k) \neq (b,l)$	(C4)	$\text{cond}_k(a)[d](\varphi,\psi) \xrightarrow{\overline{(b,l)}} \psi,$ $(b,l) \neq (a,k)$	
(P5)	$\mathcal{P}_k(a)[d] \overset{d'}{\rightsquigarrow} \mathcal{P}_k(a)[d-d'],$ $0 < d' \leqslant d$	(C5)	$\text{cond}_k(a)[d](\varphi,\psi) \overset{d'}{\rightsquigarrow}$ $\text{cond}_k(a)[d-d'](\varphi,\psi),$ $0 < d' \leqslant d$	

Fig. 1. Operational Semantics transition rules 1/2

2   Contracts and Agents

In this section, we present some previous definitions published in [2]. We include them here to make the paper self-contained. We will assume a time domain $\mathbb{T}$

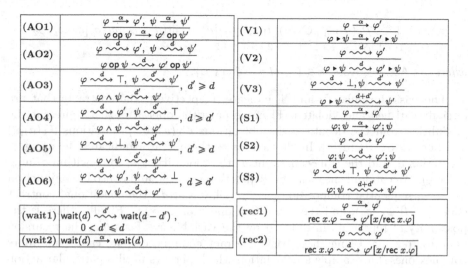

Fig. 2. Operational Semantics transition rules 2/2

ranging over the non-negative reals[1]. In order to deal with the recursion operator, we assume a set of variables fvars over which recursion will be defined.

Contracts regulate the behaviour of a number of agents, or parties running in parallel. In this section we present the notation we will use to describe these agents and their behaviour in order to be able to formalize contracts in the following sections.

Structurally, the underlying system consists of a number of indexed agents running in parallel, using variables A, A' to represent the individual agents. The system as a whole will consist of the parallel composition of all agents indexed by a finite set $\mathcal{I}$ i.e. the system will be of the form $\|_{i \in \mathcal{I}} A_i$. We will use variables $\mathcal{A}$, $\mathcal{A}'$ to denote the state of the system as a whole. Agents semantics are thus assumed to be represented as *timed labelled transition systems*:

- $A \xrightarrow{a} A'$, for $a \in$ Act, indicates that agent A changes to A' upon performing action a. As it is usual in process algebrae [17], the execution of actions do not consume time. The transition $A \xrightarrow{a}\!\!\!\!\!/\,\,$ indicates that agent A cannot perform action a: $A \xrightarrow{a}\!\!\!\!\!/\,\, \stackrel{df}{=} \neg \exists A' \cdot A \xrightarrow{a} A'$.
- $A \xrightsquigarrow{d} A'$, for $d > 0 \in \mathbb{T}$, for $d > 0 \in \mathbb{T}$, indicates that agent A evolves to A' after d time units pass.

2.1 Contract Syntax

Definition 1. *The set of contract formulae denoted by $\mathcal{C}$ (with variable $\varphi \in \mathcal{C}$ to range over the contracts) is syntactically defined as follows:*

---

[1] It is worth noting that the logic we present works equally well if the natural numbers are used for a discrete time domain. However, we allow for real time values to cater for any temporal constraints.

$$\varphi ::= \top \mid \bot \mid \mathcal{P}_k(a)[d] \mid \mathcal{O}_k(a)[d] \mid \mathcal{F}_k(a)[d] \mid \mathsf{wait}(d) \mid cond_k(a)[d](\varphi_1, \varphi_2)$$
$$\mid \varphi_1; \varphi_2 \mid \varphi_1 \wedge \varphi_2 \mid \varphi_1 \vee \varphi_2 \mid \varphi_1 \blacktriangleright \varphi_2 \mid \mathsf{rec}\ x.\varphi \mid x$$

where $a \in \mathsf{Act}$, $x \in \mathsf{fvars}$, $k \in \mathcal{I}$ *and* $d \in \mathbb{T} \cup \{\infty\}$.

The basic formulae $\top$ and $\bot$ indicate, respectively, the contracts that are trivially satisfied and violated. Then we have the operators that represent the modalities from the deontic logic: obligations $\mathcal{O}_k(a)[d]$, prohibitions $\mathcal{F}_k(a)[d]$ and permissions $\mathcal{P}_k(a)[d]$. In all three cases the operator indicates the agent k, the action a, and the time constraint d (the modality is in force within d units of time). We can find the contract disjunction $\varphi_1 \vee \varphi_2$, and contract conjunction $\varphi_1 \wedge \varphi_2$, sequential composition $\varphi_1; \varphi_2$, delay $\mathsf{wait}(d)$, the conditional contract $cond_k(a)[d](\varphi_1, \varphi_2)$, and the reparation operator $\varphi_1 \blacktriangleright \varphi_2$. Finally, there is the possibility of repetition introduced by the variable $x \in \mathsf{fvars}$ and the recursion operator $\mathsf{rec}\ x.\varphi$. Using these basic contract combinators, we can define more complex ones, for example a prohibition which persists until a particular action is performed—a prohibition on agent k from performing action a until party l performs action b, written $\mathcal{F}([a, k]\mathcal{U}[b, l])$, and defined as follows:

$$\mathcal{F}([a, k]\mathcal{U}[b, l]) \overset{\mathrm{df}}{=} \mathsf{rec}\ x.(cond_k(a)[\infty](\bot, \top) \wedge cond_l(b)[\infty](\top, x))$$

In order to simplify the semantics of the language, we define a congruence in the language.

Definition 2. *We define the relation* $\equiv\ \subseteq \mathcal{C} \times \mathcal{C}$ *as the least congruence relation that includes:*

1. $\varphi \wedge \top \equiv \varphi$
2. $\top \wedge \varphi \equiv \varphi$
3. $\bot \wedge \varphi \equiv \bot$
4. $\varphi \wedge \bot \equiv \bot$
5. $\varphi \vee \top \equiv \top$
6. $\top \vee \varphi \equiv \top$
7. $\varphi \vee \bot \equiv \varphi$
8. $\bot \vee \varphi \equiv \varphi$
9. $\top; \varphi \equiv \varphi$
10. $\bot; \varphi \equiv \bot$
11. $\top \blacktriangleright \varphi \equiv \top$
12. $\bot \blacktriangleright \varphi \equiv \varphi$
13. $\mathcal{O}_k(a)[0] \equiv \bot$
14. $\mathcal{F}_k(a)[0] \equiv \top$
15. $\mathcal{P}_k(a)[0] \equiv \top$
16. $\mathsf{wait}(0) \equiv \top$
17. $cond_k(a)[0](\varphi, \psi) \equiv \psi$

The operational semantics of the language is defined by the rules appearing in Figs. 1 and 2. The operational semantics of the contracts has three kind of transitions: (i) $\varphi \xrightarrow{a,k} \varphi'$ to denote that contract φ can evolve (in one step) to φ' when action a is performed, which involves party k (and possibly other parties); or (ii) $\varphi \xrightarrow{\overline{(a,k)}} \varphi'$ indicating that the contract φ can evolve to φ' when the action a is not offered by any party other than k; or (iii) $\varphi \overset{d}{\rightsquigarrow} \varphi'$ to represent that contract φ can evolve to contract φ' when d time units pass. We will use variable α to stand for a label of either form: (a, k) or $\overline{(a, k)}$. The rules of the operational semantics are always applied to irreducible terms.

Next, define the predicate $\mathsf{vio}(\varphi)$ that indicates if a contract is *currently violated*.

Definition 3. *We say that an irreducible contract φ is in a* violated *state, written* $\mathsf{vio}(\varphi)$*, if and only if the contract has already been violated:*

$$\mathsf{vio}(\top) \overset{df}{=} f\!f$$
$$\mathsf{vio}(\mathcal{P}_k(a)[d]) \overset{df}{=} \overline{(a,k)}$$
$$\mathsf{vio}(\mathcal{F}_k(a)[d]) \overset{df}{=} (a,k)$$
$$\mathsf{vio}(\varphi \wedge \varphi') \overset{df}{=} \mathsf{vio}(\varphi) \vee \mathsf{vio}(\varphi')$$
$$\mathsf{vio}(\varphi \blacktriangleright \varphi') \overset{df}{=} \mathsf{vio}(\varphi) \wedge \mathsf{vio}(\varphi')$$
$$\mathsf{vio}(\varphi; \varphi') \overset{df}{=} \mathsf{vio}(\varphi)$$

$$\mathsf{vio}(\bot) \overset{df}{=} tt$$
$$\mathsf{vio}(\mathcal{O}_k(a)[d]) \overset{df}{=} f\!f$$
$$\mathsf{vio}(\mathsf{wait}(d)) \overset{df}{=} f\!f$$
$$\mathsf{vio}(\varphi \vee \varphi') \overset{df}{=} \mathsf{vio}(\varphi) \wedge \mathsf{vio}(\varphi')$$
$$\mathsf{vio}(cond_k(a)[d](\varphi, \varphi')) \overset{df}{=} f\!f$$
$$\mathsf{vio}(\mathsf{rec}\ x.\varphi) \overset{df}{=} \mathsf{vio}(\varphi)$$

We can now define how contracts evolve alongside a system, and what it means for a system to satisfy a contract.

Definition 4. *Given a contract $\varphi \in \mathcal{C}$ with alphabet Act' and a system $\mathcal{A}$, we define the semantics of $\varphi \| \mathcal{A}$—the combination of the system with the contract—with alphabet Act with $\mathsf{Act}' \subseteq \mathsf{Act}$ through the following rules:*

(M1)	$\dfrac{\varphi \xrightarrow{a,k} \varphi',\ \mathcal{A} \xrightarrow{a,s} \mathcal{A}'}{\varphi \| \mathcal{A} \Rightarrow \varphi' \| \mathcal{A}'} k \in s$	**(M2)**	$\dfrac{\varphi \xrightarrow{\overline{(a,k)}} \varphi',\ \mathcal{A} \models \langle a, \overline{k} \rangle}{\varphi \| \mathcal{A} \Rightarrow \varphi' \| \mathcal{A}}$
(M3)	$\dfrac{\mathcal{A} \xrightarrow{a,s} \mathcal{A}'}{\varphi \| \mathcal{A} \Rightarrow \varphi \| \mathcal{A}'} a \notin \mathsf{Act}'$	**(M4)**	$\dfrac{\begin{array}{c}\mathcal{A} \overset{d}{\rightsquigarrow} \mathcal{A}',\ \varphi \overset{d}{\rightsquigarrow} \varphi', \\ \forall d' < d \cdot \text{ if } \mathcal{A} \overset{d'}{\rightsquigarrow} \mathcal{A}'' \text{ and} \\ \varphi \overset{d'}{\rightsquigarrow} \varphi'' \text{ then } \mathcal{A}'' \not\models \mathsf{vio}(\varphi'')\end{array}}{\varphi \| \mathcal{A} \Rightarrow \varphi' \| \mathcal{A}'}$

Rule **M1** and **M2** handles synchronization between the contract and the system. If an action a performed by the system is of interest to the contract, the contract evolves alongside the system (**M1**), if the contract allows an agent to perform an action but only agent k (and no other agent) is willing to engage in the action, then only the contract evolves (**M2**). Rule **M3** handles actions on the system which the contract is not interested in. Finally, rule **M4** ensures that time cannot skip over a violation.

Definition 5. *Let $\mathcal{A}$ be a system and $\varphi \in \mathcal{C}$ be a contract.*

- *System $\mathcal{A}$ can break φ, written $\mathsf{break}(\mathcal{A}, \varphi)$, if there exists a computation that leads to a violation of the contract: for some $n \geq 0$ and contracts φ_0 till φ_n such that:*

$$\varphi \| \mathcal{A} = \varphi_0 \| \mathcal{A}_0 \Longrightarrow \varphi_1 \| \mathcal{A}_1 \Longrightarrow \ldots \varphi_{n-1} \| \mathcal{A}_{n-1} \Longrightarrow \varphi_n \| \mathcal{A}_n,$$

and $\mathcal{A}_n \models \mathsf{vio}(\varphi_n)$.
- *System $\mathcal{A}$ may fulfil φ, written $\mathsf{fulfill}(\mathcal{A}, \varphi)$, if there exists a computation of the system that fulfils the contract: for some $n \geq 0$ and contracts φ_0 till φ_n:*

$$\varphi \| \mathcal{A} = \varphi_0 \| \mathcal{A}_0 \Longrightarrow \varphi_1 \| \mathcal{A}_1 \Longrightarrow \ldots \varphi_{n-1} \| \mathcal{A}_{n-1} \Longrightarrow \varphi_n \| \mathcal{A}_n,$$

and $\mathcal{A} \not\models \mathsf{vio}(\varphi_k)$ for $0 \leq k < n$, and $\varphi_n \equiv 1$.

Note that there are contracts which may never be fulfilled. An example of such a contract is $\varphi = \mathrm{rec}\; x.[a, k, \infty](\bot, \infty)$, which may never be fulfilled since there are no transitions from this contract leading to $\top$. Nevertheless, if agent k never performs action a, then neither is the contract broken.

3   Case Study

The case study presented in this section (Fig. 3) is based on the Madrid Barajas airport regulations [1]. The contract describing our case study can be formalized using our contract calculus as follows:

1. The passenger is permitted to check in her luggage according to the stipulations of the class of ticket they purchased from their respective airline company. It is necessary that the passenger arrives at the airport, at least two hours before her flight, in order to check-in her luggage and pass the security controls. Then, the passenger is permitted to use the check-in desk within two hours before the plane takes off (t_0). φ_0
2. At the check-in desk, the passenger is obliged to present her boarding pass within 5 minutes. φ_1
3. After presenting the boarding pass, the passenger must show her passport. She has 5 minutes for this purpose. φ_2
4. The passenger is permitted to carry two pieces (of hand luggage): one personal article and one carry-on luggage. If the passenger has carry-on luggage, she is obliged to fit it into the device for hand luggage allowance, situated next to the check-in desks. φ_3
5. After presenting her passport, the passenger is permitted to board within 90 minutes and to present the hand-luggage to the airport staff within 10 minutes. φ_4 (the part before the reparation)
6. The airline company is obliged to allow the passenger to board within 90 minutes. φ_4 (the reparation part)
7. The passenger is obliged to pass the filters or security checkpoints, before they access the restricted safety areas of the airport, as boarding gates and passenger-only zones, in accordance with the safety regulations, within 60 minutes. φ_5
8. These security checkpoints consist of metal-detector arches for the passengers and X-ray detectors for their luggage. The airport security staff are permitted to carry both systems manually. φ_6
9. If the hand luggage is a personal computer or another electronic device, the airport security staff is permitted to ask the passenger to take it out of its protective case in order to be examined. φ_7
10. The passenger is obliged to take out the personal computer protection if the airport staff need to examine it. φ_8
11. The passenger is forbidden from taking articles to the security restricted area, or to the cabin

of the aircraft, which constitute a risk for the health of other passengers, the crew and the safety of the aircraft and the cargo. φ_9
12. The passenger is obliged to included risk articles at check-in as baggage and/or apply to them the relevant procedure to be accepted on board. Otherwise, the security staff can requisition the articles. φ_{10}
13. Security staff is permitted to deny access to the boarding area and the airplane cabin to any passenger in possession of an object which, even if not considered forbidden, arouses their suspicions φ_7. If the passenger is stopped from carrying luggage, the airline company is obliged to put the passenger's hand luggage in the hold within 20 minutes φ_4 (reparation part).
14. The passenger is obliged to transport the liquids in individual containers with a capacity of fewer than 100 ml. These containers must be carried in a resealable, transparent plastic bag (for its easy inspection), with a capacity of not more than 1 liter. Maximum one bag per passenger. φ_{12}
15. The passenger is obliged to accompany her medication with a corresponding receipt, a medical prescription or a specified statement about the passenger's health condition, in case the security staff requires it. φ_{13}
16. Even if the regulations for liquids do not apply in the medication case, the passenger is obliged to demonstrate all liquid medication to the security staff, apart from the transparent plastic bag, used for the transport of other liquids. φ_{14}
17. The passenger is obliged to check in all firearms, which may not be transported. φ_{15}
18. The passenger has an obligation to know her rights if she wants to file a complaint. In this case, she may ask for a document at any airport in Spain, in which his rights are described, including some advice about how to act. Over and above, the passenger may also contact the Spanish National Aviation Agency (Agencia Estatal de Seguridad Aérea — AESA). φ_{16}
19. The passenger is entitled to present a claim, in case of any violation of those rights, which can result in a financial compensation or any other kind of compensation. If a passenger is unhappy with the service during a flight but is not entitled to present a claim, he still has the option to lodge a complaint or a suggestion. φ_{17}

Fig. 3. Adaptation of the Madrid Barajas airport regulations

$$PBS ::= ((\varphi_0 \wedge \varphi_{10} \wedge \varphi_{15}); \varphi_1; \varphi_2; \varphi_3;$$
$$(\varphi_5 \wedge \varphi_6 \wedge \varphi_7 \wedge \varphi_8 \wedge \varphi_9 \wedge \varphi_{12} \wedge \varphi_{13} \wedge \varphi_{14});$$
$$(\varphi_4 \wedge \varphi_{11})) \wedge \varphi_{16} \wedge \varphi_{17})$$

Where the formulas $\varphi_1, \ldots, \varphi_{17}$ are defined in Fig. 4 such that p, S, c refer to the passenger, the security airport staff, and the airline company, respectively; while t_0 is departure estimated time. Note that the clauses φ_0 to φ_{17} are used to express the different parts of the contract, and combined in the top-level contract expression PBS. The translation is quite straightforward although it is not automated. We have attach a formula to each point of the contract indicating where it has been formalized.

$\varphi_0 ::= \mathcal{P}_p(\textbf{checkin})[t_0 - 120]$
$\varphi_1 ::= \mathcal{O}_p(\textbf{PBP})[5]$
$\varphi_2 ::= \mathcal{O}_p(\textbf{ShP})[5]$
$\varphi_3 ::= \mathcal{P}_p(\textbf{CToHL})[120]$
$\varphi_4 ::= (\mathcal{P}_p(\textbf{board})[90]; \mathcal{P}_p(\textbf{hl})[10]) \blacktriangleright$
$\quad\quad (\mathcal{O}_c(\textbf{board})[90]; \mathcal{O}_c(\textbf{hlhold})[20])$
$\varphi_5 ::= \mathcal{O}_p(\textbf{PSC})[60]$
$\varphi_6 ::= \mathcal{P}_S(\textbf{CD})[120]$
$\varphi_7 ::= \mathcal{P}_S(\textbf{EPP})[120]$
$\varphi_8 ::= \mathcal{O}_p(\textbf{TOP})[120]$
$\varphi_9 ::= (\mathcal{F}([\textbf{TRA}, p]\,\mathcal{U}\,[\textbf{landing}, p]))$
$\varphi_{10} ::= \mathcal{O}_p(\textbf{CRA})[t_0 - 120] \blacktriangleright \mathcal{P}_S(\textbf{RRA})[10]$
$\varphi_{11} ::= \mathcal{P}_S(\textbf{DRA})[10]$
$\varphi_{12} ::= \mathcal{O}_p(\textbf{liquids})[120]$
$\varphi_{13} ::= \mathcal{O}_p(\textbf{medication})[120]$
$\varphi_{14} ::= \mathcal{O}_p(\textbf{liq})[120]$
$\varphi_{15} ::= \mathcal{O}_p(\textbf{firearms})[t_0 - 120]$
$\varphi_{16} ::= \mathcal{O}_p(\textbf{rights})[120]$
$\varphi_{17} ::= \mathcal{P}_p(\textbf{complaint})[120]$

checkin:	Go to the checkin desk
PBP:	Present boarding pass
ShP:	Show her passport
CToHL:	Carry two hand luggage
board:	Board
hl:	Board with hand luggage
PSC:	Pass the security checkpoints
CD:	Carry detectors
EPP:	Examine passanger PC
TOP:	Take out PC
TRA:	Taking risk articles
CRA:	Check in risk articles
RRA:	Requisition of risk articles
DRA:	Access to boarding area
hlhold:	Put her hand luggage in the hold
board:	Board
liquids:	Liquids of 100ml
medication:	Medication with receipt
liq:	Demonstrate liquid medication
firearms:	Check in the firearms
rights:	Know her rights
complaint:	File a complaint

Fig. 4. Madrid Barajas airport regulations formulae.

Then, this approach allows us to check and determine if any of the agents involved in the plane boarding system breaks the contract. In this case, our formalism allows us to determine, for instance, if it was the passenger who violated the contract and if so why, e.g. because she did not present her boarding pass within the specified time at the check-in desk, or because she was taking articles to the restricted security area.

4 Runtime Verification

The operational semantics we give to contracts provides us with a framework for contract monitoring: to monitor contract $\psi \in \mathcal{C}$, we start the monitor in state

ψ and update the state whenever the system performs an action according to the operational semantics. A violation is reached once the violation predicate is satisfied by the system. In the rest of this section, we concretely show how our logic can be automatically monitored using a derivative-based algorithm [4].

The idea behind derivative-based or term rewriting-based monitoring is that the formula still to be monitored is used as the state of the monitoring system. Whenever an event e is received with the system being in state ψ, the state is updated to ψ' such that any trace of events es matches ψ', if and only if $e : es$ (the trace starting with e, followed by es) matches ψ. This is repeated and a violation is reported when (and if) the monitoring state is reduced to a formula which matches the empty trace. In our contract logic, the operational semantics provide precisely this information, with ψ' being chosen to be the (unique) formula such that[2] $\psi \xrightarrow{a,k} ; \longmapsto \psi'$ (where the monitoring systems observes the action a performed by party k), and $\mathsf{vio}(\psi)$ indicates whether ψ matches the empty string (immediately violates the contract).

In timed logics, this approach has to be augmented with timeout events which, in the absence of a system event, still change the formula. For example, the contract $\mathsf{wait}(d); \varphi$ would evolve to φ upon d time units elapsing. Similarly, if d time units elapse (with no system events received), we evolve the contract $\mathcal{O}_k(a)[d]; \varphi$ to $\bot; \varphi$, which is equivalent to $\bot$, thus enabling us to flag the violation as soon as it happens. If we were to wait for a system event, the violation might end up being identified too late. In our case, we use the timeout function to enable the setting of a timer to trigger the monitoring state update, evolving φ to the unique formula φ' according to the timed operational semantics $\varphi \overset{\mathsf{timeout}(\varphi)}{\rightsquigarrow} ; \longmapsto \varphi'$. Also, system events carry a timestamp, through which the contract can be moved ahead in time upon receiving the event.

In order to formalise these ideas, we need a notion of structural equivalence. Intuitively, two contracts are structurally equivalent if they only differ in the time constraints and so they can perform the same actions.

Definition 6. *Consider the relation* $\mathcal{R} \subseteq \mathcal{C} \times \mathcal{C}$ *defined as follows:*

$$\mathcal{R} \overset{df}{=} \{(\top, \top), (\bot, \bot)\}$$
$$\cup \; \{(\mathcal{F}_k(a)[d], \mathcal{F}_k(a)[d']) \mid d, d' > 0\}$$
$$\cup \; \{(\mathcal{P}_k(a)[d], \mathcal{P}_k(a)[d']) \mid d, d' > 0\}$$
$$\cup \; \{(\mathcal{O}_a(k)[d], \mathcal{O}_a(k)[d']) \mid d, d' > 0\}$$
$$\cup \; \{(\mathsf{wait}(d), \mathsf{wait}(d')) \mid d, d' > 0\}$$
$$\cup \; \{(cond_k(a)[d](\varphi_1, \varphi_2), cond_k(a)[d'](\varphi_1, \varphi_2)) \mid d, d' > 0,$$
$$\varphi_1, \varphi_2 \in \mathcal{C}\}$$

The structural equivalence congruence, *denoted by* $\equiv_s$ *is the smallest congruence containing* $\mathcal{R}$.

---

[2] We write $r; s$ to indicate the forward composition of the two relations r and s, and use $\longmapsto$ to denote the reflexive transitive closure of the timed labelled transition systems.

Proposition 1. *Let $\varphi, \psi \in C$ be two structurally equivalent contracts, $\varphi \equiv_s \psi$. Then $\mathsf{vio}(\varphi) = \mathsf{vio}(\psi)$ and $\varphi \xrightarrow{\alpha} \chi$ iff $\psi \xrightarrow{\alpha} \chi$.*

Proof. The proof follows using structural induction.

Definition 7. *The* timeout *of a contract φ, written timeout(φ), is inductively defined as follows:*

$$\mathit{timeout}(\top) \overset{df}{=} \infty \qquad\qquad \mathit{timeout}(\bot) \overset{df}{=} \infty$$
$$\mathit{timeout}(\mathcal{P}_k(a)[d]) \overset{df}{=} d \qquad\qquad \mathit{timeout}(\mathcal{O}_k(a)[d]) \overset{df}{=} d$$
$$\mathit{timeout}(\mathcal{F}_k(a)[d]) \overset{df}{=} d \qquad\qquad \mathit{timeout}(\mathit{cond}_k(a)[d](\varphi_1, \varphi_2)) \overset{df}{=} d$$
$$\mathit{timeout}(\mathsf{wait}(d)) \overset{df}{=} d \qquad\qquad \mathit{timeout}(\varphi_1 ; \varphi_2) \overset{df}{=} \mathit{timeout}(\varphi_1)$$
$$\mathit{timeout}(\varphi_1 \blacktriangleright \varphi_2) \overset{df}{=} \mathit{timeout}(\varphi_1) \qquad\qquad \mathit{timeout}(\mathsf{rec}\ x.\varphi \mid x) \overset{df}{=} \mathit{timeout}(\varphi)$$
$$\mathit{timeout}(\varphi_1 \wedge \varphi_2) \overset{df}{=} \min\{\mathit{timeout}(\varphi_1), \mathit{timeout}(\varphi_2)\}$$
$$\mathit{timeout}(\varphi_1 \vee \varphi_2) \overset{df}{=} \min\{\mathit{timeout}(\varphi_1), \mathit{timeout}(\varphi_2)\}$$

Finally, we obtain the result that we need: any timed transition taking less than the timeout of a contract preserves the structure of a contract.

Proposition 2. *Given contract φ and time $t < \mathit{timeout}(\varphi)$, advancing φ by t time units preserves the structure of the contract: if $\varphi \overset{t}{\rightsquigarrow} \varphi'$, then: $\varphi \equiv_s \varphi'$.*

Proof. The proof is simple by structural induction.

We can now define the closure of a contract φ as all formulae reachable from φ through action transitions and timeout time transitions.

Definition 8. *We define the* closure *of a contract formula φ, written closure(φ), to be the set of all contract formulae reachable through a combination of visible action transitions and timeout transitions. Formally, closure(φ) is the smallest set such that: (i) $\varphi \in \mathit{closure}(\varphi)$; (ii) if $\varphi_1 \in \mathit{closure}(\varphi)$, and $\varphi_1 \xrightarrow{a,k} \varphi_2$, then $\varphi_2 \in \mathit{closure}(\varphi)$; and (iii) if $\varphi_1 \in \mathit{closure}(\varphi)$, and $\varphi_1 \overset{\mathit{timeout}(\varphi_1)}{\rightsquigarrow} \varphi_2$, then $\varphi_2 \in \mathit{closure}(\varphi)$.*

It is easy to prove, that for a contract φ whose time constraints are non-zero constants, the closure of φ does not exhibit Zeno-like behaviour[3]. It also follows that the relations of timeout time steps and visible event steps are sufficient to characterise the operational semantics progress of a contract to a violation or otherwise.

4.1   A Monitoring Algorithm

The monitoring algorithm for our contract logic is shown in Algorithm 1. The state of the monitor is stored in variable *contract* while variable *systime* keeps

---

[3] By Zeno-like behaviour, we mean an infinite number of arbitrarily smaller time steps whose sum converges, thus blocking time from progressing.

track of the last timestamp processed by the system. Initially, these variables are set to ψ and 0 (line 1). The monitoring algorithm is effectively a loop (lines 2–17) which checks whether there was a violation upon every iteration. Upon entering the loop, any pending timer triggers are replaced (lines 3–5), enacting a process which creates a special *timeout* event (line 4) to be launched (asynchronously) after the current contract times out. In the meantime, execution is blocked until an event is received (line 6). If the event received is the *timeout* event, the monitored formula is updated accordingly using the *timestep* function which returns the unique formula satisfying $\psi \stackrel{t}{\leadsto} timestep(\varphi, t)$ with the time advanced by $timeout(\psi)$ time units (lines 7–10). If, however, the event received is a system event e with timestamp t, the monitoring state is updated by first advancing time by $(t - systime)$ time units, and then stepping forward using the *step* function which returns the unique formula such that $\psi \stackrel{e}{\longrightarrow} step(\psi, e)$ (lines 11–14). Finally, the *systime* variable is updated accordingly (line 16).

It is worth noting that the algorithm replicates the two types of transitions required to advance a contract: (i) maximally advancing time until the structure of the contract changes (the case of a timeout event); and (ii) processing a system event. This ensures that the state of the contract monitor advances steadily in correct steps (assuming that *timestep* and *step* correctly implement the rules from the semantics). Furthermore, progress is ensured since stepping along maximal time steps never results in Zeno-like behaviour.

```
 1  contract = φ; systime = 0;
 2  while ¬vio(contract) do
 3      reset timer to timeout(contract))
 4        │ createEvent(Timeout);
 5      end
 6      switch getEvent() do
 7          case Timeout do
 8            │ Δt = timeout(contract);
 9            │ contract = timestep(contract, Δt);
10          end
11          case Event e with Timestamp t do
12            │ Δt = t - systime;
13            │ contract = step(timestep(contract, Δt), e);
14          end
15      end
16      systime = systime + Δt;
17  end
18  report(Violation);
```

Algorithm 1: Algorithm to monitor timed contracts

5   Runtime Verification Using Larva

Rather than programming the runtime verification algorithm from scratch, we have built it on top of an existing runtime verification tool. We used Larva [6], which uses Dynamic Automata with Timers and Events (DATEs) as a specification language. DATEs are symbolic timed automata enriched in many aspects.

There are three main elements in DATE transitions: (i) *Events* refer to observable actions which a DATE may react to. (ii) *Conditions* are boolean expressions taking into consideration both the DATE's symbolic state and the system state, which decides whether a transition is taken or not. (iii) *Actions* are modifications that are done to the DATE or system state upon observing an event and satisfying the condition. What follows formally defines these concepts.

Events which a DATE will be able to react to are either (i) system events over an alphabet SYSTEMEVENT, corresponding to control- or data-flow points of interest during the execution of the system; or (ii) timer events which are triggered upon a timer t reaching a threshold limit L written $t@L$. Timer limits can either take the form of a time constant $T \in \mathbb{T}$ (where $\mathbb{T}$ refers to the continuous time domain), or deadline variables $D \in$ DEADLINE. Unlike constant limits, deadline variables can be dynamically modified during the traversal of the DATE.

$$\text{EVENT} ::= \text{SYSTEMEVENT} \mid \text{TIMER@}(\mathbb{T} \cup \text{DEADLINE})$$

DATE conditions and actions may also refer to the state of the system which is being monitored e.g. to react to a *login* event only if the system is in alert mode. The state of the system σ will be assumed to range over the type STATE$_s$. Besides, monitors may keep their own state, e.g. the monitor may keep track of how many users are logged in, in order to react to a *login* only when more than 100 concurrent users are using the system. The symbolic DATE state μ will be assumed to range over the type STATE$_m$.

In addition, a DATE configuration will also keep track of the timer values $\tau \in$ STATE$_T$, assigning a time value to each time such that STATE$_T =$ TIMER $\rightarrow$ $\mathbb{T}$. Similarly, it keeps track of the current value of the timer variable deadlines $\delta \in$ STATE$_D$ where STATE$_D =$ DEADLINE $\rightarrow \mathbb{T}$. We will abuse notation and write $\delta(L)$ to extend the function to work also on constant deadlines (in which case that constant deadline is returned) and $\tau + \Delta$ (where $\Delta \in \mathbb{T}$) to denote the timer state in which all timers are advanced by Δ time units. The symbolic state of a DATE is thus defined to be a combination of all these parts: STATE$_M^+ =$ STATE$_m \times$ STATE$_T \times$ STATE$_D$.

Conditions $c \in$ CONDITION are predicates over the system and full monitoring state:

$$\text{CONDITION} = (\text{STATE}_s \times \text{STATE}_M^+) \rightarrow \mathbb{B}$$

Similarly, actions $\alpha \in$ ACTION are functions which, based on the system state, may update any part of the full monitoring state:

$$\text{ACTION} = (\text{STATE}_s \times \text{STATE}_M^+) \rightarrow \text{STATE}_M^+$$

Formally Defining DATEs. A DATE is quadruple $\langle Q, q_0, K, B \rangle$ where Q is a finite set of states, $q_0 \in Q$ is the initial state, $K \subseteq (Q \times \text{EVENT} \times \text{CONDITION} \times \text{ACTION} \times Q)$ is a set of event-condition-action transitions, and $B \subseteq Q$ is a set of bad states. We will write $q \xrightarrow{e|c \mapsto \alpha} q'$ to denote a transition $(q, e, c, \alpha, q') \in K$.

The following figure shows an example of a DATE whereupon the detection of a login event on alert mode, a timer of ten minutes is started. If the ten minutes elapse before a logout, the DATE reaches a bad state.

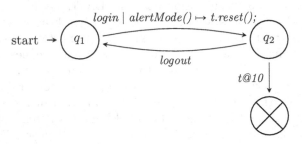

The *event triggers* from a DATE state q, written *triggers(q)*, are defined to be all events which appear on transitions outgoing from q: $triggers(q) \overset{\text{df}}{=} \{e \mid \exists q', c, \alpha \cdot q \xrightarrow{e|c \mapsto \alpha} q'\}$.

The semantics of a DATE with dynamic timer deadlines can now be defined using this notation. The configuration of the monitor consists of (i) the state $q \in Q$ of the DATE; and (ii) the symbolic monitoring state $\sigma \in \text{STATE}_M^+$ of the monitor. Given a monitoring configuration, the *earliest timer trigger* is the least time which will trigger an outgoing timer event transition if no other event is received:

$$earliest(q, (\mu, \tau, \delta)) \overset{\text{df}}{=} \min\{\delta(L) - \tau(t) \mid t@L \in triggers(q)$$
$$\wedge \; \delta(L) \geqslant \tau(t)\}$$

The semantics of DATEs will specify how the configuration of the DATE changes upon event triggering or time passing. We will have two forms of operational semantics relations: (i) $C \xrightarrow{e, \Delta, \sigma} C'$ to denote that the monitor moves from configuration C to C' upon the system receiving event e after Δ time units (from the last transition) and with the system state snapshot at that time being σ; (ii) $C \overset{\Delta, \sigma}{\rightsquigarrow} C'$ to denote that the monitor goes from configuration C to C' after Δ time units of inactivity at the end of which the system state is σ.

The first relation is defined with the implicit condition that an event e has triggered and another two preconditions: the existence of a transition triggering on e and the satisfaction of the condition c. The side-condition ensures that no timer-triggered transitions should have modified the configuration before.

$$\frac{q \xrightarrow{e|c \mapsto \alpha} q' \qquad c(\sigma, (\mu, \tau, \delta))}{(q, (\mu, \tau, \delta)) \xrightarrow{e, \Delta, \sigma} (q', \alpha(\mu, \tau + \Delta, \delta))} \; earliest(q, (\mu, \tau, \delta)) > 0$$

The second relation is similar to the previous but, while not requiring the occurrence of a system event, requires that the timer has reached its deadline.

$$\frac{q \xrightarrow{t@L|c \mapsto \alpha} q' \qquad \tau(t) + \Delta = \delta(L) \qquad c(\sigma, (\mu, \tau, \delta)) \qquad earliest(q, (\mu, \tau, \delta)) = 0}{(q, (\mu, \tau, \delta)) \xrightarrow{\Delta, \sigma} (q', \alpha(\mu, \tau + \Delta, \delta))}$$

Building on the earlier example, consider the case where the automaton is in the second state with the timer just reset: $(q_2, (\varnothing, t \mapsto 0, t \mapsto 10))$. If a logout event occurs after six minutes, then $\Delta = 6$, while $earliest(q_2, (\varnothing, t \mapsto 6, t \mapsto 10)) = 10 - 6 = 4$. Therefore the first relation would apply, updating the configuration to $(q_1, (\varnothing, t \mapsto 6, t \mapsto 10))$. On the other hand, if no logout event occurs within ten minutes, then $earliest(q_2, (\varnothing, t \mapsto 0, t \mapsto 10)) = 10 - 0 = 10$ causing the second relation to be applied resulting in the configuration $(q_\times, (\varnothing, t \mapsto 10, t \mapsto 10))$.

6   Implementation

The operational semantics given to the contracts, along with the timers and events, provide the framework to transform contracts in our calculus into DATEs which can be used to runtime verify the performance of parties involved. More details about the implementation can be found in [3] and in the Appendix.

We have adapted the derivative-based [4] runtime verification algorithm in order to obtain a DATE which reacts to the events appropriately. The resulting two-state DATE keeps track of the current contract in a variable φ and updates triggers on either an event or the timeout triggers. Initially, φ is set to the contract to monitor, while T to timeout(φ):

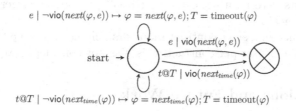

s

The function $next(\varphi, e)$ corresponds to $step(timestep(\varphi, \Delta t), e)$ while $next_{time}(\varphi)$ corresponds to $timestep(\varphi, \Delta t)$—in both cases Δt is the time elapsed since the last processed event. Using this construction, a trace leads to the bad state of the DATE if and only if it violates the initial contract. It is worth noting that since any computable function can be embedded as the action of a DATE transition, the translation is made possible by the computability of derivatives over time and event steps.

Practical Evaluation. To test our approach, we implemented the case study in Java with each action represented as a method call. When evaluated empirically, runtime verification tools, typically (e.g. [5]) get evaluated by comparing the time needed to run the system with and without monitoring. In this case, this is not practical since the system is simply a sequence of dummy method executions. Instead, the purpose of this quantitative evaluation is (i) to verify the correct behaviour of the monitor, i.e., that a violation is indeed reported when it actually occurs and vice versa; and (ii) to verify our intuition that the monitor will scale linearly with the size of the execution of the underlying system.

A number of test cases were generated, each representing the interactions of a single user involving a varying number of actions. In each case, the monitor verdict was as expected. Subsequently, different levels of traffic were generated by launching several users in parallel ranging from 100 to 100,000 users. The experiment[4] was run on a laptop with an Intel i7-855U processor, 16 GB RAM.

Thousands of users	0.1	0.5	1	5	10	50	100
No monitoring (s)	0.0556	0.231	0.261	0.736	0.811	7.00	12.1
With monitoring (s)	0.104	0.433	0.595	2.16	4.05	18.1	38.4
Difference (s)	0.0480	0.202	0.334	1.43	3.24	11.1	26.4
Difference per user (ms)	0.480	0.404	0.334	0.285	0.324	0.223	0.264

The results in the table above show that as the number of users increases, the CPU time per user stabilises at around 0.3 ms. This confirms our reasoning that since the individual user monitors do not interact, the monitoring effort scales linearly to the number of users. One would only expect this trend to stop when reaching a large number of users such that the performance of an underlying framework starts deteriorating, e.g., the thread pool grows larger than what is efficiently manageable.

Regarding memory, since contract monitors only need to keep track of a state of bounded size per user per contract, this was not considered to be an issue.

7   Conclusions and Future Work

In this paper, we have presented a runtime verification algorithm for a real-time contract calculus, proved to be correct. Also, we presented an implementation of the algorithm as part of an established runtime verification tool Larva.

It is worth noting that despite the fact that there is much work on real-time deontic logics (see [2] for a summary and comparisons of such works), and limited work on monitoring of deontic logics (e.g. see [7,8,16]), the overlap between the two has been largely neglected.

---

[4] Code is available at: https://github.com/aarandag/larva-timedcontracts.

There are various research directions this research opens. Regarding the runtime verification aspect, an interesting challenge is how we can use our techniques for runtime enforcement: starting from a specification, how we can synthesise algorithmic machinery to ensure that the system under scrutiny does not violate the specification, e.g. by delaying or injecting events. In particular, there is a body of work on runtime enforcement of timed properties, e.g. [9] which could offer insight on how our work can be extended to build contract enforcement engines, a notion that has not been widely explored in the deontic logic world.

References

1. Madrid-Barajas Airport. Airport Regulations (2020). https://www.aeropuertoma drid-barajas.com/eng/air-passenger-rights.htm. https://www.aeropuertomadrid-barajas.com/eng/regulations-hand-luggage.htm. https://www.aeropuertomadrid-barajas.com/eng/checkin-madrid-airport.htm. Accessed 25 May 2020
2. García, A.A., Cambronero, M.E., Colombo, C., Llana, L., Pace, G.J.: Themulus: a timed contract-calculus. In: Proceedings of the 8th International Conference on Model-Driven Engineering and Software Development, pp. 193–204 (2020)
3. García, A.A., Cambronero, M.E., Colombo, C., Llana, L., Pace, G.J.: Themulus: a timed contract-calculus. Technical Report TR-01-20, Universidad Complutense de Madrid (2020)
4. Brzozowski, J.A.: Derivatives of regular expressions. J. ACM **11**(4), 481–494 (1964)
5. Chen, F., Rosu, G.: MOP: an efficient and generic runtime verification framework. In: Proceedings of the 22nd Annual ACM SIGPLAN Conference on Object-Oriented Programming, Systems, Languages, and Applications, OOPSLA 2007, Montreal, Quebec, Canada, 21–25 October 2007, pp. 569–588 (2007)
6. Colombo, C., Pace, G.J., Schneider, G.: Dynamic event-based runtime monitoring of real-time and contextual properties. In: Cofer, D., Fantechi, A. (eds.) FMICS 2008. LNCS, vol. 5596, pp. 135–149. Springer, Heidelberg (2009). https://doi.org/10.1007/978-3-642-03240-0_13
7. Cranefield, S.: A rule language for modelling and monitoring social expectations in multi-agent systems. In: Boissier, O., et al. (eds.) AAMAS 2005. LNCS (LNAI), vol. 3913, pp. 246–258. Springer, Heidelberg (2006). https://doi.org/10.1007/11775331_17
8. Dastani, M., Torroni, P., Yorke-Smith, N.: Monitoring norms: a multi-disciplinary perspective. Knowl. Eng. Rev. **33**, e25 (2018)
9. Falcone, Y., Jéron, T., Marchand, H., Pinisetty, S.: Runtime enforcement of regular timed properties by suppressing and delaying events. Sci. Comput. Program. **123**, 2–41 (2016)
10. Wright, G.H.V.: Deontic logic. Mind **60**(237), 1–15 (1951)
11. Governatori, G., Rotolo, A., Sartor, G.: Temporalised normative positions in defeasible logic. In: The Tenth International Conference on Artificial Intelligence and Law, Proceedings of the Conference, Bologna, Italy, 6–11 June 2005, pp. 25–34 (2005)
12. Hashmi, M., Governatori, G., Wynn, M.T.: Modeling obligations with event-calculus. In: Bikakis, A., Fodor, P., Roman, D. (eds.) RuleML 2014. LNCS, vol. 8620, pp. 296–310. Springer, Cham (2014). https://doi.org/10.1007/978-3-319-00870 1_22

13. Pace, G.J., Schapachnik, F.: Contracts for interacting two-party systems. In: FLA-COS 2012. ENTCS, vol. 94, pp. 21–30 (2012)
14. Pace, G.J., Schneider, G.: Challenges in the specification of full contracts. In: Leuschel, M., Wehrheim, H. (eds.) IFM 2009. LNCS, vol. 5423, pp. 292–306. Springer, Heidelberg (2009). https://doi.org/10.1007/978-3-642-00255-7_20
15. Prisacariu, C., Schneider, G.: A dynamic deontic logic for complex contracts. J. Logic Algebraic Program. **81**(4), 458–490 (2012). Special Issue: NWPT 2009
16. Testerink, B., Dastani, M., Meyer, J.-J.Ch.: Norm monitoring through observation sharing. In: Proceedings of the European Conference on Social Intelligence, ECSI-2014, Barcelona, Spain, 3–5 November 2014, pp. 291–304 (2014)
17. Yi, W.: CCS + time = an interleaving model for real time systems. In: Albert, J.L., Monien, B., Artalejo, M.R. (eds.) ICALP 1991. LNCS, vol. 510, pp. 217–228. Springer, Heidelberg (1991). https://doi.org/10.1007/3-540-54233-7_136

Sound C Code Decompilation
for a Subset of x86-64 Binaries

Freek Verbeek[1,2]([⊠]), Pierre Olivier[3], and Binoy Ravindran[1]

[1] Virginia Tech, Blacksburg, VA, USA
[2] Open University of The Netherlands, Heerlen, The Netherlands
fvb@ou.nl
[3] University of Manchester, Manchester, UK

Abstract. We present FoxDec: an approach to C code decompilation that aims at producing sound and recompilable code. Formal methods are used during three phases of the decompilation process: control flow recovery, symbolic execution, and variable analysis. The use of formal methods minimizes the trusted code base and ensures soundness: the extracted C code behaves the same as the original binary. Soundness and recompilablity enable C code decompilation to be used in the contexts of binary patching, binary porting, binary analysis and binary improvement, with confidence that the recompiled code's behavior is consistent with the original program. We demonstrate that FoxDec can be used to improve execution speed by recompiling a binary with different compiler options, to patch a memory leak with a code transformation tool, and to port a binary to a different architecture. FoxDec can also be leveraged to port a binary to run as a unikernel, a minimal and secure virtual machine usually requiring source access for porting.

1 Introduction

Research in program analysis, verification, and engineering often assumes a context where source code is available. However, numerous safety-critical systems in automotive, aerospace, medical and military domains are built out of components whose source code is unavailable [40]. In the case of proprietary software, a customer is dependent on the vendor for maintenance, patching, and verification [41]. In such contexts, *decompilation* can be useful. Decompilation ideally produces *sound* (functionally equivalent to the binary) and *recompilable* C code.

The majority of existing decompilation tools do not satisfy these two properties [1,11,14–17,19,25,32]. These papers do not evaluate soundness, focusing on other metrics such as readability and code size [9]. It is a well-known issue in many existing tools that decompiled C code is not functionally equivalent to the binary [9,41]. The only exception is Phoenix [9], which provides decompilation based on semantics-preserving control-flow recovery. Phoenix, however, does not define its soundness, nor does it provide a soundness proof of its control-flow recovery algorithm. We refer to Sect. 5 for a more detailed comparison to existing decompilation tools.

© Springer Nature Switzerland AG 2020
F. de Boer and A. Cerone (Eds.): SEFM 2020, LNCS 12310, pp. 247–264, 2020.
https://doi.org/10.1007/978-3-030-58768-0_14

This paper presents FoxDec (Formal x86-64 Decompilation): sound and recompilable C code decompilation from x86-64 binaries. During three key stages of decompilation formal methods are used. First, we formally verified a control-flow recovery algorithm using the Isabelle/HOL theorem prover [33]. Second, we present a symbolic execution engine that uses rewrite rules – formally proven correct using the Isabelle/HOL theorem prover – to aggregate small state-changes induced by assembly instructions to higher-level programming constructs. Third, we show how the Z3 theorem prover [13] can be used to formally establish a relation between symbolic memory regions in the binary and variables in the decompiled C code. Taken together, these three uses of formal methods increase the trustworthiness that the decompiled C code is sound.

We show that soundness and recompilability allow FoxDec to be useful in the following contexts, each of which is discussed on Sect. 3:

Binary Patching. When source code is unavailable, performing a patch at the machine code or assembly level is highly complex [41]. By decompiling a binary as C code, one can patch at the source code level, which is significantly easier. As an example, we take a binary with a memory leak. We decompile to C, apply the code transformation tool Coccinelle [36] to patch the leak, and recompile [36].

Binary Porting. Using FoxDec, one can take an x86-64 binary, decompile, then recompile it for any other little-endian architecture. It can thus be an alternative to software emulators such as QEMU [5], which suffers from significant slow-downs ranging from 5 to 1000x [10]. FoxDec also enables porting binaries to run as *unikernels* [28]. Most of the existing unikernel models require recompilation or relinking to port an existing application, thus requiring source code [34]. As examples, we port binaries from x86 to ARM, and a binary of the PARSEC [6] Blackscholes program to a unikernel.

Binary Analysis. Verification and analysis tools typically operate on source code. The low-level intricacies occurring in binaries make analysis difficult. We show that through C code decompilation, FoxDec enables the application of standard off-the-shelf source code analysis tools on binaries. For example, we use Frama-C to determine ranges for variables and check for buffer overflows in the binary of the GNU Coreutils word-count (wc) program [24].

Binary Improvement. Different compilers offer variable program performance, compilation speed, binary sizes, etc., which vary with the compiled program and the compilation options. C decompilation enables recompiling a binary with different settings. As an example, we show that it is possible to improve execution speed of functions in a binary containing implementations of floating-point functions, simply by decompiling and recompiling them.

The approach has limitations. User-interaction is required for 1) providing information on function signatures, and 2) inclusion of header files. Soundness of a specific step – namely, introducing references to variables – cannot be guaranteed since without type-information it is undecidable whether a value is a pointer. In that case, the decompiled variable reference is annotated with a

```
1:  push rbp                              10: imul qword ptr [rbp], 3
2:  mov rbp, rsp                          11: add dword ptr [rbp - 0x4], 1
3:  mov dword ptr [rbp - 0x10], edi       12: mov eax, dword ptr [rbp - 0x4]
4:  mov dword ptr [rbp - 0x8], 1          13: cmp eax, dword ptr [rbp - 0x8]
5:  mov dword ptr [rbp - 0x4], 0          14: jb 9
6:  mov dword ptr [rbp - 0xc], 0          15: mov rax, qword ptr [rbp]
7:  sub rbp, 8                            16: pop rbp
8:  jmp 12                                17: ret
9:  shl qword ptr [rbp], 1
```

Fig. 1. Running example

soundness warning and further user-interaction is mandated. Moreover, we cannot deal with indirect branching and thus consider only a subset of all possible x86 binaries.

The research contributions of this paper are: 1) C code decompilation such that for key stages soundness criteria have been formalized; 2) the demonstration that this produces efficiently executable code: to the best of our knowledge, no related work exists that provides numbers on execution speed of the recovered code; 3) the demonstration that sound and recompilable C code recovery can be used for binary patching, porting, analysis, and improvement. To the best of our knowledge, no previous decompilation tool targets soundness, recompilability *and* is based on formal methods. Project information can be found at: https://llrm-project.org/; all code and proofs are available at: https://doi.org/10.5281/zenodo.3952034.

2   C Code Extraction

We demonstrate the steps of decompilation on the assembly code in Fig. 1. The code first initializes local variables. It then loops over lines 12-14-9-12 until the carry flag is false (`jb` looks at that flag).

2.1 Step 1: Binary to Control-Flow Graph

The Control-Flow Graph (CFG) is a graph with basic blocks (i.e., lists of instructions) as vertices and edges with labels from a set F of flags. In order to obtain a CFG from a binary, two steps are required: *disassembly* and *CFG recovery*. Both these steps have been extensively studied in literature [2–4,7,22,23,43].

In order to express the soundness of a CFG, we use the notion of paths. A *path in the binary* is defined as any list of instructions such that there exists a possible execution of the binary that visits exactly these instructions. Let I denote the set of instructions, and let $[I]$ denote lists of instructions. We use $\text{is\_path}_{\text{bin}}(\pi)$ to denote that a list π of instructions of type $[I]$ is a path in the binary. A *path in the CFG* is a list of lists of instructions. Let $\text{is\_path}_{\text{cfg}}(\pi, q)$

denote that π of type $[[I]]$ is a path in CFG g. The following notion of soundness is a reformulation of the concept of an ideal CFG from [43].

CFG Soundness: CFG g is sound, if and only if:

$$\text{is\_path}_{\text{bin}}(\pi) \Longleftrightarrow \exists \pi' \cdot \text{is\_path}_{\text{cfg}}(\pi', g) \wedge \text{flatten}(\pi') = \pi$$

FoxDec Implementation and Argument for Soundness: We use Ramblr for disassembly [41]. A generic and provably sound approach to disassembly is outside the scope of this paper. However, we limit the applicability of FoxDec to binaries without indirect branching. As result, the disassembler knows at all times at which addresses it needs to disassemble instructions. Under this limitation, disassembly can be done in a provably sound way. Similarly, CFG extraction is done by a reimplementation similar to angr's CFGFast [39]. The algorithm straightforwardly produces a CFG, by starting at a known entry point and considering for each encountered instruction its effect on the instruction pointer. Again, the limitation of no indirect branching ensures soundness.

2.2   Step 2: CFG to Abstract Code

We formulate a datatype for *abstract code* that is able to represent the decompiled program at all stages of decompilation. This datatype expresses a program as a combination of control flow, basic blocks, and branching decisions. Each basic block is represented by a polymorphic type β; branching decisions are represented using a polymorphic type ϕ.

$$\text{acode}(\beta, \phi) := \text{Block } \beta \mid \text{Skip} \mid \text{Continue} \mid \text{Break ID} \mid \text{acode}(\beta, \phi) ; \text{acode}(\beta, \phi)$$
$$\mid \text{If } \phi \text{ Then acode}(\beta, \phi) \text{ Else acode}(\beta, \phi) \text{ Fi}$$
$$\mid \text{Loop acode}(\beta, \phi) \text{ Pool Resume}\{(\text{ID}, \text{acode}(\beta, \phi))\}$$

Abstract code consists of basic blocks, skips, sequential execution, if statements, and loops. There is only one type of loop that has no exit condition and thus loops infinitely if it does not contain a break. A Continue has the same semantics as the C continue statement, i.e., forcing the next iteration of a loop. A Break is also similar to the C break, but it optionally has an argument. In case of a loop with multiple exit points, the Break can use an ID to identify which exit has been used. After the loop, a Resume statement can execute code based on which exit was taken. For example, if a loop breaks due to a Break i statement and the loop is followed by a Resume that contains the pair (i, a), then abstract code a is executed. If the set of Resume is empty, we will omit it.

Let $a = \text{acode}(\beta, \phi)$ be abstract code. A *path of the abstract code* is a list of elements of type β. Let $\text{is\_path}_{\text{ac}}(\pi, a)$ denote that π of type $[\beta]$ is a path of abstract code a.

Step 2 consists of generating abstract code with $\beta = [I]$ and $\phi = F$, i.e., with the same basic blocks and branching decisions as the CFG. It is thus a function cfg_to_ac that takes as input a CFG and produces an element a of type $\text{acode}([I], F)$.

Abstract Code Extraction Soundness: Abstract code extraction is sound, if and only if:

$$\text{is\_path}_{\text{cfg}}(\pi, g) \iff \text{is\_path}_{\text{ac}}(\pi, \text{cfg\_to\_ac}(g))$$

FoxDec implementation and Argument for Soundness: Yakdan et al. provide an algorithm for extracting control flow structures from a CFG [44]. The algorithm considers a certain subgraph. Initially, this subgraph is the entire CFG, but for each loop the body forms a new subgraph. This recursive nature allows extraction of nested loops. The function breaks down the current subgraph into sequential statements. Edges back to the entry node of the subgraph are Continue statements, edges exiting the subgraph are Break statements.

We modeled an adopted version of the method of Yakdan et al. in the Isabelle/HOL theorem prover. This provides a formalized function cfg_to_ac, which was proven sound (the proof files are made available). Subsequently, we implemented the exact algorithm as formalized in Isabelle/HOL.

Example 1. Control flow reconstruction produces the following for the running example:

```
Block 1 -> 12
Loop
  Block 12 -> 14
  If CF Then Block 14 -> 12 Else Break Fi
Pool
Block 14 -> ret
```

A block $1 \rightarrow 1'$ consists of the instructions from 1 up to (excluding) $1'$. One loop has been identified, which is exited if the carry flag is false. The final block runs until and including the ret instruction.

2.3 Step 3: Symbolic Execution

The next step is to transform the basic blocks in the abstract code to symbolic state changes. We achieve this by running symbolic execution. The purpose is twofold: a) to aggregate the state changes induced by the individual instructions to a set of larger state changes, and b) to express those state changes in a more architecture-independent fashion.

Formally, symbolic execution is a function symb that takes as input a basic block b of type $[I]$ and produces an element of type $\{A_{SP}\}$. Here elements of type A_{SP} are *assignments* over state parts, i.e., $A_{SP} = \{(SP, E_{SP})\}$. An assignment is denoted by $sp := v$. The left-hand-side is an element of type SP, i,e, a state part. A state part is either a register, a flag, or a *memory region* represented by an address a and a number of bytes s. The latter is denoted by $[a, s]$. An assignment $[a, s] := v$ of a value to a memory region is done in little-endian fashion, i.e., value v is split up into a byte list and then reversed. All assignments are mutually independent.

The right-hand side is an element of type E_{SP}, i.e., expressions over state parts. These expressions consist of common bit-vector operations including taking bit subsets and concatenation as introduced above, logical operators, casting operators, and floating-point, signed and unsigned arithmetic operators. The expression $*[a, s]$ denotes dereferencing: reading s bytes from memory address a.

To express soundness, we need to compare 1) the actual behavior of executing assembly instructions with 2) the semantics of the symbolic expressions. First, let $\text{exec}(b, \sigma)$ denote execution. It takes as input a basic block b of type $[I]$ and a concrete state σ and runs each instruction consecutively. Function calls are treated symbolically (this models non-deterministic user-input). Second, let $\text{eval}_E(e, \sigma)$ denote an evaluation function for expressions. It evaluates the expression as much as possible, but again leaves results of function calls symbolic. The execution of an assignment evaluates both the left and the right-hand side in the current state, and then updates the current state. This leads to a function $\text{eval}_{\{A_{SP}\}}$ that evaluates a set of assignments, i.e., that evaluates symbolized basic blocks.

Symbolic Execution Soundness: Symbolic execution is sound, if and only if, for any basic block b of type $[I]$:

$$\forall \sigma \cdot \text{exec}(b, \sigma) = \text{eval}_{\{A_{SP}\}}(\text{symb}(b), \sigma)$$

This notion of soundness is context-insensitive, i.e., it considers each block separately. Let $\text{symb}_{ac}(a)$ apply symbolic execution to all blocks. It thus takes as input abstract code a of type $\text{acode}([I], F)$ and produces symbolized abstract code of type $\text{acode}(\{A_{SP}\}, E_{SP})$. This ensures that:

$$\text{is\_path}_{ac}(\pi, a) \iff \text{is\_path}_{ac}(\text{map symb } \pi, \text{symb}_{ac}(a))$$

Here map is the standard map function. Moreover, soundness of symbolic execution implies that for any path π of type $[[I]]$ (produced by Step 2):

$$\forall \sigma \cdot \text{exec}(\text{flatten}(\pi), \sigma) = \text{eval}_{\text{path}}(\text{map symb } \pi, \sigma)$$

Here function $\text{eval}_{\text{path}}$ consecutively runs evaluation on the given list of symbolized basic blocks. It formulates that executing paths from the CFG is equivalent to evaluating the symbolized abstract code.

FoxDec Implementation and Argument for Soundness: The key elements of symbolic execution are *instruction semantics* and *rewrite rules*. Instruction semantics consists of a set of symbolic assignments per instruction. For example, the **add** instruction updates flags and its first operand with symbolic expressions. We use the formal semantics of Roessle et al. [38]. They leverage the work of Heule et al. [21] which produces machine-learned semantics for a large set of instructions. Their semantics have been proven to be highly reliable. Roessle et al. translated these into a bitvector language and formalized them in the Isabelle theorem prover [33]. We have taken the semantics of this model and programmed them as symbolic assignments. Aggregating the semantics of individual instructions leads to large expressions. Simplification rules are necessary to maintain scalability and readability. We have written a simplification engine that uses arithmetic, logical, and bit-vector based simplification rules. Each of these rules has been proven correct in the Isabelle/HOL theorem prover.

Example 2. Symbolic execution produces the following for the running example:

```
Block {rbp := rsp − 8, *[rsp − 8, 4] := 1, *[rsp − 16, 4] := edi, ...}
Loop
    Block {CF := *[rbp − 4, 4] > *[rbp − 8, 4], ...}
    If CF Then Block {*[rbp, 8] := *[rbp, 8] * 6, ...} Else Break Fi
Pool
Block {rax := *[rbp, 8], ...}
```

First, one can see that the basic blocks have become sets of mutually independent assignments. For example, the first block assigns the 4-byte value 1 to address $rsp - 8$. This is due to instructions 2 and 4. Second, one can see that semantics have been aggregated, e.g., multiplication by 6 instead of left-shifting and times 3. Also, instructions 12 and 13 have been aggregated into a single assignment to the carry flag.

2.4 Step 4: Variable Analysis

The key purpose of variable analysis is to establish which memory regions correspond to which variables. Three types of variables exist: local, global, or heap variables. Local variables are stored in the stack frame, relative to either the stack pointer (rsp) or the frame pointer (rbp). Global variables are stored in the data sections of a binary. Their addresses are typically immediates, i.e, constant values that represent a certain offset with respect to where the binary is stored in memory. Heap variables are represented by pointers.

Before memory regions can be matched to variables, any address computation must be expressed relative to the initial state. Consider the running example. Within the loop, region $[rbp, 8]$ actually overlaps with region $[rsp - 8, 4]$ from the first block. This is because during the loop, the following invariant holds: $rbp = rsp_0 - 8$. Expressed in initial values it is easy to see these two regions should be mapped to the same variable: $[rsp_0 - 8, 8]$ and $[rsp_0 - 8, 4]$.

The first step of variable analysis is thus *invariant propagation*. In the running example, the invariant assigned to line 1 will contain $rsp = rsp_0$. At line 12, it will contain $rbp = rsp_0 - 8$. In similar fashion, initial values of the form x_0 are propagated for all registers and memory regions. After invariant propagation, it is checked whether all addresses are expressed in terms of initial values.

The second step replaces memory regions with variables. Local variables are identified by finding regions whose address computation includes the stack- or frame pointer. For example, the symbolic expression $*[rsp_0 - 4, 4]$ is replaced by a symbolic expression consisting of some 32-bit local variable lv. Global variables are identified by finding symbolic expressions of the form $[i, s]$ with both i and s immediates. For example, the symbolic expression $*[4257968, 8]$ is replaced by a 64-bit global variable gv. For each global variable, we retrieve the initial value of the global variable from the data sections of the binary. The remaining set of memory regions constitute heap variables. These require no modification during variable analysis. For example, $*[\text{rax}, 4]$, dereferencing the pointer in register rax, is not modified by this step.

Generally, regions may be different but still map to the same variable. This happens if the regions are *necessarily overlapping*. Two regions $[a, s]$ and $[a', s']$ are necessarily overlapping, notation $[a, s] \sim [a', s']$, if and only if in *any* state addresses a and a' resolve to regions that share at least one byte. Such regions are merged during variable analysis.

Variable Analysis Soundness: Assume that the addresses of all memory regions are expressed in terms of the initial state. Let $var[a, s]$ return the variable that is being substituted for region $[a, s]$. Variable analysis is sound, if and only if, for any two accessed memory regions $[a, s]$ and $[a', s']$, anywhere in the abstract code:

$$[a, s] \sim [a', s'] \iff var[a, s] = var[a', s']$$

FoxDec Implementation and Argument for Soundness: Invariants are established via a standard forward propagation algorithm [18]. For loops, the current invariant is iteratively weakened until a fix-point is reached. To establish whether two regions are necessarily overlapping, the Z3 theorem prover is used [13]. The regions are necessarily overlapping if them being separate is unsatisfiable.

Example 3. Variable analysis produces the following for the running example:

```
Block {lv_0 := 1, lv_1 := 0, lv_2 := p_0 ...}
Loop
  Block {b := lv_1 > lv_2, ...}
  If b Then Block {lv_0 := lv_0 * 6, ...} Else Break Fi
Pool
Block {ret := lv_0]}
```

During the loop $\text{rbp} = \text{rsp}_0 - 8$. As result, the region $[\text{rbp}, 8]$ in the blocks in the loop were necessarily overlapping with the regions $[\text{rsp} - 8, 4]$ and $[\text{rsp} - 4, 4]$ in the first block. All these regions were thus merged into one variable lv_0. Variable b has been introduced as a Boolean variable for the carry flag. Moreover, the function signature maps registers edi to parameter p_0, and the function returns a value via variable $ret = \text{rax}$.

2.5   Step 5: References

After variable analysis, there can still be symbolic expressions that are references to variables. Step 5 identifies such expressions and replaces them. For example, if region $[\text{rsp}_0 - 4, 4]$ has been substituted with variable lv, symbolic expression $\text{rsp}_0 - 4$ is replaced by symbolic expression $\&lv$. In case the region was not encountered, a fresh variable lv_f is introduced and the region is translated as a reference to that fresh variable. Since the size cannot be established, it is assumed to be 8 bytes. The code is annotated with a possible unsoundness.

References to global variables pose a problem with respect to automation. Consider the occurrence of an immediate 4257968, and assume that this immediate value is within the address range of the data sections of the binary. This may or may not be the address of some global variable. By default, this is considered *not* to be a reference to a global variable. However, the code is annotated with a message indicating that an immediate occurred whose value indicates that it is likely to be a global variable pointer. The user can then manually modify a config file, ensuring that 4257968 is translated to &*gv*.

2.6   Step 6: C Code Generation

The abstract code produced by variable analysis is the base for C code generation. The main difference between the abstract code and C is *types*. For the abstract code, we know the size of each variable, but not the type.

Consider the C expression $a - b/c$. Its semantics depend on whether the variables are floats, signed, or unsigned ints. The $+$, and $-$ operator behave the same for unsigned and signed ints, but division does not. The semantics of the operators are thus dependent on the types of the variables. In the abstract code, this is not the case. The operators are well-defined, e.g., the operator in the symbolic expression is the result of a `div`, `idiv`, or `fdiv` assembly instruction (division of signed, unsigned, floating point). This means that we do not need type information for variables.

We thus rely on *type punning* to translate variables. Consider a 64-bit variable. Depending on which operator is applied to it, it must be accessed in different ways. This is achieved using a `union`. When translating an operator, we first establish the types expected by the operator. For example, an `fdiv` assembly instruction expects two doubles. A `sub` expects (un)signed ints (note that subtraction is equal for unsigned/signed arithmetic). We arbitrarily pick unsigned out of the two options. We then translate the operands and *pun* them – if necessary – to the types expected by the operator. Punning one type to another means casting without modifying its contents.

Example 4. The running example produces the following C:

```
var64_t f(var32_t p0) {
  var64_t lv0.u = 1; var32_t lv1.u = 0, lv2 = p0;
  while (1) {
    bool b = lv1.s > lv2.s;
    if (b) lv0.s = lv0.s * 6; else break;
  }
  return lv0;
}
```

In contrast to using type punning and unions to derive C, it is also possible to use type inference [30]. The major advantage of using type inference with respect to our approach is that the produced C code is much more readable and humanly understandable. The drawback is that it is not always possible (i.e., it is undecidable). Type punning thus produces in more cases code that is recompilable, at the cost of readability.

3   Applications

We have applied C code extraction to binaries containing functions of the FDLIBM library. We have considered both non-optimized code (O0) and fully optimized (O3). FDLIBM provides mathematical floating-point functions such as sin, fmod and log that satisfy the IEEE754 standard. We have chosen FDLIBM as a case-study for the following reasons:

Complexity: The functions provide highly optimized implementations of advanced mathematical functions. They contain advanced flow control, including nested loops and if-statements, goto's, switches, and both in- and external function calls. They execute a plethora of floating-point, signed and unsigned arithmetic operations and frequently cast between types. Advanced pointer-arithmetic is used, both on arrays and on addresses of variables (e.g., splitting up the high and low part of a 64-bit floating point variable). Type punning is used, even in the original (vanilla) C code.

Testability: Even though the implementation is complex, the interfaces to the functions are all simple. They generally are side-effect free functions that take either one or two floating-points parameters and return a floating point. Some functions do produce side effects, such as writing certain results into an array that is passed as a parameter. For all functions, these are well-documented. The functions are typically fast, allowing execution of millions of test-cases.

The FDLIBM library comprises 84 functions and 8.543 lines of C code. 23 of these functions are simple wrappers that only call other functions. We exclude them from our evaluation, since they do not do anything interesting on their own. One function, __ieee754_lgamma_r, uses indirect branching, which is not supported. The text sections of the remaining 61 functions comprise 13.744 (10.221) lines of assembly code (respectively O0 and O3), not including any data sections. For each of these 61 functions, we have decompiled C code. In this case study, all warnings on pointers to global variables were trustworthy, i.e., they actually were pointers and not constants. At four places, the decompiled C code has been modified due to fixed-size local arrays. The decompiled C code has been recompiled. For each function f we thus have the vanilla function f_v in the original binary and the function f_r in the recompiled binary.

Test Setup. Testing consists of running both functions f_v and f_r on randomly generated values and comparing their results. For each function, we have run 100.000.000 test cases. All experiments in this section were run on a 1.2 GHz Intel Core m3 machine with 8 GB RAM. The test setup first requires generation of random values of type double. We build a random-generator that at the top-level randomly (but uniformly) calls one of five different random double generators. Four of the random double generators randomly pick a double from 1) the range $[-2.0, 2.0]$, 2) the range $[-20000.0, 20000.0]$, 3) the range of subnormals, 4) a

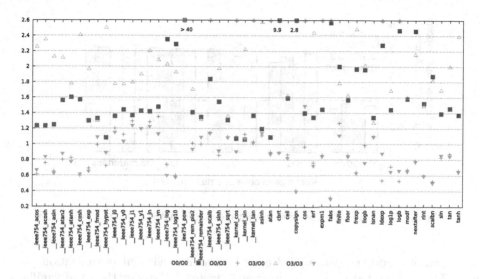

Fig. 2. Ratios of execution speed, capped of at a factor 2.6. Series x/y means that the original binary had been compiled with optimization x, and the recompiled C is compiled with optimization y. For series 00/00, factors higher than 2.6 have been labelled. Excluding __ieee754_pow, the average factor for series 03/00 is 2.3 with a maximum of 6.6.

set of specific values such as plus- and minus infinity, plus- and minus zero and one, plus- and minus NaN, and values such as maximal and minimal doubles. The fifth random double generator produces a bit pattern from 64 random Bools and casts it to a double. The purpose of this test setup is thus to test random values, likely values and corner cases.

Results. We measure running times of the vanilla and the recompiled version for a comparison. For each function, an array of 50.000 elements is initialized with random test data for 50.000 test cases. Two arrays are allocated to store output data. Subsequently, a loop is run that calls the vanilla function f_v for each test case and writes its output to one of the output arrays. Then, a loop is run for the recompiled function f_r. Of both loops, the running times are measured. After having run both loops, the output data is compared for equality, to ensure that the functions produced the same results. This is then repeated until a total of 100.000.000 test cases have been run, accumulating the running times. The reason to do it in batches of 50.000 is to prevent measurement inaccuracy. One batch of 50.000 function calls typically takes about 5.000 μs, which is accurately measurable.

Figure 2 shows running times for 50 out of 61 functions. The remaining 11 functions are each called by at least one of the 50 functions and therefore not shown. Let t_v and t_r denote respectively the running times of all test cases on the vanilla and recompiled functions. The graph shows the ratio $\frac{t_r}{t_v}$. The series 00/00 is the case where the vanilla binary had been compiled without

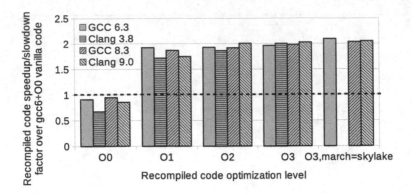

Fig. 3. Original and recompiled performance of PARSEC Blackscholes.

optimizations, and the decompiled code is compiled without optimizations as well. The regenerated code is on average a factor 1.5 slower then the vanilla. There are two notable exceptions: __ieee754_pow and cbrt. The recompiled version of the first is, for all four series in Fig. 2, about a factor 40 times slower. This function consists of a series of if-statements (no loops). Its CFG consists of a largely irreducible CFG of 93 basic blocks and 144 edges, leading to an exponential blow-up during control flow extraction. The second is a factor 9.9 slower in this series.

If, however, the decompiled code is compiled with optimizations, then the decompiled code is generally either faster than the vanilla, or is at most 50% slower. This is shown by series 00/03 and 03/03 (respectively for a non-optimized and fully optimized original binary). As expected, the series 03/00, which decompiles code from an optimized binary and recompiles it without optimizations, produces decompiled code that is significantly slower than its original (Fig. 3).

3.1 Use-Cases of C Decompilation

Binary Improvement: Decompiling as C code allows us to recompile a program with higher optimizations or a different compiler in order to get performance gains. We used the PARSEC [6] Blackscholes benchmark which is representative of modern compute-intensive data analytics applications. We compile the vanilla source code with gcc 6.3 and the default optimization level, i.e. 00. We then decompile that binary and recompile the resulting code varying the compiler and the level of optimizations. We use gcc 6.3 and clang 3.8, the default versions available on Debian 9, as well as gcc 8.3 and clang 9.0 which are the latest versions released. We varied the optimization level from 00 to 03, and added a fourth case with both 03 and march=skylake which produces binaries optimized for the particular CPU used for this test: a Xeon E3-1270 v5 clocked at 3.6 GHz. Blackscholes's largest data set was used (native size).

We compare the speedup/slowdown of the recompiled code over the original Blackscholes code compiled with gcc 6.3/00. As one can observe, the capacity to decompile and recompile with O1 or higher can bring significant speedups. Across all compilers, the average speedup is 1.81x for O1, 1.93x for O2, 1.99x for O3 and 2.01x for O3 with march=skylake. Note that clang 3.8 with this last option produced invalid code so no result is presented for that particular case.

Binary Patching. Coccinelle is a C transformation tool use for software patching [35]. It takes as input a *semantic patch* and one or a set of C files, and produces a patch. As example, we take a binary that contains a function allocating an array on the heap with malloc(), then initializing it and performing some computations within that array. The function returns without calling free() on that array which is a memory leak. We write a Coccinelle semantic patch formulating that the array manipulated by that function should be freed before it returns. We decompile C from the binary, apply the patch, and recompile, producing a patched binary.

Binary Porting. We have run the x86 binary containing the FDLIBM library on an ARM64 Cavium ThunderX server machine, by recompiling the decompiled C, and successfully reran all test cases. Moreover, we have taken an x86 binary containing the Blackscholes benchmark and run it as a unikernel. Unikernels [28] are minimal and single-purpose VMs tailored for cloud execution and presenting numerous benefits such as low image size, memory footprint, and fast instantiation times. Porting an application to unikernel models typically requires access to the application's sources [34]. Using FoxDec we can decompile an application for which the sources are not available, and recompile it as a unikernel.

We decompiled PARSEC Blackscholes and recompiled it as a unikernel, using the HermitCore [27] unikernel model. To demonstrate unikernel benefits, we measured the image size, boot time, and memory footprint of the resulting VM. We compared these numbers to a regular Linux VM (a minimal Ubuntu 16.04 from Vagrant repositories), which can be used to deploy in the cloud an application whose sources are not available. The image size, boot time, and memory footprint for the recompiled unikernel vs. the Linux VM were resp 2.1 MB vs. 781 MB, 20 ms vs. 26 ms, and 12 MB vs. 87 MB. We came to similar data for a Docker container [29] (resp. 116 MB, 1500 ms, 2 MB).

Binary Analysis. Frama-C is a tool suite dedicated to source code analysis of C software. It can be used for, among others, program slicing, test-case generation, and verification. We have applied Frama-C to the binary of the word-count program. It indicated one loop with a possible buffer overflow. Manual analysis showed that this was a false negative.

4   Discussion and Limitations

This section summarizes issues related to soundness and automation and discusses limitations.

Let a be the abstract code produced after Step 3 (symbolic execution). Soundness of these steps provides as a corollary:

$$\text{is\_path}_{\text{bin}}(\pi) \iff \exists \pi' \cdot \text{is\_path}_{\text{ac}}(\pi', a) \land \forall \sigma \cdot \text{exec}(\pi, \sigma) = \text{eval}_{\text{path}}(\pi', \sigma)$$

Table 1. Decompilation tools. FM = Based on Formal Methods; RC = recompilability

Name	Output	FM	RC	Types	Supports	Soundness
FoxDec	C	✓	Partial	Punning	x86-64 with SIMD	Yes
Phoenix	C		Partial	Yes	32 bit: x86	Yes
Ghidra	C		No	Partial	All	
RetDec	C/Python		Partial	Yes	32 bit: x86, ARM, MIPS	
Ramblr	Assembly		Yes		x86-64	
DiL	HOL	✓	No		32 bit: x86, ARM, MIPS	
IDA PRO	Assembly		No		All	
Hex-Rays	Pseudo C		No	Partial	All	
SmartDec	C++		Partial	Yes	x86-64	
McSema	LLVM IR		Yes		All	

Executions of the binary are represented by the symbolized abstract code. Steps 4 to 6 concern the translation to C. Sound variable analysis ensures that the assignments in the symbolized state blocks are executed on the proper variables. Step 5 is possibly unsound, but C code annotations are provided. Step 6 is a matter of translating symbolized expressions to their C equivalent. Universally, if the resulting C code does not contain annotations, it is sound.

The subset of supported binaries is limited to binaries without indirect branching, variadic functions, self-modifying code, `setjmp/longjmp`, and concurrency.

Some parts of our C code decompilation are x86-64 specific. The symbolic execution engine is based on semantics for x86 instructions. Variable analysis is largely generic, but it requires knowledge on which registers are used to relate local variables to (in x86: `rsp` and `rbp`). CF extraction and C code generation are generic. We thus argue that implementing this approach for other architectures is a matter of engineering.

5   Related Work

Decompilation, and C decompilation in particular, has been an active research field for decades [9,11,12,20,37,42]. Table 1 provides an overview of some of the available tools. The table does not show disassemblers, such as CapStone or BAP [8]. Column RC provides information on recompilability. Ramblr and McSema provide decompilation into a language lower-level then C, but with recompilation. The bulk of the C code decompilation tools produce pseudo C or C that requires manual inspection for it to be sound and recompilable. The notable exception is Phoenix, discussed below [9]. Column Types provides an overview of how types are dealt with, if applicable. As discussed in the previous section, we use type punning to enable recompilability, at the cost of readability.

To the best of our knowledge, the only existing C decompilation tool that targets soundness is Phoenix [9]. Phoenix uses control-flow recovery and type recovery to produce structured and readable C code. The key difference between FoxDec and Phoenix is that for Phoenix, soundness is not defined, nor is an argument provided on why the approach is sound. For example, an algorithm is provided for control-flow recovery without a soundness criterion or proof. In contrast, this paper is based on formally proven correct control-flow recovery. Second, Phoenix uses type recovery, producing much better and readable code. However, they themselves state that this leads to soundness failures, whereas type punning does not introduce any soundness issues. Finally, Phoenix works for x86 in 32-bit and does not support floating-point operations. We have not been able to install Phoenix for a direct comparison.

Very recently, Ghidra has been released by the US National Security Agency (NSA) [1]. It is an open-source framework that aims at analyzing malicious code. It provides a robust C multi-architectural decompilation framework. Moreover, it supports indirect branching and its C generation relies not on punning and unions. However, the code it produces is not necessarily sound or recompilable.

RetDec (Retargetable Decompiler) provides an end-to-end binary-to-C decompilation suite [15,25]. Their work considers binaries from various 32-bit architectures and provides decompilation via LLVM. Their output is either C or a Python-like language. Their work has some unique characteristics. First, the use of LLVM enables the application of LLVM based tools. Second, they have put a great effort in producing humanly readable source code. Thirdly, they combine their work with type inference [30], producing C code with arrays and structs. Finally, they provide an *unpacker* as a preprocessor [26], that is able to take a packed binary (e.g., malware) and make it suitable for decompilation.

Ramblr [41] is part of the angr binary analysis framework [39], which provides binary analysis tools such as CFG recovery. The focus of Ramblr is on symbolized disassembly, i.e., deriving assembly with symbolic labels instead of immediate addresses. This allows binary patching, since the assembly can be reassembled.

A special kind of decompilation is *decompilation-into-logic* (DiL) [31,32]. DiL embeds disassembled machine code into Higher-Order-Logic. Blocks are given formal pre- and postconditions and loops are translated to recursive functions. DiL enables formal verification of binaries in a theorem prover.

Various commercial tools for binary analysis and decompilation exists. IDA-PRO [16] supports all mainstream architectures and is build on years of research into binary analysis. An extension of IDA-PRO is Hex-Rays [19]. Hex-Rays extracts humanly readable C-like pseudocode text. It is extremely fast, providing a result virtually on-the-fly for many functions. Other commercial tools include SmartDec [17], which targets C++ code, and McSema [14] which extracts LLVM.

6 Conclusion

This paper presents FoxDec: a C decompilation framework that is based on formal methods and that aims at soundness and recompilability. We show that C decompilation allows the application of source-level tools on binaries. We apply, e.g., a C code patching tool to patch a binary, or we apply a C code verification framework to verify the binary. Moreover, C decompilation can be useful for binary porting. We show this by porting an x86-64 binary to a unikernel and to an ARM machine. We have shown that FoxDec provides decompiled C code with little overhead in terms of execution speed with respect to the original binary. FoxDec will be made available online under an open-source license.

In the near future, we want to strengthen the formal relation between the decompiled C code and the binary. Instead of proving formal correctness of each individual step, we aim at producing a formal certificate that provides a theorem prover with all the information necessary to establish a simulation relation between the binary and C code. Moreover, we want to focus on formally verified type inference algorithms. The result would be a way to largely automatically retrieve formally proven correct C code from a subset of x86-64 binaries.

Acknowledgments. This work is supported in part by the US Office of Naval Research (ONR) under grants N00014-17-1-2297, N00014-16-1-2104, and N00014-18-1-2022.

References

1. National Security Agency. Ghidra (2019). https://www.nsa.gov/resources/everyone/ghidra/
2. Andriesse, D., Chen, X., Van Der Veen, V., Slowinska, A., Bos, H.: An in-depth analysis of disassembly on full-scale x86/x64 binaries. In: 25th USENIX Security Symposium (USENIX Security 2016), pp. 583–600 (2016)
3. Balakrishnan, G., Gruian, R., Reps, T., Teitelbaum, T.: CodeSurfer/x86—a platform for analyzing x86 executables. In: Bodik, R. (ed.) CC 2005. LNCS, vol. 3443, pp. 250–254. Springer, Heidelberg (2005). https://doi.org/10.1007/978-3-540-31985-6_19
4. Bauman, E., Lin, Z., Hamlen, K.W.: Superset disassembly: statically rewriting x86 binaries without heuristics. In: NDSS (2018)
5. Bellard, F.: QEMU, a fast and portable dynamic translator. In: USENIX Annual Technical Conference, FREENIX Track, vol. 41, p. 46 (2005)
6. Bienia, C., Kumar, S., Singh, J.P., Li, K.: The PARSEC benchmark suite: characterization and architectural implications. In: Proceedings of the 17th International Conference on Parallel Architectures and Compilation Techniques, pp. 72–81. ACM (2008)
7. Bonfante, G., Kaczmarek, M., Marion, J.-Y.: Control flow graphs as malware signatures (2007)
8. Brumley, D., Jager, I., Avgerinos, T., Schwartz, E.J.: BAP: a binary analysis platform. In: Gopalakrishnan, G., Qadeer, S. (eds.) CAV 2011. LNCS, vol. 6806, pp. 463–469. Springer, Heidelberg (2011). https://doi.org/10.1007/978-3-642-22110-1_37
9. Brumley, D., Lee, J.H., Schwartz, E.J., Woo, M.: Native x86 decompilation using semantics-preserving structural analysis and iterative control-flow structuring. In: Presented as part of the 22nd USENIX Security Symposium (USENIX Security 2013), pp. 353–368 (2013)

10. Bugnion, E., Nieh, J., Tsafrir, D.: Hardware and software support for virtualization. Synth. Lect. Comput. Archit. **12**(1), 1–206 (2017)
11. Cifuentes, C., Gough, K.J.: Decompilation of binary programs. Softw. Pract. Exp. **25**(7), 811–829 (1995)
12. Cifuentes, C., Simon, D., Fraboulet, A.: Assembly to high-level language translation. In: Proceedings of International Conference on Software Maintenance (Cat. No. 98CB36272), pp. 228–237. IEEE (1998)
13. De Moura, L., Bjørner, N.: Z3: an efficient SMT solver. In: Ramakrishnan, C.R., Rehof, J. (eds.) TACAS 2008. LNCS, vol. 4963, pp. 337–340. Springer, Heidelberg (2008). https://doi.org/10.1007/978-3-540-78800-3_24
14. Dinaburg, A., Ruef, A.: Mcsema: static translation of x86 instructions to LLVM. In: ReCon 2014 Conference, Montreal, Canada (2014)
15. Durfina, L., et al.: Design of a retargetable decompiler for a static platform-independent malware analysis. In: Kim, T., Adeli, H., Robles, R.J., Balitanas, M. (eds.) ISA 2011. CCIS, vol. 200, pp. 72–86. Springer, Heidelberg (2011). https://doi.org/10.1007/978-3-642-23141-4_8
16. Ferguson, J., Kaminsky, D.: Reverse engineering code with IDA Pro. Syngress (2008)
17. Fokin, A., Derevenetc, E., Chernov, A., Troshina, K.: SmartDec: approaching C++ decompilation. In: 2011 18th Working Conference on Reverse Engineering, pp. 347–356. IEEE (2011)
18. German, S.M., Wegbreit, B.: A synthesizer of inductive assertions. IEEE Trans. Softw. Eng. **1**(1), 68–75 (1975)
19. Guilfanov, I.: Decompilers and beyond. Black Hat USA (2008)
20. Hecht, M.S., Ullman, J.D.: Characterizations of reducible flow graphs. J. ACM (JACM) **21**(3), 367–375 (1974)
21. Heule, S., Schkufza, E., Sharma, R., Aiken, A.: Stratified synthesis: automatically learning the x86-64 instruction set. In: ACM SIGPLAN Notices, vol. 51, pp. 237–250. ACM (2016)
22. Horspool, R.N., Marovac, N.: An approach to the problem of detranslation of computer programs. Comput. J. **23**(3), 223–229 (1980)
23. Khadra, M.A.B., Stoffel, D., Kunz, W.: Speculative disassembly of binary code. In: 2016 International Conference on Compliers, Architectures, and Sythesis of Embedded Systems (CASES), pp. 1–10, October 2016
24. Kirchner, F., Kosmatov, N., Prevosto, V., Signoles, J., Yakobowski, B.: Frama-C: a software analysis perspective. Formal Aspects Comput. **27**(3), 573–609 (2015). https://doi.org/10.1007/s00165-014-0326-7
25. Křoustek, J.: Retargetable analysis of machine code. Ph.D. thesis, Brno, FIT BUT (2014)
26. Křoustek, J., Kolár, D.: Preprocessing of binary executable files towards retargetable decompilation. In: 8th International Multi-Conference on Computing in the Global Information Technology (ICCGI 2013), pp. 259–264 (2013)
27. Lankes, S., Pickartz, S., Breitbart, J.: Hermitcore: a unikernel for extreme scale computing. In: Proceedings of the 6th International Workshop on Runtime and Operating Systems for Supercomputers, p. 4. ACM (2016)
28. Madhavapeddy, A., et al.: Unikernels: library operating systems for the cloud. ACM SIGPLAN Not. **48**(4), 461–472 (2013)
29. Merkel, D.: Docker: lightweight Linux containers for consistent development and deployment. Linux J. **2014**(239), 2 (2014)

30. Mycroft, A.: Type-based decompilation (or program reconstruction via type reconstruction). In: Swierstra, S.D. (ed.) ESOP 1999. LNCS, vol. 1576, pp. 208–223. Springer, Heidelberg (1999). https://doi.org/10.1007/3-540-49099-X_14

31. Myreen, M.O., Gordon, M.J.C., Slind, K.: Machine-code verification for multiple architectures - an application of decompilation into logic. In: Formal Methods in Computer-Aided Design, pp. 1–8, November 2008

32. Myreen, M.O., Gordon, M.J.C., Slind, K.: Decompilation into logic - improved. In: 2012 Formal Methods in Computer-Aided Design (FMCAD), pp. 78–81. IEEE (2012)

33. Nipkow, T., Wenzel, M., Paulson, L.C. (eds.): Isabelle/HOL: A Proof Assistant for Higher-Order Logic. LNCS, vol. 2283. Springer, Heidelberg (2002). https://doi.org/10.1007/3-540-45949-9

34. Olivier, P., Chiba, D., Lankes, S., Min, C., Ravindran, B.: A binary-compatible unikernel. In: Proceedings of the 15th ACM SIGPLAN/SIGOPS International Conference on Virtual Execution Environments (VEE 2019) (2019)

35. Padioleau, Y., Lawall, J., Hansen, R.R., Muller, G.: Documenting and automating collateral evolutions in Linux device drivers. In: Proceedings of the 3rd ACM SIGOPS/EuroSys European Conference on Computer Systems 2008, Eurosys 2008, pp. 247–260. ACM, New York (2008)

36. Padioleau, Y., Lawall, J.L., Muller, G.: Semantic patches, documenting and automating collateral evolutions in Linux device drivers. In: Ottawa Linux Symposium (OLS 2007), Ottawa, Canada (2007)

37. Proebsting, T.A., Watterson, S.A.: Krakatoa: decompilation in Java (does bytecode reveal source?). In: COOTS, pp. 185–198 (1997)

38. Roessle, I., Verbeek, F., Ravindran, B.: Formally verified big step semantics out of x86-64 binaries. In: Proceedings of the 8th ACM SIGPLAN International Conference on Certified Programs and Proofs, pp. 181–195. ACM (2019)

39. Shoshitaishvili, Y., et al.: SoK: (state of) the art of war: offensive techniques in binary analysis. In: IEEE Symposium on Security and Privacy (2016)

40. Sulaman, S.M., Orucevic-Alagic, A., Borg, M., Wnuk, K., Höst, M., de la Vara, J.L.: Development of safety-critical software systems using open source software - a systematic map. In: 2014 40th EUROMICRO Conference on Software Engineering and Advanced Applications (SEAA), pp. 17–24. IEEE (2014)

41. Wang, R., et al.: Ramblr: making reassembly great again. In: NDSS (2017)

42. Wei, T., Mao, J., Zou, W., Chen, Y.: A new algorithm for identifying loops in decompilation. In: Nielson, H.R., Filé, G. (eds.) SAS 2007. LNCS, vol. 4634, pp. 170–183. Springer, Heidelberg (2007). https://doi.org/10.1007/978-3-540-74061-2_11

43. Liang, X., Sun, F., Zhendong, S.: Constructing precise control flow graphs from binaries. University of California, Davis, Technical report (2009)

44. Yakdan, K., Eschweiler, S., Gerhards-Padilla, E., Smith, M.: No more gotos: decompilation using pattern-independent control-flow structuring and semantic-preserving transformations. In: NDSS (2015)

Statically Checking REST API Consumers

Nuno Burnay[ID], Antónia Lopes[(✉)][ID], and Vasco T. Vasconcelos[ID]

LASIGE, Faculdade de Ciências, Universidade de Lisboa, Lisbon, Portugal
malopes@ciencias.ulisboa.pt

Abstract. Consumption of REST services has become a popular means
of invoking code provided by third parties, particularly in web applications. Nowadays programmers of web applications can choose TypeScript
over JavaScript to benefit from static type checking that enables validat-
ing calls to local functions or to those provided by libraries. Errors in
calls to REST services, however, can only be found at runtime. In this
paper, we present SRS, a language that extends the support of static
analysis to calls to REST services, with the ability to statically find
common errors such as missing or invalid data in REST calls and misuse
of the results from such calls. SRS features a syntax similar to JavaScript
and is equipped with a rich collection of types and primitives to natively
support REST calls that are statically validated against specifications of
the corresponding APIs written in the HeadREST language.

1 Introduction

During the last decades web services have become an important building block
in the construction of distributed applications. REST web services in particular
have become quite popular [16,30]. These services, through specific application
programming interfaces, allow consumers to access and manipulate representations of web resources, identified by Unique Resource Identifiers, by using the
operations offered by HTTP. Nowadays a very large number of APIs are interfaces of REST services [24] and many software companies expose REST APIs
for their services.

Since so many applications are designed to offer REST APIs, the consumption
of REST services has become a popular means of invoking code provided by
third parties. However, the support available to programmers for writing code
that consumes these services is extremely limited when compared to the sort of
support offered when invoking external libraries provided by third parties. The
practical impact of this problem is attested by a study on a large-scale payment
company which concluded that errors in invocations of REST services, related
to invalid or missing data, cause most of the failures in API consumer code [2].

The fact that programmers have no way of knowing whether their calls to
REST APIs are correct until runtime was identified as one of the four major
research challenges for the consumption of web APIs [38]. This state of affairs
led to an inter-procedural string analysis proposal to statically check REST calls
in JavaScript [37]. The solution checks whether a request to a service conforms

© Springer Nature Switzerland AG 2020
F. de Boer and A. Cerone (Eds.): SEFM 2020, LNCS 12310, pp. 265–283, 2020.
https://doi.org/10.1007/978-3-030-58768-0_15

to a given API specification written in OpenAPI[1], and involves checking whether the endpoint targeted by the request is valid and the request has the expected data. Since OpenAPI has severe limitations on what can be expressed about the exchanged data, there are many errors related to invalid or missing data in requests that cannot be addressed by this approach. Moreover, since the models of response data are not taken into consideration, misuse of the result to REST calls cannot be addressed.

This paper presents an approach to API consumer code development based on two new languages: HeadREST—a specification language for REST APIs with a rich type system that supports the specification of semantic aspects of REST APIs—and SRS (short for SafeRESTScript)—a subset of JavaScript equipped with (i) types and strong static analysis and (ii) primitives to natively support REST calls that are statically validated against HeadREST specifications of the corresponding APIs. The validation system of SRS is based on a general-purpose verification tool (Boogie). SRS compiler generates JavaScript code for valid SRS programs, making it easy to use the two languages together and providing a solution for the execution of SRS programs in many different execution environments. The SRS compiler comes in the form of an Eclipse plugin which is publicly available for download. Alternatively, HeadREST and its validator can be exercised directly from a browser [8].

The main contributions of this work are an approach to statically check REST API consumption, and SRS, a type-safe JavaScript-like language, together with its compiler.

The paper starts with a tour through our approach (Sect. 2) and a brief introduction to THE HeadREST specification language (Sect. 3). Then, we present the SRS programming language and its validation system (Sect. 4). The validation system guarantees the detection of errors in REST calls as well as common runtime errors (including null dereference, division by zero and accesses outside arrays bounds). Section 5 presents the evaluation of SRS, Sect. 6 discusses related work, and Sect. 7 concludes the paper by pointing towards future work.

2   Overview of the Approach

This section presents the motivation for SRS and walks through our approach by means of an example. First we show how HeadREST allows us to specify REST APIs and capture properties that are important and cannot be expressed in currently available Interface Description Languages (IDL) such as OpenAPI. Then we show how SRS allows programming clients of REST services and how to rely on the compiler to check whether (i) REST calls conform to the specified service interface and (ii) the response data is correctly used, thus avoiding runtime errors.

---

[1] https://swagger.io/specification.

```
1  // Get Location ID from lat/long coordinates
2  function getLocation() {
3      var client_id = '813efa314de94e618290bc8bfcbbb1ac';
4      // URL for API request to find locations
5      var locationUrl =
6          'https://api.instagram.com/v1/locations/search?lat='+LAT
7              +'&lng='+LNG+'&distance=5000&client_id='+client_id;
8      var result = $.ajax({
9          url: locationUrl,
10         dataType: "jsonp",
11         type: "GET",
12     })
13     .done(function(result){
14         //grab first ID from results
15         var locationId = result.data[0].id;
16         return locationId
17     })
18 }
```

Fig. 1. Excerpt of JavaScript code with a call to an endpoint of the Instagram API

2.1 Background

Applications that consume REST APIs communicate with the service provider through calls to the API endpoints, that is to say, by sending requests for the execution of a HTTP method over an URL. The URL of the request identifies a web resource and additionally can provide values for some optional parameters; additional data can be sent in the request body. The service provider sends back a response that carries, among other data, a response status code indicating whether the request has been successfully completed.

Figure 1 shows an excerpt of a JavaScript application [20] that performs a call to an endpoint of the Instagram API to search for locations by geographic coordinates. According to the API documentation [19], this endpoint has several optional parameters, including lat, lng, and distance. The center of the search must be defined and there are three different ways of doing it. Although lat and lng are optional, if one is used, the other is also required. The distance is optional and its maximum value is 5000. In the success case—signalled by response code 200—the response body is an object with field data containing an array of objects with field id, among others.

Code that consumes this endpoint may contain different sorts of errors. Calls may not conform to the specified interface: for instance the request may contain a value for lat but not for lng, or it may contain a value for distance that exceeds the maximum value or simply that is not an integer. Moreover, the response data may not be correctly used. This is the case in the example: if the call succeeds, then line 15 accesses a possibly non-existent element of the array in field data.

The fact that the model of the response data might depend on the provided input is an additional source of errors. For example, the endpoint in the GitLab API to get all wiki pages for a given project [17] features an optional boolean parameter with content to indicate whether the pages' content must

```
 1  specification Instagram
 2
 3⊝ type SearchLocation = (o: {
 4       ?distance: (x: Integer where x>0 && x<=5000),
 5       ?lat: Integer,
 6       ?lng: Integer,
 7       ?facebook_places_id: String,
 8       ?foursquare_id: String
 9  } where
10⊝      isdefined(lat) <=> isdefined(lng) &&
11       (isdefined(lat) || isdefined(facebook_places_id) || isdefined(foursquare_id))
12  )
13
14  type Location = {id: String, name: String, lat: Integer, lng: Integer}
15
16⊝ { !(request in {template: SearchLocation}) }
17       get `/locations/search{?distance,lat,lng,facebook_places_id,foursquare_id,client_id}`
18  { response.code != 200 }
19
20⊝ { true }
21       get `/locations/search{?distance,lat,lng,facebook_places_id,foursquare_id,client_id}`
22  { response.code == 200 ==> response in {body: {data: Location[]}} }
```

Fig. 2. A HeadREST specification for an Instagram API endpoint

be included in the response. Hence, the response body is an array of objects that contains field **content** only when the request has value **true** for field **with-content**.

In order to avoid such errors programmers must carefully read the API documentation. The situation is worsened as this sort of documentation tends to be vague and imprecise, even when available in a formal document. Limitations in the expressiveness of existing IDLs—and in particular of OpenAPI, the de facto standard for specifying REST APIs—make programmers resort to natural language for conveying extra information. In the case of the two endpoints considered here this is in fact what happens since most of the properties under discussion are not expressible in the IDLs used for the documentation.

Such state of affairs lead us to develop an approach to support the detection of common errors at compile-time by statically checking that calls match APIs' requirements and that data obtained in the response is correctly used.

2.2 SRS in Action

Our approach builds on two pillars: HeadREST, a specification language for REST APIs, and SRS, a language with an expressive type system for programming the code that consumes REST APIs.

HeadREST resorts to types to express properties of states and of data exchanged in interactions and pairs of pre and post-conditions to express the relationship between data sent in requests and those obtained in responses, as well as the resulting state changes. Two type primitives account for its expressiveness: refinement types, $(x\!:\!T \text{ where } e)$, consisting of values of type T that satisfy expression e; and a predicate, $e \text{ in } T$, for checking whether the value of e is of type T.

```
 1 specification "./specs/Instagram.hrest" of "https://api.instagram.com/v1"
 2
 3 var string client_id = "813efa314de94e618290bc8bfcbbb1ac";
 4
 5 type Error = {error: string};
 6
 7●async string|Error getLocation(int lat, int lng) {
 8       SearchLocation searchLocation = {lat= lat, lng= lng, distance= 5000, client_id= client_id};
 9       Request request = {template = searchLocation};
10●      Response result = await get
11              "/locations/search{?distance,lat,lng,facebook_places_id,foursquare_id,client_id}"
12              request;
13●      if (result.code != 200) {
14              return {error = "No locations found!"};
15      }
●16 |Index out of bounds| result.body.data[0].id;
17 }

 7●async string|Error getLocation(int lat, int lng) {
● 8 |Expression does not match declared type|rchLocation = {lat= lat, lng= lng, distance= 50000, client_id= client_id};
 9       Request request = {template = searchLocation};
```

Fig. 3. Example of SRS code consuming an Instagram API endpoint

The endpoints exposed by an API, together with their behaviour, are specified by assertions of the form $\{\phi\}$ m u $\{\psi\}$ where ϕ is the pre-condition, m is the HTTP method; u is a URI template and ψ is the post-condition.

Figure 2 shows a specification of the endpoint discussed before. It starts with the declaration of type `SearchLocation` that represents the search data. Note how refinement types capture the endpoint requirements for search data; e.g., line 10 says that fields `lat` and `lng` must be both present or absent; the question marks in front of these two fields indicate that they are optional.

The behaviour of the endpoint is specified by two assertions (lines 16–22). The first says that, if the requirements for the search data sent in the request are not met, then the call does not succeed (the response code is different from 200). The second assertion says that, if the request is successful, then the response body consists of an array of `Location`, a type defined in line 14.

HeadREST also supports the specification of conditions concerning resources, their representations and their identifiers (see [34] for details). For instance, in the second triple (lines 20–22), we can specify that each `Location` in the response is the representation of a resource that can be individually obtained through the endpoint. Since these properties do not help in avoiding errors in consumer code (individually, clients have no control over the state of the resources), in this paper we limit our presentation to a resource-less version of HeadREST.

Figure 3 shows an SRS program similar in spirit to the JavaScript code in Fig. 1. SRS adopts HeadREST types, while featuring direct support for REST operations. We can see that the type checker spots an error in the use of the response data in line 16. The specification ensures that the effective type of `result` in that execution point is `{body:{data:Location[]}}` (Fig. 2, line 22). This means that it is safe to access `result.body.data[i].id` only if $i <$ `length(result.body.data)` and, hence, line 16 is incorrect. Would the specification be stronger and, in Fig. 2 line 22, read instead `response.code == 200 ==> response in body:{data:{v·`

Scalar types	G	::=	Integer | String | Boolean | {} | Regexp | URITemplate
Types	T	::=	Any | G | $\{l\colon T\}$ | $T[]$ | $(x\colon T\,\text{where}\,e)$
Constants	c	::=	n | s | true | false | {} | u | r | null
Expressions	e	::=	x | c | $f(e_1,\ldots,e_n)$ | $e\,?\,e\colon e$ | $e\,\text{in}\,T$ | $\{l_1 = e_1,\ldots,l_n = e_n\}$
			$\|\,e.l\,\|\,[e_1,\ldots,e_n]\,\|\,e[e]\,\|\,\text{forall}\,x\colon T.e\,\|\,\text{exists}\,x\colon T.e$
Verbs	m	::=	get | put | post | delete
Declarations	D	::=	$\{e\}m\,u\{e\};D$ | ϵ

Fig. 4. The syntax of HeadREST

`Location[] where length(v) > 0)`}, then the program would be valid. Note that the use of type `SearchLocation` in line 8 makes sure that the data sent in the request meets the stated necessary conditions for the request be successful (Fig. 2, line 16). The figure also shows the type checker signaling an error if, in line 8, the value given for distance exceeds the maximum value allowed. SRS further supports assert statements that are statically validated. They are useful to check, immediately before a call to an endpoint, that a necessary condition for the request to be successful holds. In the example, we could add **assert(request in {template: SearchLocation})** immediately before line 10.

3   The HeadREST Specification Language

HeadREST was designed to support the specification of REST APIs and to capture important properties that cannot be expressed in currently available interface description languages. This section briefly introduces the resourceless version of HeadREST [34].

The syntax and validation system of HeadREST are influenced by the Dminor language [7]. Extensions and adaptations to Dminor types, expressions and their respective validation rules were adapted to address the specific needs of REST. The syntax of HeadREST is in Fig. 4. It assumes a countable set of identifiers (denoted by f or x, y, z), a set of constants (c), a set of labels ($l, l_1, l_2, \ldots$), integer literals (n), string literals (s), a set of URI template literals (u), and a set of regular expression literals (r).

Scalar types include standard Integer, String, Boolean, the REST-specific URITemplate to represent a service endpoint or a group of URI resources and Regexp for regular expressions. Any is the top type. For *types*, we additionally have arrays, refinement types, and the singleton object type $\{l\colon T\}$.

Constants include integer, string, and boolean literals, to which null was added. The null value is of type Any but not of object types. The empty object type, {}, describes empty objects and constitutes the super type of all objects. To inhabit Regexp and URITemplate types, two sorts of literals were added: regular expressions and URI templates values. Regular expressions form a subset of those in JavaScript. The syntax of URI Templates is conform to RFC-6570 [18].

Expressions include variables and constants, (primitive) function calls, a conditional, arrays and object operations, quantification, and the e in T operator that allows checking whether a given expression e belongs to type T. Useful derived expressions include $\text{isdefined}(e.l) \triangleq e \text{ in } \{l : \text{Any}\}$ and $e \,\&\&\, f \triangleq e \,?\, f : \text{false}$.

Although HeadREST features a small core of types, the type language is quite expressive due to the interplay between refinement types and the in predicate. A few examples of derived types follow, where x is a variable taken freshly.

$$T \,\&\, U \triangleq x : \text{Any where } (x \text{ in } T \,\&\, x \text{ in } U) \qquad\qquad\qquad !T \triangleq x : \text{Any where }!(x \text{ in } T)$$

$$\{?l : T\} \triangleq x : \{\} \text{ where } x \text{ in } \{l : \text{Any}\} \Rightarrow x \text{ in } \{l : T\} \quad \text{Natural} \triangleq x : \text{Integer where } x \geq 0$$

The operator e in T is essential for the expressiveness of the type system. The intersection, union and negation types are derived using this operator, and these types are the basis for many other derived types. The important multi-field object type can be derived thanks to the intersection type; e.g., $\{l : \{\}, m : \text{String}\}$ abbreviates $(x : \text{Any where } (x \text{ in } \{l : \{\}\} \,\&\, x \text{ in } \{m : \text{String}\}))$ which only uses core types. An important derived type is the optional field type, $\{?l : T\}$, asserting that if an object has a field l then its type is T. For example, if e is an expression of type $\{?l : \text{Boolean}\}$, then expression e in $\{l : \text{Any}\} \,\&\&\, e.l$ is valid since, according to its type, if e has field l its type is Boolean and the good formation of $e.l$ is only ensured in this case.

Specifications consist of a collection of assertions (triples), each of which describe part of the behavior of an endpoint. Currently HeadREST supports the four main HTTP verbs: get, post, put and delete. For the specification of pre- and post-conditions three variables are added: request and response that correspond to the call and the reply, and root, the absolute URL of the entry point of the service. The types of the request and response variables are as follows.

$$\text{Request} \triangleq \{\text{location}: \text{String}, ?\text{template}: \{\}, \text{header}: \{\}, ?\text{body}: \text{Any}\}$$

$$\text{Response} \triangleq \{\text{code}: \text{Integer}, \text{header}: \{\}, ?\text{body}: \text{Any}\}$$

Algorithmic type checking is based on a bidirectional system, composed of two main relations: one that synthesizes the type of a given expression and one that checks whether an expression is of a given type [13,15,29]. At the intersection of these two relations lies *semantic subtyping*, a relation that establishes that a type T is subtype of a type U when all values that belong to T also belong to U. Types and contexts are translated into first-order logic (FOL) formulae. The thus obtained FOL formulae are then evaluated using an SMT solver. Our implementation uses Z3 [26].

Constants	$c ::= \dots \mid$ undefined
Expressions	$e ::= \dots \mid$ await$^{?}\, m\, u\, e$
Locations	$w ::= x \mid w.l \mid w[e]$
Statements	$S ::= w = e \mid$ if (e) then S else $S \mid$ while (e) inv $e\, S \mid$ return $e \mid S; S \mid \epsilon$
Declarations	$D ::=$ specification s of $u \mid$ var $T\, x = e \mid$ async$^{?} T\, x\, (\overline{T\, x})\, \{\overline{T\, x = e}; S\}$
Programs	$P ::= D; P \mid \epsilon$

Fig. 5. The syntax of SRS (extends Fig. 4)

4   The SRS Programming Language

The SRS language (a shorthand for SAFERESTSCRIPT) is a type-safe variant of JavaScript with direct support for REST calls. It was designed to be, at the syntactic level, as close as possible to JavaScript. It transpiles to JavaScript, making it easy to integrate REST API consumer code written in SRS with JavaScript code, namely code of web applications for manipulating the DOM.

Compared with other typed extensions of JavaScript, such as TypeScript [6], the main novelty of SRS is the incorporation of refinement types, the in-type predicate and, most importantly, REST endpoints as external functions. More precisely, a REST endpoint is seen as an impure, external function that receives a value of type Request, possibly changes a global resource set state, and then returns a result of type Response. REST calls are then just calls to such functions. Additional properties of these endpoints-as-functions, namely their specific return type, are inferred from the HeadREST specification of the REST API endpoints. Each triple in the specification specifies a relation between the input (the request) and the output (the response) of an endpoint: if the request meets the pre-condition, then the response meets the pos-condition. From triple $\{\phi\}\, m\, u\, \{\psi\}$, the return type of endpoint-as-function $m\, u$ is extracted as $\{r\colon \mathsf{Request}$ where $\phi \Rightarrow \psi\}$. Note that endpoints-as-functions are, hence, total: they accept any input of type Request, even those that do not meet the precondition of any of their triples (in the vein of Hoare Logic [21] and as opposed to that of Design by Contract [25]). JavaScript is single threaded and, hence, function calls that take time to execute should ideally be executed asynchronously. REST calls fall into this category; SRS supports asynchronous in addition to synchronous REST calls.

SRS adopts the HeadREST type system, not only for its support for REST operations, but also to provide precise static type checking. In SRS, each variable is declared with a type that restricts the values that can be assigned to the variable. Each variable also features an *effective type* that corresponds to the set of values the variable may have at a given point in a program. The effective type changes with program flow, but is necessarily a subtype of the declared type.

4.1 Syntax

The syntax of SRS, presented in Fig. 5, extends that of HeadREST in Fig. 4. The language includes a new *constant* undefined. Functions that return undefined are of type void, an abbreviation of $(x:$ Any where $x ==$ undefined$)$.

At the level of *expressions*, SRS introduces REST calls $m\,u\,e$, composed of an HTTP method m (see Fig. 4), an URI template literal u describing the relative URL of the target resource, and an expression e that should evaluate to a value of type Request. The endpoint needs to be specified in the SRS specification imported by the program. Functions can be declared with the async keyword; calls to these functions are asynchronous while REST calls are asynchronous if they are preceded by keyword await.

Statements include variable assignment. The left hand side w of an assignment statement (a *location*) is a variable x, an object field $w.l$, or a position in an array $w[e]$. An assignment can thus update a specific element of an object or an array. Moreover, statements include conditional statements, while loops, and return statements. Loops may declare an invariant, i.e., an expression that is true at loop entry and after each loop iteration. Invariants are sometimes necessary to prove that certain expressions have the right type, for instance, whether the effective type of the expression used in a return statement matches the return type of the function. Statement return abbreviates return undefined.

An SRS *program* is a sequence of *declarations*: import clauses, global variable and function declarations. The implementation of SRS further supports type abbreviations in the form of type $x = T$. Function definitions are composed of a return type T, the function name f, a comma-separated list of parameters with their respective types $\overline{U\,x}$, and the function body. In order to simplify variable scope validation, the body opens with the declaration and initialization of all local variables: $\overline{V\,y = e}$ is a semi-colon-separated list of variable declarations. The initialization is mandatory since some types, such as refinement types, may not have a default value. The function's body consists of a statement S that defines the control flow and the return value.

4.2 Type Checking

Statically type checking SRS programs is a major challenge given the rich type system of SRS and global imperative variables. It requires flow-sensitive typing (the effective type of an expression depends on its position in the program).

SRS programs are translated into verification conditions, i.e., logical formulae whose validity entails the correctness of the program. Following a popular approach initiated by Spec# [4], these conditions are not generated directly but instead obtained through a translation into Boogie [5], an intermediate language for program verification. Once a SRS program is translated into a Boogie program, it is up to the Boogie validator to generate the verification conditions and, resorting to an SMT solver, verify whether they hold.

At the basis of the translation is an axiomatization of the typing relation that is inspired by Whiley [28]. Values and types are modelled as sets. All SRS values, independently of their type, belong to the Boogie type `Value`. For each type, we introduce functions and axioms that define its subset of values. More concretely, given a type `X` (for example, `Integer`) and its internal representation `Y` in Boogie (`int`, in the example), the base functions and axioms are the following.

```
function isX(Value) returns (bool);
function toX(Value) returns (Y);
function fromX(Y) returns (Value);
axiom (forall y: Y :: isX(fromX(y)));
axiom (forall y: Y :: toX(fromX(y)) == y);
axiom (forall v: Value :: isX(v) ==> fromX(toX(v)) == v);
```

Function `isX` checks whether a value belongs to type `X` and returns a Boogie boolean. Function `toX` converts the Boogie value to its internal representation `Y`, and `fromX` performs the inverse operation. The axioms define the properties of the functions. The first asserts that all values constructed from type `Y` belong to type `X`. The second and third axioms assert that `toX` and `fromX` are inverse functions. More complex types, such as arrays and objects, are represented by Boogie maps and require the introduction of additional functions and axioms.

Functions `isX`, `toX` and `fromX` are used for defining the translation of expressions and the predicate that checks whether the value of an expression is of a given type. This is illustrated below in simple cases: the translation of an SRS integer literal and an array access, and the predicate for the integer type.

$$\mathbf{V}[\![n]\!] = \mathsf{fromInt}(n) \qquad\qquad \mathbf{F}[\![\mathsf{int}]\!](e) = \mathsf{isInt}(e)$$
$$\mathbf{V}[\![e_1\,[e_2]]\!] = \mathsf{getIndexValue}(\mathbf{V}[\![e_1]\!], \mathsf{toInt}(\mathbf{V}[\![e_2]\!]))$$

The translation of SRS to Boogie is based on the collection of functions presented below. We discuss some cases that convey the main ideas of how the translation works. The full set of rules is available in the extended version of this paper [9].

$$
\begin{aligned}
\mathbf{V}[\![e]\!] &\equiv \text{Boogie expression of type } \mathtt{Value} \text{ that represents expression } e \\
\mathbf{F}[\![T]\!] &\equiv \text{Boogie predicate that checks whether an expression is of type } T \\
\mathbf{V}^*[\![e]\!]_x &\equiv \text{Sequence of Boogie statements that validates expression } e \\
&\quad\ \text{and places the corresponding Boogie expression in variable } x \\
\mathbf{W}[\![T]\!] &\equiv \text{Sequence of Boogie statements that validates type } T \\
\mathbf{B}[\![S]\!] &\equiv \text{Boogie statement that represents statement } S \\
\mathbf{B}[\![D]\!] &\equiv \text{Boogie declaration that represents declaration } D
\end{aligned}
$$

The translation of REST calls and of specification triples to Boogie are the most interesting elements of the translation, as they accomplish the view of endpoints-as-functions discussed before. REST calls are translated to Boogie using a function, named restCall, that receives as parameters the REST method, the translation of a string u' representing the URI template relative path u, and the request object, and returns the response object. Each specification triple is translated into an axiom relating the return value of restCall with the request call argument as follows.

$$\mathbf{B}[\![\{e_1\}m\,u\{e_2\}]\!] = \mathbf{axiom}\ (\mathbf{forall}\ \text{request}: \text{Value, response}: \text{Value}::$$
$$\text{restCall}(m, \mathbf{V}[\![u']\!], \text{request}) == \text{response} \wedge$$
$$\mathbf{V}[\![e_1]\!] == \mathbf{V}[\![\text{true}]\!] \Rightarrow \mathbf{V}[\![e_2]\!] == \mathbf{V}[\![\text{true}]\!])$$

The translation of REST calls is defined by the following rules:

$$\mathbf{V}^*[\![m\,u\,e]\!]_x = \mathbf{V}^*[\![e]\!]_y;\ \mathbf{assert}\ \mathbf{F}[\![\text{Request}]\!](y);$$
$$x := \text{restCall}(m, \mathbf{V}[\![u]\!], y);\ \mathbf{assume}\ \mathbf{F}[\![\text{Response}]\!](x)$$
$$\mathbf{V}^*[\![\mathbf{await}\,m\,u\,e]\!]_x = \mathbf{V}^*[\![m\,u\,e]\!]_x;\ \mathbf{havoc}\ g_1, \dots, g_p$$

Expression e in a synchronous REST call is validated and placed in a fresh variable y. Then an **assert** checks whether y is of type Request. Function restCall is called and its response is stored in variable x. The response is assumed to be of type Response. Note that when the request does not meet the pre-condition of any triple for the target endpoint, the axiomatization of restCall does not ensure anything about the response; it is only known that it belongs to type Response. In asynchronous REST calls, the execution is suspended and, when resumed, the global variables may have changed. This is captured by the **havoc** statement, which assigns arbitrary values to variables (while respecting their declared types).

The type validation takes into account that types may contain expressions by descending the abstract syntax tree of types. The most important rule is the rule for where types (y, z are variables taken freshly).

$$\mathbf{W}[\![(x: T\ \text{where}\ e)]\!] = \mathbf{W}[\![T]\!];\ \mathbf{assume}\ \mathbf{F}[\![T]\!](y);\ \mathbf{V}^*[\![e[y/x]]\!]_z;\ \mathbf{assert}\ \mathbf{F}[\![\text{Boolean}]\!](z)$$

We complete this brief presentation by addressing the translation of global variable declaration and functions.

$$\mathbf{B}[\![T\ x = e]\!] = \mathbf{var}\ x: \text{Value}\ \mathbf{where}\ \mathbf{F}[\![T]\!](x);\ \mathbf{V}[\![T\ f()\ \{\ \mathbf{return}\ e\ \}]\!]$$
$$\mathbf{B}[\![T\ f\ (T_1\,x_1, \dots, T_n\,x_n)\ \{\ U_1\ y_1 = e_1;\ \dots;\ U_m\ y_m = e_m;\ S\ \}]\!] =$$
$$\mathbf{procedure}\ f(x_1: \text{Value}, \dots, x_n: \text{Value})\ \mathbf{returns}\ (\text{result}: \text{Value})$$
$$\quad \mathbf{requires}\ \mathbf{F}[\![T_1]\!](x_1) \wedge \dots \wedge \mathbf{F}[\![T_n]\!](x_n);\ \ \mathbf{ensures}\ \mathbf{F}[\![T]\!](\text{result});$$
$$\quad \mathbf{modifies}\ g_1, \dots, g_p;$$
$$\{$$
$$\quad \mathbf{var}\ y_1, \dots, y_m, w_1, \dots, w_n: \text{Value};\ w_1 := x_1; \dots; w_n := x_n;$$
$$\quad \mathbf{W}[\![T_1]\!]; \dots; \mathbf{W}[\![T_n]\!]; \mathbf{W}[\![U_1]\!]; \dots; \mathbf{W}[\![U_m]\!]; \mathbf{W}[\![T]\!]$$
$$\quad \mathbf{B}[\![y_1 = e_1;\ \dots;\ y_m = e_m;\ S[w_1/x_1]\dots[w_n/x_n]; \mathbf{return}]\!]$$
$$\}$$

In the first rule, the declared type is captured by a Boogie **where** clause while the initialization is ignored as it is not relevant: whenever a procedure is called, nothing can be assumed about any global variable besides its declared type. The validation of T and e is achieved via an additional, dummy, procedure f.

In the second rule, the immutability of procedure parameters in Boogie requires the declaration of new variables to use instead of the parameters in the function body. The **requires** clause checks whether the arguments belong to the parameters types and the **ensures** clause checks whether in all returning points of the procedure the result of the function matches the function type. The **modifies** clause asserts that all global variables can be modified by the procedure. The body of the procedure makes the validation of parameters types T_i, local variables types U_k and the return type T. The validation order allows that the validity of T and U_k depend on T_i and the validity of T_i depend on the T_j, for $j < i$, as in $\{x\colon \mathsf{int\ where}\ x > b/a\}\ f(\{x\colon \mathsf{int\ where}\ x! = 0\}\ a, \mathsf{int}\ b)\{...\}$.

4.3   Transpiling to JavaScript

Valid programs are transpiled to JavaScript. The translation of REST calls is achieved by calling auxiliary functions, one for synchronous and another by asynchronous calls. The URL to the call is the expansion of the URI template; its parameters are defined by the field template of the request object. The expansion follows the RFC 6570 [18], only for the level of URI templates supported by SRS. The content-type JSON is added to the request headers, so objects sent and received in the body are ensured to be of JSON format, and therefore having a direct translation to JavaScript objects. The calls use `XMLHttpRequest`, an object that is supported by all browsers and devices.

5   Evaluation

This section addresses the evaluation of our approach. Ideally, we would like to compare the bug finding efficacy of our approach in "real code" with that of Wittern et al. [37], the unique approach to statically checking REST calls that we are aware of. However, this turned out not feasible, since translating JavaScript code into SRS requires annotating all the libraries used and/or write adaptors that monitor the interface with libraries.

In this way, to evaluate our approach, we used HeadREST to specify a variety of REST APIs and SRS to write and validate programs that exercise the different elements of the language while consuming REST APIs. The goal is to evaluate *to what degree can SRS be used in examples which include complex REST calls that can be found in real examples*.

We used SRS to write programs that consume publicly available APIs and do not require authentication, including PetStore[2] and DummyAPI[3] as well

---

[2] https://petstore.swagger.io.
[3] http://dummy.restapiexample.com.

as programs that consume real-world off-the-shelf services such as Instagram, GitHub and GitLab. Since API calls in SRS are checked against HeadREST specifications, we also developed HeadREST specifications for the chosen APIs describing the behaviour of the relevant endpoints. In what follows we provide details about three of these case studies. The complete examples are available in the supplementary material [8].

Instagram. We developed in SRS a solution alternative to the JavaScript function in Sect. 2. The application allows users to find Instagram photos by tag or location and calls the different endpoints of the Instagram API which supports search for (i) locations by geographic coordinate, (ii) photos by location and (iii) photos by tag. The solution is based on a SRS program defining asynchronous functions for calling the API, similar to that presented in Fig. 3. These functions are available in the generated JavaScript code and used by the program that manipulates the DOM. We additionally developed a program for showing the recent comments on media for a user, given its identifier, which requires to call three other endpoints: one to get the ids of recent media, another to get the comments for each of them and a third one to get information about the user. Both programs use the same specification with the behaviour of the six endpoints.

GitHub. We developed an SRS program that offers a function `getUserById(int id)` to obtain a GitHub user given its `id` with return type `(u: User where u.id == id)|NotFoundError`. Since the GitHub REST API does not have an endpoint that supports this operation (to get the representation of individual users, one needs to provide the username), our program sends a `GET` request to `/users?since=id-1` if `id` is a positive integer. According to the API documentation, this endpoint lists all users, in the order that they signed up on GitHub. Retrieval is by pagination: each call retrieves a sublist of all users. The start of the sublist is defined by the optional parameter `since`. If case the parameter is not present, then its value is assumed to be zero. In the HeadREST specification of GitHub we were able to precisely express this behaviour. One of the assertions included in the specification states that if the request provides a value for `since` that is a natural number, then the array of users provided in the response body starts with a user whose `id` is equal to `since+1`. This assertion is essential to prove that if a user is obtained, it has the id provided in the function argument and, hence, that the return type of the function is valid.

The endpoint **`/get users{?since}`** can also be used for searching for an user with certain characteristics. We used it to define a function `getSiteAdmin()` with return type `(u: User where u.site_admin)|AdminNotFound` that searches over the GitHub users to find an administrator. The search code gets the various pages of users and stops when one of them contains an user with admin privileges, or when no admin was found on all pages, in which case `AdminNotFound` is returned. The fact that the function type checks ensures that the returned user representation (if any) is an indeed an administrator.

In GitHub each user has a set of repositories, and each repository has a set of collaborators and a list of commits, each with its author. We programmed

Table 1. Case studies of consuming REST APIs with SRS

	HeadREST				SRS			
	#EndP	#Types	LOC	Check (s)	#EndP	#Func	LOC	Check (s)
Instagram#app1	6	9	225	1.3	3	4	82	1.5
Instagram#app2	6	9	225	1.3	3	3	65	1.8
GitHub	5	9	93	0.8	5	3	86	1.3
GitLab	10	20	435	1.7	8	10	250	50.5

a function that gets the collaborators of a repository that did not contribute to a project, i.e., did not make a commit. The function crosses the information obtained in two different endpoints: one for retrieving the collaborators of a given repository for a given user and another for retrieving the list of commits of the repository. As the repository may be private, the function receives a key that must give authorization to access the repository information, and that is added to the request header.

GitLab. is the Git manager used by our students to develop their course projects. We wrote functions that automate tasks we recurrently perform manually. For instance, we programmed a function to remove a user from all projects owned by another user. This function uses three endpoints, one of them involving request and response types particularly large—the request has more than 10 optional parameters and the response body is an array of an object type with more than 30 fields, several of them also objects. The type of the response is used, for instance, to validate the expression `response.body[i].namespace.name` that occurs in the body of the function. Another interesting example is the function `getWikisFromProject(string token, int|string id, boolean withContent)` we defined in SRS to get the wikis from a project, identified by its integer id or a string that is the URL-encoded path of the project (and, hence, of type `int|string`). The function uses an endpoint that features an optional parameter to indicate whether the response should contain the content of the wikis. The behaviour of GitLab at this endpoint was specified in HeadREST as shown below and allows the SRS validator to find errors in accesses to `response.body[i].content`, such as when the SRS code does not guarantee that accesses are performed only if the value sent in `request.template.with_content` is true.

```
{ request in {template: {id: String|Integer, ?with_content:
    Boolean}} }
        get '/projects/{id}/wikis{?private_token,with_content}'
{ (response.code == 200 ==> response in {body: Wiki[]}) &&
    (response.code == 200 && request.template in {with_content:
    Boolean}
    && request.template.with_content ==>
        response.body in (Wiki & {content:String})[]) }
```

Table 1 presents additional information about the three case studies. The first group of columns addresses HeadREST specifications and shows the number of endpoints that were specified, the number of types that were defined, the number of lines and the validation time, in seconds. The second group of columns, which addresses SRS client programs, shows the number of endpoints that were consumed, the number of functions that were defined, the number of lines of code and the validation time, in seconds. The validation the time of SRS programs presented in the table does not consider the validation time of the specification. Benchmarking was performed on a machine with an Intel Core i7-7700HQ CPU, 2.80 GHz and 16 GB of RAM memory, under Windows 10. The times reported are the average of three runs.

Overall, these examples demonstrate that HeadREST supports the specification of a variety of API endpoints found in real examples and is able to capture important properties of these endpoints that were previously available only in natural language. During the development of the client programs we could witness that the formalisation of properties allowed SRS to find all sort of errors in our code, in particular, errors in the invocations of the underlying services (invalid or missing data in the requests or use of incorrect URLs) and errors in the use of the data received in the response. We also noted that were we programming the same client code in JavaScript, most of the errors we made would not be found by Wittern at al. [37]. On the one hand, errors caused by invalid data in the requests were often caused by restrictions on data that are simply not expressible in OpenAPI. On the other hand, several errors lied in the usage of the data received in the response, a type of error that is not addressed by the analysis performed by the tool.

In terms of performance, we witness what is also evident in the results in Table 1: the complexity of the types involved in REST calls significantly slows the validation process when the correctness of the code strongly depends on these types. This problem can be alleviated by placing functions whose validation is too demanding in separated source files. Because the validator ignores files that have not changed, these functions do not need to be validated again if they have not changed.

6   Related Work

Static verification of JavaScript code has been the main research topic for client-side coding in the last few years [31]. Nevertheless, research concerning the verification of consumer code of REST APIs for JavaScript-like client-side languages is slim and the solutions proposed tend to be quite limited.

Solutions for helping finding bugs in scripts come in the form of a varied set of languages and tools. JSHint [22] scans JavaScript code for suspicious usage; Thiemann [32] and Anderson et al. [1] propose type system for subsets of JavaScript; TypeScript [6], Dart [11] and Flow [14] are languages that were developed with the goal of statically detecting type-related errors in JavaScript-like languages. Languages such as Dependent JavaScript [10] and Refined TypeScript [35] incorporate sophisticated type systems, but the power of the e in J predicate and semantic subtyping (supported by SRS) seems to be particularly suited for programming REST clients. Whiley [28] is a programming language that features a rich type system and flow typing; it uses Boogie only to check the verification conditions [33]. Contrary to SRS, neither of these solutions specifically addresses REST calls.

TypeScript$_{\text{IPC}}$ [27] extends TypeScript with the ability to describe the presence or absence of properties in objects, a feature that HeadREST and SRS can easily describe and for which a derived predicate isdefined was introduced (cf. Sect. 3). Like all the languages discussed above, TypeScript$_{\text{IPC}}$ does not provide explicit support for REST calls.

The tool by Wittern et al. [37], discussed in the introduction, statically checks web API requests in JavaScript code, focusing on ajax requests made via jQuery[4]. The tool uses a field-based call graph to make the necessary string analyses on the JavaScript method calls and is able to check whether calls to endpoints match a valid URI template in the API specification and the request has the expected data. Such errors are easier to check in SRS since the construction of URIs is limited to URI template instantiation (thus ruling out the construction of new URIs via string operations such as concatenation). In contrast, the verification supported by SRS that the request has the expected data is beyond reach of Wittern et al. for the rich, non-OpenAPI, data definitions. RESTyped Axios [12] is a client-side tool that verifies REST calls in TypeScript against RESTyped specifications, with requests made via the Axios framework [3]. RESTyped allows to define strongly-typed routes and Axios checks at compile time whether the URLs are valid and whether the types of the members passed on requests and accessed on responses correspond to the ones declared in the specification. These two approaches fail to detect many of the defects at the reach of SRS, including those related to complex restrictions on input data of REST calls (not expressible in the adopted specification languages) or the misuse of the return data.

Whip [36] is a contract system for services that uses a dependent type system to monitor services at runtime and check whether they respect their advertised interfaces. Whip offers a high-order contract language that, similarly to HeadREST, addresses the lack of expressiveness of IDLs to capture non-trivial properties that can be found in the documentation of popular services. Whip focus is on the specification of properties that cross-cut more than one service (e.g., properties that describe how a client of one system should use a reply to interact with another) and, by using contracts, addresses the specification of the expectations and promises of a service to other services.

7   Conclusion

We present a framework for statically checking code that consumes APIs. Relevant aspects of APIs are described with HeadREST, a specification language featuring refinement types and semantic subtyping. The consumer code itself is written in SRS, a variant of JavaScript with explicit primitives for synchronous

[4] https://api.jquery.com.

and asynchronous REST calls. HeadREST specifications are validated by resorting to an SMT solver to discharge semantic subtyping goals. API consumer code is checked via a translation to Boogie. We validate our approach by writing in SRS various benchmarks from the literature. We further report on three case studies of consumer code for popular APIs (Instagram, GitHub, and GitLab).

Much remains to be done; we sketch a few ideas for future work. The lack of references is the most relevant difference between SRS and JavaScript. Introducing references in objects and arrays is not trivial and adds additional complexity to the Boogie translation. Dafny [23] devised a clever solution using object references in its translation to Boogie, but the technique does not carry straightforwardly to refinement types. A preliminary experience showed that this extension substantially increases the validation time.

Since SRS compiles to JavaScript, programmers may take advantage of its standard libraries. To use JavaScript functions in SRS code, their signatures are required. We plan to address this issue, possibly by following the TypeScript approach, that is, by introducing declaration files where external JavaScript can be declared and annotated with the SRS types so they can be used in SRS code.

HeadREST specifications may feature inconsistent triples. This aspect does not influence the validation of HeadREST specifications, since each triple is validated independently, but it can affect the validation of SRS programs. Specifications featuring inconsistent triples induce inconsistent Boogie axiomatizations, allowing programs with typing errors to be validated. It is therefore important to detect inconsistent HeadREST specifications.

Acknowledgements. This work was supported by FCT through the LASIGE Research Unit, ref. UIDB/00408/2020, and by project Confident ref. PTDC/EEI-CTP/4503/2014.

References

1. Anderson, C., Giannini, P., Drossopoulou, S.: Towards type inference for JavaScript. In: Black, A.P. (ed.) ECOOP 2005. LNCS, vol. 3586, pp. 428–452. Springer, Heidelberg (2005). https://doi.org/10.1007/11531142_19
2. Aué, J., Aniche, M.F., Lobbezoo, M., van Deursen, A.: An exploratory study on faults in web API integration in a large-scale payment company. In: Proceedings of the 40th International Conference on Software Engineering: Software Engineering in Practice, ICSE, pp. 13–22. ACM (2018). https://doi.org/10.1145/3183519.3183537
3. Axios: Promise based HTTP client for the browser and node.js. https://github.com/axios/axios
4. Barnett, M., Fähndrich, M., Leino, K.R.M., Müller, P., Schulte, W., Venter, H.: Specification and verification: the Spec# experience. Commun. ACM **54**(6), 81–91 (2011)
5. Barnett, M., Chang, B.-Y.E., DeLine, R., Jacobs, B., Leino, K.R.M.: Boogie: a modular reusable verifier for object-oriented programs. In: de Boer, F.S., Bonsangue, M.M., Graf, S., de Roever, W.-P. (eds.) FMCO 2005. LNCS, vol. 4111, pp. 364–007. Springer, Heidelberg (2006). https://doi.org/10.1007/11804192_17

6. Bierman, G.M., Abadi, M., Torgersen, M.: Understanding TypeScript. In: Jones, R. (ed.) ECOOP 2014. LNCS, vol. 8586, pp. 257–281. Springer, Heidelberg (2014). https://doi.org/10.1007/978-3-662-44202-9_11

7. Bierman, G.M., Gordon, A.D., Hritcu, C., Langworthy, D.E.: Semantic subtyping with an SMT solver. J. Funct. Program. **22**(1), 31–105 (2012). https://doi.org/10.1017/S0956796812000032

8. Burnay, N., et al.: Communication contracts for distributed systems development. http://rss.di.fc.ul.pt/confident

9. Burnay, N., Lopes, A., Vasconcelos, V.T.: SafeRESTScript: statically checking REST API consumers. arXiv:2007.08048 (2020). http://arxiv.org/abs/2007.08048

10. Chugh, R., Herman, D., Jhala, R.: Dependent types for JavaScript. In: Proceedings of the 27th Annual ACM SIGPLAN Conference on Object-Oriented Programming, Systems, Languages, and Applications, OOPSLA, pp. 587–606. ACM (2012). https://doi.org/10.1145/2384616.2384659

11. Dart: The Dart programming language. https://www.dartlang.org/

12. Dezfuli-Arjomandi, A.: Introducing RESTyped: end-to-end typing for REST APIs with TypeScript (2017). https://blog.falcross.com/introducing-restyped-end-to-end-typing-for-rest-apis-with-typescript/

13. Dunfield, J., Krishnaswami, N.R.: Complete and easy bidirectional typechecking for higher-rank polymorphism. In: ACM SIGPLAN International Conference on Functional Programming, ICFP, pp. 429–442. ACM (2013). https://doi.org/10.1145/2500365.2500582

14. Facebook: Flow: a static type checker for JavaScript. https://flow.org/

15. Ferreira, F., Pientka, B.: Bidirectional elaboration of dependently typed programs. In: Proceedings of the 16th International Symposium on Principles and Practice of Declarative Programming, pp. 161–174. ACM (2014). https://doi.org/10.1145/2643135.2643153

16. Fielding, R.T., Taylor, R.N.: Principled design of the modern web architecture. ACM Trans. Internet Technol. **2**(2), 115–150 (2002). https://doi.org/10.1145/514183.514185

17. GitLab: GitLab OpenAPI documentation. https://gitlab.com/gitlab-org/gitlab-foss/blob/swagger-api/doc/api/wikis.md

18. Gregorio, J., Fielding, R.T., Hadley, M., Nottingham, M., Orchard, D.: URI template. RFC 6570, pp. 1–34 (2012). https://doi.org/10.17487/RFC6570

19. Harmony, A.: Instagram API. https://apiharmony-open.mybluemix.net/public/apis/instagram#get_locations_search

20. Herman, M.: Instagram search app. https://github.com/mjhea0/thinkful-mentor/blob/master/frontend/instagram-search/app.js

21. Hoare, C.A.R.: An axiomatic basis for computer programming. Commun. ACM **12**(10), 576–580 (1969). https://doi.org/10.1145/363235.363259

22. JSHint: JSHint, a static code analysis tool for JavaScript. https://jshint.com/about/

23. Leino, K.R.M.: Dafny: an automatic program verifier for functional correctness. In: Clarke, E.M., Voronkov, A. (eds.) LPAR 2010. LNCS (LNAI), vol. 6355, pp. 348–370. Springer, Heidelberg (2010). https://doi.org/10.1007/978-3-642-17511-4_20

24. Levin, G.: The rise of REST API (2015). https://blog.restcase.com/the-rise-of-rest-api/

25. Meyer, B.: Object-Oriented Software Construction, 2nd edn. Prentice-Hall, Upper Saddle River (1997)

26. de Moura, L., Bjørner, N.: Z3: an efficient SMT solver. In: Ramakrishnan, C.R., Rehof, J. (eds.) TACAS 2008. LNCS, vol. 4963, pp. 337–340. Springer, Heidelberg (2008). https://doi.org/10.1007/978-3-540-78800-3_24

27. Oostvogels, N., Koster, J.D., Meuter, W.D.: Static typing of complex presence constraints in interfaces. In: 32nd European Conference on Object-Oriented Programming, ECOOP. LIPIcs, vol. 109, pp. 14:1–14:27. Schloss Dagstuhl - Leibniz-Zentrum für Informatik (2018). https://doi.org/10.4230/LIPIcs.ECOOP.2018.14

28. Pearce, D.J., Groves, L.: Whiley: a platform for research in software verification. In: Erwig, M., Paige, R.F., Van Wyk, E. (eds.) SLE 2013. LNCS, vol. 8225, pp. 238–248. Springer, Cham (2013). https://doi.org/10.1007/978-3-319-02654-1_13

29. Pierce, B.C., Turner, D.N.: Local type inference. In: POPL 1998, Proceedings of the 25th ACM SIGPLAN-SIGACT Symposium on Principles of Programming Languages, San Diego, CA, USA, 19–21 January 1998, pp. 252–265. ACM (1998). https://doi.org/10.1145/268946.268967

30. Richardson, L., Ruby, S.: RESTful Web Services - Web Services for the Real World. O'Reilly, Sebastopol (2007)

31. Sun, K., Ryu, S.: Analysis of JavaScript programs: challenges and research trends. ACM Comput. Surv. **50**(4), 59:1–59:34 (2017). https://doi.org/10.1145/3106741

32. Thiemann, P.: Towards a type system for analyzing JavaScript programs. In: Sagiv, M. (ed.) ESOP 2005. LNCS, vol. 3444, pp. 408–422. Springer, Heidelberg (2005). https://doi.org/10.1007/978-3-540-31987-0_28

33. Utting, M., Pearce, D.J., Groves, L.: Making Whiley boogie!. In: Polikarpova, N., Schneider, S. (eds.) IFM 2017. LNCS, vol. 10510, pp. 69–84. Springer, Cham (2017). https://doi.org/10.1007/978-3-319-66845-1_5

34. Vasconcelos, V.T., Martins, F., Lopes, A., Burnay, N.: HEADREST: a specification language for RESTful APIs. In: Boreale, M., Corradini, F., Loreti, M., Pugliese, R. (eds.) Models, Languages, and Tools for Concurrent and Distributed Programming. LNCS, vol. 11665, pp. 428–434. Springer, Cham (2019). https://doi.org/10.1007/978-3-030-21485-2_23

35. Vekris, P., Cosman, B., Jhala, R.: Refinement types for TypeScript. In: Proceedings of the 37th ACM SIGPLAN Conference on Programming Language Design and Implementation, PLDI, pp. 310–325. ACM (2016). https://doi.org/10.1145/2908080.2908110

36. Waye, L., Chong, S., Dimoulas, C.: Whip: higher-order contracts for modern services. PACMPL **1**(ICFP), 36:1–36:28 (2017). https://doi.org/10.1145/3110280

37. Wittern, E., Ying, A.T.T., Zheng, Y., Dolby, J., Laredo, J.A.: Statically checking web API requests in JavaScript. In: Proceedings of the 39th International Conference on Software Engineering, ICSE, pp. 244–254. IEEE/ACM (2017). https://doi.org/10.1109/ICSE.2017.30

38. Wittern, E., et al.: Opportunities in software engineering research for web API consumption. In: 1st IEEE/ACM International Workshop on API Usage and Evolution, WAPI@ICSE, pp. 7–10. IEEE Computer Society (2017). https://doi.org/10.1109/WAPI.2017.1

A Layered Implementation of DR-BIP Supporting Run-Time Monitoring and Analysis

Antoine El-Hokayem[✉], Saddek Bensalem, Marius Bozga, and Joseph Sifakis

University of Grenoble Alpes, CNRS, Grenoble INP, Verimag, Grenoble, France
`antoine.el-hokayem@univ-grenoble-alpes.fr`

Abstract. Reconfigurable systems are emerging in many application domains as reconfiguration can be used to cope with unpredictable system environments and adapt by delivering new functionality. The Dynamic Reconfigurable BIP (DR-BIP) framework is an extension of the BIP component framework enriched with dynamic exogenous reconfiguration primitives, intended to support rigorous modeling of reconfigurable systems. We present a new two-layered implementation of DR-BIP clearly separating between execution of reconfiguration operations and execution of a fixed system configuration. Such a separation of concerns offers the advantage of using the mature and efficient BIP engine as well as existing associated analysis and verification tools. Another direct benefit of the new implementation is the possibility to monitor a holistic view of a system's behavior captured as a set of traces involving information about both the state of the system components and the dynamically changing architecture. Monitoring and analyzing such traces poses interesting questions regarding the formalization and runtime verification of properties of reconfigurable systems.

1 Introduction

The current trend for adaptive and resilient systems changes the perspective of system designers who have to consider systems that are reconfigurable and self-organizing. This requires conceptual models to better understand and properly take into account the different types of dynamism and corresponding coordination mechanisms for their description. In particular, it is desirable to have a rigorous and disciplined approach that would allow envisioning how a system with static coordination structure can be progressively modified to enhance its adaptivity and resilience.

Consider a platoon system of an automated highway where an arbitrary number of autonomous cars are moving in the same direction, in a single lane, at different cruising speeds. Cars dynamically organize into platoons, i.e., groups

Grenoble INP—Institute of Engineering University of Grenoble Alpes.
The research performed by these authors was partially funded by H2020-ECSEL grants CPS4EU 2018-IA call - Grant Agreement number 826276.

F. de Boer and A. Cerone (Eds.): SEFM 2020, LNCS 12310, pp. 284–302, 2020.
https://doi.org/10.1007/978-3-030-58768-0_16

of cars cruising at the same speed and closely following a leader car. Platooning confers advantages such as increasing the road capacities, providing a more steady-state traffic flow, and reducing the risk of traffic congestion [4]. Organizing as platoons requires non-trivial dynamic coordination between cars. All the cars belonging to a platoon must agree on a common cruising speed dictated by the leader car. Platoons may dynamically merge or split. A merge can take place if two platoons are close enough, i.e., the distance between the tail car of the first platoon and the leader car of the second is reaching some minimal distance K. After the merge, the speed of the new platoon is updated consistently for all cars. A platoon may also split upon the request of a car to leave the platoon. This results in the creation of two platoons. A leading platoon that increases its speed whereas the newly formed tail platoon decreases its speed to achieve some separation distance. However, not all cars can initiate a split, as they may leave other cars stranded. After splitting, the resulting platoons should have at least some minimal size S. For such traffic systems, the global system dynamics depends both on the behavior of individual cars as well as the organization into platoons and their coordination.

Providing insight into the interplay between static coordination and various types of dynamism and reconfiguration has been a driving concern for the design of the DR-BIP component framework [9]. DR-BIP is an extension of the BIP framework which has been used for more than a decade for modeling component-based systems with static architectures. In BIP, a system is built from architecture-agnostic components coordinated using interactions and priorities. We have thoroughly formalized operational semantics for BIP and studied results comparing its expressiveness with respect to existing modeling formalisms [5]. The theoretical framework has been implemented by a toolset integrating an execution engine, code generators for different types of execution platforms, and verification tools. DR-BIP supports an incremental modeling methodology considering that a system consists of a set of motifs, a kind of "worlds" where components "live". Motifs are dynamic architectures integrating components coordinated according to specific rules. To model component mobility, a motif is equipped with a data structure which is a graph representing a map. An addressing function is used to associate with each component a node of the map. *Reconfiguration rules* deal with: 1) component dynamism e.g., creation/deletion of components; 2) map dynamism e.g.., updating the map structure; 3) component mobility e.g., changing the addressing function, and 4) modifying connectors that define interactions between components. Furthermore, it is possible to express reconfiguration between motifs e.g., component migration, which confers the ability for system self-organization.

The paper presents the DR-BIP *language* for constructing dynamic reconfigurable systems using BIP components and connectors as well as a *layered implementation* of DR-BIP that re-uses the BIP Engine. Our previous work on DR-BIP introduced the concepts for programming reconfigurable systems [8,9], nonetheless, its implementation was limited to a restricted abstract language of simple components and motifs, and had little support for executing reconfiguration rules.

The DR-BIP language has been designed to integrate full-fledged components and connectors described in BIP, arbitrary motif maps and addressing functions described as external C++ structures, and a high-level declarative syntax for reconfiguration rules. The implementation of DR-BIP semantics relies on code generation (for motifs, reconfiguration rules, components, etc.) and clearly separates reconfiguration issues from the execution of static configurations. It involves two separate computational phases: the first deals with the execution of reconfiguration rules that determine the overall static coordination structure which we refer to as the *instantiated BIP model*; the second executes for the instantiated BIP model, the interactions between components using the BIP Engine. The two phases alternate in a global computation cycle synchronized by a well-defined protocol. The present implementation offers the advantage of using the mature and efficient BIP execution engine. Furthermore, the underlying separation of concerns allows better comprehension and management of the intricate semantics of DR-BIP and enhances confidence in the reconfiguration engine implementation. Another direct benefit from the studied implementation is the possibility to monitor a holistic view of the system behavior as a set of traces involving dynamic configurations in addition to component states. The proposed implementation of DR-BIP provides insight into system behavior as the combination of both architectural and component state information, as well as monitoring execution traces at different levels of detail. Analyzing such traces poses interesting questions regarding the formalization and verification of properties of reconfigurable systems. Nonetheless, the development of a specific logic for expressing reconfiguration properties and the synthesis of monitors are beyond the scope of this paper.

Automatic code generation for implementation and/or analysis purposes is one of the most prominent features of model-based design methodologies. There exists a tremendous number of modeling formalisms and associated code generation flows dedicated to static systems. On one hand, general purpose formalisms such as UML/PAPYRUS [12], AADL/OSATE [11], TASTE [18], PTOLEMY [7] are state-of-the-art tools oriented towards design and implementation. On the other hand, domain specific formalisms and/or software libraries such as GENOM [14] and ROS [21] focus on simulation, rapid prototyping and implementation targeting only specific application domains.

Code generation and runtime analysis is becoming more challenging for reconfigurable systems. Approaches have been explored for several general-purpose architecture description languages with reconfiguration capabilities such as π-ADL [6], ARCHJAVA [1], C2SADEL [16] to cite only a few. Nonetheless, these approaches did not reach the same level of acceptance as for static systems. Architecture dynamism and reconfiguration is of much interest for domain specific languages as well. Formalisms such as BUZZ [19] for swarm robotics and PARACOSM [13] for autonomous driving systems are gaining popularity. However, most of the concepts supported are ad-hoc and hardly re-usable beyond their domain. We position DR-BIP as a general-purpose architecture description language for the description of dynamic reconfigurable systems.

The paper is structured as follows. Section 2 recalls the DR-BIP concepts and introduces the key features of the DR-BIP language. Section 3 presents the DR-BIP layering principle and its concrete implementation. Section 4 provides insights on the software architecture and the tooling for generating code used to execute DR-BIP models. Section 5 presents the provided monitoring support and illustrates its application to the analysis of a platoon system as presented earlier. Section 6 discusses challenging future work directions on modeling and analysis of dynamic reconfigurable systems. Finally, Sect. 6 concludes about the benefits from the presented layered implementation. We provide an online artifact with the tools, the simulation experimental data, and the documentation needed to recreate it [22].

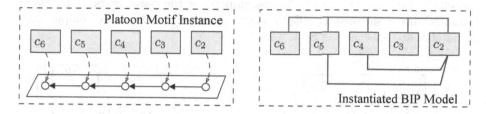

Fig. 1. An example motif and its instantiation in BIP. (Color figure online)

2 DR-BIP Overview

We consider DR-BIP models integrating (1) components and connector types described in the BIP language and (2) motif types and reconfiguration rules described in the DR-BIP language. We recall that in BIP, connector types specify interactions between components along their interfaces. This section introduces the concepts underlying DR-BIP and key features of the language.

2.1 Motifs and Reconfiguration Rules

Motifs are dynamic structures consisting of (i) a set of components, (ii) a map and (iii) an addressing function [9]. Maps are underlying data structures (typically a directed graph) used to organize interactions between components. Addressing functions provide an association between the components and the nodes of maps.

Example 1. Figure 1 showcases on the left an instance of a motif type named Platoon. It consists of the set of five components $\{c_2 \ldots c_6\}$, the map consisting of a chain of five nodes, and the addressing function associating each component with one node in the chain. Component c_2 is associated with the head of the chain, thus giving it the role of the leader. Components $c_3, \cdots c_6$ are associated with other nodes and have the role of followers of the platoon.

Motifs are associated with local reconfiguration rules dictating their evolution. These rules define how components are interconnected, and modify the motif i.e., add/remove components, update the map, and update the addressing function. Rules are executed depending on conditions evaluated on the motif and component states. More precisely, local reconfiguration rules have the general form:

rule rule-name $(arg_1, \dots arg_n)$
  when $(cond_1, \dots cond_n)$ { $action_1(args), \dots action_m(args)$ }

Their execution consists in selecting a set of components of the motif and assigning them to formal parameters arg_i. Assignments are constrained by a "**when**"-clause, providing a Boolean condition $cond_i$ for each formal parameter. For each valid assignment to formal arguments $args$, a sequence of actions $action_j$ is executed modifying the motif. An assignment of the parameters such that a "**when**"-clause is satisfied, is called a *match*. Further details on the computation of matches are presented in Sect. 3.2.

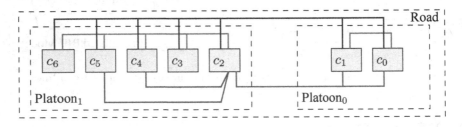

Fig. 2. An example platoon system consisting of 7 cars organized in 2 platoons. (Color figure online)

We distinguish between two types of configuration rules: 1) *connecting rules* whose actions deal solely with the creation of connectors, and 2) *updating rules* whose actions deal with the creation or deletion of components and the modification of the map or of the addressing function. The distinction is important because connecting rules do not change the motif; they affect solely the instantiated BIP model.

Example 2. Figure 1 illustrates the Platoon motif (left), and the instantiated BIP model resulting from the application of connecting rules (right). Connector **SpeedUpdate** (pink) is used to synchronize speed with the leader. Furthermore, cars that are allowed to split from the platoon are connected with the leader, as they need to adjust speeds. We call this connector **SplitStep**. For example, c_3 cannot split, since by doing so, it will leave c_2 stranded. Since both c_4 and c_5 can split, two connectors (shown in brown) of **SplitStep** are created.

While local reconfiguration rules apply to a single motif and are given access to that motif only, global reconfiguration rules apply to more than one motif. In this case, the formal parameters can be assigned any motif or component. Moreover, actions can perform migration of components between motifs as well as the creation or deletion of motif instances. The execution of all reconfiguration rules both local and global results in creating an instantiated BIP model containing components interconnected by a set of connectors.

Example 3. Figure 2 illustrates a fully instantiated BIP model of the platoon system. We have one Road motif grouping all 7 cars, and two platoons: $Platoon_0$ grouping two cars, and $Platoon_1$ grouping five. We notice two `SpeedUpdate` connectors (pink), one for each platoon, and two `SplitStep` connectors (brown) in $Platoon_1$, as no car is allowed to split in $Platoon_0$. The `GlobalStep` connector (blue) allows all cars to move synchronously. Finally, to perform a merge, the two platoons can interact using connector `MergeForward` (green) resulting from the execution of a global connecting reconfiguration rule between the two platoons. This connector involves the leader of the heading platoon, the tail and the leader of the second platoon. It allows checking proximity and updating the speed.

2.2 The DR-BIP Language

The DR-BIP language is a declarative language for the description of: (1) imports that expose all building blocks for the dynamic model (i.e., component types, connector types, additional BIP predicates, map types and addressing functions); (2) a set of motif types with their associated local and global reconfiguration rules; and (3) a designated "initializer" global reconfiguration rule to initialize the system.

Imports. The DR-BIP language allows component and connector types to be imported from a BIP model. Additionally, external general purpose data structures and functions from the host language (C++) can be used for the implementation of maps and addressing functions. Listing 1.1 provides an example of imports. It includes the reference to the BIP package containing component and connector types (Line 1) which can be used in DR-BIP rules. The listing also includes specifications of signatures of the data structures used to build maps and addressing functions that can be found in a file `platoon.cpp`. We distinguish methods that modify objects from those that do not (using keyword `const`). We see in lines 3–9 the declaration of the data structure `PlatoonMap` used as a map. The methods prefixed with `const` do not modify the map. For example, the method `allowedSplit` checks whether a split of the platoon by the car assigned to that node is allowed. The method `assign` replaces all nodes of the current map with those of another `PlatoonMap`. Finally, we import the signature of additional BIP predicates, described as Boolean functions over elements of the BIP model. Line 11 introduces the predicate `AtSplitLocation` which checks if a given `Car` component (whose type is described in BIP) is in a control location where a split is allowed.

Motif Types and Reconfiguration Rules. The definition of a set of motif types follows the declaration of imports in a DR-BIP specification. For each motif, the

Listing 1.1. DR-BIP external declarations.

```
1  model platoon
2  import from "platoon.cpp" {
3    map PlatoonMap {
4        const bool isLeader(Node)
5        const bool allowedSplit(Node)
6        const PlatoonMap[] splitAt(Node)
7        void   assign(PlatoonMap)
8        ...
9    }
10   addressing PlatoonAddressing { ... }
11   predicate AtSplitLocation(Car)
12 }
```

types of map and addressing functions are declared, along with their associated
reconfiguration rules.

As explained previously, each reconfiguration rule consists of (1) a label specifying its name, (2) a list of formal parameters referring to components or motifs
affected by the rule's actions (3) a "when"-clause consisting of a list of Boolean
conditions used to filter the relevant components and assign them to formal
parameters, and (4) one or more reconfiguration actions.

The concrete specification of reconfiguration rules in the DR-BIP language
uses the following predefined symbols for every motif: the set of managed components (C), the map (S), and the addressing function (@). These variables can
be used in the "when"-clause by calling the const methods of the map and
addressing functions[1]. Furthermore, all methods for S and @ can be used as
reconfiguration actions.

Listing 1.2. The Platoon motif and the SplitIR connecting rule.

```
1  motif Platoon<PlatoonMap, PlatoonAddressing> {
2    connecting rule SplitIR(Car leader, Car follower)
3      when ((C.size() > 3) && S.isLeader(@leader),
4        follower != leader && S.allowedSplit(@follower)) {
5          new SplitStep(follower, leader)
6  }}
```

Example 4. Listing 1.2 displays the motif Platoon along with the local connecting rule SplitIR. Line 1 declares the motif with the identifier Platoon, and associates with it the map PlatoonMap and addressing function PlatoonAddressing
(which are imported as explained in Listing 1.1). Platoon has a connecting reconfiguration rule SplitIR. It creates a connector (of type SplitStep) between each
follower and the leader to allow the follower to split. Thus, it is parametrized
by a *follower* and a *leader*. The "when"-clause provides two conditions, one for

[1] The set of components (C) is a C++ std::set, and relevant methods can be used.

each parameter. The first condition (line 3) specifies that there must be at least
3 components in the component set and queries the map to ensure that the node
associated with *leader* is the head of the platoon in the map. Since function
`isLeader` expects a node, the addressing function is used (`@leader`) to get the
associated node. In the second condition (line 4), we ensure that the *follower*
is any other car in the platoon where a split is allowed. To check if splitting is
allowed, we make use of the method `allowedSplit` associated with the map. For
every match, we create a new connector (`SplitStep`) with the two associated
components.   ∎

3   Layered Implementation

We adopt a two-layered approach for the execution of DR-BIP models. The first
layer is the *interaction layer*. It deals with an instantiated BIP model involving a
fixed number of components and their connectors. This model can be simulated
and executed using the BIP engine, and analyzed using existing tools of the
BIP toolset. The second layer is the *reconfiguration layer*. It deals with dynamic
changes of the set of components and the way they are connected. It includes
the reconfiguration rules that determine how the instantiated BIP model evolves.
We note that this implementation principle is general and can be applied to any
kind of dynamic reconfigurable system.

Our approach is driven by two main goals: *separation of concerns* and *simplicity*. Separation of concerns means that we reason separately about each layer.
We reuse predefined elements from the interaction layer such as types of components and connectors as well as existing engines for execution, analysis, and
verification (cf. [2]), while adequately extending all the concepts of BIP. Simplicity means that we ease the learning and use of the language by introducing
a minimal set of new concepts and constructs. For the reconfiguration layer, we
only provide constructs for building the rules modifying the instantiated BIP
model that is used by the interaction layer. In the reconfiguration layer, elements of the BIP model and all necessary topological structures are external to
the language and are imported.

3.1   Execution Principle

The execution of a DR-BIP model uses a protocol for the collaboration between
two engines (shown in Fig. 3): the reconfiguration engine handling the reconfiguration layer, and the BIP engine handling the interaction layer. The two engines
share an instantiated BIP model which consists of: the set of components, the set
of connectors between these components, and a set of interrupt conditions. An
interrupt condition is a predicate on a given state of the instantiated BIP model.
When an interrupt condition becomes true, the system needs to be reconfigured.
Normal execution is stopped in the BIP engine, and control is transferred to the
reconfiguration engine so that it applies reconfiguration. Two signals determine

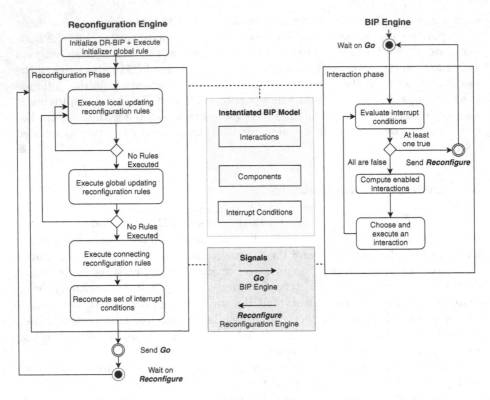

Fig. 3. Interplay between the reconfiguration engine and BIP engine.

which layer is to execute: *Go* and *Reconfigure*, respectively, initiate phases of execution of the BIP engine and the reconfiguration engine.

The BIP engine evaluates all interrupt conditions, and if *none* of them holds, it computes *enabled* interactions. If an interrupt condition holds, control is transferred to the reconfiguration engine until a *Go* signal is received. In BIP, interactions are specified by connectors. They represent synchronized state changes of several components. An interaction is *enabled* if all inter-connected components are able to synchronize. The BIP engine finds all enabled interactions and, if any, one is selected for execution. Following the execution, the states of all inter-connected components are updated. If no enabled interaction is found, the BIP engine has reached a deadlock state of the instantiated BIP model and the entire execution of the dynamic reconfigurable system is halted. Otherwise, it continues executing as long as no interrupt condition holds.

The reconfiguration engine executes the reconfiguration rules and modifies the instantiated BIP model. First updating reconfiguration rules are executed iteratively until stabilization. They consist in adding/removing components and updating the structure of the motifs. In our implementation, local updating reconfiguration rules execute first until stabilization, followed by global updating reconfiguration rules. When stabilization is reached, connecting rules are executed to re-create the connectors between components, and then the set of interrupt conditions is updated. Control is then passed to the BIP engine. It is important to note that to avoid interference, reconfiguration rules are executed *sequentially*.

3.2 Reconfiguration Engine Details

We present additional details about the reconfiguration engine and the way it computes matches and modifies the set of interrupt conditions.

Computing Matches. The computation of matches constitutes the core operation in the reconfiguration phase. It can be computationally expensive as generally, a condition for a given parameter can depend on other parameters. For efficiency reasons, in our implementation, we restrict conditions to reference only previous parameters in the list (i.e., a condition for parameter at index n can reference only parameters $[0..n]$). This ensures that matches can be computed incrementally without the need to backtrack, stopping immediately if no assignment is found.

Example 5. We revisit the connecting rule in Listing 1.2 applied on Example 1. The `Platoon` motif shown in Fig. 1 has the set of components C = $\{c_2, c_3, c_4, c_5, c_6\}$, where c_2 is the leader and c_6 is the tail of the platoon. This rule has two formal parameters of component type `Car` namely, `leader` and `follower`. Since it is a local reconfiguration rule, parameters are assigned components of type `Car` belonging to the motif (in our case C). The "when"-clause consists of 2 conditions, one for each formal parameter. The computation begins by evaluating the first condition to calculate the possible assignments for `leader`. The predicate $|C| > 3$ holds for all possible assignments. However, `S.isLeader(@leader)` is true only for c_2. The final set of assignments for `leader` is therefore $\{c_2\}$.

We now evaluate the possible assignments for `follower`. Note that it is possible to reference also `leader` as the set of possible assignments is computed. Indeed the condition `leader != follower` is evaluated for each component assigned to `leader` (i.e., for all elements in $\{c_2\}$). Furthermore, since no split can result in a platoon with less than 2 cars, `S.allowedSplit(@follower)` holds only for c_4 and c_5. The possible assignments for the second parameter are thus $\{c_4, c_5\}$. The rule executes for each of the following two matches: $\langle c_2, c_4 \rangle$ and $\langle c_2, c_5 \rangle$, creating two `SplitStep` connectors (shown on the right of Fig. 1 in brown). ∎

Executing Rules. After finding possible matches for a given rule, it is possible to execute it multiple times. In the case of updating reconfiguration rules (both local and global), the rule is executed with the first match, before stopping and re-evaluating all the reconfiguration rules. This is important, as a rule action can modify the state of (one or more) motif component set, map, or addressing function, requiring all respective clauses to be recomputed. However, in the case of connecting rules, the rule is executed for all possible matches, as connecting rules only add connectors to the model without modifying the motifs.

Modifying the Set of Interrupt Conditions. Interrupt conditions are predicates on the state of the instantiated BIP model that initiate reconfiguration. For each rule, we construct the conjunction of all conditions in the "when"-clause, and instantiate it to account for all possible assignments of parameters, adding each instantiation as an interrupt condition. The set of interrupt conditions models the disjunction over all such interrupt conditions, as when one holds at least one rule has a match and can execute. Since the sets of components and motifs change dynamically after reconfiguring, the set of possible assignments changes, and the set of interrupt conditions is updated to account for it. Recall that during the execution of the instantiated BIP model, motifs remain unchanged, when generating interrupt conditions, only BIP predicates are considered to change values. Therefore, optimizations by partial evaluation are applied to minimize the number of instantiated interrupt conditions.

4   Software/Code Architecture

The two-layered execution principle (Fig. 3) is mirrored in the software code, where BIP and the reconfiguration layer are written separately, and compiled separately to generate all necessary C++ files. Then, all C++ files are compiled together to form a single executable process. Figure 4 showcases the compilation scheme for DR-BIP models. Note the clear separation between BIP language, DR-BIP language, and external code.

BIP Compiler Modifications. We modified the BIP compiler to generate the BIP engine code that accounts for interrupt conditions. As shown in Fig. 4, the BIP compiler also generates a separate file containing all type information on connectors and components. The BIP engine itself has been modified to work on a dynamic number of components and connectors. Related connectors and interrupt conditions are grouped according to the rules that generate them. In this way, a group acts as a "namespace" for the corresponding rule allowing (1) dynamic change in connectors and interrupt conditions to be done in bulk for performance gains; and (2) isolation of connectors and interrupt conditions of one rule from those of other rules. In BIP, connectors are originally conceived to operate on a fixed number of components. To overcome this limitation, an extra annotation to the BIP model has been introduced to specify connector types with a variable number of components.

Reconfiguration Compiler. The reconfiguration compiler performs the parsing, analysis, and code-generation for the reconfiguration layer. It re-uses the BIP compiler to load information on interaction and component types for the considered BIP model. Furthermore, it parses the elements from the input reconfiguration file to generate the reconfiguration engine code. Type-checking is done at this phase using information from the BIP model and the external signatures of BIP predicates, maps, and addressing functions. To analyze, and eventually generate code, the reconfiguration compiler provides an infrastructure for executing a sequence of passes on the model. The reconfiguration compiler performs two passes: the first annotates rules and motifs with necessary information to minimize the number of interrupt conditions; the second pass generates C++ code. It outputs the necessary code to (1) create data-structures to manage components; (2) compute matches, execute, and generate interrupt conditions for rules; and (3) initialize and destroy motifs dynamically.

Execution Control Flow. The DR-BIP implementation compiles both engines in one executable. In the resulting executable, the BIP engine begins executing, and yields control to the reconfiguration engine using the two function calls `init` and `reconfigure`. Function `init` is called once to initialize the reconfiguration engine. Function `reconfigure` is called whenever reconfiguration is needed. Alongside the reconfiguration compiler, a template (C++ file) provides an implementation for functions `init` and `reconfigure`. The `init` implementation calls the "initializer" global reconfiguration rule, then performs a reconfiguration phase, while `reconfigure` performs the reconfiguration phase as described in Fig. 3. So, control flow goes from the BIP engine main loop to the template, which then invokes the relevant methods for the rules and motifs generated by the configuration layer compiler to perform reconfiguration. By providing the general execution infrastructure in a template separately from the rules specific to the dynamic model, it is possible to manage, inspect, and customize the DR-BIP state and execution independently of a given model. Template modification is key for instrumenting DR-BIP and outputting traces for analysis and monitoring, as we will discuss in Sect. 5.

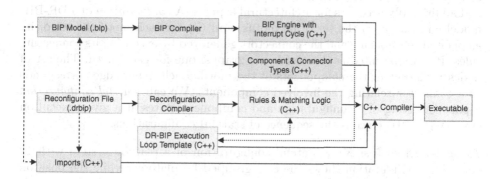

Fig. 4. Compilation scheme for the reconfiguration engine alongside BIP. Solid arrows indicate input/output relation, dashed arrows indicate logical dependencies and dotted arrows highlight the control-flow between the various elements.

5   Monitoring, Analysis and Profiling Support

In Sect. 4, we introduced the two elements allowing DR-BIP modular support for tracing, inspection, and run-time monitoring and analysis. On the one hand, the reconfiguration compiler provides a modular pass on the model that can be used to generate further code and "hooks" for tracing and generating run-time events. On the other hand, the DR-BIP template provides all the structures and control flow primitives needed to inspect, analyze and log relevant elements of the model: the instantiated BIP model shown in Fig. 3, including all BIP component instances internals, sets of all active motif instances and their reconfiguration rules, as well as global reconfiguration rules.

In addition to execution, our implementation provides the key ingredients that enable profiling, analyzing, and monitoring the execution of DR-BIP models. In this section, we describe our approach for inspecting dynamic reconfigurable architectures and generating a trace for analysis and profiling. We first present the concept of DR-BIP traces. Then, we evaluate quantitative properties on two scenarios of platoon system, we profile the execution time of these scenarios, and report on performance metrics.

5.1   DR-BIP Traces

The *state* of the instantiated BIP model is usually represented as a tuple giving for each component its current control location and a valuation of its variables [3,10]. Nonetheless such a concept of state is not adequate for dynamic reconfigurable systems as it ignores their structure represented by the motifs and the outcome of applying reconfiguration rules. For this reason we use the concept of *configuration* which encompasses the usual notion of component state and additionally accounts for architectural aspects. A *configuration* of a DR-BIP model consists of (i) the set of its motifs, and (ii) for each motif the set of its associated components and the connectors generated by executing its connecting rules. It is represented as a set of hyper-graphs, one for each motif. The set of nodes is the set of the components of the motif. Each hyper-edge corresponds to a connector relating the involved components. We call *stateful configuration* a pair consisting of a configuration and component states at a given execution step. A DR-BIP trace is the sequence of stateful configurations.

Example 6. Fig. 5 shows a stateful configuration of a platoon system with 12 cars. The configuration shows the cars grouped by platoons while the position of the cars is part of their state. Combining information from both makes it possible to calculate distances between platoons, and the space occupied by all the cars. Our example has 4 platoons (shown different colors) occupying a total of 10.41 units. We infer from the respective positions that two platoons are about to merge as they are separated by 0.41 units.   ∎

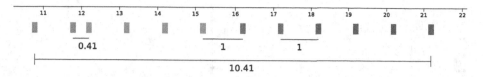

Fig. 5. Stateful configuration of a 12 car platoon system with 4 platoons (each platoon is assigned a unique color). (Color figure online)

5.2   Properties for Dynamic Reconfigurable Systems

By analyzing DR-BIP traces we are able to check properties not only about components and their states, but also about the evolution of configurations as a result of reconfiguration actions. Monitoring and checking such qualitative or quantitative properties requires the evaluation of predicates on stateful configurations.

Qualitative properties can be formalized in logics. Clearly, a propositional formula can be checked on a given stateful configuration. If a formula involves modalities, it should be evaluated on sequences of stateful configurations. While formalizing qualitative properties for dynamic reconfigurable systems is not in the scope of this paper, we present an example safety property ensuring that a car can belong only to one platoon, and all cars in the same platoon have the same speed as the leader. The property can be expressed as:

$$\Box \, \forall p, p' \in \text{Platoon} \; \forall c \in \text{Car} \; \exists c' \in p.C \; \exists X \subseteq p.C :$$
$$(p' \neq p \wedge c \in p.C) \implies (c \notin p'.C \wedge (\text{SpeedUpdate}(c', X)) \wedge c.\text{speed} - c'.\text{speed})).$$

This means that for any sequence of stateful configurations, the argument of $\Box$ holds. For a given stateful configuration, we can verify if a car belongs to a platoon ($c \in p.C$) by checking if it is a vertex in the hypergraph of the motif. Furthermore, the leader is determined by verifying the presence of the edge associated with the connector ($\text{SpeedUpdate}(c', X)$) in the corresponding hypergraph. Using the state of each car, we verify that the cars have the same speed as the leader ($c.\text{speed} = c'.\text{speed}$).

Quantitative properties can be evaluated in a similar manner. We specify the degree of satisfaction of a quantitative property by using score functions normalized in the interval $[0..1]$. We assume that the degree increases as the scores get close to zero.

Example 7. To analyze quantitative properties of the platoon system in Example 6, we define three score functions: (1) uniform separation (US), (2) target size (TS), and (3) road occupancy (RO). Uniform separation is used to assess how uniform the distance between platoons is. It is computed from the set of distances between platoons, normalized in an interval $[0..1]$ to obtain a set of distances d_i, for which we compute their mean $\overline{d}$, and the standard deviation as follows: $\text{US} = \sqrt{\frac{\Sigma((d_i - \overline{d})^2)}{|J|}}$. Thus, for uniform distances the score converges to 0.

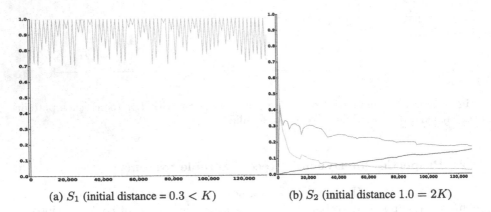

(a) S_1 (initial distance $= 0.3 < K$)   (b) S_2 (initial distance $1.0 = 2K$)

Fig. 6. The evolution of scores in two scenarios of platoon systems. The Y-axis shows the score (in the range $[0..1]$), while the X-axis shows the number of steps of the system (number of rules and interactions executed). The scores are: uniform separation (blue), target size (orange), and road occupation (purple). (Color figure online)

TS is used to estimate how close the size of platoons is to an ideal target size. It is computed similarly to the score US as the deviation from the ideal size. For this example, we fix the ideal size to be 2. Lastly, RO measures the total space occupied by all cars on the road. It is computed as follows: $RO = 1 - ((L - \Sigma d_i)/L)$ where L is the distance between the leading car of the first platoon and the tail car of the last platoon. By combining the three scores we aim to measure deviation with respect to configurations where the platoons have a specific size, while maintaining similar distances between them that are not too large, so as to not waste road space. The scores computed for the stateful configuration in Fig. 5 are as follows: $US = 0.34, TS = 0.14$ and $RO = 0.23$. Indeed, we observe that the distance between the left-most two platoons (0.41) significantly differs from the distance between the two others (1). Additionally, we see two platoons of size 4, and a total separation distance of 2.41 units between platoons (23% of the total distance occupied by the cars).

We consider two different large platoon systems: S_1 and S_2 differing only in the initial distance between cars. Both S_1 and S_2 start with a single platoon of 1,000 cars. In S_1 cars are initially separated by $K = 0.3$ which is less than the minimal distance needed to merge platoons, while in S_2 cars are initially separated by $2K$. By taking the initial distance between cars smaller than the merge distance, platoons have very little possibility to diverge, as they will be merged very soon after a split. On the contrary, with an initial distance much larger than K, platoons are not likely to be merged soon after a split. We illustrate the evolution of scores in Fig. 6. In the case of S_1, cars form at most 2 platoons during the simulation, and we are unable to reach platoon size 2, as splits are rapidly followed by merges. In addition, distances between platoons remain equal in S_1 as splits are rapidly followed by merges allowing no possibility for the cars to separate. For S_2, we see a convergence towards the target platoon size. However, we observe larger and diverging separation between platoons, as well as differentiation of the distances between platoons.   ∎

Table 1. Fixed-length simulation of 5,000 interactions of platoon system capturing maximum number of motifs (**M**) and execution times (**BIP, DR-BIP**) when varying initial distance, number of cars (**N**), and number of reconfiguration phases (**RP**).

N	S_1				S_2			
	RP	M	BIP (s)	DR-BIP (s)	RP	M	BIP (s)	DR-BIP (s)
100	48	4	0.16	0.05	178	77	0.18	0.52
	13	4	0.13	0.01	30	40	0.14	0.05
500	48	4	0.68	0.59	569	306	0.83	30.40
	14	4	0.72	0.18	47	65	0.75	0.77
1000	48	4	1.40	2.08	729	504	1.52	118.00
	14	4	1.44	0.62	51	73	1.44	1.94

5.3   Profiling DR-BIP Performance for Platoon System

We use performance metrics to profile the behavior of both DR-BIP and the system being executed. Measurements of reconfiguration frequency and time allow fine-tuning rules and models so as to enhance performance.

Recall from Example 7, we have two platoon systems that differ only in the initial distance between cars: S_1 and S_2. Both S_1 and S_2 start with a single platoon of N cars. Cars are initially separated by $0.3 < K$ for S_1 and $2K$ for S_2, where K is the minimal distance needed to merge platoons. We performed a fixed-length simulation up to 5,000 BIP interactions for S_1 (resp. S_2), and report the result in Table 1 averaging values over 10 simulations. To control the number of reconfiguration phases, we modify the model so that a car cannot split before moving for a certain amount of time.

Consider the case of 1000 cars and high reconfiguration rate (row 5). The average total execution time for S_1 (resp. S_2) is 3.48 s (resp. 119.52 s). A reconfiguration phase occurs after executing 104 (resp. 7) interactions. The percentages of the time spent reconfiguring are respectively 60% and 99%. For S_1, we can see that the maximum number of motifs present after each reconfiguration phase (**M**) is 4, indicating the presence of at most 2 platoons (with 1 road and 1 motif responsible to merge platoons). For S_2, we see the creation of multiple motifs, increasing to 729 motifs, which results in an increase of execution time for DR-BIP. Growing number of car and motif instances increases the time required for matching motif rules and global reconfiguration rules. When reconfiguration is less frequent, and with fewer motif instances, we observe reasonable execution times. For S_2, when a reconfiguration phase occurs every 98 interactions (row 6), the runtime is reduced from 119.52 s to 9.98 s.

6   Conclusion

We presented a two-layered approach for the specification, execution and monitoring of DR-BIP models integrating a reconfiguration and an interaction layer. DR-BIP extends BIP with the concepts and primitives needed for modeling dynamic reconfigurable systems. It supports modeling reconfiguration involving motifs along with their maps and addressing functions as well as reconfiguration rules for the dynamic change of local and global coordination patterns. We elaborated on the interplay between the reconfiguration engine which manages motifs and executes reconfiguration rules to modify an instantiated BIP model, and the BIP engine which executes the interactions of the latter. We also presented the necessary extensions to the BIP compiler and engine in order to reuse them in the context of dynamic and reconfigurable systems.

Another key contribution is the definition of traces for DR-BIP models allowing a natural high level interpretation of system behavior and run-time monitoring and analysis. Using information from stateful configurations, we can analyze properties characterizing the complex collective behavior of the system components. We demonstrated all these concepts for both qualitative and quantitative properties on a platoon system example inspired from autonomous traffic systems.

We focus on two complementary directions for future work. The first is to improve the current implementation. The second is to provide enhanced support for analysis and controlled experimentation through model simulation. We plan to increase the efficiency of the execution of the reconfiguration phase, by allowing the incremental evaluation of reconfiguration rules. For instance, static dependencies between rules can be exploited to avoid the costly global re-evaluation of all rule constraints and computation of matches at every step. Moreover, symbolic representations and/or searching techniques inspired from SAT/SMT solving can be used to isolate the impact of a rule on the system and therefore to restrict the focus of application of rules to that part.

Regarding the support for analysis at runtime, our simulation infrastructure provides all the needed introspection capabilities to extract both architecture (i.e, hypergraph of interconnected components and connectors) and state information (i.e, component state vectors). We plan to integrate the monitoring of behavior and/or configuration properties by introducing temporal modalities [20] into configuration logics [15]. Beyond monitoring, statistical model checking can be used to evaluate properties over multiple traces of the system and to compute levels of confidence for their satisfaction. However, the application of statistical model checking would require the definition of a stochastic semantics for the DR-BIP model. As a first alternative, this can be achieved by keeping non-stochastic the execution of the reconfiguration engine, while leaving stochastic aspects at the BIP level to be handled only by the (statistical) BIP engine [17]. A more challenging alternative would consist in proposing and implementing a stochastic semantics for the reconfiguration engine to be combined with the BIP engine.

Finally, in addition to monitoring and analysis, we plan to develop support for controlled experimentation allowing to bring reconfigurable dynamic systems into specific configurations and check their behavior. This is particularly important for the definition of coverage criteria and validation through the exploration of corner cases and critical situations. It will additionally require the refinement of the BIP model into a model distinguishing between observable and controllable features and their integration.

References

1. Aldrich, J., Chambers, C., Notkin, D.: ArchJava: connecting software architecture to implementation. In: Tracz, W., Young, M., Magee, J. (eds.) Proceedings of the 24th International Conference on Software Engineering, ICSE 2002, Orlando, Florida, USA, 19–25 May 2002, pp. 187–197. ACM (2002)
2. Basu, A., et al.: Rigorous component-based system design using the BIP framework. IEEE Softw. **28**(3), 41–48 (2011)
3. Basu, A., Bozga, M., Sifakis, J.: Modeling heterogeneous real-time components in BIP. In: Fourth IEEE International Conference on Software Engineering and Formal Methods (SEFM 2006), pp. 3–12. IEEE Computer Society (2006)
4. Bergenhem, C.: Approaches for facilities layer protocols for platooning. In: 2015 IEEE 18th International Conference on Intelligent Transportation Systems (ITSC), pp. 1989–1994. IEEE (2015)
5. Bliudze, S., Sifakis, J.: A notion of glue expressiveness for component-based systems. In: van Breugel, F., Chechik, M. (eds.) CONCUR 2008. LNCS, vol. 5201, pp. 508–522. Springer, Heidelberg (2008). https://doi.org/10.1007/978-3-540-85361-9_39
6. Cavalcante, E., Oquendo, F., Batista, T.: Architecture-based code generation: from π-ADL architecture descriptions to implementations in the go language. In: Avgeriou, P., Zdun, U. (eds.) ECSA 2014. LNCS, vol. 8627, pp. 130–145. Springer, Cham (2014). https://doi.org/10.1007/978-3-319-09970-5_13
7. Eker, J., et al.: Taming heterogeneity - the Ptolemy approach. Proc. IEEE **91**(1), 127–144 (2003)
8. El Ballouli, R., Bensalem, S., Bozga, M., Sifakis, J.: Four exercises in programming dynamic reconfigurable systems: methodology and solution in DR-BIP. In: Margaria, T., Steffen, B. (eds.) ISoLA 2018. LNCS, vol. 11246, pp. 304–320. Springer, Cham (2018). https://doi.org/10.1007/978-3-030-03424-5_20
9. El Ballouli, R., Bensalem, S., Bozga, M., Sifakis, J.: Programming dynamic reconfigurable system. In: Bae, K., Ölveczky, P.C. (eds.) FACS 2018. LNCS, vol. 11222, pp. 118–136. Springer, Cham (2018). https://doi.org/10.1007/978-3-030-02146-7_6
10. Falcone, Y., Jaber, M., Nguyen, T.-H., Bozga, M., Bensalem, S.: Runtime verification of component-based systems in the BIP framework with formally-proved sound and complete instrumentation. Softw. Syst. Model. **14**(1), 173–199 (2013). https://doi.org/10.1007/s10270-013-0323-y
11. Feiler, P.H., Gluch, D.P.: Model-Based Engineering with AADL - An Introduction to the SAE Architecture Analysis and Design Language. SEI Series in Software Engineering. Addison-Wesley, Boston (2012)
12. Lanusse, A., et al.: Papyrus UML: an open source toolset for MDA. In: Proceedings of the Fifth European Conference on Model-Driven Architecture Foundations and Applications (ECMDA-FA 2009), pp. 1–4 (2009)
13. Majumdar, R., Mathur, A.S., Pirron, M., Stegner, L., Zufferey, D.: Paracosm: a language and tool for testing autonomous driving systems. CoRR abs/1902.01084 (2019)

14. Mallet, A., Pasteur, C., Herrb, M., Lemaignan, S., Ingrand, F.F.: GenoM3: building middleware-independent robotic components. In: IEEE International Conference on Robotics and Automation, ICRA 2010, Anchorage, Alaska, USA, 3–7 May 2010, pp. 4627–4632. IEEE (2010)
15. Mavridou, A., Baranov, E., Bliudze, S., Sifakis, J.: Configuration logics: modeling architecture styles. J. Log. Algebraic Methods Program. **86**(1), 2–29 (2017)
16. Medvidovic, N., Rosenblum, D.S., Taylor, R.N.: A language and environment for architecture-based software development and evolution. In: Boehm, B.W., Garlan, D., Kramer, J. (eds.) Proceedings of the 1999 International Conference on Software Engineering, ICSE 1999, Los Angeles, CA, USA, 16–22 May 1999, pp. 44–53. ACM (1999)
17. Nouri, A., Mediouni, B.L., Bozga, M., Combaz, J., Bensalem, S., Legay, A.: Performance evaluation of stochastic real-time systems with the SBIP framework. IJCCBS **8**(3/4), 340–370 (2018)
18. Perrotin, M., Conquet, E., Delange, J., Schiele, A., Tsiodras, T.: TASTE: a real-time software engineering tool-chain overview, status, and future. In: Ober, I., Ober, I. (eds.) SDL 2011. LNCS, vol. 7083, pp. 26–37. Springer, Heidelberg (2011). https://doi.org/10.1007/978-3-642-25264-8_4
19. Pinciroli, C., Beltrame, G.: Buzz: an extensible programming language for heterogeneous swarm robotics. In: 2016 IEEE/RSJ International Conference on Intelligent Robots and Systems, IROS 2016, Daejeon, South Korea, 9–14 October 2016, pp. 3794–3800. IEEE (2016)
20. Pnueli, A.: The temporal logic of programs. In: 18th Annual Symposium on Foundations of Computer Science, pp. 46–57. IEEE Computer Society (1977)
21. Quigley, M., et al.: ROS: an open-source robot operating system. In: ICRA Workshop on Open Source Software, Kobe, Japan, vol. 3, p. 5 (2009)
22. Verimag: DR-BIP Artifact, February 2020. https://gricad-gitlab.univ-grenoble-alpes.fr/verimag/bip/artifacts/drbip-feb2020

Formal Verification of Human-Robot Interaction in Healthcare Scenarios

Livia Lestingi[1]([✉]), Mehrnoosh Askarpour[2]([✉]), Marcello M. Bersani[1]([✉]),
and Matteo Rossi[1]([✉])

[1] Politecnico di Milano, Milan, Italy
{livia.lestingi,marcellomaria.bersani,matteo.rossi}@polimi.it
[2] McMaster University, Hamilton, Canada
askarpom@mcmaster.ca

Abstract. We present a model-driven approach for the creation of formally verified scenarios involving human-robot interaction in healthcare settings. The work offers an innovative take on the application of formal methods to human modeling, as it incorporates physiology-related aspects. The model, based on the formalism of Hybrid Automata, includes a stochastic component to capture the variability of human behavior, which makes it suitable for Statistical Model Checking. The toolchain is meant to be accessible to a wide range of professional figures. Therefore, we have laid out a user-friendly representation format for the scenario, from which the full formal model is automatically generated and verified through the Uppaal tool. The outcome is an estimation of the probability of success of the mission, based on which the user can refine the model if the result is not satisfactory.

Keywords: Human-robot interaction · Service robots · Healthcare robotics · Model-driven approach · Statistical Model Checking

1 Introduction

Robots are becoming increasingly widespread in non-industrial contexts. Future applications range from autonomous means of transportation [28] to personal assistants [14]. If on one hand factory workers are specifically trained to interact with this type of machinery and grow familiar with safety practices over time, on the other hand a much wider range of users awaits robots in the near future [22] and this poses a new set of challenges. In the area of safety, strong guarantees of people's health preservation will be required, beginning from compliance with the standards. ISO 12100 [18] and ISO 13849-1 [20] provide general guidelines, whereas ISO 13482 [19] is specifically targeted to service robots. It is common knowledge for researchers in the field that testing techniques are not sufficient given the complexity of these systems [25], and there already exist works in literature that resort to formal verification for safety-critical scenarios [16,30].

© Springer Nature Switzerland AG 2020
F. de Boer and A. Cerone (Eds.): SEFM 2020, LNCS 12310, pp. 303–324, 2020.
https://doi.org/10.1007/978-3-030-58768-0_17

In this paper, we focus on human-related aspects in scenarios involving inter-actions between humans and robots. Service robots will support people in every-day life situations, and it is, therefore, crucial that human factors are accounted for in the robot decision-making process. To this end, we have developed a model-driven approach for the creation and formal verification of scenarios related to human-centric robotic applications. Target scenarios feature mobile robots and their controllers interacting with humans in a defined environment. Separate scenarios tackle different interaction strategies, depending on what specific service the human is requesting. To ease the modeling process, we have identified a set of usual coordination patterns involving a human and a robot, which the user of the approach can customize and re-use with minimum effort. The *mission* of the robot, as more thoroughly discussed in Sect. 4, will be to provide all the services requested in a specific scenario, and the purpose of the approach is to allow the designer of the application to verify the feasibility of the mission.

The approach considers some physiological features of humans that make it particularly suited for the healthcare domain, but it is still general enough to befit a broader range of applications. The policies of the robot controller that drive the mission to success are designed to prioritise human needs over efficiency. This can make a difference when robots interact with people in dis-comfort or in pain, or when human lives are at stake and the controller has to make a decision—something that can happen in healthcare settings. Another key issue for practitioners is that modeling the volatility of human behavior is often considered beyond the capabilities of formal methods [25]. As a first step towards solving this issue, in our approach humans are not treated as rational agents that unmistakably execute their mission. Instead, their model features a stochastic component to simulate free will, that causes them to occasionally make autonomous decisions.

In our approach, scenarios are formally modeled through Hybrid Automata [4], with the addition of stochastic components. The model is formally verified through Statistical Model Checking (SMC) [3] against a set of relevant proper-ties. The toolchain is meant to be used by professional figures with a technical background, though not necessarily in robotics nor in formal models. Therefore, the entry point is a user-friendly representation of the key parameters of the sce-nario that the application designer can smoothly produce and refine. The tool processes this input, automatically generates the complete formal models, and performs verification through the Uppaal tool [11,24].

We have selected a use case from the healthcare domain to evaluate the effectiveness of the approach. Some significant experimental results drawn from the use case are presented in the paper. The experiments are run using a publicly available prototype of the tool [1].

The paper is structured as follows: Sect. 2 surveys related works; Sect. 3 out-lines the background; Sect. 4 presents the approach; Sect. 5 describes the formal model; Sect. 6 presents the use case and the experimental results; finally, Sect. 7 concludes. Appendix A presents additional details about the formal model, and Appendix B describes additional experiments.

2   Related Work

Formal modeling and verification of systems that involve interactions between humans and robots is a long-standing issue. The work by Webster et al. [31] analyses the dynamics of a person assisted by a personal care robot in a smart home. All the elements of the scenario are modeled as *agents* using Brahms, and then verified through the SPIN model-checker: in particular, the human non-deterministically selects the action to perform from a pre-determined set, and the robot must act accordingly. Vicentini et al. [30] focus on the risk assessment procedure of industrial collaborative tasks. The authors propose a framework based on LTL formulae to verify that the overall level of risk of the system does not exceed a certain threshold. The work has been extended to also include manifestations of erroneous human behavior, handled in a black-box manner [7]. Bersani et al. [9] address applications involving robots and humans working in a shared environment, modeled as networks of Timed Game Automata. Humans are modeled as *uncontrollable* agents, to capture the uncertainty of the real world. A robot controller that also accounts for unpredictable human moves is then automatically synthesized through the Uppaal-TIGA tool.

Porfirio et al. [27] explore how formal verification can be used to ensure that robots adhere to *social* norms while interacting with humans. Norms, expressed as LTL formulae, constitute the properties to be verified, whereas the sequence of interactions is modeled as a composition of state machines. Concerning the social robotics field, Adam et al. [2] propose a framework based on the BDI architecture to make human-robot interaction feel more natural. The authors build upon models of human cognition to develop a perception and deliberation process that drives the robot towards making decisions in a human-like fashion.

Some works exploit SMC to verify robotic systems. Arai and Schlingloff [6] use SMC to make predictions on the performance of autonomous transport robots in production plants. Foughali et al. [13] apply SMC to formally verify real-time properties, like schedulability and readiness, of robotic software. Herd et al. [17] focus on multi-agent systems, and on swarm robotics in particular: in this case, SMC helps deal with the size of the problem, which cannot be handled by traditional model checking techniques.

Finally, Zhao et al. [12] perform probabilistic model-checking of UAV missions, focusing on advanced aspects of battery prognostics and health management.

As this brief survey shows, although the issue of verifying human-robot interaction has been tackled with different techniques, the combination of sound formal methods with the modeling of human behavior unpredictability is still an open question. To the best of the authors' knowledge, the work in this paper is the first attempt at formally verifying an explicit model of human-related aspects, such as free will. In addition, as mentioned in Sect. 1, service robots will come into contact with people with different backgrounds, who may not be able to create complex models while designing their application. Therefore, the accessibility of a tool is a key factor in assessing its effectiveness. The work presented in this paper addresses these issues and is a first step towards filling the gaps.

3   Background

The formal models presented in this work are expressed through Hybrid Automata (HA) enriched with a stochastic component, indicated as HA+ in the rest of the paper. HA are an extension of Timed Automata. In Timed Automata, time is modeled through variables (*clocks*), whose value increases linearly with time unless they are reset [5]. Conditions on clocks govern the transitions between states. In HA, locations are also endowed with sets of differential equations (*flow conditions*) that constrain the derivatives of real-valued variables of the model, thus allowing for the modeling of systems with complex dynamics [4].

Automata can be organized in *networks*, where synchronization between different automata occurs through *channels*. Given a channel e and two automata with complementary enabled transitions labelled as $e?$ and $e!$—whose guards are both satisfied—the two transitions fire at the same time and the two automata synchronously change their locations. Non-deterministic choices in the model can be refined by probabilistic distributions. These constitute the stochastic component of the formalism and are modeled via probabilistic transitions, as exemplified in Fig. 1. This type of transition is marked with a probability weight, that determines how much the system will be biased to evolve in a certain direction rather than its alternatives.

The stochastic component of the formalism enables the application of statistical techniques, and SMC in particular. As opposed to traditional model checking, SMC relies on Hypothesis Testing or Estimation to evaluate the probability that a property holds on paths starting from a generic state s of the system [3]. Therefore, it does not fully explore the state space, and is feasible also for complex systems. The properties to be checked are expressed in the PCTL logic, whose syntax, shown in Table 1, allows us to express quantitative constraints on probabilities through the $P_{\geq\theta}(\phi)$ operator. Given a HA+ automaton and a PCTL property ψ, the possible outcomes of SMC are: (a) a binary value, 1 or 0, depending on whether $P(\psi) \geq \theta$ holds or not, where $P(\psi)$ is the probability of ψ holding, and θ is a threshold; or (b) a probability interval to which $P(\psi)$ is guaranteed to belong. Section 6 presents some examples of SMC experiments.

The features of HA+ are used for the robot and human models presented in detail in Sect. 5. In particular, given the emphasis of the work on human physiology, the model of the human includes differential equations describing the time-dynamics of fatigue. Although human fatigue can take different forms [21], at the moment we focus on the physical strain originated from non-stop

Table 1. PCTL Syntax

Fig. 1. Automaton with probabilistic transitions: 0.4 and 0.6 are the probabilities of reaching s_2 and s_3 starting from s_1.

$\phi ::= a \mid \neg\phi \mid \phi \vee \phi' \mid \phi \wedge \phi'$
$\psi ::= \phi \mid \mathbf{X}\phi \mid \phi\mathbf{U}\phi' \mid P_{\geq\theta}(\psi)$
$a \in AP$ atomic proposition
$\theta \in [0,1]$ probability bound

walking. According to Konz [23], the alternate fatigue/recovery cycles can be modeled as exponential curves, as in Eq. 1. Low values of coefficients λ and μ mean slower fatigue accumulation and recovery, while F_0 corresponds to the value of fatigue at the start of the current cycle (it is 0 when the human starts walking for the first time). Full exhaustion corresponds to $F(t) = 1$, full recovery to $F(t) = 0$.

$$F(t) = \begin{cases} 1 - (1 - F_0)e^{-\lambda t} & \text{(walking)} \\ F_0 e^{-\mu t} & \text{(resting)} \end{cases} \tag{1}$$

Concerning the model of robot velocity, we use the typical trapezoidal velocity profile [10] with three phases: acceleration, constant maximum speed, and deceleration. Maximum acceleration a_{max} and maximum velocity v_{max} are design parameters of the robot. For the robot battery, we assume an exponential charge/discharge cycle typical of electronic devices with lithium batteries [29]. Equation 2 shows the battery charge time-dynamics: ρ and σ represent the charge/discharge rates, whereas C_0 is the starting charge value for the current cycle. The times required for a full charge and a full discharge cycle (T_{chg} and T_{dchg}) are known a-priori given the battery model, therefore rates ρ and σ are approximated with precision ϵ as in the following: $\rho = \frac{1}{T_{dchg}} ln(\frac{100}{100-\epsilon})$, $\sigma = \frac{1}{T_{chg}} ln(\frac{100}{100-\epsilon})$.

$$C(t) = \begin{cases} 100 - (100 - C_0)e^{\rho t} & \text{(discharging)} \\ 100 - (100 - C_0)e^{-\sigma t} & \text{(charging)} \end{cases} \tag{2}$$

4   Approach

The main contribution of this paper is a model-driven approach for the analysis of human-robot interaction through formal verification. The approach is tailored to non-industrial settings, and in particular to the healthcare environment. Indeed, we focus on scenarios in which the volatility of human behavior is at its peak, which may not be the case for industrial workers who are methodically trained to perform a set of actions during their shift. Furthermore, modeling physiology-related aspects is crucial for healthcare applications, since people in need of a medical service may find themselves in diverse, even critical, physical conditions. The toolchain is meant to be used by professionals possibly with some technical background, but not necessarily in robotics or in formal methods. Hospitals are subject to a tremendous flow of people on a day-to-day basis, and this requires dedicated professional figures to be efficiently handled. For example, clinical workflow analysts [26], who design and analyze work shifts for medical facilities, perfectly fit this profile.

The application designer is in charge of assigning each of the currently requested services to one of the available robots. Therefore, a group of humans served by a robot will constitute the atomic operational unit (referred to as the *scenario* hereinafter). Serving everybody in the group will constitute the *mission*, i.e., the high-level goal [8], for the robot. The boundaries of the mission

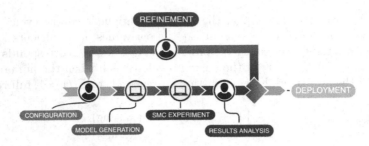

Fig. 2. Diagram representing all the phases of the approach. Different shades of gray indicate the current progress of implementation: the darker phases are fully implemented, the lighter ones are to be expanded in the future.

also include any other parameters that, were they to be modified, the overall outcome would change accordingly, e.g., the enclosed environment where the agents operate or the robot starting conditions. Through the tool, the designer can try different configurations until the estimated probability of success is reasonable. Figure 2 depicts the steps of the design process: (i) configuration of the scenario, performed by the designer; (ii) automated model generation; (iii) execution of the SMC experiment; (iv) critical assessment of the verification results, followed by application deployment if the results are satisfactory, otherwise by model refinement. In this paper, we focus on the scenario configuration and on the formal model, whereas the deployment phase will be elaborated in future works.

4.1   Configuration

The user of the toolchain has the option to customize all the parameters of the scenario depicted in Fig. 3 and described in the following.

A scenario includes N_h humans to be served and a robot from the fleet that will serve them. Robots are characterized by maximum speed and acceleration (v_{max} and a_{max} in Fig. 3) and are each associated with a battery. An association between a robot and a battery constitutes a robotic system with its own id.

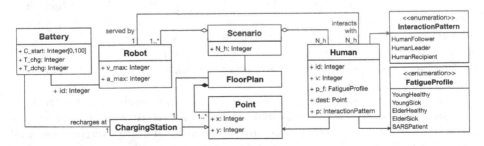

Fig. 3. Class diagram of the user-customizable portion of the model.

Table 2. Human-robot interaction patterns

Pattern	Description
Human follower	The human follows the robot while the robot moves towards the destination. Because of *free will*, the human can decide to walk freely and whether to follow or not when the robot issues its command. If they get too far, the robot stops and waits for them
Human leader	The robot follows the human that moves towards the destination (unknown to the robot). The human is free to start and stop whenever they want and the robot follows accordingly
Human recipient	The human waits for the robot to fetch an item from a specific location. While the robot is delivering the object, the human is free to move and the robot has to track them. Synchronization occurs when the human and the robot are close and the human stops to pick up the item

Batteries possess an initial charge value $C_{start} \in [0, 100]$, and the two parameters T_{chg} and T_{dchg} that determine the duration of full charge/discharge cycles. For each scenario, it is also essential to model the environment in which services will be carried out. Specifically, the operational environment is modeled as a two-dimensional layout. The designer may specify the Cartesian coordinates of specific points of interest—e.g., wall corners and doorposts. The model capturing robot navigation takes these elements into account to drive the agent towards their correct destination and to prevent collisions with walls or humans.

Together with robots, humans are a basic component of the scenario that needs to be configured by the designer. Each human is identified by a unique id that determines the order in which they will be served. Furthermore, the user can specify the human's walking speed v and the destination point dest. A fundamental aspect of humans in the scenario is the way in which they are going to interact with the robot. We have identified a set of patterns for recurrent human-robot synchronization mechanisms, focusing on a particular subset suitable for the mobile robots with a predefined set of functionalities covered by our work. Currently implemented patterns are described in Table 2. Different patterns impact how the system will evolve while a certain service is being carried out and the condition that the system needs to verify to state that the service has been provided. As shown in Fig. 3, the designer can specify the parameter p for each human to set up how the interaction with the robot will play out.

Finally, it is also possible for the designer to customize the physiological traits of the humans in the scenario through the p_f parameter (see Fig. 3). This draws from a set of profiles that aggregate potential subjects by *age* and *medical condition*. Since the physiological property currently included in the model is fatigue, particular care is given to conditions that specifically target the respiratory functions of patients, thus their ability to walk. Providing the designer with this predetermined set of profiles allows them to match the specific individuals from their scenario with medically recognized significant cases. This also allows them to save time while designing the application, although the manual specification of a different set of parameters is still possible if necessary. Referring to the model of fatigue introduced in Sect. 3, different profiles mean different values for parameters λ and μ. Therefore, they determine the time needed by a specific subject to reach full exhaustion and full recovery. With this feature, the professional assessing the results has the guarantee that the physical condition of the patient has been taken into account while estimating the outcome of the mission.

4.2   Model Generation and SMC Experiment

The HA+ models are handled as templates customizable by the user. This subset is, indeed, the result of the configuration phase. By doing so, the designer is only required to arrange the main elements of the application in a user-friendly format, which is more suited to their technical background than creating formal stochastic models from scratch. This input is fed to a script that automatically generates the formal model with the values laid down by the designer. Once the generation of the model is completed, the tool initiates the verification process. The user also has the option to choose whether the tool should produce a simulation of the system or estimate the probabilities of the mission ending in failure or success—i.e., a typical SMC experiment.

4.3   Result Analysis and Refinement

If the user decides to run an SMC experiment, this yields a probability value. If the probability of success is smaller than a desirable threshold, the user may refine the model in one of the following ways: (a) reduce the workload of a robot, for example, if its current battery charge value is not sufficient to carry out all the requested services; (b) change the order in which humans are to be served, which could improve the overall efficiency, e.g., by reducing robot movements between a service and the next one; (c) choose different services to be included in the scenario; (d) choose a different robot from the fleet, with different speed/acceleration parameters or with a different battery charge value. A different robot model may be useful in case the previous one moved too fast for the human, whereas issues related to the battery may involve complete discharge before the mission is done.

5   Model

In this section, for each type of component of a scenario (robots, batteries, humans) we present the corresponding HA+. The model also features an *orchestrator*, which plays the pivotal role of managing the synchronization among all other components through *channels* (see Sect. 3). The decisions of the orchestrator are based on the state of the system. In particular, specific features of the model capture the behavior of sensors measuring physical properties of the system, which drive the decisions of the orchestrator. Each property is modeled via a *dense counter* variable that changes over time as a result of *update* instructions on transitions, but does not possess an explicit time-dependency. We also assume that these sensors periodically repeat the measurement: constant T_{poll} captures the refresh period and clock t_{upd} measures the time elapsed since the last update. As mentioned in Sect. 3, the robot movement follows a trapezoidal velocity profile, whereas the human moves with constant speed. As for human free will, we have chosen the straightforward approach [15] of modeling it as a random phenomenon whose behavior is comparable to a Bernoulli variable X. Finally, to dampen the complexity of the model, we assume that humans are only free to choose *when* to start or stop, and not an arbitrary trajectory. Interested readers can find additional details about the models in Appendix A.

Robot: The HA+ in Fig. 4 represents the three operating conditions of the robot, corresponding to idleness, motion and battery recharging. We introduce two time-dependent variables V and r_{dist} that model, respectively, the velocity of the robot at a generic time instant t and the distance covered since the beginning of the motion. The automaton features locations r_{idle}, r_{start}, r_{mov}, r_{stop}, and r_{rec} corresponding, respectively, to: (1) the idleness of the robot with $V = 0$; (2) the acceleration phase of the motion, thus $\dot{V} = a_{max}$; (3) the travel phase with constant speed, $V = v_{max}$; (4) the deceleration phase with $\dot{V} = -a_{max}$; (5) the battery recharging phase, thus $V = 0$. In every location, $\dot{r}_{dist} = V$ holds. When the orchestrator fires the commands to start or stop recharging (b_{start} and b_{stop}), if the robot is at the recharging station, the automaton transitions from r_{idle} to r_{rec} and back. The switch from r_{idle} to r_{start} takes place when the command to start moving (r_{start}) is issued. Similarly, the automaton switches from r_{mov} to r_{stop} when r_{stop} is fired. It is also possible to start and stop the robot while it is accelerating or decelerating, so two transitions are added between r_{start} and r_{stop}. In location r_{start}, velocity is increasing linearly from 0 to v_{max}, thus when $V = v_{max}$ the automaton switches to r_{mov}. While decelerating, the robot stays in r_{stop} as long as $V > 0$ and goes back to r_{idle} when $V = 0$. We model as dense counters the Cartesian coordinates of the robot in space (r_{pos_x} and r_{pos_y}), and the angle θ_r for the orientation with respect to the x-axis. On every self-loop, and on all transitions in Fig. 4 marked with a ξ_R, the corresponding update instruction of Table 3 is executed.

Robot Battery: Figure 5 shows the HA+ representing the behavior of the battery. The time-dependent variable in the model is the charge value C. The

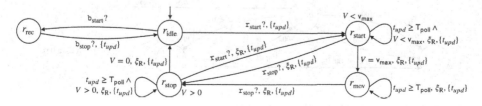

Fig. 4. Robot automaton.

robot battery can be in one of three states, modeled by as many locations: discharging (b_{dchg}), charging (b_{chg}), and fully discharged (b_{empty}) in which case the robot cannot move autonomously. The constraints on the derivative of charge C stemming from the model introduced in Sect. 3 are shown in Eq. 3.

$$\dot{C} = \begin{cases} -(100 - C_0)\rho e^{\rho t} & (b_{\mathrm{dchg}}) \\ (100 - C_0)\sigma e^{-\sigma t} & (b_{\mathrm{chg}}) \end{cases} \tag{3}$$

The switch from b_{dchg} to b_{chg} and vice versa occurs when the orchestrator decides that a robot needs to start/stop recharging, firing events b_{start} and b_{stop}, respectively. An additional location b_{full} is needed to model the case in which the battery is back to full charge (condition $C = 100$) and immediately stops recharging. This happens thanks to the *urgent* channel b_{full} [24] that fires as soon as the automaton enters location b_{full}. The sampled charge value is modeled by dense-counter b_{ch}, whose update instructions ξ_{BC} and ξ_{BD} are shown in Table 3 and correspond, respectively, to the charge and discharge operating conditions.

Human-Follower: The model is depicted in Fig. 6. The time-dependent variables are h_{dist}, which represents the distance covered by the human, and F, which corresponds to the value of the fatigue at a generic time instant. Their temporal dynamics are given in Eq. 4: h_{dist} is either constant, or it increases linearly with time (with coefficient v, which is the human's constant speed) when the human is moving, whereas F adheres to the model in Eq. 1.

$$h_{\mathrm{idle}} = \begin{cases} \dot{F} = -F_0\mu e^{-\mu t} \\ \dot{h}_{dist} = 0 \end{cases} \qquad h_{\mathrm{busy}} = \begin{cases} \dot{F} = F_0\lambda e^{-\lambda t} \\ \dot{h}_{dist} = v \end{cases} \tag{4}$$

The operating conditions modeled for this component are the idleness of the human (location h_{idle}) or walking (h_{busy}). The switch from h_{idle} to h_{busy}, and back, occurs when the orchestrator orders it or as a result of the human's free will. In the first case, the orchestrator fires h_{start} or h_{stop}. This leads to a probabilistic transition (the dashed arrows in Fig. 6) whose possible outcomes represent the human *obeying* the order, thus reaching the prescribed destination, or *disobeying* it, thus staying in the same location. The transition is governed by the two constant weights obey and disobey. In the second case, two additional transitions between h_{idle} and h_{busy} capture autonomous decisions as a result of free will:

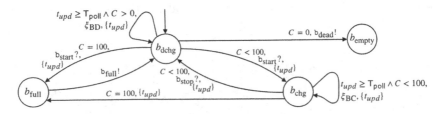

Fig. 5. Battery automaton.

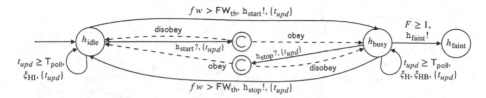

Fig. 6. Human-follower automaton.

Table 3. Update instructions

ξ_R :	$r'_{pos_x} := r_{pos_x} + V(t)\mathsf{T}_{\mathsf{poll}}\cos(\theta_r)$	ξ_H :	$h'_{pos_x} := h_{pos_x} - \mathsf{v}\mathsf{T}_{\mathsf{poll}}\cos(\theta_h)$
	$r'_{pos_y} := r_{pos_y} + V(t)\mathsf{T}_{\mathsf{poll}}\sin(\theta_r)$		$h'_{pos_y} := h_{pos_y} - \mathsf{v}\mathsf{T}_{\mathsf{poll}}\sin(\theta_h)$
ξ_{BC}:	$b'_{ch} := 100 - (100 - b_{ch})e^{-\sigma\mathsf{T}_{\mathsf{poll}}}$	ξ_{BD}:	$b'_{ch} := 100 - (100 - b_{ch})e^{\rho\mathsf{T}_{\mathsf{poll}}}$
ξ_{HI}:	$h'_{ftg} := h_{ftg}e^{\mu\mathsf{T}_{\mathsf{poll}}}$	ξ_{HB}:	$h'_{ftg} := 1 - (1 - h_{ftg})e^{-\lambda\mathsf{T}_{\mathsf{poll}}}$

thus, the human fires $\mathbf{h}_{\mathsf{start}}$ and $\mathbf{h}_{\mathsf{stop}}$. Sample points of the random variable X are observations of local variable fw. A *success* is the decision of the human to start or stop freely and it occurs when $fw > \mathsf{FW}_{\mathsf{th}}$, which is the guard condition of the transitions between h_{idle} and h_{busy}. $\mathsf{FW}_{\mathsf{th}}$ is a constant threshold, and variable fw is updated every $\mathsf{T}_{\mathsf{poll}}$ instants with a random value in range $[0, \mathsf{FW}_{\mathsf{max}}]$. Therefore, the probability of making an autonomous decision is $E[X] = p = 1 - \frac{\mathsf{FW}_{\mathsf{th}}}{\mathsf{FW}_{\mathsf{max}}}$. If the p-value is close to 1, humans will behave more erratically, and vice versa if it is close to 0. Location h_{faint} models the case in which the human is too exhausted to proceed: it is reached when $F \geq 1$, where 1 corresponds to the maximum value of fatigue, and it causes *urgent* channel $\mathbf{h}_{\mathsf{faint}}$ to fire immediately. The dense counters are h_{ftg} (for the fatigue), and h_{pos_x}, h_{pos_y}, θ_h for the Cartesian coordinates and orientation of the human with respect to the x-axis. Table 3 shows the update instructions (ξ_{HI}, ξ_{HB}) for the fatigue, which adhere to the model in Eq. 4, and also those (ξ_H) of the position, where h_{pos_x}, h_{pos_y} represent the projections of the displacement since the last update.

Orchestrator: The automaton is displayed in Fig. 7a. The purpose of this component is to orchestrate the synchronization among the other agents and drive the system towards mission accomplishment. This is realized by monitoring the sensor outputs described in previous sections, and deciding whether the current state of the system requires a certain event to be fired. We have identified three operational paradigms implemented by as many sub-machines: r_rech controls the recharging phase of the robot; r_move controls the start and the end of the movement when, based on the interaction pattern between the human and the robot carrying out the service, it is initiated by the robot; h_move controls the dual case, in which the movement is initiated by the human. The orchestrator features both r_move and h_move since both designs can be included in the same scenario. Sub-machines in Fig. 7a are endowed with *ports*; these are not part of

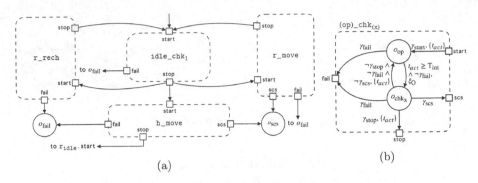

Fig. 7. Orchestrator automaton and $\langle op\rangle\_chk_{\langle x\rangle}$ pattern.

the formalism, but a visual representation of the transitions entering and leaving the component (arrows in and out of a port constitute the *same* transition).

Figure 8 shows the details of the sub-machines. They are all built using the $\langle op\rangle\_chk_{\langle x\rangle}$ pattern of Fig. 7b, which includes a location modeling the current operating condition of the entire system (e.g., $o_{r_{rech}}$, $o_{r_{flw}}$), generically identified by o_{op}, and a location o_{chk_x} modeling the orchestrator monitoring the state of the system, where x is a numerical index. Ports highlight the transitions entering and leaving the pattern sub-component, guarded by γ_{start}, γ_{stop}, γ_{fail} and γ_{scs}, where each γ condition is associated with a component-specific formula. The semantics of the pattern is described in the following.

The orchestrator moves to operating condition o_{op} when the corresponding condition γ_{start} is true. The transition from o_{op} to o_{chk_x} is governed by clock t_{act}, and it periodically occurs every T_{int} time instants. Upon entering o_{chk_x}, the orchestrator runs the monitoring routine (ξ_O of Fig. 8). If condition γ_{stop} holds, the orchestrator moves to the following operating condition—i.e., a different sub-component—otherwise it goes back to o_{op}. Table 4 shows the guards for each sub-machine. Locations o_{fail} and o_{scs} of Fig. 7a correspond to the end of the mission with failure or success, respectively, and are reached when conditions γ_{fail} and γ_{scs} hold. Failure occurs if the battery charge drops to 0 (event b_{dead}), hence the robot cannot recover autonomously, or if the human fatigue exceeds 1 (event h_{faint}). Location o_{scs} is reached when the mission has been successfully completed—i.e., when all humans in the scenario have been served.

The first instance of the pattern is idle_chk$_1$ in Fig. 7a, which models the situation in which the system is idle and periodically checks whether an action can start. The system enters this component first when the execution starts, and returns to it whenever an action stops (and the corresponding sub-component is left). Similarly, the orchestrator exits this component if one of the γ_{start} conditions for the other sub-machines is true.

The recharging routine of Fig. 8a starts when a robot is idle and its current battery charge b_{ch} is below a threshold B_{th_1}. Sub-machine r_rech models two operating conditions: the movement of the robot towards the charging station ($r_{mov}\_chk_2$), and the robot recharging its battery ($r_{rech}\_chk_3$). Upon entering

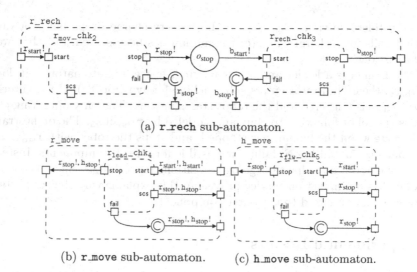

(a) r_rech sub-automaton.

(b) r_move sub-automaton.   (c) h_move sub-automaton.

Fig. 8. Sub-machines of the orchestrator automaton.

Table 4. Orchestrator guard conditions

	γ_{start}	γ_{stop}
idle_chk$_1$	$r_{\text{rech}} \cdot \gamma_{\text{stop}} \vee r_{\text{lead}} \cdot \gamma_{\text{stop}} \vee r_{\text{flw}} \cdot \gamma_{\text{stop}}$	$r_{\text{mov}} \cdot \gamma_{\text{start}} \vee r_{\text{lead}} \cdot \gamma_{\text{start}} \vee$ $r_{\text{flw}} \cdot \gamma_{\text{start}}$
r_mov_chk$_2$	$r_{\text{idle}} \wedge (b_{ch} < B_{\text{th}_1})$	$(r_{pos_x} = RS_x) \wedge (r_{pos_y} = RS_y)$
r_rech_chk$_3$	$t_{act} \geq T_{\text{int}}$	$(b_{ch} > B_{\text{th}_2}) \wedge r_{\text{rec}}$
r_lead_chk$_4$	$r_{\text{idle}} \wedge \neg(h_p = 1)$	$(h_{ftg} > H_{\text{th}_1}) \vee (b_{ch} < B_{\text{th}_1}) \vee (h_{svd} \wedge \neg \forall_h h_{svd})$
r_flw_chk$_5$	$h_{\text{busy}} \wedge (h_p = 1)$	h_{idle}
$\langle op \rangle$_chk$_{\langle x \rangle}$	$\gamma_{\text{scs}} : \forall_h \ h_{svd}$	$\gamma_{\text{fail}} : b_{\text{dead}}? \vee h_{\text{faint}}?$

r_rech, the orchestrator fires r_{start} to instruct the robot to reach the charging station (Cartesian coordinates RS_x and RS_y), then r_{stop} when the dock has been reached. Location o_{stop} bridges the two operating conditions and models the deceleration phase of the robot (r_{stop}): this is why the orchestrator *waits* T_{int} time instants before moving on, with $T_{\text{int}} > v_{\text{max}}/a_{\text{max}}$. When the robot has stopped completely, it can start recharging, and the orchestrator fires b_{start}. The robot stops recharging, thus b_{stop} is fired, when variable b_{ch} is above a threshold B_{th_2}, then the orchestrator switches back to o_{idle}.

The r_move sub-machine of Fig. 8b is entered to initiate the robot movement when the robot is idle and the human is not a leader. Upon entering r_move, the orchestrator fires r_{start} and h_{start} since the human is a follower. The only operating condition modeled by this sub-component is the robot movement (component r_lead_chk$_4$ in Fig. 8b). The robot movement stops (events r_{stop} and h_{stop} fire, since the human is a follower) if: (a) human fatigue h_{ftg} exceeds a maximum tolerable value H_{th_1}, or (b) the battery charge drops below a value B_{th_1} that calls for recharging, or (c) the human has been served, but they were not the last one.

If the human is a leader and starts moving, hence its automaton is in location h_{busy}, the orchestrator enters sub-machine h_move (Fig. 8c). Upon entering h_move, r_{start} is triggered and the robot starts moving. The only operating condition is the robot following the human, modeled by r_{flw}-chk$_3$. The orchestrator exits h_move when the human has stopped, and stops the robot with r_{stop}.

As per Fig. 7a and Fig. 8, failure is possible for all sub-components. Instead, only r_move and h_move have outgoing transitions towards o_{scs}, since recharging the robot has no impact on service provision: this explains why the scs ports in Fig. 8a are not connected to the outer component.

6   Experimental Results

As previously discussed, use cases are conveniently found within the healthcare domain, specifically for the purposes of efficient patient flow handling. The experimental setting chosen to test the approach involves a human patient who needs to reach a doctor's office. The mobile robot is aware of the floor plan and the patient's characteristics, and it is able to guide the human towards the destination. When the service is successfully provided, the robot will have achieved its *mission*. Instances of classes and attributes of Fig. 3 are provided by the designer through a JSON file. The portion of the model that is not customizable by the user is stored in an XML template. The tool automatically processes the input of the user to generate a verification-ready version of the HA+ model. The tool selected for the verification is Uppaal and its extension for SMC [11, 24]. In this work we use Uppaal version 4.1.24 to implement the automata, and run SMC experiments[1] with the default set of statistical parameters. Each experiment yields the probability for mission success: formula $P_{\geq \theta}^{\leq \tau}(\diamond\ o_{success})$ is verified, with probability bound θ and time-bound τ.

With this experiment, we are able to test how different fatigue profiles impact the completion of the mission. The experimental setting features a mobile robot with $v_{max} = 20$ cm/s, $a_{max} = 5$ cm/s^2, with a fully charged battery ($C_{start} = 100$) and approximately 2.5 h of full charge/discharge time ($T_{chg} = T_{dchg} = 9000$ s). Listing 1.2 shows the portion of the JSON file defining these parameters. The floor plan used for this experiment, depicted in Fig. 9a, reproduces a T-shaped hallway of a hospital, with doors leading to different offices. The entrance and starting point for both agents is on the left-end side (coordinates $(200, 300)$) close to the charging station ($RS_x = 250, RS_y = 375$). Listing 1.3 shows a snippet of the JSON file defining the coordinates for the points of the layout.

The mission for this robot is to lead a single human to their destination in $(1300, 500)$. Therefore, the interaction pattern is **Human-Follower**. To test the effectiveness of the fatigue-related policies of the orchestrator, we repeat the

---

[1] On a machine with 128 cores, 515 GB of RAM and Debian Linux version 10.

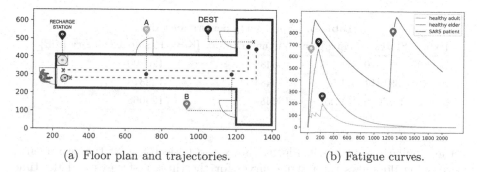

(a) Floor plan and trajectories.   (b) Fatigue curves.

Fig. 9. On the left, the floor layout for Exp A, with initial positions and destination marked by a ×, and intermediate points by a •. On the right, the fatigue curves for all the profiles tested in this experiment (colors as in the legend). Location markers indicate the time each human has reached the corresponding point of the trajectory. (Color figure online)

experiment with three different versions of the human, with different fatigue profiles and values of walking speed. Listing 1.1 shows how these data are specified. In the first case, the human is young and in fine health ($p_f = 1$). Their Maximum Endurance Time (MET)—i.e., how long they can walk non-stop before $F = 1$— is approximately 23 min (with reference to Eq. 1, it leads to $\lambda = \mu = 0.005$) and their walking speed is $v = 18$ cm/s. In the second case, the human is an elder in good health ($p_f = 3$), with MET $= 14$ min ($\lambda = 0.008$, $\mu = 0.0035$) and $v = 8$ cm/s. In the third case, the human is affected by a severe respiratory disease ($p_f = 5$, $v = 5$ cm/s) with MET $= 4.6$ min ($\lambda = 0.025$, $\mu = 0.001$).

Listing 1.1. Humans	Listing 1.2. Robot	Listing 1.3. Floor Plan

```
1  "humans":[          "robots": [           "floorPlan": [
2   {"id": 1,           {"id": 1,             {"name":"HALL1",
3    "v": 5,             "v_max": 20,          "x": 200,
4    "p": "follower",    "a_max": 5,           "y": 400},
5    "p_f": 5,           "c_start": 100,       {"name":"HALL2",
6    "dest": {           "T_chg": 9000,        "x": 1200,
7     "x": 1300,         "T_dchg":9000},       "y": 400},
8     "y": 500}},[..]]   [..]]                 [..]]
```

For the first case study, we have verified through the tool that $P(\diamond\, o_{success}) \in [0.717, 0.817]$ with $\tau = 300$ s. With the second setting, the property that has been verified is $P(\diamond\, o_{success}) \in [0.8, 0.9]$ with $\tau = 300$ s, and in the last case $P(\diamond\, o_{success}) < 0.098$ with $\tau = 1000$ s. Furthermore, a simulation trace with $\tau = 2000$ s has also been produced for each test case. These results prove that in the first two cases the destination can be reached in approximately 5 min with a high degree of confidence. In the last case, instead, it is practically impossible to complete the mission even in 16 min. The reason behind this result is highlighted

318   L. Lestingi et al.

Table 5. Experiments performance data

Exp.	States	Time [min]	Virtual memory [KiB]	Resident memory [KiB]
$\mathsf{p_f} = 1$	212570	≈ 1	166488	120800
$\mathsf{p_f} = 3$	391311	≈ 1.5	166484	122376
$\mathsf{p_f} = 5$	2927009	≈ 11.5	166484	123068

by the simulations in Fig. 9: Fig. 9a shows the trajectories of the two agents, whereas Fig. 9b shows the fatigue curves for the three test cases and the time instants in which the destination or intermediate points of the trajectory have been reached within the simulation. The orchestrator commands every agent to stop walking if human fatigue exceeds a certain threshold, set to $\mathsf{H_{th_1}} = 0.9$. In the last test case, motion stops at $t = 200\,\mathrm{s}$, it resumes at $t = 1200\,\mathrm{s}$ when fatigue drops to an acceptable value ($\mathsf{H_{th_2}} = 0.3$) and stops again at $t = 1400\,\mathrm{s}$ when the destination is yet to be reached. This behavior is caused by the orchestrator trying to prevent human exhaustion, which inevitably slows down the entire mission. In the other two cases, thanks to the different $\mathsf{p_f}$ parameter values, when the human reaches the destination the value of fatigue is still acceptable, thus they are not stopped by the orchestrator.

Performance data for each experiment can be found in Table 5. The experiment demonstrates how the tool can predict the outcome of the mission for various scenarios with little effort on the designer-side. Moreover, it constitutes a preliminary step towards assessing the soundness of the models presented in Sect. 5, specifically the ability of the orchestrator to enable corrective actions if required by the state of the system.

7 Conclusion

We have presented a model-driven approach for the verification, through SMC, of human-robot interactions in healthcare scenarios. There are two main future development directions for the approach presented here. The model can be enriched with new interaction patterns to widen the range of applications that can be assessed. It is also possible to refine the model of human behavior by creating a correlation between environmental factors and the likelihood of autonomous decisions, which are a purely random phenomenon in the current version of the work. The maximum degree of scenario flexibility could also be enhanced by having the human and the robot dynamically shift from one pattern to another in particular situations as a result of the orchestrator's policies. We envisage the creation of a Domain-Specific Language that designers can use to model the mission, with finer-grained details and a richer set of physiological factors. Simultaneously, we plan on developing the deployment phase of the toolchain. Through a code generation procedure, the orchestrator could be transformed into executable code to be deployed on real mobile platforms. This would allow us to test if the robot can effectively accommodate real people's needs and comply with the human-oriented nature of the work. The deployment-ready controller could also be simulated in a 2D/3D environment: beyond the testing purposes, this could also help professionals with a different or non-technical background in visualizing the potential capabilities of the approach.

Aknowledgements. The Italian Ministry of Education, University and Research is acknowledged for the support provided through the Project "Department of Excellence LIS4.0 - Lightweight and Smart Structures for Industry 4.0".

We would also like to thank the reviewers for their comments and suggestions for the improvement of our work.

Appendix A   Additional Models

A.1   Human-Leader Model

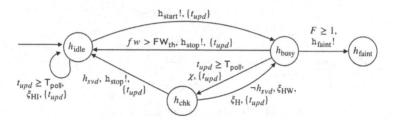

Fig. 10. Human-leader automaton.

The automaton modeling the second pattern in Table 2 is depicted in Fig. 10. Operating conditions, time-dependent variables and dense counters are the same as the ones described for the **Human-Follower** pattern in Sect. 5. In this pattern, the human is leading the task, thus they are in charge of checking when the task is complete, and, in that case, end it. This checking mechanism is modeled by location h_{chk}. The automaton enters this location every time the value of clock t_{upd} equals T_{poll}. The model includes a boolean variable h_{svd}, which has value 1 when the service requested by human h has been provided, 0 otherwise. Upon entering location h_{chk}, the automaton checks whether the destination has been reached or not (update indicated by χ in Fig. 10). If this is the case, h_{svd} is set to true, h_{stop} is triggered and the automaton switches back to h_{idle}. Otherwise, the automaton returns to h_{busy} and the human keeps walking. If the human is a leader, their free will manifests itself by stopping even if the destination is yet to be reached, which is modeled through a transition from h_{busy} to h_{idle}, with the guard condition $fw > \mathsf{FW}_{th}$. Free will is modeled as described in Sect. 5. Similarly, what is stated about update instructions in Table 3 for the **Human-Follower** pattern stands correct for this pattern as well.

A.2   Human-Recipient Model

Figure 11 represents the automaton for the **Human-Recipient** pattern. Locations h_{idle} and h_{busy} model the same situations described for the previous two patterns. In this case, there is an additional contingency corresponding to the moment in which the human collects the item from the robot, modeled by location h_{rec}. This occurs when the robot has fetched the item and reached the human location: at this point, the orchestrator triggers h_{start} to prompt the synchronization. Event h_{stop} is then triggered to signal the end of the task. Free will is also taken into account for this pattern, with the same characteristics described in Sect. 5. The human can freely decide to walk or stop while the robot is fetching the object. Therefore, two transitions are added between h_{idle} and h_{busy}, enabled by the condition $fw > \text{FW}_{\text{th}}$, which trigger events h_{start} and h_{stop}. All variables (time-dependent, dense counters and parameters) have the same semantics described for the first pattern.

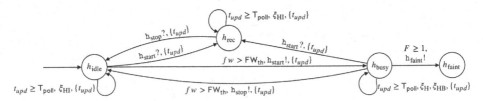

Fig. 11. Human-recipient automaton.

Appendix B   Additional Experiments

The additional experimental setting, presented in the following, demonstrates how the two patterns in Appendix A work in practice, and how the robot battery is managed by the orchestrator. The floor layout is the same as in Fig. 9a. In this case study, the robot needs to serve two humans: one adhering to the **Human-Recipient** (see A.2) pattern, and one to the **Human-Leader** pattern (see A.1). The specific parameters for the first human are: $v = 15\,\text{cm/s}$, $p_f = 3$ and dest $= (1250, 100)$. Since this is a recipient pattern, in this case the dest parameter represents the location of the item needed by the human. For the second human, they are: $v = 10\,\text{cm/s}$, $p_f = 1$ and dest $= (1250, 500)$. The robot has the same characteristics as the one used for the experiment in Sect. 6, but we are going to run two versions of the experiment: one with $C_{\text{start}} = 100\%$ and one with $C_{\text{start}} = 11\%$.

The experiments are run on the same machine used for the experiment in Sect. 6, with the same version of Uppaal and the same statistical parameters. Performance data can be found in Table 6.

Figure 12 and Fig. 13 show two simulation traces, one for each value of C_{start}. When the battery is fully charged, the robot immediately moves towards the location of the object to fetch and then returns to the location of the first

Table 6. Experiments performance data

Exp.	States	Time	Virtual memory [KiB]	Resident memory [KiB]
$C_{start} = 100\%$	1138343	≈4.5 min	166972	126304
$C_{start} = 11\%$	75339267	≈6.5 h	166968	124752

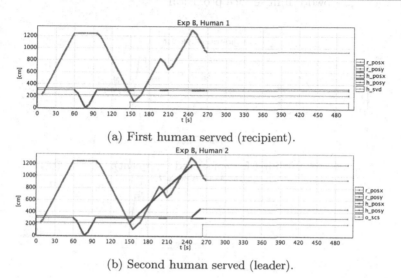

(a) First human served (recipient).

(b) Second human served (leader).

Fig. 12. Simulation trace of the experiment with $C_{start} = 100\%$: robot trajectory is in both plots, human 1 is in (a) and human 2 in (b).

human, who never moves from the starting point (Fig. 12a). As in Fig. 12a, the first human is served ($h_{svd} = 1$) at $t = 150$ s. Figure 12b shows the behavior of the second interaction pattern: since the second human is a leader, they immediately start moving as soon as their turn comes. The robot follows and, when it ends up ahead of the human (e.g., $t \approx 190$ s), it steps back and resumes the trailing. The whole mission ends successfully after approximately 270 s (see Fig. 12b).

In the second case with low battery charge, the robot initially starts moving towards the location of the object, but, as soon as $b_{ch} < B_{th_1}$, with $B_{th_1} = 10\%$, the orchestrator orders it to stop and start moving towards the recharge station instead. This is allowed since the human is a recipient, thus the robot is entitled to start and stop the action whenever necessary. The recharging phase lasts until $b_{ch} > B_{th_2}$, with $B_{th_2} = 70\%$ for this experiment ($t = 1400$ s), as in Fig. 13c. When the battery has sufficiently recharged, the robot resumes all its operations: it fetches the item from point (1250, 100), brings it to the first human ($t \approx 1600$ s), then follows the second human to the destination. The whole mission ends successfully at $t \approx 1700$ s.

The verified property in both cases is $P^{\leq \tau}_{\geq \theta}(\diamond\, o_{\text{success}})$. With $C_{\text{start}} = 100\%$, the property is verified with $\tau = 500\,$s and $\theta = 0.9$. With $C_{\text{start}} = 11\%$, we have verified that $P(\diamond\, o_{\text{success}}) \in [0.4, 0.5]$ with $\tau = 2000\,$s.

The experiment demonstrates how the orchestrator successfully manages the battery recharge policy to prevent the failure of the mission, even though this causes a general slowdown in service provision.

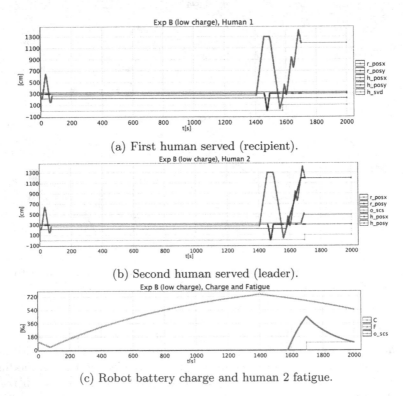

(a) First human served (recipient).

(b) Second human served (leader).

(c) Robot battery charge and human 2 fatigue.

Fig. 13. Simulation trace of the experiment with $C_{\text{start}} = 11\%$: robot trajectory is in both plots, human 1 is in (a) and human 2 in (b), battery charge and fatigue of human 2 in (c).

References

1. HRI Toolchain (2020). https://github.com/LesLivia/hritoolchain
2. Adam, C., Johal, W., Pellier, D., Fiorino, H., Pesty, S.: Social human-robot interaction: a new cognitive and affective interaction-oriented architecture. In: Agah, A., Cabibihan, J.-J., Howard, A.M., Salichs, M.A., He, H. (eds.) ICSR 2016. LNCS (LNAI), vol. 9979, pp. 253–263. Springer, Cham (2016). https://doi.org/10.1007/978-3-319-47437-3_25
3. Agha, G., Palmskog, K.: A survey of statistical model checking. ACM Trans. Model. Comput. Simul. (TOMACS) **28**(1), 1–39 (2018)

4. Alur, R., et al.: The algorithmic analysis of hybrid systems. Theoret. Comput. Sci. **138**(1), 3–34 (1995)
5. Alur, R., Dill, D.L.: A theory of timed automata. Theoret. Comput. Sci. **126**(2), 183–235 (1994)
6. Arai, R., Schlingloff, H.: Model-based performance prediction by statistical model checking an industrial case study of autonomous transport robots. In: Concurrency, Specification and Programming (2017)
7. Askarpour, M., Mandrioli, D., Rossi, M., Vicentini, F.: Formal model of human erroneous behavior for safety analysis in collaborative robotics. Robot. Comput.-Integr. Manuf. **57**, 465–476 (2019)
8. Askarpour, M., Menghi, C., Belli, G., Bersani, M., Pelliccione, P.: Mind the gap: robotic mission planning meets software engineering. In: Proceedings of the 8th International Conference on Formal Methods in Software Engineering (2020)
9. Bersani, M.M., Soldo, M., Menghi, C., Pelliccione, P., Rossi, M.: PuRSUE-from specification of robotic environments to synthesis of controllers. Formal Aspects Comput. 1–41 (2020). https://doi.org/10.1007/s00165-020-00509-0
10. Chettibi, T., Haddad, M., Lehtihet, H., Khalil, W.: Suboptimal trajectory generation for industrial robots using trapezoidal velocity profiles. In: IROS, pp. 729–735. IEEE (2006)
11. David, A., Larsen, K.G., Legay, A., Mikučionis, M., Poulsen, D.B.: UPPAAL SMC tutorial. Int. J. Softw. Tools Technol. Transfer **17**(4), 397–415 (2015). https://doi.org/10.1007/s10009-014-0361-y
12. Zhao, X., et al.: Towards integrating formal verification of autonomous robots with battery prognostics and health management. In: Ölveczky, P.C., Salaün, G. (eds.) SEFM 2019. LNCS, vol. 11724, pp. 105–124. Springer, Cham (2019). https://doi.org/10.1007/978-3-030-30446-1_6
13. Foughali, M., Ingrand, F., Seceleanu, C.: Statistical model checking of complex robotic systems. In: Biondi, F., Given-Wilson, T., Legay, A. (eds.) SPIN 2019. LNCS, vol. 11636, pp. 114–134. Springer, Cham (2019). https://doi.org/10.1007/978-3-030-30923-7_7
14. de Graaf, M.M., Ben Allouch, S., van Dijk, J.A.: Why would I use this in my home? A model of domestic social robot acceptance. Hum.-Comput. Interact. **34**(2), 115–173 (2019)
15. Hadley, M.: A deterministic model of the free will phenomenon. J. Conscious. Explor. Res. **9**(1), 01–19 (2018)
16. Halder, R., Proença, J., Macedo, N., Santos, A.: Formal verification of ROS-based robotic applications using timed-automata. In: International FME Workshop on Formal Methods in Software Engineering (FormaliSE), pp. 44–50. IEEE (2017)
17. Herd, B., Miles, S., McBurney, P., Luck, M.: Quantitative analysis of multiagent systems through statistical model checking. In: Baldoni, M., Baresi, L., Dastani, M. (eds.) EMAS 2015. LNCS (LNAI), vol. 9318, pp. 109–130. Springer, Cham (2015). https://doi.org/10.1007/978-3-319-26184-3_7
18. ISO 12100: Safety of machinery - General principles for design - Risk assessment and risk reduction. ISO (2010)
19. ISO 13482: Robots and robotic devices - Safety requirements for personal care robots. ISO (2014)
20. ISO 13849–1: Safety of machinery - Safety-related parts of control systems - Part 1: General principles for design. ISO (2006)
21. Jaber, M.Y., Givi, Z., Neumann, W.P.: Incorporating human fatigue and recovery into the learning-forgetting process. Appl. Math. Model. **37**(12–13), 7287–7299 (2013)

22. Jacobs, T., Virk, G.S.: ISO 13482 - the new safety standard for personal care robots. In: International Symposium on Robotics, pp. 1–6. VDE (2014)

23. Konz, S.: Work/rest: Part ii-the scientific basis (knowledge base) for the guide 1. In: Ergonomics Guidelines and Problem Solving, vol. 1, no. 401, p. 38 (2000)

24. Larsen, K.G., Pettersson, P., Yi, W.: Uppaal in a nutshell. Int. J. Softw. Tools Technol. Transfer 1(1), 134–152 (1997). https://doi.org/10.1007/s100090050010

25. Luckcuck, M., Farrell, M., Dennis, L.A., Dixon, C., Fisher, M.: Formal specification and verification of autonomous robotic systems: a survey. ACM Comput. Surv. (CSUR) 52(5), 1–41 (2019)

26. Payne, P., Lopetegui, M., Yu, S.: A review of clinical workflow studies and methods. In: Zheng, K., Westbrook, J., Kannampallil, T.G., Patel, V.L. (eds.) Cognitive Informatics. HI, pp. 47–61. Springer, Cham (2019). https://doi.org/10.1007/978-3-030-16916-9_4

27. Porfirio, D., Sauppé, A., Albarghouthi, A., Mutlu, B.: Authoring and verifying human-robot interactions. In: Proceedings of ACM Symposium on User Interface Software and Technology, pp. 75–86 (2018)

28. Rasouli, A., Tsotsos, J.K.: Autonomous vehicles that interact with pedestrians: a survey of theory and practice. IEEE Trans. Intell. Transp. Syst. 21, 900–918 (2019)

29. Sinkaram, C., Rajakumar, K., Asirvadam, V.: Modeling battery management system using the lithium-ion battery. In: International Conference on Control System, Computing and Engineering, pp. 50–55. IEEE (2012)

30. Vicentini, F., Askarpour, M., Rossi, M.G., Mandrioli, D.: Safety assessment of collaborative robotics through automated formal verification. IEEE Trans. Rob. (2019). https://doi.org/10.1109/TRO.2019.2937471

31. Webster, M., et al.: Formal verification of an autonomous personal robotic assistant. In: AAAI Spring Symposium Series (2014)

Author Index

Printed in the United States
By Bookmasters